Socia

...ral change and the middle classes

Social change
and the middle classes

Edited by

Tim Butler and Mike Savage

UCL
PRESS

First published in 1995 by UCL Press

UCL Press Limited
University College London
Gower Street
London WC1E 6BT

and

1900 Frost Road, Suite 101
Bristol
Pennsylvania 19007-1598

The name of University College London (UCL) is a registered
trade mark used by UCL Press with the consent of the owner.

British Library Cataloguing in Publication Data
A catalogue record for this book is available from the British Library.

Library of Congress Cataloging-in-Publication Data are available

ISBN: 1-85728-271-X HB
       1-85728-272-8 PB

Typeset in Baskerville.
Printed and bound by
Page Bros (Norwich) Ltd, Norwich, England.

Contents

Preface

Who cares about the middle classes? They are not, or are least do not at first glance appear to be, a "social problem". They do not appear to have spectacular amounts of power or influence. Worst of all, might not studying the middle classes encourage navel-gazing and complacency amongst "middle class" academics themselves? Yet the study of the middle classes actually poses a variety of interesting challenges. Traditionally, the social scientific gaze has been directed either downwards, to the working classes, the poor and the dispossessed, or upwards, to the wealthy and powerful. Despite the currently fashionable interest in "reflexive" approaches to social inquiry (e.g. Beck 1992) research has only sporadically focused upon the more mundane types of people who go to make up the middle classes: the sort of people who tend to write and read books such as this! In recent years, however, a series of arguments have appeared that claim that the middle classes play a key role either as a dynamic force changing contemporary societies (Lash & Urry 1987) or as bulwarks of the traditional order (Goldthorpe 1982). More generally, given current controversies about whether the concept of social class retains any relevance, it is interesting that recent attempts to defend the concept have done so by explicit reference to the middle classes (e.g. Savage et al. 1992). For all these reasons, a collection of original papers on various aspects of the British middle classes seems an important venture that will cast valuable light on the course of social change in Britain more generally.

This book therefore has a number of objectives. Most obviously it is designed to bring together a series of accessible, high-quality research papers on various aspects of the British middle classes. We hope that readers of this book, even those who are not specifically interested in the fortunes of the middle classes, will learn things that interest them about how contemporary Britain is changing. Secondly, this book is designed to shed light on the general state of "class analysis" in social research. By focusing on the middle classes, which are rising in numbers and (arguably) social importance, rather than the (declining, at least in numerical terms) working class we seek to give a new slant to debates about class, which have traditionally tended to conflate the idea of class with images of the "traditional working class" (see further,

Savage, Ch. 1). We therefore hope that, by assembling together a variety of very different articles under one cover, it will be possible to judge the contemporary relevance of class by the quality and timeliness of academic research being done, however loosely, under the rubric of class.

In pursuing these objectives, we are particularly concerned to see if research on class can counter the fragmentation of social science research into different research communities with different methodologies and perspectives. Much class analysis, especially the research associated with Goldthorpe and his colleagues, adopts quantitative techniques, which in itself may be one reason why it is unpopular in some circles. However, as we seek to show in this book, there is also interesting qualitative research being carried out on social class, and we want to demonstrate some of the strengths of quantitative analyses. Our hope is that, by drawing together papers with a variety of research techniques, both quantitative and qualitative, we will encourage readers to think about how boundaries between different research traditions might be bridged. We are genuinely excited that we have been able to bring together well-known contributors from very different research traditions, and hope that this book may valuably encourage interchange and debate.

The papers for this book were all specially commissioned by the editors. Contributors were asked to report on their research in the context of debates about the nature and changing character of the British middle classes. Authors were asked to pay particular attention to a number of competing approaches to both class analysis in general and specifically the middle classes – in particular the concept of the service class developed in different ways by Goldthorpe (1982) and Urry with various collaborators (Abercrombie & Urry 1983, Lash & Urry 1987); the asset-based approach to the middle class pioneered by the American Marxist Erik Wright (1985) and developed in the British context by Savage et al. (1992); as well as Marxist, culturalist, feminist and race-sensitive approaches to class.

We have been concerned, at all stages, to make this book both interesting to the specialist but also accessible to a general readership. We want this book to be read widely by undergraduates studying not only sociology but also other disciplines such as geography and cultural studies. We think that the specialist will find the new research appealing, and the fact that this book contains important statements on social class by some of the central figures in the field should provoke much of interest. In order to help those unfamiliar with debates about class, we have included two introductory chapters by the editors, on the current debates and research. We have also provided editorial introductions to the various sections of the book in order to explain to readers how the specific papers fit into wider debates.

We cannot claim that this book – long though it is – is comprehensive. Particularly glaring is the omission of studies of health and education. Nonetheless, if you feel you have learnt something about how Britain is changing and about some of the current issues in social science research, then the book will have served its purpose.

Acknowledgements

We would first like to thank UCL Press, and especially Justin Vaughan, for their enthusiasm for this book, and their support and advice throughout. Secondly, would like to thank the contributors for their papers. Unlike most edited collections, this book been a genuinely collective endeavour. Early drafts of nearly all the papers were discussed at a specially convened conference in Danbury Park near Chelmsford in June 1994, and we are grateful to everyone who made the meeting an enjoyable and lively one. In addition to the contributors to this volume, the following commented in detail on each of the sections that make up the book: Fiona Devine, David Lockwood, Andrew Miles, Sophie Watson and Rosemary Crompton. David Lockwood and Rosemary Crompton subsequently agreed to contribute to the book itself. We would also like to acknowledge the generous assistance of the Research Committee of the Sociology Department of the University of East London which made it possible to invite contributors who were unable to obtain financial support from their own institutions. Thanks also to Joan Tremble from the University of East London for carrying out the administration of the conference with such efficiency and within budget. Tim Butler is grateful to Susan Fitzgerald and the Internet, who helped ensure that this book appeared despite his disappearance to Peru. Mike Savage would like to thank the University of North Carolina at Chapel Hill for its support (notably, extensive use of the fax machine!) during the period when this book was actually assembled in a finished state, and also Joe Gerteis, a graduate at Chapel Hill, who worked bravely on assembling the bibliography and checking papers.

Notes on contributors

Paul Bagguley is Lecturer in Sociology in the School of Sociology and Social Policy at the University of Leeds. He is the author of *From protest to acquiescence? political movements of the unemployed* (1991), and co-author of *Restructuring: place, class and gender* (1990).

Tim Butler is Principal Lecturer in Sociology at the University of East London. His research interests are in the fields of urban sociology and stratification, and he has published on gentrification in *Society and Space*.

Bob Carter teaches in Adult Education at the University of Leicester. His most recent books include *Capitalism, class conflict and the new middle class* (1985), and, jointly with Peter Armstrong, C. Smith and T. Nichols, *White collar workers, trade unions and class* (1986). Recent articles have appeared in *Capital and Class*.

Paul Cloke is Professor of Geography at the University of Bristol, and has written widely on rural issues. He is co-author of *Approaching Human Geography* (1991) and of *The rural state? Limits to planning in rural society* (1990).

Rosemary Crompton is Professor of Sociology at the University of Leicester, having previously worked as Senior Lecturer and Reader at the University of Kent at Canterbury. She has written and researched widely in a number of areas, including class, stratification, and women's employment. Her most recent book is *Class and stratification* (1993), and she has also edited *Gender and stratification* (1986) with Michael Mann.

Peter Fairbrother teaches in the Department of Sociology and is Director of the Centre for Comparative Labour Studies at the University of Warwick. He is the author of *All those in favour: the politics of union democracy* and *Politics and the state as employer* (1994), and joint author, with S. Clarke, M. Burawoy, and P. Krolov of *What about the workers: workers in the transition to capitalism in the USSR* (1993) and, with S. Clarke and U. Borisov, of *The workers' movement in Russia* (1995).

Tony Fielding is Professor of Economics at Ritsumeikan University, Kyoto (at other times he is Reader in Geography at the University of Sussex). His research interests are in inter-regional and international migration in Britain and Western Europe. He is also interested in urban and regional development in western Europe and Japan and in the politics of West European integration.

John Goldthorpe is an Official Fellow of Nuffield College, Oxford. He is a leading international authority on the study of social mobility, and is the author of *Social mobility and class structure in modern Britain* (1987) and, with Robert Erikson, of *The constant flux: a study of class mobility in industrial societies* (1992).

Nicky Gregson is Lecturer in Geography at the University of Sheffield. She has researched and written on a variety of issues, including Anthony Giddens' structuration theory and the concept of locality. Her most recent research has been concerned with gender and the domestic division of labour in middle-class households, the results of which have been published as *Servicing the middle classes* (1994, with Michelle Lowe).

Susan Halford is Lecturer in Sociology at Southampton University. She has published on women and local politics, the local state, and feminism and the state, and has recently completed a book with Mike Savage and Anne Witz, *Gender, careers and organisation* (1996).

Chris Hamnett is Professor of Human Geography at King's College London, having formerly been Professor of Urban Geography at the Open University. Amongst his recent publications are, with Bill Randolph, *Cities, housing and profits: flat break up and the decline of private renting* (1988).

Anthony Heath is an official Fellow of Nuffield College, Oxford, and a Joint Director of the ESRC Centre for Research into Elections and Social Trends. His most recent (co-authored) works include *How Britain votes* (1985), *Understanding political change* (1991) and *Labour's last chance?* (1994).

David Lockwood is Research Professor at the University of Essex and has for many years been one of the most distinguished British sociological theorists. His most recent work is *Solidarity and schism: "The problem of disorder" in Durkheimian and Marxist Sociology* (1992).

Michelle Lowe is Lecturer in Geography at the University of Southampton. Amongst her recent publications is *Servicing the middle classes* (1994), with Nicky Gregson.

Doreen Massey is Professor of Geography in the Faculty of Social Sciences at the Open University. Her most recent books are *High tech fantasies*, with Paul Quintas and David Wield, (1992), *Space, place and gender* (1994), *Spatial divisions of labour* (2nd edition 1995), *Geographical worlds* (1995, edited with John Allen) and *A place in the world* (1995, edited with Pat Jess).

Colin Mills is Lecturer in Sociology at the London School of Economics. His interests lie in social stratification and the application of quantitative techniques to sociological problems, and he has authored or co-authored recent articles in *British Journal of Sociology*, *Sociological Review* and *Rationality and Society*.

Deborah Phillips is Lecturer in the School of Geography at the University of Leeds. She has researched widely in the field of "race" and ethnicity. Her publications include *What price equality?* (1987), and she is co-author of *Ethnic minority housing: Explanations and policies*.

Martin Phillips is Lecturer in Geography at the University of Leicester, having previously worked at the University of Coventry. He has published extensively on social change in rural Britain.

Phil Sarre is Senior Lecturer in Geography at the Open University. He has written extensively on issues of ethnicity, especially in relation to housing.

Mike Savage is Professor of Sociology at the University of Manchester and has an associate position at the University of North Carolina, USA. He was previously Reader in Sociology at Keele University. His most recent publications include *Property, bureaucracy and culture: Middle class formation in contemporary Britain* (1992, with James Barlow, Peter Dickens and Tony Fielding) and *Urban sociology, capitalism and modernity* (1993, with Alan Warde)

Nigel Thrift is Professor of Geography at the University of Bristol. Amongst his many publications are *Class and space* (edited with Peter Williams 1987), and *Money, power and space* (with Andrew Leyshon 1994).

Mark Tomlinson is a Research Officer at Nuffield College, Oxford. He is currently researching employment relations in Britain and Eastern Europe. He has previously written about employment patterns and British food habits.

John Urry is Professor of Sociology and Dean of Research at Lancaster University. He is author or co-author of *Capital, labour and the middle classes* (1983), *The end of organised capitalism* (1987), *The tourist gaze* (1990), *Economies of signs and spaces* (1994) and *Consuming places*, (1995). He is editor of the Routledge International Library of Sociology series.

Alan Warde is Reader in Sociology at Lancaster University. His recent publications include a paper on theoretical approaches to consumption in *Sociology* (1994), and papers on food habits in *Sociological Review* (1994) and *The British Food Journal* (1993 and 1994). A study of changing British taste will be published in 1996. Amongst his other recent publications is *Urban sociology, capitalism and modernity*, jointly with Mike Savage.

Anne Witz is Lecturer in Sociology at the University of Birmingham. She has worked on various aspects of women and employment and is the author of *Professions and patriarchy* (1992), and co-editor with Mike Savage of *Gender and bureaucracy* (1992).

Introduction

Marking out the middle class(es)

David Lockwood

The papers brought together in this book take forward some of the ideas introduced in an earlier work by Savage and his colleagues (1992), which originated as an investigation of the "service class". This term was coined by Renner, but given a much sharper meaning and applicability by Goldthorpe's (1982) widely influential hypothesis that professional, managerial and administrative employees constitute a class because they share a distinctive employment status, whose principal feature is the "trust" that employers necessarily have to place in these employees whose delegated or specialized tasks give them a considerable autonomy. This concept, developed in connection with the study of social mobility, which revealed the remarkable intergenerational staying power of the upper service class, quickly became the major reference point of further investigations of the middle class as a whole. It has also been the focus of much fruitful debate, well represented in the work in this volume, in which a chief issue is the usefulness or otherwise of counterposing to the idea of a unitary service class that of there being three middle classes – namely, the entrepreneurial, managerial and professional, differentiated mainly by their respective command of property, organizational and cultural assets. Nevertheless, both parties to this dispute agree that the question of the terms by which this subject matter is defined is less important than their relevance to the understanding of whatever may be established through systematic research into the process of the formation of the middle class; or, as it might be, the middle classes. In this respect, it is noteworthy that Goldthorpe, as a true Popperian, is quite willing to have the service class re-labelled as the "salariat" – if only to avoid confusion with the service sector of employment.[1] It is also generally agreed that the self-employed groups of the petite bourgeoisie are a distinctive section of the lower middle class, socially quite separate from the class, or classes, of managerial, administrative and professional employees. This means that the debate has come to centre on the question of whether the latter form a unitary class or one divided into professionals on the one hand and managers and administrators on the other.

All of this marks an important new venture in class analysis. Hitherto, British sociologists have paid little attention to the formation of the middle classes proper. This is all the more striking when set against the body of historical research documenting the emergence of these groups from the late eighteenth century onwards. What sociological studies there have been have focused mainly on lower white-collar workers, who have tended to be treated throughout the twentieth century, from Lederer down to contemporary Marxist theorists such as Wright, Braverman and Poultantzas, as an essentially residual group, and one especially liable to proletarianization.

Until relatively recently, then, there has been very little theoretically inspired research into the middle class proper, that is, as a social category possessing a structural and social identity distinct from such marginal groupings as lower non-manual workers and small-scale entrepreneurs. This is not to say that there has been a shortage of descriptive historical studies of specific professions and their associations, such as those of teachers, higher civil servants and many others – an approach that also characterized Carr-Saunders and Wilson's earlier treatment of professions in general (1933). In addition, there have been several investigations of managers, concentrating mainly on social origins and career paths. But what for a long time was missing in these and subsequent studies was a broader sociological conceptualization of the middle classes from the viewpoint of class analysis. Indeed, in his introduction to *Social mobility in Britain* (1954) – which itself was originally planned as a research project on the middle classes – Glass could point only to the work of Lewis and Maude, *The English middle classes* (1949) This was a well-informed piece of social commentary that in retrospect is chiefly interesting for its separation of the middle classes into broadly the same three groups that are represented almost half a century later in the most recent systematic overview of the subject (Savage et al. 1992).

Contemporary disputes about the nature of middle-class formation are now conducted in much more precisely defined terms, both conceptual and methodological; and yet in large part their vitality thrives on a lack of firm evidence. So any intervention in this debate must cautiously attend to both these features of it. More than 30 years ago, in responding to an invitation to write a piece on the "new" working class, which had been singled out as a rapidly growing section of well-to-do manual workers, and which market researchers, journalists and not a few academics supposed to be middle class oriented and conservatively inclined, it seemed that, in dealing with this hypothesis, it was necessary, first, to take an historical perspective, in order to discover what was actually "new" about this development; and, secondly, to distinguish between changes in economic circumstances, norms and social relations (Lockwood 1960). These viewpoints may still be useful in trying to identify the major issues at stake in current debates on the formation of the middle class(es), which, although much more sophisticated in their conceptualization of class structure, lead to much the same sort of problems relating to social class formation as did those raised by announcements of a "new" working class.

First of all, the most obvious sense in which the problematic of the new service class has replaced that of the new working class is to be found in the fact that the rapid growth of white-collar, and especially of professional, managerial and administrative, employment over the last 20 or 30 years (not least as a result of the extension of the welfare state) has been mirrored by a corresponding diminution of the working class, and particularly its more traditional representatives. Not only is the working class now outnumbered by the middle class (if routine non-manual workers are included) but its centre of social and moral gravity has shifted decisively from Barnsley to Basildon. On the other hand, the "new" middle class, or service class, defined as having a distinctive and privileged employment by contrast with other employees (whether lower white-collar workers or the mass of the manual working class), has also come to be seen as having the potentiality of becoming a well-formed class with its own distinct social identity, and interests that lead on the whole to "conservative" political leanings. There are therefore considerable similarities between the problematic of the new working class of the 1960s and that of the new middle class of the late 1990s and beyond.

Taking first the historical view, it is fairly clear that the chief ways in which the middle classes have always sought to realize their family and group interests are not particularly new. For a long time, at least since the reform of the higher Civil Service (Banks 1954), the core groupings of the upper middle class, such as professionals and administrators, have fairly successfully secured their social reproduction by seeing to it that their children got the right kind of education. Moreover, what is very striking is their continuing success in this respect down to the present time. As Goldthorpe and his colleagues have shown (Goldthorpe 1980a), upper service class fathers have continued to have relatively undiminished chances of passing their positions on to their sons during a period that has also seen very considerable upward mobility into this region of the class structure.

The second point that needs to be made from an historical perspective is that although the groups making up the core of middle classes, or the "service class", have been neglected by class theory, this does not mean that the middle classes have not been very well "formed" right from their inception (Davidoff & Hall 1987, Morris 1990) – perhaps not as a class, but certainly corporatively, through various national associations, professional bodies and trades unions; through appointments or elections to the membership of innumerable representative and consultative bodies at local, regional and national levels; through informal local networks and cliques (including those of Rotarians and Freemasons). For a long time, they have also used to the full their own personal resources, moral as well as material, in seizing opportunities afforded by both private and public educational and medical services. In these various ways, middle-class groups and individuals have defended and promoted their sectional and family interests in a much more direct, continuous and effective manner than by the periodical casting of votes in parliamentary or local elections. This is the "stuff" of which class formation is made up. From this perspective, then, the middle classes have probably always been much better formed than all but the most skilled sections of the working class; and in turn probably less well interconnected than the upper classes (Heald 1985, Scott 1982). At the same time, this aspect of middle-class formation is clearly in need of much closer study – especially one that might establish the structural bases of different types of collective action.

In class theory, the fact that the large amount and variety of associational activity and informal networking – especially at the local level – is central to anything that might be called class formation has been obscured by the idea of classes as unitary actors. Savage (below) is correct in pointing out that the idea of class formation has been almost entirely associated with the fate of the working class, which in turn has been heavily influenced by the Marxian theory of the proletariat and its historical mission. There are two chief reasons why this concept of a "class in itself" becoming a "class for itself" as a collective self-conscious actor is no longer adequate even in its most qualified versions. One is that the institutional nexus of bureaucratiz-ation, citizenship and market relations characteristic of modern capitalist, welfare state democracies has (in a manner too complicated to go into here) produced not only new forms of structured social inequality, but also associated patterns of their legitimation that together make it extremely unlikely that these societies will experi-ence the kind of large-scale "class movements" predicated by Marxian class theory. Secondly, with the benefit of historical insight, it is possible to see that, instead of the class-wide identities and collective actions envisaged by Marxian theory, an equally if not more important feature of working-class formation was its diverse associational life, which was shaped as least as much by the particularities of trade, craft, profession and place and which, because it was bound up with the formation of the middle class, was aimed as much at gaining social position as at economic advantage. By comparison with this ground-level class formation, marked by con-stant redefinitions of local solidarities and hierarchical relations, episodes of any-thing approximating national class conflicts or "class war" have been relatively rare, mostly belonging to a period after the First World War. This is not to try to diminish the significance of past labour movements, but merely to suggest that un-der present-day conditions the so-to-speak "infrastructure" of class formation is likely to be more and more the typical form.

Against this background, it is useful to consider the formation of the contemporary service class or the middle classes by reference to the following benchmarks: the economic, relational and normative. It may be thought odd that this leaves out what has just been identified as the meat of class formation: collective action, which in the case of the middle class has mainly involved strategies of social closure (Parkin 1979). But this is a complicated subject, and in recent debates, as the chapters below well confirm, not one that has received much attention.

It is rather class formation at the *economic* level that is now seen as the key issue, because this is what bears most directly on the validity of the concept of the service class in its most fundamental respect. Inter- and intra-generational patterns of recruitment acquire their significance only on the assumption that the specific employment status of professional, managerial and administrative employees, which engenders and meets expectations of a secure and progressive career, is in fact still the enduring feature of their common class situation.

Against this hypothesis must be set the process of delayering (in US parlance: "rightsizing") and outplacing of middle management functions, which has been frequently reported in the past five years. Equally well publicized have been the anxieties about job security and career prospects among those who have not yet lost their jobs as a result of these measures (the "survivor syndrome") as well as complaints about increasing workloads placed on lower management by corporate directorates in both the private sector and the public sector, perhaps especially in the privatized utilities. Delayering middle management functions has the effect of destroying the hierarchy onto which career expectations are latched – as well as leaving a gulf between top and lower management. If these downward pressures are at all widespread, then there could be no doubt that employees' "loyalty", the reciprocal of employers' "trust", would become less and less the distinctive, defining property of service class jobs. In the public sector, too, new forms of management or external intervention have produced increasing protests among, for example, health and educational professionals about the harsher climate of accountability, which not only goes against the idea of trust but is even seen as an invasion of professional competence and authority.

At the moment, however, there is insufficient evidence to judge whether these kinds of changes (some of which are documented in particular sectors of employment in Ch. 8 by Carter and Fairbrother and Ch. 7 by Halford and Savage) mark the beginnings of a new trend in service class employment, or whether, as Goldthorpe (Ch. 18) suggests, members of the service clas, who have been jettisoned into the ranks of the self-employed will still enjoy "continuity of employability" by taking on outplaced tasks that some of them previously performed as regular employees. As it is, the number of this new breed of managers and professionals who are hired to fill the gaps created by delayering is unknown; as is, more importantly, how many of them are on short-term and part-time contracts. The scale on which these processes are occurring, the extent to which there is a growing differentiation between core and peripheral jobs, and the consequences of all of this for the careers of both kinds of managers and professionals are questions of the utmost importance for the viability of the service class concept.

This is the context within which to consider "demographic" class formation, a term introduced by Goldthorpe to refer primarily to the extent to which the service class is self-recruiting intergenerationally. But an important sub-theme that has emerged in the course of recent discussions is the ease of lifetime movement between professional and managerial jobs (see, for example, Mills in Ch. 6 and Buck et al. 1994). This might very well indicate the growing identity of these two sections of the service class, or at least the blurring of the lines between professional and managerial functions. It is, however, far from clear what interpretation can be put on this. It is not difficult to grasp how professionals are able take on managerial functions. But it is less easy to understand managers being able to enter the traditional and well-established professions that make up the core of the upper service or middle class. Therefore, it must be that their career switch involves retraining for lower, and perhaps less well certified, professional jobs. Moreover, as the research of Fielding (Ch. 10) reveals, in the course of their careers managers are much more likely than professionals to sink into the ranks of the petite bourgeoise and lower-level white-collar workers, or even into the working class and the unemployed. There is obviously much volatility in the managerial region of the service class, a broad and rather indistinct category that has expanded quite remarkably in recent years (Elias 1995). This may be the result of what some experts in the field suspect: namely, that the title of manager is now being rather freely bestowed, perhaps without much change in work routines and earnings. And it is also the case that an increasing number of lower or associate professionals are now taking on managerial duties and responsibilities.

The *relational* aspect of class formation refers to the extent to which a class can be identified through its more or less exclusive patterns of informal social interactions, of which the principal indices are intermarriage and informal association (Scott 1994). Such information, although hard to get, has an important bearing on the question of whether or not there exists a more or less homogeneous service class that possesses definite social as well as economic boundaries, or whether or not within such a class, there are clear subdivisions, whether of situs (such as managerial versus professional, or public versus private sector, employment) or of status (such as between the upper and lower service class). The relational aspect of class formation is therefore distinct from the demographic and the economic. The latter have to do with the extent to which certain occupations constitute a class or a potential class by reason of their having a common employment status and more or less distinct boundaries identifiable by patterns of intergenerational and lifetime mobility. But the extent to which this level of class formation results in social class formation, as measured by such things as intermarriage, friendship networks and associational memberships, is a different matter. It is also one that is closely connected to the problem of class formation at the normative level; that is, the extent to which a class is united by shared values and beliefs or divided into different subcultures. It is at this juncture that the question of whether or not class formation coincides with status formation is most obscure and intriguing. But it is not one to which there is a ready answer. The relational and normative aspects of class formation are now more than ever an open field of investigation, partly because the tradition of local community studies, which once provided some insights into these matters, however partial they may have been, has long since lapsed.

From the small amount of research into the subject of class-related social interactions, it would seem that there is no impermeable barrier between professional and managerial groups as far as intermarriage is concerned (Savage et al. 1992). There also seems to be considerable intermarriage between higher service class men and women in service class jobs, as well as women in lower white-collar jobs (Marshall et al. 1988: 69) and the same broad pattern seems to be apparent from data relating to wives' social backgrounds (Heath 1981: 112). This is perhaps not surprising, given the overall distribution of women's and men's employment. As far as informal association is concerned, there is remarkably little information. In fact, the only reliable data come from the Oxford Mobility Study of 1972. These showed that both the upper and cadet service class drew their friends mainly from within the service class; that lower white-collar workers figured most prominently among their friends from lower social classes; and, interestingly enough, that more of the lower service class had friends in the upper service class than vice versa (Heath 1981: 230). This would suggest that the service class as a whole has fairly distinct social class boundaries – at least in comparison with the social origins of its members – and that there is no marked division between its upper and lower echelons. In contrast to this, a more significant intra-service class social boundary was recorded by a recent German study of the *Dienstklasse* (Herz 1990). It was found that the upper service class was distinct from the lower service class not only in terms of rewards and educational level, but also in its social origins and friendship patterns.[2] Beyond such meagre statistics, there is little evidence of social formation at this level. In this book, Chapter 11 on "gentrification" (Butler) and Chapter 13 on "constructs of rural living" (Cloke et al.) touch on this subject, mainly by illustrating what might possibly prove to be significant differences between the urban-centred and the urban-fleeing middle classes.

The *normative* aspect of class formation refers to the extent to which a class shares common values and beliefs that are manifested in specific norms and forms of behaviour. Setting aside journalism and fiction, information bearing on this subject is sparse. Data on consumption patterns throw some light on lifestyles and cultural orientations of different classes – an approach represented by Warde (Ch. 14), whose research indicates the need for further investigation into the differing lifestyles of professional and managers, in line with the findings of Savage et al. (1992) But the main source is studies of party affiliation, voting and related socio-political attitudes.

Within the salariat or service class, the relationship between class and vote is far from being a very close one, with all major parties finding some support, and Conservative loyalties by no means the dominant tendency (Marshall et al. 1988: 253, Herz 1990: 43). In line with previous studies, the work of Heath and Savage (Ch. 16) shows that the most important divisions within the service class are between the higher and lower sections of professional, administrative and managerial employees, and most especially between those in public versus private employment. Conservative voting is especially low among schoolteachers, social workers, and junior civil servants, and still not very high among such groups as nurses and local government officials. Most of them prefer other parties or express no firm identification.

This distribution seems most likely to be explained by a process of self-selection (see Bagguley Ch. 17), whereby certain kinds of employment are sought by people who have retained or acquired left-wing, collectivist or altruistic values and beliefs as a result of their social origins, their choices of subjects in further or higher education, or their choice of spouse or partner. Such orientations are most prevalent in the "cadet" service class of caring professionals in health, education and the social services, which together make up a large proportion of the service class as a whole.

The same hypothesis is offered by Rose (1994) in presenting his findings that these selfsame groups tend to score low on a scale of individualism, especially in comparison with private sector managers.

Whether differences in consumption patterns, political preferences and wider socio-cultural orientations are finally to be understood as no more than situs or status divisions within a service class identifiable by its common employment status, or else as manifestations of class divisions, based on the command of different kinds of assets within the middle classes, must surely be for the moment a matter of conceptual preference and therefore the impetus to further research. The real test will be which of these approaches proves to be the more useful in accounting for class formation at which particular level. Their ramifications are fully explored by Butler (Ch. 2).

There is a further possibility, favoured by German students of "social milieus": namely that lifestyles and subcultures are becoming increasingly "decoupled" from class position. The thesis of this "new inequalities" school (for an overview, see Hradil 1987, Berger & Hradil 1990, Schulze 1990) is that class analysis, which assumes that the occupational hierarchy is the key to understanding closely related forms of socially structured inequality and corresponding attitudes and behaviour, is now very much at odds with the fact that new lines of inequality have appeared both within, but especially outside, this narrow "economic" or occupational sphere – particularly those associated with gender, ethnicity, age, unemployment, region and family composition, as well as those created by the allocation of welfare state benefits. As a consequence, it is claimed that life-situations and life-courses, far from being determined exclusively by gainful employment and stable careers, are being replaced by a great variety of multiply resourced positions, and of more and more autonomously chosen goals. The final part of the thesis is that, in this changing context, there now flourishes a plurality of subcultures and life-styles that reflect postmaterialist as well as traditional values, and through which people seek to make sense of, and bridge, the various aspects of their lives.[3]

A major defect of this approach, resulting from its methodology, is that the various social milieus have no clear structural location.[4] This precludes the possibility that they may turn out to be related to different employment conditions within broader social classes, such as the various middle-class lifestyles identified by Savage et al. (1992) or the patterns of social consciousness suggested by Crompton (1992).

The ways in which other forms of inequality, such as gender and ethnicity, bear upon the formation of the middle classes still await conceptual clarification. It is now generally recognized that the very process of lower service class and routine white-collar job creation is heavily gendered. And the fact that men's superior access to upper service class jobs results partly from women being disadvantaged in the competition for them is equally uncontentious. But these facts would become significant for class formation only if it were found that service class women had very different social and political beliefs from service class men that were specifically the result of gender, rather than, say, of their different location within the service class, their social origin or "cross-class" marriages and partnerships. So far there is no evidence that this is the case. However, approaching this subject from a rather different perspective, the chapters in this book by Crompton (Ch. 4), Gregson and Lowe (Ch. 9) and Witz (Ch. 3) raise very interesting questions about the effects of domestic arrangements on social mobility, such as the way in which middle-class families who can afford to employ nannies and cleaners might thereby enjoy superior chances of reproducing themselves socially by virtue of what these domestic arrangements contribute to their children's socialization and educational achievement.

What these various pieces of evidence add up to is far from clear. Data on patterns of intermarriage and informal sociability and, to some extent, those relating to lifetime job mobility might be taken to support the service class hypothesis. On the other hand, nothing is known about how social interaction is related to differences in socio-political attitudes within the service class; for example, whether or not in this connection there is a social as well as an ideological boundary between managers in private industry and lower welfare state professionals. Moreover, the evidence that will be most decisive for accepting or rejecting the service class thesis – that relating to the effects of changes in employment relations – is as yet quite insufficient for this purpose.

In the end, the opposition between those who emphasize distinctions within the middle class, such as those between the upper and lower, the professional and managerial, and public and private employment, and those who favour the idea of a unitary service class having structurally well-defined common interests in secure employment and career prospects revolves around the question of the criteria by which a class can be said to be "well formed". This then raises the further question of what degree of internal differentiation is compatible with the use of the term "class". For example, Goldthorpe's defence (Ch. 18) of the continuing relevance of the idea of a unitary service class emphasizes the easy mobility between managerial and professional employment, whereas Herz (1990) is led to the opposite conclusion on the grounds that the upper service class is distinct from the lower service class in terms of educational level, social origins and friendship patterns. At some stage, the judgement as to whether the middle class should be seen as a single service class or one made up of distinct subclasses, turns on what amount of internal differentiation, in respect of which levels and measures of class formation, counts as a difference in kind rather than a difference in degree.[5]

The term "working class" has long been the subject of the same kind of controversy. On the one hand, there are those who tend to see the history of the working class as a sequence of ever new forms of division along the lines of skill and industry, predominantly as a pattern of constantly changing sectional interests, interrupted only very infrequently by episodes of anything remotely resembling unitary class action. From this perspective, it is questionable whether in the light of such variety – all the way down from the "labour artistocracy" to "Essex Man" – it is at all useful to refer to *the* working class. At the other extreme are those who, at least until very recently, have found in the same story support for the idea of a class steadily and progressively gaining in cohesion and coming to recognize that its interests are irreconcilably opposed to those of the capitalist class.

Put in this way it might be thought that there is some resemblance between the latter interpretation and the view that the basic unity of the service class inheres in distinctive employment relations. But the idea of the service class does not entail any corresponding notion of fundamental class opposition. Nor need it imply that it is the class now in the process of replacing the proletariat as the new collective subject on the historical stage – though this is a theme identifiable in the work of Abercrombie & Urry (1983). The service class is more usually seen as a group very much in the middle of contending forces – simultaneously seeking to safeguard its advantages against those who seek to join its ranks from below as well as against those who seek to undermine its privileges from above. Moreover, the ways in which these interests are pursued are very various. Just in respect of collective action, the middle class is surely much more internally differentiated than the working class, in that its modes of representation range all the way from traditional professional associations to militant trade unions. And, quite apart from this, a great many of the service class, principally managers in private industry, have to seek to realize their interests individually rather than collectively.

Of course, personal initiative is the hallmark of the middle classes. They have always used their superior moral and material resources to full effect, above all by giving their children a competitive edge in the main site of social selection: the educational system. And "material resources" deserves emphasis, because even at this level of the class structure the advantages deriving from the possession of substantial wealth, and from the exclusive social circles it gives access to, should not be underestimated. Among the upper reaches of the middle or service class there certainly are some who are able to buy the "right" kind of education for their children and in this way (as well as perhaps more directly) link them with social networks that might be useful for their subsequent careers. In this respect, the social reproduction of some sections of the service class is probably similar to that of the upper class.

One final comment is necessary in this connection, although it refers to a quite different consequence of the concentration of wealth. This is that, among those who by definition have to be assigned to the top service class, there is a very small minority who are what Mouzelis (1991) calls *mega-actors*: namely, the chief executives and top investment managers of the 40 or 50 largest pension and insurance funds that now "own" well over half the value of UK quoted equities. This places them on the frontier, if not at the very centre, of capitalist reproduction. Whom exactly they "serve", to what ends, and by which means, are matters of the utmost importance not only for middle-class formation but for class formation in general.

But all aspects of a subject cannot be followed up all at once. Some discipline is needed. This comes from theory, and is most productive when theories predict contrary and researchable events. The following contributions are distinguished by just such a common focus. The question of which of the two chief, currently competing perspectives on the constitution of the middle class casts more light upon the subject is what gives the several essays their coherence and sharpens their particular lines of enquiry. In this way, the book is a model of how sociological research should be done, and will undoubtedly be a major reference point of further investigation.

Notes

1. As Kocka has pointed out, the terms used to refer to this middle region of the class structure carry very different national connotations, and are therefore "not very useful analytical tools if used outside the type of intellectual or historical context in which they originated" (Kocka, 1980: 9). From this viewpoint, it is worth commenting on the social conditions of pre-war Germany and Austria, which must have influenced Renner's introduction of the term "service class" to refer to the growing numbers of white-collar employees in private employment, whom he saw as agents performing the delegated functions of the capitalist class. The model for this new *Dienstklasse* was Prussian officialdom, whose ethos of service to the state went hand in hand with an almost caste-like, quasi-militaristic social honour, shared all the way down from the higher civil servant and professor to the postman. What was chiefly remarkable about this state bureaucratic hierarchy was that superiors commanded the loyalty of their subordinates because of a shared "service" *ethos* rather than having to trust them because of their specialized skills. A lot of this rubbed off on the new white-collar workers employed in large-scale private industrial and commerical establishments, who entered into a society still very much imbued with an estate consciousness. A major consequence was that the new *Privatbeamte* and *Angestellte* were legally as well as socially identified not so much as a "middle class" in the Anglo-American sense, but rather as a part of the *Mittelstand*. This estate, and even that designated by the inferior title of *Kleinbuergertum*, had a very clear and negative reference point: namely, the proletariat. So, above this line, everyone knew more or less where they stood in a complex social hierarchy. During the Weimar Republic, these status-charged professional identities formed the bases of a multiplicity of associations and parties, which, in turn, robbed the major centre parties of much of their support and became a rich recruiting ground for the NSDAP (Childers 1991). It may be thought that this context of Renner's notion of the "service class" is with difficulty transferrable to a late twentieth-century context in which not only private but also many public, managerial and professional employees' reciprocation of loyal dedicated service for their employers's trust is a relationship that is not at all of the same order.
2. The research, which attempted to apply Goldthorpe's class schema, was based on a sample of men and women respondents, drawn from three national representative surveys in West Germany (including West Berlin) between 1980 and 1984.
3. A similar line of argument is presented in the contribution of Cloke, Phillips and Thrift (Ch.13), which documents the various culturally mediated "lifestyle strategies" of middle-class groups in the context of what is held to be their ever more extensive "colonization" of rural life.
4. "Social milieus" are first identified by means of cluster analysis of a variety of data relating to attitudes and lifestyles, and then presented in a two-dimensional space: one axis being some kind of traditional/post-materialist continuum, and the other one a scale of socio-economic status, with broadly defined "classes", such as upper, middle and lower. The result is that "social milieus" have no clear structural location in employment relations. This in turn does nothing to discomfort the guiding hypothesis that lifestyles are

becoming progressively "decoupled" from class or status positions.

5. For example, here are some of the figures by which Herz seeks to make his case, and in brackets the corresponding ones from the Oxford Mobility Study as presented by Heath (1981: 63, 230). A recalculation of the figures in Herz's Table 1 shows that 49% of the upper service class came from service class backgrounds (37%) compared with 30% in the case of the lower service class (23%). As regards informal association, 59% of the friends of the upper service class were in *mainly* upper service class occupations (44%) compared with 36% in the case of the lower service class (22%). The point is not whether or not the German and English data are exactly comparable, which they are not, but rather that these figures are susceptible of different interpretations, one of which might be that the German salariat of the 1980s is on both counts more socially exclusive than the English salariat of the 1970s. But the chief question is whether the recorded differences between the upper and lower sections of the service class in either country might or might not be taken to signify an internal *class* boundary.

Part One
Orientations

Chapter One

Class analysis and social research

Mike Savage

> . . . in the traditional models, people were socialised into worlds of home
> and work in which they "knew their place". They joined a class, learned its
> values, developed its attitudes and behaved accordingly – again through-
> out their lifetimes. Those fairly rigid boundaries have now gone. (Thrift &
> Johnston 1993: 84)

As this rather apocalyptic comment implies, the status of class analysis is in doubt as
we approach the twenty-first century. There is a feeling amongst social scientists
that the pace and scope of contemporary social change is making the concept of
social class redundant. What value does the idea of class, fashioned by Marx and
Weber to explore the tensions of industrial capitalism, have for investigating the
putatively postmodern, post-industrial, information societies that some observers
currently detect?

Indeed, it might even be argued that the supposed "death of class" is one of the
very few themes shared by the varied writers arguing that major social change is
occurring, because there is certainly no broader consensus on how they interpret
current developments. Accounts range from "economy-centred" analyses such as
those associated with neo-Marxist writers discussing post-Fordism (Aglietta 1979
and Harvey 1987; see Amin 1994 for an overview) to more "cultural" accounts,
such as the arguments of Giddens, Beck and Bauman concerning the development
of "reflexive modernity" (Giddens 1990, Beck 1992, Lash & Urry 1994) or "postmodernity" (Bauman 1991). It is not the purpose of this paper to discuss and evaluate these different views (see Smart 1992). Rather, it is interesting to note their
common objection to the contemporary relevance of class. For Beck (1992: 100),
"class society will pale into insignificance"; for Bauman (1985: 112), "it is increasingly difficult to maintain that class membership remains a major key to the mechanism of reproduction of societally-inflicted deprivations (and more generally, social
differentiation as such)", and similar ideas are echoed by Giddens, Lash & Urry,
and others.

And yet, despite this tide of negative opinion, social class is an obstinate concept that refuses to make a dignified exit from the social scientific agenda. Some sociologists, such as the English sociologists John Goldthorpe, Anthony Heath and Gordon Marshall, the American Erik Wright, or – in a rather different tradition – the Frenchman Pierre Bourdieu, have insisted on the continued centrality of social class divisions to the analysis of social relations. Indeed some would argue that class analysis has only recently attained unprecedented conceptual clarity and achieved major research breakthroughs. Thus it would be possible to trace an evolutionary history from the early days when social enquirers such as Booth and Rowntree documented the nature and extent of poverty at the turn of the century to the sophistication evident in current analyses, such as that of Erikson and Goldthorpe's *The constant flux* (1992b). The argument might run that, with the introduction of Weberian theory from the 1950s and Marxist theory from the 1960s, the study of class took a more analytical focus, and landmark studies such as Glass's *Social mobility in Britain* (1954), Lockwood's *The blackcoated worker* (1958), and Goldthorpe, Lockwood et al.'s *The affluent worker in the class structure* (1968/69) appeared to give class analysis a new theoretical clarity and empirical rigour that placed it at the centre of British social science. The promise of class analysis lay in its ability to offer a viable theoretical alternative to functionalism while opening up whole new areas of empirical research. The field of social mobility was especially affected by the development of the "class structural" approach, which marked a major break from the individualistic assumptions of previously dominant status attainment models common in the USA (see Goldthorpe 1980a, Erikson & Goldthorpe 1992b), but there were other examples. Studies of the relationship between class and politics (Heath et al. 1985) and between social class and popular attitudes (Marshall et al. 1988) seemed to confirm such promise. For researchers within this "class analysis programme" (to adopt the terminology of Goldthorpe & Marshall 1992), the growing scepticism towards class appeared at the very same moment that its importance was being demonstrated through substantive research.

In recent years something of a debate between critics and supporters of the value of the class concept has spluttered along (Pahl 1989, Mullins 1990, Goldthorpe & Marshall 1992, and see the overview in Crompton 1993). However, it has succeeded only in revealing that various writers have such different conceptions of what social science is all about that they find it difficult to understand each other's arguments. One of the principal objectives of this book is to allow the debate about the merits of class analysis to continue in a more profitable and stimulating vein through the collection of a range of empirically focused papers on various aspects of the British middle classes. The aim is partly to use the middle classes as a "frame" on which to hang observations about the nature of contemporary British society. But underlying this we also have a deeper conceptual interest in the value of class analysis itself. A question raised in every paper, in different ways, is the extent to which some concept of social class can be used to shed light on current dynamics of change and persistence.

This first chapter is an attempt to clear the ground so that the terms of the debate are clear. The intention is less to advance a particular view of the status of class analysis, than to try and provide a guide round a contested terrain, though some of my own prejudices will inevitably be displayed in the process. I begin by showing that the debate about class has, in Britain, been conducted in the shadow of a particular view of the "traditional working class". Views about the changing character of the working class are all too readily transported into claims about the status of class analysis and there has been a persistent tendency to assume that class analysis as a whole is brought into question because of the alleged decline of the "traditional working class" (indeed echoes of this can be found in the quote from Thrift and Johnston that began this paper). In the second section I propose that it is necessary to examine the merits of class analysis on its own terms, and I indicate some of the conceptual choices and options facing social scientists. I suggest that the concept of class occupies a "force field" between structural and cultural analyses and between views that see class as the central as opposed to one possible axis of social division. Finally, I discuss how the recent rise of attention to the processes of gender and ethnicity affects the "class analysis programme".

1.1 The political context

In order to understand the contours of the current debate on social class it is essential to comprehend the peculiarly British obsession with class. The most important point to make here is that in Britain, since at least the early twentieth century and arguably for much longer, there has been a strong tendency to conflate class in general with the working class in particular. The working class has traditionally been the crucial reference point that people have used to identify themselves in class terms. This partly reflects the cohesiveness, strength and visibility of the working class and its organizations in the first half of the twentieth century, especially as manifested through the labour movement. But it is important to recognize that this "traditional working class", as it has later been termed (Stedman-Jones 1973), was actually a particular social construction. As McKibbin (1990) has shown, Conservative politicians after the First World War tried to define a particular notion of a "middle-class public" by counterposing it to a version of the "working class" that they defined as being trade union based, disloyal, unpatriotic and so forth. By this means the construction of middle-class identities was primarily related to a claim that you were *not* working class.

The result of this was twofold. First, it led to a particular preoccupation with a highly stereotyped "traditional working class", when in reality manual workers were much more divided and heterogeneous than that image of them. Secondly, and more important for us, people's views of the general value of class analysis tended to be coloured by views about the significance of this stereotype of the traditional working class. Even if one is prepared to accept some of the pertinence of the traditional view of the working class in the early years of the twentieth century (see the overview in Savage & Miles 1994), there can be little doubt that there have been significant changes to the working class since the mid-twentieth century. Even the most cautious on this point, for example John Goldthorpe, are prepared to admit that the working class has shrunk in size as a result of the decline of manufacturing industry, while others point to much more far-reaching economic, social and cultural changes, related to such issues as the rise of working-class affluence, consumerism and home-ownership, the development of distinct working-class youth cultures, the proliferation of ethnic cultures and so forth. Whatever one's view about such developments, the important point is that they should not be assumed *a priori* to be indications that "class is not important". The general merits or otherwise of class analysis should not be confused with the fortunes of a particular view of working class.

But, in fact, confusion is legion. Perhaps the best example of this is the debate over "class dealignment" (see Crewe & Sarlvik 1981, Heath et al. 1985, 1991, Marshall et al. 1988). Strictly speaking, class dealignment refers to the declining propensity for members of given social classes to vote for their allegedly "natural" class party: Labour in the case of the working class and Conservative for the middle class. There do seem to be important shifts here: in the 1960s, 63% of manual workers voted Labour, compared with only 43% in the 1980s (Dunleavy 1989: 173). In a period such as the early and mid-1980s, however, when the Labour Party is generally less popular amongst the electorate, one would expect a smaller proportion of the working class – as of any other class – to vote for it. What needs to be shown if the class dealignment thesis is to be upheld is that workers are proportionately less likely to vote Labour than other social classes are, and research suggests that the trends here are by no means unilinear (Heath et al. 1991, Dunleavy 1989). In the ensuing debate over this issue, however, it has become clear that some writers regard the idea of class dealignment as virtually synonymous with the decline of the Labour Party. Kavanagh's (1990: 178) observation that, "in all the rarefied debate over whether we should measure absolute or relative class dealignment . . . we are in danger of throwing out the baby with the bathwater, overlooking the dramatic decline in Labour support", is a remarkable admission of this fact.

The same point can be made concerning the recent debate about the "underclass", which has been the subject of considerable speculation and research both in America and more recently in Britain. Proponents of the underclass theory argue that a significant sector of the population is deprived of access to regular (or even irregular) employment and is ghettoized into "redundant" social spaces, frequently slums and council estates, and is becoming increasingly marginalized from the rest of society (see Saunders 1990, Westergaard 1992, Lash & Urry 1994). The evidence concerning the underclass issue is hotly debated, and a number of writers contest the idea that it can be clearly distinguished from the working class, pointing to a relatively high degree of mobility into and away from "underclass" positions (Gallie 1989, Morris 1994). But what is revealing about the importation of the underclass idea to Britain is the way that it is seized upon by some writers to show that the working class is now no longer homogeneous and therefore to cast doubt on the value of class analysis *per se* (Saunders 1990). There is no reason to suppose, however, that the existence of the underclass really has fundamental implications for class analysis (as opposed to implications for our understanding of the working class). It is interesting, in fact, to point out that in the American context the idea of the underclass has been used to explore the declining significance of race rather than of class. For Wilson (1986) it is the ability of affluent middle-class blacks to leave ghetto locations which allows those left behind to form a distinct underclass, and in this respect appears to indicate the growing importance of class.

A final example of this issue is evident if the question of new forms of politics is broached. Today there are numerous claims that "class politics" is giving or has given way to other types of political movements. The sorts of movements mentioned here are various. They include new forms of politics arising out of consumption divisions, especially in relation to housing tenure (Saunders 1990); concerns with environmental risks that are common to members of all classes (Beck 1992); people's growing concerns with expressive issues as evidenced through ideas of "postmaterialism" (Inglehart 1971), and with "self-identity" and lifestyle (Giddens 1991). Related to these developments, it is sometimes claimed that solidaristic class-based political organizations are giving way to new social movements that tend to be organized around specific issues and have a more diffuse constituency (Scott 1991).

What is again interesting about these sorts of arguments is how they suggest a contrast not with class politics *per se* but with a specific form of political organization based on the labour movement. Indeed this contrast is directly drawn by Giddens (1990: 159), for instance, when he seeks to distinguish labour movements, democratic movements, peace movements and ecological movements. It is all too easy for a typology such as this to drift into the quite erroneous assumption that class is most important in relation to labour movements. But just as it is vital to register that labour movements are not "pure" class movements, because they also rest upon gendered, ethnic and nationalist bases, it is equally important to recognize that class may be pertinent to other political forms.

In general I have suggested that we need to liberate contemporary discussions about class analysis from specific concerns with the "traditional working class" and Labour politics. The working class organized through the labour movement is not the litmus test against which the virtues (or otherwise) of class analysis should be judged. It is this that gives particular general interest to this collection of papers on the middle classes.

1.2 Issues in class analysis

The papers in this book use a variety of means for understanding and analyzing the middle classes. Some of the specific issues in the way they understand the middle classes are examined in the next chapter. Here, I focus on some of the broad tensions evident in their handling of the class concept. Let me begin by noting that it has always been difficult to find ways of carrying out theoretical "closure" round the concept of class. This is indeed one of its strengths, since it serves as a point of intersection between different frameworks of analysis and between social scientific and lay terms of reference. Indeed, it is one of the few terms that appears both to be widely used by people in their "everyday life" (at least in contemporary Britain (see Marshall et al. 1988), for we obviously need to be wary about assuming it has any pertinence in other societies, (see Reddy 1987, Joyce 1990)), and to be the subject of systematic social scientific enquiry. However, the inevitable concomitant of this is that the term lacks precision. In this section I seek not to delineate what class is "really" about, but to indicate some of the possible ways of handling it within social scientific analyses.

Let me begin by noting that most perspectives on class tend to adopt some sort of structural approach that focuses on the way that social classes are rooted in the division of labour and, in particular, employment relations. This perspective can be traced back to the theoretical framework laid down by Marx and Weber and in current usage has led to the focus on social class as defined by employment and occupational location (Edgell 1993, Crompton 1993). In the course of the 1980s, however, many social theorists became critical of structural approaches to social explanation that rooted social causation in disembodied and abstract social structures. Within sociology, the work of Giddens (e.g. 1984) was especially influential in redirecting attention to the need to overcome the duality between structure and agency through a recognition that structures exist only insofar as they are drawn upon by human agents in their everyday lives. But Giddens' theoretical objectives have been overshadowed by an even more radical critique influenced by post-structuralist and postmodernist currents in which any attempt to delineate "objective" social structures is regarded as illegitimate. The arguments of Derrida (1976) pointing to the way that "reality" can become an object only through language have had wide repercussions here (e.g. Laclau & Mouffe 1985). From a more sociological perspective, the writings of Bauman (1987) alert us to some of the political stakes involved in attempting to define "truth" and "reality". He sees this as part of the general tendency of modern thought to reject ambivalence and establish certainty. For Bauman, the attempt to specify objective social structures is related to the traditional role of the intellectual as "legislator", able to decree what is right or wrong by intellectual pronouncement.

From these points of view it is easy to see how social class appears as a problematic concept, tied to a modernist, "objectivist" perspective. Hindess (1987) raises two particular criticisms. First, class analysis sees classes as actors, wrongly imputing agency to otherwise heterogeneous groups of people. Although Hindess agrees that organizations can be seen as agents, he regards it as illegitimate for researchers to define a social class by theoretical fiat and then to suggest that the resulting group of people are collective actors. Secondly, Hindess argues that class analysis rests upon a notion of "objective interests", that is to say, the interests that govern social classes are defined by virtue of objective social structures, with the result that human agents have only a minimal role in defining their interests.

The sorts of problems I have outlined have been dealt with in three different ways, which I want to explore below. First, it can be denied that social class is a structuralist, "objective" concept in the way Hindess suggests. There is in fact a distinguished tradition, whose best-known exponent is E. P. Thompson, that argues that social classes can be recognized only in the cultural activities and beliefs of social agents. Thompson's best-known statement of this position is his claim that "class happens when some men [sic], as a result of common experiences (inherited or shared) feel and articulate the identity of their interests as between themselves, and as against other men whose interests are different from (and usually opposed to) theirs" (Thompson 1968: 9–10). In the absence of such identities, class cannot be said to exist in any meaningful way.

One of the problems with Thompson's formulation is that it may radically restrict the relevance of the concept of class. Indeed, in recent social history, this "culturalist" turn has been widely taken up by historians emphasizing that the idea of class has only limited provenance, even in those capitalist industrial societies previously assumed to be based around it. Stedman-Jones (1983) has argued that even the Chartists of the 1840s – assumed by Thompson to be a class-based political movement – did not deploy a clear notion of class in their writings, and this argument has been taken further by Joyce (1990), who contends that late-Victorian textile workers had only a limited awareness of class.

Another problem with Thompson's formulation it that it reiterates the distinction between structure and agency without finding a clear way of seeing how they interrelated. Despite himself, Thompson was led to a voluntarist account in which awareness of class seemed unrelated to economic or social context. A number of Marxists criticized Thompson for being unable to examine how forms of class awareness were linked to various forms of economic and social relationship (e.g. Johnson 1978: Anderson 1980).

This suggests a second response to the problem of class determinism. This involves finding a way of conceptualizing structure and agency that does not involve either a crude determinism or a crass voluntarism. This is the response developed by Anthony Giddens in his attempts to develop "structuration theory". Giddens (1973) coined the term "structuration" in a book on class that tried to specify how economic class relations give rise to forms of class identity and action, though in his later work he developed his arguments more generally. Giddens (1984) argued that sociology needs to explore the duality of structure. This duality refers to the "essential recursiveness of social life as constituted in social practices. Social life is both medium and outcome of the reproduction of practices" (Giddens 1979: 4).

Although this notion of duality is attractive, it can be argued that it is too ambitious, in that it attempts to "resolve" an issue through epistemological formulation rather than by recognizing how specific structures and agents interrelate in particular contexts (see, generally, Mouzelis 1991). It is indeed noteworthy that little empirical research has actually deployed Giddens' framework in practice (see Gregson 1988). The reasons for this have been suggested by Margaret Archer (1987), who argues that the structure–agency issue should be seen as a dualism that exists in the social world, and by Mouzelis (1991), who points out that structures can be dualisms at different times. Mouzelis emphasizes that when people want to change or monitor social relations they need to step back from such structures in order to question or evaluate them, with the result that "actors as subjects take up a certain distance from the rules, in order to view them as social objects requiring strategic intervention" (Mouzelis 1991: 29). The point is that the tension between structure and agency is not a specifically sociological problem that can be resolved purely at the level of social theory; rather it is one that we routinely confront in various ways every day of our lives, but whose precise nature and the ways in which we handle it will vary. For this reason the aim of analysis should be to provide a framework that allows the study of the structure–agency interface but that does not lay down *a priori* what will be found.

This suggests a third and final response to the criticism of determinism. This is that the relationship between structure and agency (along with related tensions between macro and micro, and economic and cultural relations) needs to be studied empirically, and that research should address the question of how different sorts of relationships are established concretely. This may sound as if it is the response of an empiricist, but this would be a mistaken claim, for it is still vital to develop a conceptual framework that allows the relationship to be explored, and it is precisely here that the study of class may be important.

It can in fact be argued, contrary to Hindess and other critics of class analysis, that most research on class, since at least the 1950s, has endeavoured to find ways of understanding the complex inter-linkages between class structures and class formation that attempt to avoid class determinism while still being attuned to the manner in which classes are "rooted" in economic relationships. Thus it is widely accepted that membership of a class does not guarantee any particular form of social action. Lockwood (1981) shows that the only viable theory of action readily available to class theory is an instrumental one in which people pursue their maximum self-interest as defined by their class position. This poses problems in explaining non-instrumental action, and also in finding a way of resolving the "free-rider problem", since instrumentally rational individuals will tend not to act collectively to pursue their interests because this will entail costs without the guarantee of benefits (Lash & Urry 1984).

This position is rather similar to that of Goldthorpe (1980a), who distinguishes class situations from social classes themselves, which he defines as social collectivities. This distinction allows the authors at least to claim to avoid determinism. For Goldthorpe and Marshall,

> . . . the occupancy of class positions is seen as creating only potential interests, such as may also arise from other structural locations. Whether, then, it is class, rather than other, interests that individuals do in fact seek to realise will depend in the first place on the social identities that they take up . . . (Goldthorpe & Marshall 1992: 384)

The point here is that, if class formation does not take place, then it is not possible for the class positions to have any independent effects on social relations (which is not to say that there may not be strong associations between them and a range of other practices), and therefore they do not really exist.

Rather than assume any direct relationship between class structure and class action, most research has focused on how forms of collective action can nonetheless be sustained by exploring the sorts of resources that agents can draw on (Lash & Urry 1984) or the capacities that allow them to pursue their interests (Savage 1987). In some respects this means that the purity of class analysis is substantively weakened since it has to incorporate presuppositions from outside its original theoretical remit. But if the goal is to provide convincing accounts of the relationship between class structures and forms of social action, the gains seem considerable.

The sort of research that might be held up as examples of the virtues of this research tradition includes the relationship between images of society and social location sparked off by Lockwood (1966) and discussed by Bulmer (1975), Newby (1977) and many others; the relationship between class structures and demographic class formation (Goldthorpe 1980a, Heath 1981); the relationship between class and voting (Heath et al. 1985, Marshall et al. 1988); the examination of the sorts of capacities that might facilitate class based collective action (Wright 1978, Lash & Urry 1984, Savage 1987); and so on. In all these cases it is recognized that the mere fact of class explains very little and that it is much more significant to explore the sorts of intervening factors that might facilitate class formation, and these examples all point to how a class analysis can be sensitive to context and particularity.

1.3   The class formation problematic

In recent years the notion that a "class formation" problematic is emerging that uses a focus on class as a way of establishing links between diverse social phenomena is becoming rather more popular. It is evident (in different ways) in Goldthorpe and Marshall's (1992) call for a "research programme" of class analysis, in Savage et al.'s (1992) framework for class analysis, and in Crompton's (1993 and this volume) account of the pitfalls and promise of recent class analysis. The main task of research within the class formation problematic is to establish whether structurally based relationships are socially meaningful and, if so, how and why they become significant. Some of the papers in this volume examine the extent to which employment-based social class does appear a significant feature in explaining given social outcomes: notably Warde and Tomlinson's examination of food preferences (Ch. 14), Hamnett's study of housing and class (Ch. 15), and Heath and Savage's study of political identification (Ch. 16). Other papers discuss some of the processes that might explain how class formation does or does not occur. Some of the most important of these general issues are as follows.

Class, gender and ethnicity

Until the 1980s an emphasis upon class tended to be associated with a repudiation of the significance of gender and ethnicity (see e.g. Lockwood 1986). One of the striking features about most of the papers in this book is that few would seek to defend class in these terms. The main point at issue is whether gender and ethnicity are to be held analytically separate from class, or whether they are to be seen as linked. The decision will affect whether one examines class formation as a process that also involves forms of gender and ethnic mobilization. These issues are discussed theoretically in Part II of this book, and are taken up empirically in some of the chapters, notably by Gregson and Lowe in their study of domestic labour and the middle classes (Ch. 9), and by Mills and Fielding in their respective studies of social mobility (Ch. 6) and migration (Ch. 10), and are discussed further in the conclusions, especially by Massey (Ch. 19).

Social mobility

The work of Goldthorpe has done most to establish the idea that social mobility plays a key role in class formation. Goldthorpe (1980a, with Lewellyn & Payne 1987) argues that patterns of social mobility have an important function in ascertaining whether social classes might emerge as collectivities. If a particular social class is largely composed of people who were brought up in other social classes, it will comprise heterogeneous types of people, with the result that it is unlikely to be the base for a common identity. Goldthorpe adds the important rider that, even if there is a high rate of self-recruitment it does not follow that collective action need ensue – political organization and cultural mobilization are separate elements of class formation (e.g. Goldthorpe & Marshall 1992: 384–5). In this book, three papers contain material relevant to this analysis of social mobility. Using different datasets, Mills (Ch. 6) and Fielding (Ch. 10) examine the work-life mobility of professionals and managers, while Halford and Savage (Ch. 7) explore how the bureaucratic career is being redefined in some large organizations. The early parts of Mills's (Ch. 6) paper also discuss some of the general issues in studying social mobility.

Spatial processes

The notion of class formation implies that classes reach a level of fixity and stability that allows them to engage in cohesive, routinized social actions. This notion of stability is clearly present in Goldthorpe's analysis of social mobility, but it also has a spatial dimension. Do members of the same social classes tend to live together? Do their patterns of spatial mobility – whether this be mobility of residence (migration), or mobility in the course of working routines or leisure activity – tend to undermine or consolidate patterns of solidarity with others? Part IV of this book comprises a series of studies of this issue: Fielding (Ch. 10) examines how patterns of migration affect middle-class mobility, Urry (Ch. 12) and Cloke et al. (Ch. 13) consider whether the middle class relationship to the countryside plays an important role in their formation as a class and, finally, Butler (Ch. 11) considers the distinctive lifestyles of middle-class gentrifiers to examine whether they constitute a distinctive middle-class fraction.

Consumption

One of the main arguments developed by various writers exploring contemporary social change is that consumption practices are increasingly independent of the world of employment (and class?). This notion reaches its apogee with Baudrillard's arguments concerning the hyper-reality of consumer societies. The two chapters in Part V, by Warde & Tomlinson (Ch. 14) and Hamnett (Ch .15), are sensitive explanations of the extent to which food consumption and housing can be linked to features of class position.

Political mobilization

Goldthorpe emphasizes that political mobilization cannot be read off from social class position, an argument that now sounds uncontroversial. This raises the question of how forms of political mobilization can be seen as linked to social class in any way. The two papers in Part VI explore this issue by examining the extent to which "new social movements" and political identification with established political parties can usefully be seen as class-based forms of politics.

1.4 Conclusions

In this introductory paper I have argued that it is often assumed that class analysis is primarily a tool to study the working class. This reflects the peculiarities of British history, and gives the term "social class" a dated feel, as a concept that may have limited value today. In this chapter I have contended that we should not see class analysis as simply being *about* the fortunes of particular social classes. Rather it should be defended as an empirically based attempt to explore the complex interrelationships and interdependencies between social structures and forms of agency on the one hand, and as an enquiry into the relationship between mechanisms that produce inequalities and various forms of cultural identity on the other. As an analytical tool committed to the value of empirical research, class analysis has had a distinguished history and it is by no means clear that it is played out. Indeed, as Crompton (1993) suggests, its ability to prevent theoretical "closure", to be totally incorporated into one theoretical or methodological framework, is a real strength well suited to these allegedly postmodern times.

In order to provide a broad defence of class analysis here, I have chosen to skate over more specific arguments concerning how the middle classes can be conceptualized and understood. In Chapter 2, therefore, Tim Butler examines the various theoretical approaches to the middle classes, that helps introduce many of the more specific issues discussed in the chapters of this book.

Chapter Two

The debate over the
middle classes

Tim Butler

2.1 Introduction

Chapter 1 suggested that if class analysis is to remain a live area of enquiry it needs to examine emerging social groups such as the middle classes, rather than keep the lens focused on groups such as the working class. Traditionally, however, historians, sociologists and geographers have found it much easier to examine the working class or the "ruling class" than the more messy and fragmented middle class. However, in the past few years a number of important and significant contributions have been made to the task of thinking about the position and role of the middle class, or middle classes, in modern societies, and this chapter reviews the basic features of various relevant approaches as an introduction to some of the specific issues discussed in the following chapters.

The problem of understanding the middle classes is an old one. Here is the historical sociologist Michael Mann (1993: 547):

> Defining the middle class has always been contentious. The rise of "middling groups" immediately presented conceptual problems for nineteenth century observers. Most used the plural "middle classes", impressed by their heterogeneity . . . contemporaries left definitions to us, but our historians have been no great help . . . Sociologists provide more concepts – the petit bourgeoisie with its old, new and traditional fractions; the middle class, old, new and decomposed; the new working class; the service class; the professional and managerial class – all of these may be in "contradictory class locations" . . . this plethora embodies five alternative theories. Middling groups are
> 1. In the working class – the conclusion of orthodox Marxism
> 2. Part of the ruling bourgeois or capitalist class – an occasional, pessimistic Marxian response
> 3. In an ambiguous, contradictory class location (Wright 1985: 42–57)
> 4. "Decomposed", as various middling groups fall into different classes,

or Stande – the most common view (e.g. Dahrendorf 1959)
5. A separate middle class (e.g. Giddens 1973)

It is probably true to say that in more recent years attention has shifted from the early to the later options that Mann presents. Classical Marxism argued that, as capitalist societies polarized between capitalists and proletariat, the middle classes would either be squeezed into the working class (option 1), or become co-opted into the capitalist class proper (option 2), or, in Wright's option 3, come to occupy a rather ambiguous class position between the two key classes. Recently, however, such views have been challenged by arguments that the middle classes cannot easily be seen either as surrogate members of the working class or as a direct part of the capitalist class – they have their own distinctive role and position in society.

This leads to Mann's options 4 and 5. If option 5 – the suggestion that the middle classes are indeed a separate class – is adopted, it becomes essential to be able to specify its distinctive foundations and character. Another possibility, Mann's option 4, is to see the middle classes as "decomposed" between different sorts of fragmented classes, but this still raises the question of what sort of classes the middle class is decomposed between. Most current writers (including Mann) take some sort of hybrid approach between these last two options. Let me briefly lay out the details of the most important of these.

2.2   The concept of the service class

Perhaps the most important recent contribution to the understanding of the middle classes has been the development and popularization of the concept of the "service class", principally by John Goldthorpe (1982), and also by John Urry with various co-authors (Abercrombie & Urry 1983, Lash & Urry 1987). The key point in both these accounts is that what are often loosely termed "the middle classes" are in fact divided between routine white-collar workers, who in many respects are little different from manual workers, a "service class" of professionals and managers, and also a distinct class of self-employed petits bourgeois.

The term "service class" derives from the writings in the 1950s of the Austro-Marxist Karl Renner (Goldthorpe 1982, Abercrombie & Urry 1983, Crompton 1986, Lash & Urry 1987, Savage et al. 1988, 1992).

> The expression "service class" marks a fundamental distinction from the traditional "serving class" which performed real labour, if only at a rudimentary technical level, and was for the most part paid in kind. Three basic forms can be distinguished: economic service (managers etc.), social service (distributive agents of welfare services), and public service (public, official agents). (Renner 1978: 250)

Dahrendorf (1959) was responsible for introducing Renner's work into English-language sociology, largely, it would appear, to buttress his own attempt to develop a non-Marxist (or anti-Marxist) analysis of the conflicts in industrial society,

> Renner developed a kind of "theory of delegation". In post-capitalist society, "the functions" of capitalists appear subdivided into a steadily growing number of salaried employees of the very highest and of high and of lower rank . . . these new aids [*sic*] are neither capitalists nor workers, they are not owners of capital, they do not create value by their work, but they do control values created by others. Renner calls this stratum the "service class". It has fashioned itself on the model of public civil service and has been transformed from a caste into a class. Although it participates in authority, it does not exercise absolute authority but is subject to the norms and values of society. (Dahrendorf 1959: 94)

For Renner, the service class – unlike the working class – is not in a wage relationship with capital but rather in a contractual one for which a salary is awarded. The service contract is a measure of the trust placed in the official not only to carry out the instructions of the employer but also to proffer advice that is in the employer's best interest. Although the origins of the service class might have been in public administration, its membership, according to Renner, has now spread to those running private enterprises and organizing welfare services.

The concept of the service class remained unpopular, however, until its use by Goldthorpe (1980a) in the course of his enquiries into social mobility, and its subsequent adoption by Urry to examine various facets of social and economic change (notably Lash & Urry 1987), at which point it began to be more commonly used in British social research (e.g. Thrift 1987, Savage et al. 1988), though it has rarely been adopted by researchers from other countries, such as the USA. The service class became a term for distinguishing the more powerful members of the middle class from less powerful and more menial non manual workers. Let me now discuss the arguments of Goldthorpe and Urry in more detail.

2.3   The service class: a dominant and conservative class?

Goldthorpe identifies trust as the key concept in defining the class position of the service class. In the same manner that the working class is defined, in Marxist terms at least, by its wage relationship to capital, so for Goldthorpe (as for Renner) the key issue is the "service contract", that involves a set of moral obligations between the employer and employee. This is important because, if employers are to delegate authority and also if they are to seek professional advice, then they must know that their employees are acting in their best interests (Goldthorpe 1982: 169). As a result, the service class employee is rewarded with more favourable remuneration, conditions of service, security of tenure and, crucially, career advancement prospects than the ordinary employee. In essence, according to Goldthorpe, there is a long-term set of moral obligations between the two and, whereas the wage employee receives a wage for a fairly tightly defined task, the service relationship is less specific and refers to "compensation" and "consideration" in return for the acceptance of an obligation to discharge trust "faithfully" (Goldthorpe 1982: 169). Both their work and market situations distinguish them from other groups of employees.

Goldthorpe denies that this definition of the service class embraces disparate groups who occupy different positions in the division of labour, notably professionals on the one hand and managers and administrators on the other. Despite the fact that these groups perform often quite different functions, he argues that it is the trust to carry out their role faithfully for the employing class both in terms of delegated authority (managers/administrators) and as providers of specialist advice (professionals) that defines them as members of a common class. The boundary problem he identifies as being between them and the classes above and below them (1982: 170). Following Renner, he argues that members of the service class are ultimately propertyless employees and so are separated from the class that appoints them. The nature of this dominant class is unimportant and can, he suggests, be conceived of as a ruling or capitalist class or a series of ruling elites without weakening the case for the existence of a service class. The boundary between the service class and those below it is based on the latter's lack of prospects.

Goldthorpe also discusses the question of class formation, which he sees as the intervening variable between the position the service class occupies in the class structure and its socio-political self-expression, by claiming that it is still in a process of evolution. There are, he says, two aspects to class formation: demographic and socio-cultural identity. The former refers to the extent to which classes acquire a demographic identity – that is, "become identifiable as collectivities through the continuity by which individuals and families retain their class structure over time" (1982: 172). The latter refers to the extent to which a common and identifiable lifestyle emerges together with "patterns of preferred association" (ibid.). He admits that, at least at the time of the Nuffield Mobility Survey of 1972, the service class did not exist as a cohesive, demographically formed class. This was due to the speed with which the service class has developed over recent years, growing from approximately 5% of the population in the early decades of the twentieth century to in excess of 25% in the 1980s. The reasons for its growth, he suggests, are less important than the effects, which are twofold. First, in order to grow it has had to recruit widely from other social classes, with the consequence that only about one third of its members are the offspring of parents who held similar positions. Secondly, as a result of this widespread recruitment from outside the service class, he claims that many of its members have a low level of formal qualification and thus of cultural capital; this is particularly marked in the administrative and managerial strata (Goldthorpe 1982: 175). Goldthorpe points to a class that he sees as relatively undifferentiated internally and essentially conservative in outlook. His rationale for this claim is derived from the defining characteristic of the service class, which, as he sees it, is its position of delegated authority or specialized knowledge, that is the

29

basis of favoured conditions of employment and advancement for its members. He argues that it is reasonable to assume that it will act in defence of those privileges and that its general outlook will therefore be conservative (1982: 180). Crucially, the service class will want to police the space below it in order to maintain its relative privilege. Thus Goldthorpe claims there is little chance of a political alliance with the working class, as some "new class" theorists have claimed.

2.3   The service class: a class possessed of causal powers?

In contrast to Goldthorpe (1982), Abercrombie & Urry adopt the concept of the service class within a neo-Marxist framework. They argue that the mechanisms of the capitalist mode of production require the "functions of conceptualization, control and reproduction to be performed and they produce sets of places comprising specific market and work situations, which we call classes. In the case of the service class, there is a coincidence of function and class place, though not for deskilled white–collar workers. Persons with certain market capacities are recruited to class places" (Abercrombie & Urry 1983: 126). They take the view that the service class has developed as a "class in itself" with "causal powers" concerned with "control, conceptualization and reproduction", and it is these causal powers that define the service class and give it a degree of autonomy from the ruling class. A key claim made by Abercrombie & Urry for the service class is that its exercise of causal powers affects the constitution of capital and may in significant ways change the dynamics of capital accumulation itself (1983:123); this marks a significant departure from the work of both Renner and Goldthorpe. This theme is taken up by Lash & Urry (1987), who argue that:

> Once attaining a certain threshold of development and mobilization, this new class itself begins to have a dislocating effect on the relationship between capital and labour and an irredeemably disorganizing effect on capitalist society in general. (Lash & Urry 1987: 162)

A major sub-theme of *The end of organized capitalism* (Lash & Urry 1987) is the rise of the service class; its authors elucidate a series of key points about the service class that largely restate those arrived at in Abercrombie & Urry (1983). They retain conceptualization, control and regulation of reproduction as the key functions of the service class in "servicing" the needs of capital. They reiterate the key distinction of the possession of credentials as marking the "boundary" between themselves and "deskilled white-collar workers".

The service class did not really emerge in Britain, according to Lash & Urry, until the 1960s, and it is this that accounts for some of its distinctive features.

> When the British service class began to form itself [in the 1960s], it did so heavily under the sway of what Bernice Martin calls the expressive profes-

sionals, mainly employees within the state and concerned with extending and protecting the welfare services. Such employees in Britain gave a particular direction to the British service class and made it less obviously tied into private capital, private foundations and private educational institutions. When the British service class did develop it was very much something that was state–sponsored and occurred during the period in which British political culture was peculiarly "progressivist" and when the long post-war boom ensured fairly high levels of welfare expenditure. (Lash & Urry 1987: 186)

In their most recent book, *Economies of signs and space* (1994), Lash & Urry distance themselves somewhat from the view, expressed in *The end of organized capitalism* (1987), that the service class is the bearer of postmodern culture by arguing that, at least in the case of Anglo-American cultures, consumption and consumer services have become a major force in reshaping capitalism.

While the earlier book attempted to understand cultural post modernism through the mediation of the link between culture and the economy via the new middle classes, this book understands the link through the ways in which economic life is itself becoming cultural and aestheticized. (Lash & Urry 1994: 109)

In the USA and the UK, social and economic restructuring has resulted in the remarkable growth of consumer services and a much swollen service class recruited from an expanded higher education system. Although the service class, or the middle classes as they begin to call them, are significant actors, they are so more as individuals and less as members of classes. In pointing to the disorganization and globalization of social and economic life, Lash & Urry claim:

Social classes, which are conventionally taken as focused around place, national spaces and organized hierarchies, are one of the victims of such disorganization. They are simultaneously localized and globalized, transformed by the flows of people, images and information. Classes in the sense of hierarchically organized national entities are rapidly dissolving, at the very time that social and spatial inequalities rapidly increase. (Lash & Urry 1994: 323)

It might therefore be argued that the middle classes have been reborn as individual consumers in a world where one's only position is an address on the Internet. They have now moved beyond the position stated in *The end of organized capitalism* (1987), which, *inter alia*, saw the members of the service class as the bearers of postmodern culture but also as simultaneously the pallbearers for organized capitalism and the midwives of its successor. This earlier analysis was, however, an analysis loyal not only to the concept of class but to an occupationally based definition of class; postmodernism was seen as the culture of the service class. In *Economies of signs and space* (1994) they have gone well beyond this; whether they have gone over the top, time will tell. The implication of their argument would appear to be that not only Marx's "monstrous" class structure but the concept of class more generally has melted, thawed and resolved itself into the ethernet. The infrastructure of this world is the "wide area network" and optic fibre as opposed to the timetable and road/rail/airline network of organized capitalism, that, even in its later multinational phase, grouped classes into fixed and national spaces corresponding to the asset locations of industrial capital.

2.4   Beyond the service class . . . beyond occupational class?

These various characterizations of the "service class" are examined in many papers of this book. But it would be misleading to think that the concept of the service class has gained universal support, even amongst those who still think class is a useful concept. Crompton criticizes both Goldthorpe and Lash & Urry for being too narrowly concerned with occupational issues and not taking into account sectoral, sectional, gender and other divisions. The origins of the service class, she feels, are considerably broader than the conflict between labour and capital: "there is a constant tendency in their account to discuss industrial managerialism as a proxy for the 'service class' as a whole" (Crompton 1990b: 7). This warning is aimed particularly at Lash & Urry (1987) and, it would seem, has been heeded in *Economies of signs and space* (1994). Moreover, she argues, by concentrating on the homogeneity of the service class, these authors have not satisfactorily accounted for the increase in professional and higher-level managerial occupations.

Her own argument is that there are likely to be different sections of the service class with different worldviews and these may "impact" differently on the course of events. She argues that there is no one way of organizing capitalism and that the service class is likely to reflect this. A range of influences will determine its members' social consciousness, which include occupation but also family of origin, social background, gender and experience of higher education. Like Lockwood (1966), she argues that people's consciousness will vary according to their experience. In particular, though, she argues that there are two main ways of regulating "expert labour": professionalism and organizational corporatism. The first is organized around the occupation and depends on what she terms "institutionalized altruism", whereas the second is based around the organization and is derived from "the human relations school" of industrial relations. Each has rather different outcomes as far as the development of social consciousness is concerned and, she suggests, this may be a major dimension of "difference" within the service class.

2.5   Asset-based approaches to the middle classes

Criticism of the concept of the service class has also been directed at those influenced by the other leading approach to class analysis, that derived from Marxist debates. From the early 1970s Marxists began to explore ways of reconciling the Marxist stress on the centrality of the division between capital and labour with the seemingly enhanced role of the middle classes in contemporary capitalism. Carchedi (1977) emphasized the way that groups within the middle classes carried out distinctive "control" functions for capital (a formulation that was partly drawn upon by Urry in his analyses of the service class). More influential were the attempts of the American Marxist Erik Wright to examine the nature of the middle classes. His early work (Wright 1978) attempted to situate the middle classes in a variety of contradictory class locations between capital and labour, which allowed him to emphasize both the centrality of the capital–labour division but also the existence of groups that did not neatly map onto it. During the 1980s Wright changed his approach to Marxism fundamentally, from a form of macro-structuralism drawing (albeit critically) upon Althusser and Poulantzas, to a form of micro-Marxism, based upon the methodological individualist approaches of Roemer and Elster. The result was a considerable reformulation of his approach to class, that no longer emphasized the centrality of property relations alone, but also pointed to the salience of other bases of exploitation deriving notably from organizational hierarchies and from skill scarcities (Wright 1985).

The implications of this approach suggested that there were fundamental axes of division within the service class itself that needed full and proper recognition. This argument seemed interesting in the view of empirical research also pointing to entrenched division amongst the ranks of professionals and managers. And, indeed, even Lash & Urry's definition of the service class – as performing three distinctive roles for capital (conceptualization, control and orchestration of welfare) – suggests that, far from being a cohesive grouping, it is likely to be internally divided. "There is in fact no reason to believe that people who orchestrate the provision of services will tend to act in similar ways to those who control the labour process" (Savage & Fielding 1989: 204). Savage & Fielding note that most studies of the service class tend to use the term in a more descriptive than analytical sense, "as a shorthand for senior administrative, professional and managerial workers" (Savage & Fielding 1989: 204). There is a fair measure of consensus about who is included but, since these groups do not necessarily share a common economic position, it is difficult to justify the argument that the service class constitutes a single social class formation (Savage & Fielding 1989: 205). It may well be non-economic factors that account for its claimed coherence (Goldthorpe 1982, Abercrombie & Urry 1983, Lash & Urry 1987). In other words, its social identity lies in "civil society" or elsewhere in the non-economic sphere (Urry 1981). Goldthorpe (1982) identifies trust as the hegemonic force, Lash & Urry (1987) imply that education and "cultural capital" are important sources for cohesion, whereas Savage & Fielding (1989), following Goldthorpe (1980a), identify social mobility as a key element in social formation.

This emphasis upon the systematic forces fragmenting the service class is developed by Savage et al. (1992), who, having flirted with the term "service class" for much of the later 1980s, decided to call their subjects the middle classes; at the core of their argument lies the claim that there is not a single middle class but three different middle classes. They identify three groupings formed around property (the petite bourgeoisie), bureaucracy or organization (the managers) and cultural capital (the professionals).

The argument draws on the work of Wright (1985) and Bourdieu (1984) but also upon an older tradition in British sociology (Parkin 1968, Roberts et al. 1977). Their argument was that the three causal entities "property, bureaucracy and culture" are deployed as "assets" in a process of class formation and that different sections of the middle class rely on different assets. For the traditional petite bourgeoisie it is property that is translated into economic and social status; in Britain this has been, at least until recently, a relatively unimportant grouping. The real division that Savage et al. highlight is between managers and professionals. Managers in Britain – and the position in France, Germany and the United States has been very different, as they and others have shown (e.g. Mann 1993, Lash & Urry 1987) – have depended very heavily on their position within the organization. Such people have lacked skills independent of the organization and they have little to hand on to their children because organizational skills, unlike property, "are not transmittable". Professionals, on the other hand, have relied heavily on credentialism, and these skill assets are – unlike organizational assets – the property of the individual holding them. The problem facing the professionals has been to translate this into social and economic status: "professionalism can best be understood as an attempt to translate cultural assets into material rewards." Savage et al. resolve the problem of how skills are transmitted intergenerationally by adopting Bourdieu's concept of cultural capital (for example, higher educational qualifications), that can be "stored" and then translated into privileged jobs in the occupational structure. The education system is therefore crucial for the professional middle class; managers, dependent on their organization assets, can attempt to advantage their children by either passing on property and/or providing them with the cultural capital they themselves lack, although in this strategy they are likely to be at a disadvantage compared with the professionals, who are more adept at gaining benefit from the education system. Owner-occupation has been the main source of property assets. It has also, for some managers dependent on organization assets, allowed them the capital to branch out into self-employment and so become less dependent on the organization for which they work.

Interestingly, this approach to understanding middle-class formation is rather similar to that developed independently by the historical sociologist Mann. Mann also points to three systematic bases on which the middle classes have developed:

> Three variably "impure" relations of production impinge on middling groups: (1) capitalist property ownership, (2) hierarchies specific to capitalist corporations and modern state bureaucracies, and (3) authoritative state-licensed professions. (Mann 1993: 549)

Mann locates these within a wider concept of the distinction that he draws between "authoritative" and "diffused" power relations and notes that capital consists not just of authoritative employment organizations but also of other "diffused circuits of capital, including consumption" (Mann 1993: 549). These in turn are embedded in his model of social power, which comprises networks of ideological, economic, military and political power:

> All three of these criteria – employment relations, diffused power relations, and all the sources of social power – confer an additional common quality on middle class persons: they have predominantly segmental relations with dominant classes above, reinforcing their loyalty – if for some generating a worrying "superloyalty". Thus they are fractions of a single middle class defined by the formula: segmental middling participation in the hierarchies of capitalism and nation state. (Mann 1993: 549–50)

2.6 Conclusions

The debate on the middle classes I have briefly rehearsed above is interesting in a number of ways. First, it does not map at all well onto preconceptions about any fundamental division between Marxist and Weberian approaches to class. The service class concept was originally developed by a Marxist (Renner), then popularized by a Weberian (Dahrendorf), and in the 1980s was championed by Goldthorpe, who is usually thought of as a neo-Weberian, as well as by Urry, who has been more influenced by Marxist debates. On the other hand, the "asset" model developed by Wright and used by Savage et al. (1992) owed something to methodological individualistic currents of Marxism, but also echoed typical Weberian themes concerning the distinction between class, status and party, as well as drawing eclectically on writers such as Bourdieu. Some might regard this as an indication that these approaches are not theoretically pure. It is, however, possible to argue that they indicate that class analysis is managing to free itself from its founding debates and may be able to renew itself in the context of current social changes (see also Savage 1994).

Another exciting feature of these debates, and in many ways the key reason for bringing this book together, is that – unlike many current debates in the social sciences – they are amenable to some sort of empirical examination. Rather than being meta-theoretical discussions of class at such a general level that it is not clear how claims could be proved or disproved by empirical research, both the various proponents of the service class concept as well as those arguing for the asset-based approach spell out a number of empirical implications of their arguments that allow some sort of adjudication between them to take place. Many of the papers in this book are indeed reflections on how empirical research bears upon the key theoretical issues laid out above. It will be helpful to the reader to gain a sense of what some of the key issues at stake are.

First, how significant are structural divisions within the "service class", and what sorts of trends are acting either to strengthen or to weaken such divisions as do exist? Is the service class a potentially homogeneous class, or are there clear divisions between groups within it that might be explained in terms of the distinction between property, bureaucracy and culture? Also, how marked are the boundaries between the "service class" and other classes, and are such boundaries growing stronger or weaker? These debates are particularly evident in the chapters on social mobility (Mills, Ch. 6), migration (Fielding, Ch. 10), food consumption (Warde, Ch. 14), housing (Hamnett, Ch. 15) and political identification (Heath and Savage, Ch. 16) but are also found elsewhere. Some general discussion of the overall implications are found in the concluding chapters.

Secondly, to what extent are the middle classes conservative or radical forces in contemporary society, taking these terms both in their narrower, political sense, but also in a broader cultural sense here. Goldthorpe's stress, as well as that of some Marxists such as Carchedi, is on the conservative role of the service class because they are the subaltern force for their employers and have vested interests in the status quo. Urry, on the other hand, has suggested a rather more dynamic role for them, whilst Savage et al. emphasize the internal conflicts within their ranks. These issues are clearly centre stage in the papers by Heath and Savage (Ch. 16), and by Bagguley (Ch. 17), but also pop up, in interesting ways, elsewhere, for instance in Gregson and Lowe's paper on domestic workers (Ch. 9), Carter and Fairbrother's study of the Civil Service (Ch. 8), Urry's study of the middle classes and the countryside (Ch. 12) and so forth.

Thirdly, what changes are taking place in the realm of employment that impact on our conceptualizations of the middle classes? Can we still rely on notions of the middle classes as depending on bureaucratic employment, which is implicit in many ideas of the service class (see Halford and Savage Ch. 7, Mills Ch. 6, Carter and Fairbrother, Ch. 8). Or, in line with the asset approach of Bourdieu, as adopted by Savage et al., can one usefully conceive of classes being formed in other areas, such as cultural life?

Finally, in this chapter we have discussed some of the salient issues in debates about the middle classes. We have, however, by no means exhausted them, and in particular we have sidestepped some of the most controversial general issues, that are to do with the implications of gender and race. This is deliberate. It would not be adequate to discuss these in passing. It is for these reasons that, before passing on to the more empirical chapters, we have a series of three papers on how the issue of gender, race and class affects discussions of the middle classes.

Part Two
Class, gender and ethnicity

Understanding the relationship between class, gender and race has long been problematic and, arguably, is becoming more so as the centrality of class analysis to social research is becoming more uncertain. We include three papers in this section, two of which (by Witz and Crompton) deal with the issue of class and gender, whilst the third (by Phillips & Sarre) tackles the relationship between class and race. This introduction provides an orientation to some of the general issues, and in particular whether gender and ethnicity should be seen as independent social processes from those of class, or whether there are interdependencies between them.

Both Witz's and Crompton's papers assume some knowledge of the prior debate on gender and class, the key issues of which were first raised in the early 1970s. One of the main starting points for the debate was reflections on Marxist stratification theory, in particular the Marxist emphasis on the way that relations of production take precedence over other social relations, with the resulting stress that the exploitation of workers through capitalist employment relations was more fundamental than the "oppression" of women in the family. It should be pointed out, however, that it was not just Marxism that underwrote the marginalization of gender relations within stratifcation theory, and that similar emphases could be found in the work of Weberians, for instance Lockwood (1986). Much feminist writing from the 1970s was therefore concerned to counter the "conventional view" of the priority of class by showing that gender needed to be taken seriously as a stratifying system independent of social class (e.g. Acker 1973; Hartmann 1979).

And in fact there were signs during the 1970s that both Marxists and Weberians were beginning to take gender more seriously. Within Marxist theory the "domestic labour debate" addressed the relationship between domestic relations and the capitalist employment relationship head on (e.g. Seccombe 1974). From a Weberian perspective Parkin (1979) argued that mainstream groups (which might exclude the organized working class) maintained their relative social and economic power by operating policies of closure and exclusion against other groups, and that race and gender were one of the means by which closure could occur. By the end of the 1970s, then, there were clear signs of a rapprochement between gender and class theory, perhaps the most sophisticated example being the dual systems approach of Hartmann (1979) and Walby (1986b) which saw class and gender relations as independent stratifying principles which none the less interacted in crucial ways.

However, in the early 1980s this trend was shattered by Goldthorpe's (1983) paper which controversially defended the "conventional" view of gender and class. Goldthorpe claimed that households should be seen as the correct "unit" of class analysis and that it made most sense to understand the class position of households by the occupation of its male head. It is possible to recognize two types of feminist response to Goldthorpe's position: one of outright rejection and critique (e.g. Stanworth 1984), to a more measured, though still critical, assessment of Goldthorpe's claims (e.g. Dex 1990; McRae 1990). Both Witz and Crompton can be seen as following this latter course in that both of them are not just concerned to emphasize the salience of gender alone (the fact that gender "matters" and is not reducible to class is not a controversial statement, and would in fact be readily accepted even by Goldthorpe), but rather to reflect on how gender and class interlink. Witz's contribution emphasises that a more dynamic, historical approach to class and gender may force us to unpick the rather arid polarities and distinctions in class analysis which Goldthorpe draws, whilst Crompton argues in related vein that there are different ways of thinking about class to that endorsed by Goldthorpe.

Given the subject matter of this book it is also worth emphasising here that the issue of women and the "middle classes" is of crucial importance in reflecting generally on the class and gender relationship. In fact, Goldthorpe's original (1983) arguments rested upon his claim that where women were employed they were usually in lower social classes to "their" men, and hence that they were rarely employed in the middle classes. This raises a number of issues. Why, historically, were middle class jobs created largely as male jobs? This is one of the issues explored by Witz. Also, how are things changing in contemporary Britain given the marked increase in the number of women employed in managerial and professional jobs? This point is examined by Crompton, both in her paper in this volume and elsewhere (e.g. Crompton & Sanderson 1990).

Turning now to the relationship between race and class, it is notable that a rather different type of discussion has taken place. Whereas the issue of gender and class has been discussed – however unsatisfactorily it might seem to some – within "mainstream" (or "malestream") stratification theory, the issue of race and ethnicity has been altogether absent. In some respects this is rather odd, given that it is certainly possible to detect a lineage of Weberian inspired stratification theory which was interested in issues of race (notably, Rex & Moore 1967; Parkin 1979). It might also be pointed out that the situation is very different in the US where researchers like Wilson (1980, 1986) have made the relationship between class and race central to their work. In fact, in Britain it is only specialist researchers on race and ethnicity who have explored this question. Here a variety of formulations have been developed, including the idea of "racialized class fractions" (Miles 1982), and the notion that "race is the modality through which class is lived" (Hall 1980). More recently books such as *The empire strikes back* (Centre for Contemporary Cultural

Studies 1982) and Paul Gilroy's *There ain't no black in the Union Jack* (1987) have emphasized the need to take "whiteness" seriously in studies of race and class, and not to "pathologize" blackness as a departure from an otherwise unproblematic norm. What has been missing from existing work, however, is any attempt to consider if there is any possible way in which some of the theoretical issues in class analysis can usefully be related to questions of ethnicity. In their chapter Phillips and Sarre carry out a careful excavation of this particular question, with particular emphasis on how the question of race and ethnicity can be made more central to studies of the middle classes.

Chapter 3

Gender and service-class formation

Anne Witz

3.1 Introduction

The focus of this chapter is on gendered processes of service-class formation, which I regard as an issue worthy of further sociological debate. The substantive focus is historical, and two conceptual issues are highlighted. First, the relatively under-theorized status of the family within sociological accounts of class formation, and secondly the *a priori*, taken-for-granted status of the structure of occupational positions, that provides the raw material for charting class maps and deducing statements about socio-demographic and socio-political class formation, and about social closure. The second of these issues forms the central concern of this chapter, as it is the specifically gendered processes and mechanisms embedded in the occupational structure with which I am preoccupied. I shall argue that we might usefully work with a third dimension of class formation, which I shall call the socio-structural, in order to instate gendered processes into historical and contemporary analyses of service-class formation. Specifically in relation to the issues of service-class formation, I shall suggest that a more adequate definition of the service class is possible if we uncover the gendered dynamics embedded in the historical formation of the classic service class.

3.2 Gender and class formation

The occupational structure as well as the family are sites of gender relations, and both are fundamental to an understanding of processes of class formation. One might say that the significance of the gender-segregated structure of occupational positions is now well established, and can no longer be ignored by class theorists. John Goldthorpe recognizes this, particularly in relation to service-class positions, arguing that "the long term change in the occupational distribution of males, and especially the growing proportion found in professional, administrative, and managerial positions, . . . cannot be understood other than in relation to the trend and character of female employment" (Goldthorpe 1980a: 295). Marshall et al. (1988) also stress how the specific location of women in the occupational structure affects the distribution of men's life-chances, insisting that "class systems are structured by sex in ways that clearly affect the distribution of life-chances, class formation, and class action among both women and men alike . . . [T]he mobility chances of men are themselves dependent on a pronounced degree of sexual differentiation in the social division of labour, that is at the level of the class structure as whole. Classes and class phenomena are conditioned by the peculiar pattern of women's participation (however intermittent) in the market for paid labour" (Marshall et al. 1988: 73).

A recognition of this point has emerged following a prolonged "women and class" debate in British sociology during the 1980s (cf. Crompton & Mann 1986, Roberts 1993, Crompton 1993, for useful overviews). This debate entailed a series of exchanges between John Goldthorpe (1983, 1984), defending conventional methodological procedures of class analysis, and a range of critics, who argued that class analyses could no longer ignore women's employment, or for that matter women. What about the resource contributions that flow into households as a result of married women's employment? And what of the significance of gendered occupational segregation *per se*, which did not figure as a concern of class analysts and yet which seemed to suggest that men's occupational mobility was to some extent conditioned by the clustering of women into vertically segregated jobs marked by inferior market and work situations, and out of which there were no career-like trajectories (see Britten & Heath 1983, Stanworth 1984, Dale et al. 1985). Could class analysis continue to ignore women's occupational mobility (Dex 1987, 1990, Abbot & Sapsford 1987)? Critics of conventional class analyses also questioned the ways in which women's class position was defined (i.e. as marriage determined, deriving from their husbands) as well as the way in which the "class structure" was conceptualized wholly in terms of male agency (Charles 1990). One of the points at issue concerned the continued viability of sociological work that made general claims about the class structure based exclusively on studies of men's occupational activities (see Dex 1990), thus ignoring not only the ways in which gender is implicated in the production and reproduction of the class system (Roberts 1993) but also the significance of gendered power relations as a feature of the stratification order *per se* (cf. Delphy 1981, Delphy & Leonard 1986, Walby 1986a, b, 1990).

It is not entirely clear where the "women and class" debate has left us. Clearly, women are now taken into account in class analysis, in what Marshall et al. (1988) call the "revised conventional" position of Goldthorpe (cf. Erikson & Goldthorpe 1992b), which adopts a "dominance" approach to prioritizing class-determining resource flows into families and examines women's as well as men's occupational mobility, as well as in Marshall et al.'s (1988) own major study of the class map of modern Britain. We might conclude that the methodological procedures of class analysis are now more explicitly gendered in the sense of taking women into account, rather than implicitly gendered as in past androcentric practices when only men's occupational or class mobility was examined (cf. Dex 1990 for an elaboration of this latter point).

Nonetheless, there's also a strong sense in which it is still a case of tracking newly gendered persons through the *same* social scaffolding of conventional class theory – that "structure of occupational positions, associated with a specific historical form of the division of labour" (Goldthorpe 1983). But the "women and class" debate also alluded to the possibility that gender matters in a *further*, more embedded, sense that has much more to do with the processes and mechanisms underlying intergenerational class transmission, about which Stanworth (1984) raised some interesting questions (Dex 1990), *and* with those underlying the historical specificities of forms of the social division of labour, of which the occupational structure is one aspect.

To return to my earlier point about recognition of the salience of gender-segregated occupational structures to class analysis, this is something that Marshall et al. (1988) clearly recognize, leading them to raise some important questions, as Stanworth (1984) did, about the *scope* of class analysis. Marshall et al. (1988) insist that a recognition of the salience of gender for class analysis means that we can no longer treat the structure of occupational positions through which people track their career-like trajectories as beyond the concerns of class theory, as Goldthorpe would prefer. This is because, as Marshall et al. see it, "women also make a difference to precisely those aspects of social structure that John Goldthorpe considers to be the first concern of class analysis, namely those pertaining to questions of demographic class formation. People are distributed to places through time according to processes that are powerfully shaped by gender. *The structuring of opportunities itself is therefore a legitimate part of the subject matter for a class analysis* concerned with demographic as well as socio-political class formation" (1988: 84, my emphasis). In other words, gender matters in questions of class *formation* because gendered processes are embedded in the occupational structure from which are deduced statements about socio-demographic class formation (whether classes have formed as stable collectivities) and socio-political class formation (whether these, in turn, provide the basis for solidarity and shared beliefs, identities, behaviours and so on). But Marshall et al. do not go far *enough*, because they still operate within Goldthorpe's twofold distinction between demographic and socio-political class formation, although they are critical of his interest in the former only insofar as it affects the latter. However, I do not think that existing conceptualizations of class formation permit a thorough enough appreciation of its gendered dynamics. Instead, we need a new concept of class formation in order to describe the processes and mechanisms whereby occupational structures of "places" emerge and gendered "persons" come to be associated with them over time and, indeed, how these two processes are not necessarily sequential.

It seems vital to recognize that male patterns of mobility through situs positions have been critically dependent upon processes of gendered closure that operate *within* the occupational structure itself. However, to enquire how it is that men's occupational fates are tied into women's is to introduce a further dimension of class formation, which I term the socio-structural. The concept of class formation itself has emerged as a crucial one for the project of class analysis, although it remains an elusive concept in need of considerable clarification. Taking gender into account demands that we operate with a new dimension of class formation: a socio-structural one, which does not take the structure of occupational positions as an *a priori* in analyses of class formation, but treats the very structuring of these positions as something to be explained.

Socio-demographic and socio-political class formation

The notion of class formation is defined in different ways by class theorists. Wright defines it as "the actual structure of social relations within a class" (Wright 1978: 98). Used in this sense, it implies that classes "form" on the basis of an already given set of class positions. Like Wright, Goldthorpe argues that class formation takes place on the basis of a given set of class positions and similarly recognizes the significance of *socio-political* class formation. By this Goldthorpe means political mobilization in given social and political situations, although Wright addresses this through the concept of "organizational class capacities". The main difference between Wright and Goldthorpe concerns the latter's stress on the significance of *socio-demographic* class formation, which is principally concerned with social mobility and the way individuals may be linked to particular class positions through the process of social closure. Goldthorpe argues that self-recruitment into social classes is likely to make them more socially stable and cohesive, and hence it will aid their "maturity". The study of social mobility thus becomes crucial in analyzing the extent to which a given set of class positions is likely to lead to social and political solidarity, i.e. in analyzing socio-demographic class formation.

There are, then, two usages of the concept of class formation: socio-political and socio-demographic. It is possible to show that gender is integrally tied to both. As regards the concept of socio-political class formation, there is a growing body of work indicating how apparently "class-based politics" have also been mediated by gender relations. The fact that trade unions have historically been centrally concerned with issues of gender exclusion and the family wage is now well documented (cf. Hartmann 1979, Barrett 1980, Cockburn 1983, Walby 1986a, Seccombe 1986, Rose 1992, Gray 1993). The point can be put more abstractly. Offe & Wisenthal (1980) argue that there are structural problems facing atomized working-class individuals competing in the labour market that might prevent them from engaging in collective class action. However, by drawing on gender solidarities, these problems of collective action and political mobilization may be overcome. These gender solidarities may be, for instance, male camaraderie based on workplace interaction. For instance, male printing workers, notorious for their exclusion of women (Cockburn 1983), were also trade union militants and strong advocates of Labour Party and socialist politics. The same point also holds for other male-dominated trades, such as the engineers (Walby 1986a), whose common identity and politics as skilled men were forged partly out of their tenacious opposition to women in engineering, both in peacetime and in two world wars (Braybon 1980). On the other hand, female solidarity may be formed through what I have called "female professional projects"

(Witz 1990, 1992), such as women engaged in collective campaigns to bring about systems of state registration for midwives and nurses in Britain in the late nineteenth and early twentieth centuries. And of course, professional associations in medicine, law and accountancy, for example, admitted only men and took legal advice on how they could legitimately continue to exclude women during the nineteenth and into the twentieth centuries in Britain. Gender identities, then, have provided a basis of intra-class, and indeed inter-class, solidarity.

But what of the other aspect of class formation, discussed at greater length by Goldthorpe: the "socio-demographic"? The salience of the family here is not in dispute, given its well-recognized role in the intergenerational transmission of social advantage (Garnsey 1978), while of course patterns of intra- and intergenerational mobility through the occupational structure are also vital to the analysis of socio-demographic class formation. But families in conventional class analyses appear like phantoms, clearly implicated in the intergenerational transmission of social and economic advantage, and yet assuming a unitary status curiously lacking in real social content. At one level, it would simply be interesting to open up phantom families to greater sociological scrutiny, in terms of the family–labour market nexus of its individual members, of resource flows into families, and of the gendering of these processes. Acknowledging the significance of women's employment in class analysis suggests that we cannot ignore the material effects of women's earnings in families, and particularly how these may have affected socio-demographic class formation, in ways such as facilitating expanding home-ownership or increased consumption of consumer goods (see Stanworth 1984, McRae 1990, Dex 1990). Certainly, some critics of conventional class analysis have argued that a clear recognition of gendered processes and inequalities in the family would present problems for conventional practice precisely because it must cling to a dubious naturalistic ideology of the family in order to retain the assumption that class formation depends upon familial transfers across generations (of property, status, habits, customs, educational opportunities, etc.) (see Delphy & Leonard 1986).

Women also bring their own stock of cultural capital to families, which we assume they do not keep to themselves but transmit to other family members. A recognition of the gendered dynamics of socio-demographic class formation raises some potentially interesting questions concerning gender relations within families, and the complex ways in which resource flows into households might be mediated by gender. The family is, after all, a key institutional medium for the intergenerational transmission of class culture, identities, aspirations and behaviours, as well as of property, and yet the implicitly gendered bias of the conventional origins and destinations approach only really took into account the transmission of male privileges across generations from father to son. Yet the family as the institutional medium for this transfer of cultural and material resources between men nonetheless assumed only a shadowy presence or, to borrow a phrase of Shilling's, an "absent presence" in class analysis. Paradoxically perhaps, it took centre stage in accounts of women's social class position as derived from their husbands. Yet women neither acquire their husbands' credentials on marriage (Allen 1982) nor for that matter do they lose their own education or background if they marry men less educated or well connected than themselves (Abbot & Sapsford 1987).

This poses some new challenges for conventional assumptions about the family in processes of socio-demographic class formation. Savage et al. (1992) approach this issue by looking at how individuals with different types of labour market position come together to form specific types of household. Women's entry into middle-class employment in recent years has depended largely on the mobilization of cultural, educational assets, rather than property or organizational assets, access to which is more patriarchally structured. They argue that the middle-class household may become of major significance in allowing certain assets (cultural, property and organizational) to be used and transformed, and that middle-class formation becomes crucially dependent upon household type and structure. They make two points of particular interest. One concerns the considerable fragmentation of middle-class household types, which may well be a force by which service-class formation is forestalled. The other concerns the possibility that class formation will depend increasingly not simply on the assets on which an individual can draw but on the assets upon which a household can draw.

Turning from the family to the occupational structure leads to the crucial point here, which has been developed by Crompton & Jones (1984), Crompton (1986, 1993), Marshall et al. (1988) and Savage et al. (1992): patterns of occupational and social mobility are critically dependent upon processes of gendered closure and exclusion. High rates of male mobility into "service-class" jobs may well depend upon the exclusion from these very same positions of women working in routine jobs for the same employer. Similarly high rates of male self-recruitment into skilled manual jobs may also depend upon the exclusion of women from these. Payne's argument that "male and female mobility should be analyzed separately because the genders experience such widely different lives, not least in a gender segregated labour market" (1987: 5–6), completely misses the point that male mobility may be premised upon female immobility.

But it is when we turn our attention to the structure of occupational situs positions, which is the springboard from which statements about socio-demographic class formation are deduced, that a third dimension of class formation suggests itself – socio-structural class formation. For Goldthorpe, class formation takes place on the basis of already given class positions, and the occupational division of labour is taken as given for the purpose of class analysis (Marshall et al. 1988). And yet, when we start raising questions about the gendering of these positions, it becomes increasingly difficult to sustain a position that depends upon the assumption that class positions can be specified independently of the people who occupy these positions, and thus sees the relationship between people and positions as a contingent one.

Socio-structural class formation

Class formation is about something more than the association of persons with positions over time. It is also about the very creation of those positions that might be the basis for the formation of classes as stable collectivities. This is the third, socio-structural, dimension of class formation.

A recognition of this point evokes Przeworski's (1977) analysis of class formation. Przeworski sees the process of class formation as the process of organization, disorganization and reorganization of class positions. So class formation is not simply a matter of fixing people to particular class positions, but it is also about the very constitution of these places. To insist on this point is to move beyond or stretch the conventional parameters of class analysis, as Goldthorpe (1990) insists that the task of explaining the evolution of structures of occupational positions is one for historians or historical sociologists to describe rather than for sociologists to theorize. A key point made by critics of the conventional research agenda of class analysis is that the structure of occupational positions from which men's social class is derived is occupied by women as well as men (e.g. Allen 1982, Stanworth 1984, Dale et al. 1985, Scott 1986, Walby 1986b, Abbot & Sapsford 1987, Crompton 1993). Indeed, this fact has always presented problems for class theorists when attempting to draw boundaries between non-manual occupations that may or may not warrant designation as the middle or the service class. A particularly salient aspect of this so-called "boundary problem" was the clustering of women into occupational slots that were difficult to position either side of the manual/non-manual divide or in/out of the middle. Sometimes these were conveniently dismissed as a "buffer zone" between the real stuff of class theory – men's job slots (Giddens 1973, Mann 1986). The stumbling block appears to be the existence of gender-segregated occupational structures, where not only do men and women tend to perform different jobs (horizontal segregation), but also where men cluster in the upper reaches of manual or non-manual occupational hierarchies and women in the lower echelons, with marked differences in market and work situations (vertical segregation).

3.3   Gender and service-class formation

Existing attempts to specify the basis of the service class may be seen to have been only partially successful because they fail to theorize the gendered underpinnings of service-class positions. Indeed, Crompton (1989) uses the insight that class factors cannot be separated from gender factors in the structuring of occupational positions to abandon any specific conceptualization of the service class. However, it might equally be argued that it is only by recognizing the gendered character of class formation that we can for the first time provide a more adequate conceptualization of the service class.

Gendering the concept of the service class

The service class refers to an *ensemble* of occupational groups in advantaged positions in modern societies: professionals, managers, administrators, and so forth. Definitions of the service class run into problems in specifying what the various occupational groups contained within it actually have in common that might then become the basis for socio-demographic and socio-political class formation (Savage et al. 1992). In current accounts, the service class is not only composed of a somewhat disparate set of occupational groupings, but also seen as having a number of different bases.

One absolutely crucial feature of service-class positions is that these are located in bureaucratic hierarchies, a point stressed by Dahrendorf (1959), by Goldthorpe (1982, with Llewellyn & Payne, 1987), and by Abercrombie & Urry (1983). Dahrendorf differentiates between two groups of salaried positions (originally encapsulated within Renner's classic definition of the service class) on the basis of whether or not they are in positions within a bureaucratic hierarchy, arguing that only those who are make up a service class. It is the possession or non-possession of authority, then, that distinguishes service class from non-service-class places.

Recent work on gender and bureaucracy suggests that modern, bureaucratic organizations rest upon specific configurations of gender relations that were indeed crucial to their very formation (Ferguson 1984, Pringle 1989, Witz & Savage 1992). For example, the boss–secretary relation could be taken to defy analysis in terms of Weber's classic rendering of the modern bureaucratic organization as characterized by universalism, legalistic standards, specialization, and routinization of tasks. Instead, it displays many of the elements of a patrimonial rather than a rational–legal authority relation (see Kanter 1993). As "a repository of the personal inside the bureaucratic" the boss–secretary relation is described by Kanter as a bureaucratic anomaly (1993: 101). Ferguson (1984) argues that there are historical links between the discourses of subordination within bureaucracies and within patriarchy, generating organizational arenas in which the "feminization" of subordinates becomes possible. Savage (1992) argues that the historical development of modern bureaucratic forms can be directly linked to the employment of women within them because the bureaucratic career (a central part of Weber's definition of bureaucracy, as well as of Dahrendorf's and Goldthorpe's delineation of service-class positions) was strategically constructed in gendered terms as a male career. Other work has shown how the historical construction of bureaucratic careers and the possibility of progression from junior (non service-class) to senior (service-class) jobs was premised upon large amounts of routine work being carried out by women whose mobility chances were blocked in order to permit mobility prospects for junior men (Crompton 1986, Crompton & Jones 1984, Savage 1992). Thus, rather than it being a contingent fact that the service class as superordinate workers in organizations tends to be male, it might be argued that it is the very fact that these workers are male that has historically helped establish their superordinate characteristics. The possession of authority in bureaucracies has been legitimated by masculinity.

The possession of "delegated authority" (Goldthorpe) as a key element of service-class members distinctive work situation is also linked to their distinctive market situation. This argument is by no means clear though, because the service class seems to contain employers and employees, managers and managed, workers with and without credentials, and the range of incomes of people within it could be vast – from managing directors to junior professional workers (Savage et al. 1992). Nonetheless, it is the evocation of distinctive gendered market situations that has at least enabled service-class theorists (and indeed class theorists generally, e.g. Giddens 1973) to narrow down the range of different market situations contained within the service class. The interesting point here is that the recognition that market situations are markedly gender differentiated has enabled the resolution of ambiguous class boundaries. Thus, for example, Abercrombie & Urry (1983) simultaneously establish the feminine and the proletarian character of routine white-collar work, which is then excluded from their category of the service class, but do not probe the corollary of this, which is the masculine character of those managerial, professional and administrative positions in their designated service class.

Apart from "delegated authority", Goldthorpe specifies "specialist knowledge" as one of two bases for service-class positions. Indeed, "specialist knowledge" is seen by virtually all theorists as a crucial base of service-class position. The way in which social groups control access to forms of specialist knowledge is central to neo-Weberian analyses of class formation through social closure, and "credentialism" is seen as a vital resource in strategies of collective and individual social mobility in modern societies. The collective exclusion of women from the institutional means of acquiring specialist knowledge throughout the nineteenth century and well into the twentieth century is now well documented (see Crompton 1989, Crompton & Sanderson 1990, Witz 1992), and the disproportionate increase in the numbers of women compared with men occupying expanding service-class positions today has been one result of the opening up of higher education to middle-class women since the 1940s. Thus, one key historical way of restricting access to service-class positions has been the use of credentialist tactics by men of this class.

The gendered dynamics of service-class formation

The previous section has suggested ways in which there are gendered boundaries between those who have and do not have trust, authority, relatively advantaged market positions and credentials. I now turn to an analysis of the socio-structural formation of service-class places in order to suggest how both the "form" and "content" of these positions have been gendered. In the case-study material that follows I show how gendered processes of exclusion, demarcation and segregation have helped shape the hierarchical arrangement of work and market situations that constitute the internally differentiated service class. The structure of occupational positions is not "always already there" but is historically constructed and reconstructed in complex configurations. The structure of occupational positions that might be the basis for the emergence of a stable service class has been inextricably tied up with gendered patterns and strategies of closure, both exclusionary (denying women access to certain occupations) and demarcationary (confining women's access to other occupations), which in turn produce horizontally and vertically gender-segregated occupational structures and hierarchies (cf. Bradley 1990, Crompton & Sanderson 1990, Walby 1986a, 1990, Witz 1988, 1990, 1992). The relative market and work situations, and the symbolic standing in society of different occupational groups, are also the outcome of collective processes of distributive struggle (Crompton 1989, 1993). As noted earlier, one force for cohesion in groups such as trade unions and professional associations has been gendered solidarity, and the workplace has become a key battleground in the reworking of masculine and feminine gendered identities (see Davidoff & Hall 1987, Rose 1992).

What has been the embedded gendered dynamic in processes of socio-structural service-class formation? Studies of the historical creation of service-class occupational positions in the nineteenth and early twentieth centuries suggest that this process entailed gendered strategies of exclusion and demarcation, engaged in by class-privileged and gender-privileged male agents. Indeed, one of the most distinctive features of the service class is precisely its male-dominated character, and there are considerable grounds for arguing that gender has provided a major force for cohesion in the service class. Insofar as there is a distinct service class, it developed on the basis of gendered divisions and practices, and cannot be adequately defined or understood in isolation or abstraction from these.

Historically, in the process of middle-class formation, men had a head start in arrogating citizenship rights and claiming the exclusive right to be "occupied" in the public sphere of work, whereas middle-class women were excluded from the whole gamut of citizenship rights to which their male counterparts were claiming entitlement. The early process of middle-class formation was a deeply gendered one, as was the later formation of the "service class". As Davidoff & Hall (1987) have shown, men and women of the new provincial middle class came to adopt distinctly different class *identities*: women as "private persons" and men as "public someones" (Davidoff & Hall 1987, Hall 1990). "Occupation" in the public sphere of work thus became central in the construction of middle-class, masculine identities (see Rose 1992 and Gray 1993 for similar arguments concerning working-class masculine identity).

The Civil Service mandarins are perhaps the best example of service-class exclusivity, and the Civil Service as an administrative, bureaucratic, state institution provides an instructive case study in the gendered dynamics of service-class formation. As Corrigan & Sayer (1985) show, although there were career workers in the Treasury as far back as 1400, before the mid-nineteenth century civil servants were overwhelmingly dependent upon patronage for their privileged administrative positions. This meant that the governing aristocratic classes retained a crucial hold over the recruitment of civil servants until the publication of the Northcote–Trevelyan Report in the 1850s, which was a crucial period for the formation of the modern Civil Service. This report advocated two crucial changes. The first was a separation of "mechanical" from "intellectual" tasks, so that intellectual men could be freed from "mechanical work" in the interests of "efficiency". The second was use of credentialism to govern entry into the Civil Service through a qualifying examination. In addition, clerical work was to be graded so people would perform tasks appropriate to their education and experience. As we shall see, credentialism and grading soon became means of gendering job slots.

The Northcote–Trevelyan Report was implemented slowly, but by 1870 the principles of open competition adjudicated on the basis of credentialism had been accepted and administrative grades reorganized. The crucial point to note here is that, just as the civil servants were one of the first "service-class" groups to form within a modernizing bureaucracy, the Civil Service was also one of the first employers to introduce women into bureaucratic employment in large numbers – a process that began in 1870 when the Post Office inadvertently found itself with women telegraphists in its newly nationalized telegraph companies (Martindale 1938, Zimmeck 1992).

However, in order to unpick the ways in which the socio-structural formation of service-class positions contained a gendered dynamic, it is important to recognize two distinct phases to the gendering of the bureaucratic career in the Civil Service. The first was between 1870 and 1920 when parallel hierarchies of men's grades and women's grades co-existed, as women were in effect "bolted onto" an all-male bureaucracy but in strictly non-comparable, separate and inferior grading structures. The second, from 1920 onwards, was when men's and women's grades were "assimilated" into a mixed-sex grading structure but there was an almost universal downgrading of women's grades *vis-à-vis* men's as women clerks were assimilated into the clerical grade and not, as was the case with their comparable male Second Division clerks, into the executive grade (Zimmeck 1992). As Zimmeck notes, the language of "spheres", where women were separate but inferior, was replaced by the language of pyramids, in which they were incorporated but unequal, confined to the lower levels of the pyramid – "women up to a point and men above" (Zimmeck 1992: 70). It is at *this* point that the mobility of middle-class men into service-class positions, where they enjoy delegated authority, high levels of trust and superior work and market situations, can be seen to be *directly* facilitated by the immobility of women within particular grades, with greater degrees of subordination to authority, lower degrees of trust and inferior market and work situations.

Thus, the modern Civil Service hierarchy between men that prevailed from the 1870s onwards was bureaucratically *and* culturally or socially hierarchical, but these hierarchical principles served not only to mark men off from one another, but also to use gender as a principle of differentiating occupational positions within modern organizations. The bureaucratic hierarchicalization of different types of work ("intellectual" and "mechanical") enabled men to reposition themselves *vis-à-vis* each other through the medium of credentials, which served to instate differentiated occupational slots of upper, middle and lower class men and thereby reproduce a cultural hierarchy. But the bureaucratic hierarchicalization of competencies also established a further division between men and women (see Zimmeck 1992). The overt manipulation of the gendering of skills and competencies as senior men downgraded work and moved it across the gender frontier may be seen as a response by elite, male civil servants to bureaucratic, class and gender politics, all of which coalesced in the hierarchical structuring of "positions" and the filling of those positions with "persons". The structuring of these "positions", then, is aided by gendered strategies of exclusion from some, demarcation between these and others, and the subsequent segregation between male and female jobs.

Similarly, the rapid expansion of managerial positions from the beginning of the twentieth century entailed processes of sifting, sorting and rearranging jobs, which also contained a gendered dynamic. Gender relations came to be institutionalized within occupational hierarchies, and gender became a significant structuring principle in marking off different market and work situations, as well as in constructing new managerial careers. As Savage has argued in the case of Lloyds Bank (1992, 1993), the restructuring of the managerial career during the inter-war years in Britain was a gendered affair. By the 1920s there was clearly a log-jam in promotion prospects, with fewer and fewer male clerks ever reaching managerial grades in Lloyds Bank branches. There was considerable debate about whether or not to introduce tiered entry into managerial roles, distinguishing between those who passed professional examinations by their mid-twenties and would be eligible for promotion, and the rest who would be excluded by their lack of credentials. Then in 1923 another possibility was mooted, which was to follow the example of the insurance companies and the Civil Service and employ women in the banks. By employing women, entry into management could be tiered by gender, rather than credentials, by treating all *male* clerks as potential managers but restricting women to lower-graded work. So, during the 1920s and 1930s Lloyds Bank embarked on a gendered grading and segregation strategy that restructured the male bureaucratic career. Whereas the male career in nineteenth-century banking had been based on stratifying the workforce by *age*, as increments and promotion accrued on the basis of years of service, by the 1930s it began to be based on stratifying the workforce by *gender*. Indeed, Savage (1993) uses his case study of Lloyds Bank to throw light on national differences in middle-class formation in Europe, suggesting that the retention of career mobility for men up out of the lower middle-class (from whence they were recruited into clerical bank work) into the middle-class mitigated against the formation of a cohesive, highly credentialed middle class as occurred in Germany and France. Thus the British service class was more cohesive in terms of its maleness than in terms of the class origins of its members.

The rise of professional occupations was one of the most significant social and political developments in Britain during the late nineteenth and early twentieth centuries (Perkin 1989) and has also been an important element of socio-structural service-class formation. At the core of the professional project was the attempt to secure a linkage between education and occupation through strategies of occupational and social closure (Larson 1977, 1979, Parkin 1979, Murphy 1984, 1986, 1988, Witz 1990,1992). As noted earlier, "occupation" was a central element in the construction of new, middle-class male identities. Professional projects were an important means of establishing this new identity, particularly as they utilized a discourse of the "occupied gentleman".

Neo-Weberian class theorists see the socio-structural formation of professional class positions as processes of occupational closure, which in turn generated new forms of social closure, or social classes, in modern society (see Parkin 1979, Murphy 1988, Parry & Parry 1976). But there were gendered dimensions to these occupational strategies. Parry & Parry, for example, emphasize how medical professionalization in nineteenth-century Britain constituted a strategy of social closure and collective mobility that contained both class *and* gender dimensions, as medicine strove to become a closed homogeneous group in both class and gendered terms. Professional projects were projects of occupational closure, but they were also gendered projects. The male professional project in medicine successfully used gendered collective criteria of exclusion against women, and these operated most effectively within the institutions of civil society, where educational institutions and examining bodies admitted only men and not women, some well into the twentieth century (Witz 1992). But, as Glazer & Slater (1987) argue, the emergence of modern professional occupations was also seen by middle-class women as a historical moment of incomparable opportunity for gainful employment, even as they recognized the obstacles they faced in dislocating professional ideology from its masculinist roots. Women did engage in professional projects, for example in midwifery and nursing, but here were constrained by medical men's demarcationary strategies and by the patriarchal structuring of civil society and the state, for it was within these spheres that the key institutional means of professionalization were located, namely access to educational and legislative means of occupational closure (Witz 1990, 1992). Lower professional occupations that did become feminized in the twentieth century were, as in the case of radiography, those that established education and training in institutions other than universities, for example in hospitals. The key to gendered closure in the professions, then, was credentialism, which operated on collectivist grounds against women as a group.

It is vital to see processes of occupational professionalism in Britain as a series of historically specific phases of socio-structural service-class formation, each with its own specific gendered dynamic: the first, when the "model" of profession emerged in the late eighteenth and nineteenth centuries; the second when the "ideology" of profession was deployed in different economic circumstances to justify inequalities in symbolic (status) and material rewards (Larson 1979); and the third, when social, educational and health services expanded during the latter part of the twentieth century. The first of these periods was characterized by male professional projects, as middle-class men capitalized upon and mobilized their privileged access to the institutions of civil society and the state to engage in occupational strategies of closure, marking out new "exclusionary shelters" (Parkin 1979) within an emerging order of occupations that formed the backbone of socio-structural service-class formation. During this period men secured exclusive access to professional occupations, and gendered strategies of *exclusion* provided an important means of facilitating closure, made possible by the patriarchal structuring of the institutions of civil society (particularly the modern university) and the state. The second phase of professional service-class formation, from the late nineteenth century onwards, witnessed the emergence of gendered strategies of *demarcation*, as the increasingly complex process of sifting and sorting of sometimes rapidly expanding occupational positions relative to each other was facilitated by the gender-typing of skills and competencies, and simultaneous processes of de-skilling and feminization. For example, the history of the emergence of accountancy as a distinct occupation with its own specialist knowledge base shows many similarities to the account of managerial careers above. The process whereby accountancy in Britain was transformed from an ill-defined commercial occupation into an established professional organization entailed the simultaneous downgrading *and* feminization of the occupation of clerk, together with the differentiation of a specific accountancy function. The third phase, from 1945 onwards in Britain, has been one of an expansion of professional service-class positions led by the welfare state, which has created a new hierarchy of professional functions (many of which are located in bureaucracies), where women predominate but men dominate. Thus, it is gendered strategies of *internal demarcation* within professional occupations that come to assume causal powers in socio-structural service-class formation (see Crompton & Sanderson 1990).

So my argument is that, when we look at the structure of professional, administrative and managerial positions against which we plot patterns of male mobility in and out of the service class, we are faced with the condensation of a series of historically specific occupational closure projects, within which gender has played a distinctive role. To unify into one "service class" the somewhat disparate, yet distinctly gendered, market and work situations of Class 1 and Class 2 professional occupations (defined as part of the service class primarily on the basis of "specialist knowledge") is to ignore the extent to which we are reading off "class effects" from a structure of occupational positions that is the sedimentation of class *and* gender processes, i.e. to ignore the extent to which processes of socio-structural class formation have been gendered at their very core, although in different ways at different times.

3.4 Towards a gendered research programme?

I have argued, then, that a recognition of the gendered dimensions of class formation suggests that gender-mediated class practices are a significant aspect of socio-political class formation, that the input of both men's and women's cultural and material resources into the family needs to be recognized, together with the impact of these dual resource flows on socio-demographic class formation, and finally that gender factors affect the structuring of occupational positions, in terms of a process of socio-structural class formation. I have focused mainly on the third of these issues by looking at gendered processes of socio-structural service-class formation and demonstrating how, in the nineteenth and early twentieth centuries in Britain, processes of managerial and professional occupational formation were gendered at their very core, or how, as Crompton so succinctly states, "the 'places' themselves have often been actively created as gendered occupations" (1993: 115).

Rosemary Crompton's (1986, 1989, 1993) work has been particularly important in teasing out the ways in which gender factors seep into the conventional concerns of class analysis, and she has in fact looked specifically at the service class. She actually broadens the problematic of the class research agenda considerably more than I do by identifying *two* ways in which women's labour underpins male service-class workers' privileged market and work situations. This they do both as "cadet" or "subaltern" white-collar workers such as secretaries and clerical workers performing key support functions that sustain service-class men in their work, *and* as service-class wives, whose domestic labour underpins and is often incorporated into that of their service-class husbands. Indeed, on the grounds that women's participation in both the domestic and labour market spheres is changing in important ways, Crompton suggests two vital ways in which the internal cohesion of the service class, and the link between this and socio-demographic class formation, may be destabilized. First, the use of the "credentials lever" by both "subaltern" and service-class women, together with their aspirations to reap long-term rewards from their participation in paid work, may undermine the privileged access that service-class men have enjoyed to bureaucratic careers up through service-class occupational positions (see Crompton & Jones 1984, Crompton 1986, Crompton & Sanderson 1990). Secondly, the disproportionate expansion of women's opportunities for service-class employment has implications for processes of socio-demographic class formation because increasing numbers of households contain two "service-class" individuals:

> If we assume that experience of a service class household advantages those members, such as children, who are not themselves in paid employment, then the phenomenon of the dual service-class household implies that the benefits of service-class expansion will be enjoyed by fewer household members than the actual rate of service-class expansion would seem to imply. It is paradoxical, therefore, that the expansion of opportunities for women may have the effect of widening the gulf between the most materially advantaged and disadvantaged households in Britain. (Crompton & Sanderson 1990: 166)

This latter point underscores my earlier argument about the need to look at dual resource flows into households, but pulls this through in terms of the effect this has on the differential distribution of cultural and material resources between households and, consequently, on class maps.

Where does the argument about gender and class formation leave the conventional agenda of class research and theory? Does the analysis of socio-structural class formation operate within a different and separate problematic from the agenda of conventional class analysis, as both Goldthorpe (1990) and Crompton (1993) suggest? Is it still possible conceptually and methodologically to conduct "class" analysis business as usual? I remain somewhat open on this question, recognizing the continuing ability of the conventional agenda to tell us sociologically interesting things about social mobility and social closure, albeit with some modifications (see Erikson & Goldthorpe 1992b), at the same time as feeling that the very nature of contemporary occupational change and mobility regimes, as well as of patterns of family/household formation, seem to defy sociological attempts to differentiate cleanly between "class" and "gender" processes. It could be that there is no degenerate research agenda, such as the conventional class agenda, but a number of different competing agendas, some of which are getting played out in terms of their continuing sociological utility.

There is an important sense in which we cannot consign the study of socio-structural class formation to the realm of the socio-historical, because occupational structures are never simply always already there, but are constantly changing. A recognition of the constant flux of occupational positions is, of course, central to the conventional approach, and provides the rationale for the vital distinction between "relative" and "absolute" mobility, where the latter (but not the former) is affected by the changing proportion of occupational places. But isn't there something more to "changing places"? Esping Andersen's (1993) powerful analysis of changing places in late capitalism suggests that there is and that conventional class analysis lacks the conceptual tools to grasp this.

Esping Andersen introduces a challenging, new institutional *depth* to analyses of the post-industrial trajectory of change. Indeed, his major criticism of conventional approaches is that "orthodox class theory is nested in an institutionally 'naked' world" and that the emergent structure of employment, life-chances and inequality in post-industrial societies cannot be understood with inherited theories of class. Drawing upon Goldthorpe's focus on mobility as a processual approach to class far superior to Wright's excessively static one, Esping Andersen nonetheless broadens the institutional pathway of "mobility regimes" beyond occupational slots to encompass pathways between familial and occupational places. In particular, he argues that huge sectors of the service economy are being constructed as female labour markets, as gender-distinctive mobility regimes and career trajectories are rapidly solidifying. What is more, Esping Andersen treats "housewife" as an origin, and is thus able to identify a distinct gendered mobility regime into and out of the "new service proletariat" as a mobility regime *between* households and unskilled service positions. What is particularly interesting about Esping Andersen's position is the way he tips the analytical concerns of class analysis into an almost exclusive concern with what I have termed socio-structural class formation. This he does through his focus on the "class-formative propensities of occupational groupings" (1993: 228) and an analysis of intragenerational class formation, rather than the class formative propensities of the incumbents of occupational slots through intergenerational class formation. In addition, he radically repositions the family as an institutional site of class formation by shifting the focus from intergenerational transmission of cultural and material resources to the institutional linkages between families, labour markets, welfare states, education systems, etc. that generate distinct mobility regimes, which, in turn, solidify into hierarchies of market and work situations.

By abandoning the institutionally naked world of conventional class theory, Esping Andersen operates within a conceptual framework that places the shifting institutional nexus between family, working life, and the state at the core of the post-industrial trajectory of change. There are ways, then, in which the sociological deadlock that conceptually disaggregates class, gender and race factors, identities and effects can be broken, with a view to producing sociological pictures of the historical trajectory of high modernity in its full complexity. Taking women into account poses considerable challenges to the conventional methodological procedures of class analysis, while theorizing gender and gender relations as part of the trajectory of historical and current social change challenges conventional wisdoms about what precisely constitutes the core concerns and conceptual scope of sociological theories of stratification.

Chapter 4

Women's employment and the "middle class"

Rosemary Crompton

4.1 Introduction

Until the end of the 1970s, much empirical work on social class in British sociology was taken to be broadly synonymous with studies of *men's* employment alone (Goldthorpe et al. 1968/69, Roberts et al. 1977, Goldthorpe with Llewellyn and Payne 1987, Blackburn & Mann 1979, see also for the United States Blau & Duncan 1967). In assuming this stance, sociologists in Britain and elsewhere uncritically reflected the then dominant "male breadwinner" ideology relating to the gender division of labour, in which women's paid employment (if any) was seen as "secondary" as far as the economic fate of the household was concerned, and women's domestic work within the household was not taken into account at all (Stacey 1981).

It is not surprising, therefore, that the sociology of class and stratification was one of the first arenas within which the critiques developed by "second-wave" feminism were articulated in the 1970s. The lack of attention given to women's domestic labour in the home, it was argued, in effect marginalized their productive contribution to society as a whole. By being treated as virtually invisible, this essential contribution of women was downgraded and treated as less valuable than that of men. Furthermore, the taken-for-granted "male breadwinner" assumption seemed to be increasingly out of date given the increasing number of married women who were entering paid employment. It was argued, therefore, that women should be given a "class situation" in their own right, rather than being conventionally allocated to that of their nearest male breadwinner, that is, that their "own" work, rather than that of their male partner, should be seen as determining their "class situation" (Acker 1973, Allen 1982).

The initial debates that followed were often acrimonious. (See, for example, Goldthorpe 1983, and the ensuing exchange in *Sociology* vol. 18, no. 4, 1984). However, since the 1980s, although the level of attention devoted to gender-related topics has increased enormously within British sociology, the gender/class interface, once seen as a central issue, is now rarely discussed at all. Section 2 of this chapter, therefore, will attempt to explain how this situation has come about. It will be argued that, in large part, it is a consequence of the dominance of a particular approach to "class analysis" within British sociology, which was concerned with a rather narrow range of gender-related topics and, indeed, sometimes gave the impression of a positive hostility to feminist critiques. In the light of this discussion, section 3 of this chapter will discuss contemporary developments in women's employment in Britain, particularly the increase in the number of women in higher-level occupations, and how these changes relate to sociological discussions of the middle or "service" classes.

The starting point for our examination of the service class will be a paper written ten years ago ("Women and the 'service class'" Crompton 1986). Originally, this paper was intended as a part of the attempt to rescue the "invisible woman" within class analysis. It argued that the burgeoning (male) service class could be shown to rest upon women's work in both the public and private spheres (as routine clerical and secretarial workers, and as middle-class housewives). It also suggested that the looming influx of women into "service-class" occupations might have a significant impact on male service-class careers. As we shall see, this latter point requires modification in the light of the actual events that followed, and we will be drawing upon recent census data in order to examine the empirical consequences of the changing gender composition of the middle or service classes, particularly in relation to the structuring of household types.

In the next section, however, we will first return to the sociological debates on gender and class in order to review developments over the past decade – particularly in respect of the "employment aggregate" approach to class analysis, which was a major focus of feminist criticisms throughout the 1980s.

4.2   Sociology, gender and "class"

The assumption that "classes" may themselves be adequately identified within the employment structure represents just one strategy within the sociology of "class analysis" as a whole. This approach, which will be described as the "employment-aggregate" approach, may be located within the sociology of class and stratification as shown in Table 4.1 (see Crompton & Mann 1994).[1]

Table 4.1   Levels of "class analysis".

Level of analysis	Method of investigation
(1) Class formation	Socio-historical analyses of change (e.g. Thompson 1968)
(2) Class placement in employment structures	Large data sets aggregating jobs (e.g. Goldthorpe with Llewellyn & Payne 1987, Wright 1985)
(3) Class consciousness and action	Contemporary case studies of specific groups (e.g. Newby 1977, Savage et al. 1992)

Employment-aggregate approaches (level 2) rest upon large sample surveys gathered at the national level, which proceed by assigning individuals to positions within a "class" scheme (most often on the basis of their job or occupation), then aggregating these positions into an overall class structure. The best-known sociological practitioners of this approach are Wright and Goldthorpe, who have gathered extensive survey data that have been analyzed with reference to their sociologically informed "class" schemes. However, this general strategy is also widely employed in empirical discussions of inequality employing "intuitive" or "commonsense" class schemes, such as those of the Registrar General (Marshall 1988, Crompton 1993; for an example of the latter see Reid 1981).

Feminist criticisms of the employment aggregate approach to class analysis (and it should be noted that these criticisms have also been directed at "intuitive" as well as "sociological" class schemes) revolve around two broad themes. First, it is argued that the persistence of occupational segregation (that is, the concentration of men and women into different occupations) makes it difficult, if not impossible, for a class scheme to be devised that is equally appropriate for men and for women at the individual level. In fact, most class schemes *have* tended to reflect the male occupational structure and hierarchy, given that men have been dominant in the sphere of employment. Secondly, it has been argued that the employment-based, masculinist approach to class analysis in effect ignores women's domestic work and denies women a place in the class structure by treating them as male appendages, through the common practice of (a) taking the household to be the unit of class analysis, and (b) taking the "class" of the household unit to be that of the "male breadwinner".

These criticisms need to be carefully specified, however, in view of the details of both Goldthorpe and Wright's arguments. They have both devised employment-based class schemes that they describe as "relational" – that is, reflecting the actualities of class relations rather than the commonsense categories of classifications such as those of the Registrar-General (Marshall 1988). Two elements contributed to the location of occupations within Goldthorpe's initial scheme, first, employment status (whether employed, self-employed, an employee, etc.) and, second, the "market" and "work" situation characteristic of the occupation. Goldthorpe's class scheme, therefore, has often been described as "neo-Weberian", following Weber's equation of "class situation" with "market situation". This approach treats the occupational order as gender neutral, disregarding occupational segregation. However, there are a number of well-known examples of occupations in which the "market" situation (understood particularly with reference to the nature of the work and promotion prospects) associated with an occupation depends crucially upon whether the incumbent is male or female. In such cases, it is argued that men and women cannot be said to share the same "class" situation, even if they share the same occupational label. Clerical work, the most commonly occurring female occupation, is an obvious example here (Crompton & Jones 1984). In contrast to Goldthorpe, Wright's class scheme was explicitly grounded in Marxist theoretical principles. It was originally devised with reference to job content, and on this basis classified clerical jobs (and therefore the women who occupied them) in "worker" positions.

The initial (1970s) Nuffield surveys did not sample women except as the wives of male respondents, and the "class position" of women was generally taken to be that of the most proximate male (i.e. husband or father). It was argued that this procedure was justified by the fact that the proper unit of class analysis was the household, and that the class position of the family was most reliably indicated by that of the male "head of household". Feminist critics argued that this empirical strategy both obscured the contribution made by women within the household, and took into account neither the rapidly increasing levels of women's paid employment nor the growing number of female-headed households. Here Wright's approach, in which the individual, rather than the family, is regarded as the unit of class analysis, might seem to be more appropriate. However, Wright's solution to the problem of the female domestic worker is in fact very similar to the strategy employed by Goldthorpe. Women not in paid employment, Wright argues, may be assigned a "derived" class situation, that is, they take the class position of their "male breadwinner" (Wright 1989a).

Although, therefore, Goldthorpe and Wright have often been taken to represent very different approaches to class analysis (Marshall et al. 1988), there are actually a number of parallels in their work as far as gender is concerned. Wright argues that, although gender is relevant for understanding and explaining the concrete lived experiences of people, it does not follow that gender should be incorporated into the abstract concept of class (Wright 1989b: 291). This analytical separation of class and gender may be seen as part of a more general strategy, also endorsed by Goldthorpe & Marshall (1992) within the employment aggregate approach in which the continuing relevance of "class" is demonstrated by the empirical evidence of "class effects". Both Goldthorpe and Wright have also focused upon the topic of women's political preferences, particularly as compared with those of their partners. Indeed, Erikson & Goldthorpe's (1992a) defence of the household as the unit of analysis rests in large part upon the empirical finding that women's political attitudes are more closely associated with those of their male partner than their own occupation (or class).

To many of those interested in the exploration of the class/gender interface, however, this rigid separation of "class" and "gender" seemed inappropriate – particularly in studies exploring issues of class formation (see Fig. 4.1). The structure of paid work rests upon a complementary structure of unpaid work together with a division of labour that has been constituted on gender lines. Class formation in the employment sphere, therefore, is implicated with the gender division of labour in both the public and private spheres. Feminist sociologists wishing to explore the links between gender and class, therefore, sought to explore the nature of the changing interaction of the public and the private that had been indicated by the growth of women's employment. The debates associated with the "employment aggregate" approach to class analysis did not seem particularly fruitful to those interested in these gender-related issues. The increase in the paid employment of married women, and the changes in family dynamics associated with this increase (Leiulsfrud & Woodward 1987), were seen to be two of the major social changes that had taken place in western Europe and the USA since the Second World War. Nevertheless, the employment aggregate tradition of "class analysis" had little to say about these phenomena and, indeed, sought positively to distance itself from them (Erikson & Goldthorpe 1988).

Both Goldthorpe and Wright have modified their positions considerably over the years. Wright's revisions have been largely directed at his underlying theoretical framework, and his original class scheme has been completely revised in consequence (Wright 1989b). Paradoxically, it is Goldthorpe, who has at times appeared very resistant to feminist criticisms, who has incorporated important changes in respect of gender (Erikson & Goldthorpe 1992b: 35–47). The male "head of household" approach has been replaced by the "dominance" strategy, and the class position of the household is now given by that of the "dominant" breadwinner, whether male or female. References to "work" situations have been purged from descriptions of the "class scheme", which is now described as resting upon "employment relations" alone (this is important because, as we have seen, differences in the nature of men's and women's work have been regarded as an obstacle to their placement in the same class category). The class scheme has also been partially re-jigged to take account of occupational segregation, in that class III has been divided into IIIa and IIIb (when appropriate) to take account of the preponderance of women in low-skilled, non-manual occupations (i.e. IIIb). More particularly, however, the "research programme" of "class analysis" upon which Goldthorpe and his CASMIN[2] colleagues are engaged has recently been outlined in some detail. In this exercise, the very considerable differences between their position and that of other sociologists (who would also consider themselves to be engaged in "class analysis") have been made apparent.

In brief, their approach would reject any *a priori* theory of class – such as, for example, the presence of inherently exploitative class relations – as well as any tendency to "historicism" – that is, the capacity of theory to give an account of societal development. A major empirical focus of class analysis within the research programme as described by Goldthorpe & Marshall (1992) has been upon processes of social mobility – not least because it is through the persistence and regularities of mobility patterns that the very existence of a "class structure" can be established. The class scheme it uses is not characterized by any distinctive "theoretical" underpinnings relating to the structuring of occupations (whether relations of power and domination and / or the systematic variations in market and work situations that follow from these relations), rather, in constructing the scheme, "we have drawn on ideas, whatever their source, that appeared to us helpful in forming class categories capable of displaying the salient features of mobility among the populations of modern industrial societies" (Erikson & Goldthorpe 1992b: 35). Thus the internal consistency of the categories (i.e. occupations) which go to make up the aggregates within the class scheme is not an issue. Rather, as Evans (1993) has argued, the validity of the class scheme is held to be dependent upon criterion-related validity rather than construct validity; it is dependent "not on a theory linking the concept to other variables, but on the measurement of an outcome or characteristic that represents directly . . . the concept we are trying to index". In short, the approach is judged by its empirical consequences – or, rather more unsociologically, the proof of the pudding is in the eating. As far as women are concerned, Erikson and Goldthorpe are aware that women's mobility prospects are less favourable than those of men, but this fact is not important within the research programme given the lack of sex difference in fluidity patterns – i.e. women suffer because they are *women*, and not because of "class" differences (as defined by Erikson and Goldthorpe) between women and men.

We can see, therefore, that the research programme of class analysis advocated by Goldthorpe and his colleagues is relatively narrow in scope and does not have a great deal to say about the gender/class interface. This is not because of intellectual sexism, but more because the central topic of the research programme relates to class (as they have defined it) rather than to gender (and it may be noted that Wright makes a parallel argument here). There is an ongoing debate concerning the nature of the "research programme" and the claims made on its behalf, but this is not our concern here. (See, for example, Goldthorpe & Marshall 1992, Pahl 1989, 1993, Scott 1994, Holton & Turner 1994).

Questions relating to class and gender, of course, have not been confined to debates within the framework of the employment aggregate approach. During the 1970s and 1980s, Marxist and socialist feminists engaged in extensive debates directed at the possibilities of the integration of women into class theory – notably the "domestic labour" debate. However, the theoretical assimilation of class and gender proved to be an impossibly difficult exercise (Molyneux 1979). In practice, structuralist–materialist feminism has in effect adopted a modified "dual systems" approach, in which capitalism and patriarchy are seen as separate, but interacting, systems of social organization (Hartmann 1981). For example, Walby argues from a socio-historical perspective (i.e. level 1) that "gender and class have independent historical dynamics, although of course they do have effects upon each other" (1990: 200). However, this analytical separation is difficult to achieve empirically in the case of level 2 employment aggregate approaches. This is for the very simple reason that employment structures are "gendered", reflecting the outcome of both class and gender processes, and criticisms along these lines have been made of both Wright's and Goldthorpe's work (Marshall et al. 1988, Marshall 1988, Crompton 1989, 1993).[3]

The emphasis upon the "service class" in Goldthorpe's approach has led to his work (particularly Goldthorpe 1982) becoming a significant reference point for discussions of the service class. However, our arguments above suggest that it is important to recognize that his framework might not be a particularly useful point of departure for those not sharing the assumptions of the programme of "class analysis" that he and his colleagues endorse. It has always been apparent that the theoretical assumptions of this approach are very different from those of others who have also employed the "service-class" concept (see Crompton 1990a). More particularly, however, recent clarifications have made explicit the extent of the gulf between the research programme and others who have used the "service-class" concept. For example, arguments to the effect that the heterogeneity of "service-class" positions throws doubt upon the unity of the "class" as such (see Savage et al. 1992) would not be seen as relevant within the research programme, given that the existence of the class is dependent upon a finding of constant social fluidity rather than the internal homogeneity of the occupational groups comprising the "class".

On a more positive note, however, it may be argued that Erikson and Goldthorpe's recent suggestions as to possible future developments in "class analysis" might be read as opening up the potentialities of further work at the gender/class interface. It is important to remember that the major empirical focus of the research programme has been on the topic of social mobility. The main theories against which Erikson and Goldthorpe's arguments have been directed have been liberal theories of industrialism, which have claimed that industrial societies are characterized by a greater openness and equality of opportunity, and thus enhanced rates of social mobility. In arguing against this liberal position, they assert that "even though the 'logic of industrialism' may create pressures for the fuller use of a society's stock of talent through more universalistic processes of social selection, these pressures would seem more often than not to be resisted, and by opposing forces which operate chiefly at the microlevel of 'adaptive' individual and family strategies" (1992b: 394). That is, pressures (whether structural or politico-legal) in the direction of enhanced equality of opportunity will, they argue, invariably be countered by the superior capacities of the more powerful and advantaged families to preserve the life-chances of their children (ibid.: 368).

"Bringing the family back in" might have interesting consequences as far as level 2 class analysis is concerned. It has been argued above that the developments associated with the most influential programmes of employment aggregate "class analysis" have (over the last decade) not been particularly useful in enhancing our understanding of the creeping feminization of the middle or service classes. Feminists have argued that this lack stems in large part from the masculinist, productivist, orientation that has in the past characterized sociological approaches to "class" more generally (see also Crompton & Mann 1994). However, the emphasis on the family as the major agent in the reproduction of class inequality might be seen as returning the concerns of class analysis to the gender/class interface and the kinds of questions raised by early feminist critics of class analysis. In the next section, therefore, we will focus on the question of the links between household structures and women's service-class employment, and the possible consequences of increasing differentiation within the class by *household*, as well as inter-class segregation.

4.3 The changing gender composition of the "service" or "middle" class

It has been argued (Crompton 1986) that, in the early 1980s, (a) the "service class" was predominantly male, but (b) nevertheless rested upon two crucial inputs from women: (i) women's input into male "service-class" careers via domestic support, and (ii) women's concentration in lower-level support occupations (e.g. routine clerical and administrative work) for "service-class" positions. However, signs of change were noted in the structuring of women's employment. Recent empirical work had suggested that women were showing signs of increasing resentment at their lack of promotion prospects (Crompton & Jones 1984), and levels of formal qualifications (both academic and vocational) amongst women appeared to be rising very rapidly (Crompton & Sanderson 1986, 1990, Crompton 1987). It was anticipated that these trends would result in more women moving into "service-class" positions, and that, "Were increasing numbers of women to begin to undertake – even at a relatively modest level – "service-class" careers, then this could have a very substantial impact on the internal cohesion of the service class" (Crompton 1986: 136).

In the decade that followed, there has, indeed, been a substantial increase in the proportion of women in "service-class" positions, as the "male breadwinner" model of the employment structure overall has been progressively eroded. In 1981, men were 80% of SEG (socio-economic group) 1 (employers and managers, large establishments), but this had fallen to 71.4% by 1991. For SEG 2 (employers and managers, small establishments), the relevant percentage has declined from 77 to 68.6. Men were 90% of professionals in 1981, but this had fallen to 86.8% of self-employed professionals, and 81.7% of employed professionals by 1991. Gender parity has not been achieved by any means, but nevertheless women are making substantial inroads into service-class occupations. Conversely, women are increasingly dominant in junior non-manual positions (SEG 6): 69% in 1981 but 75.8% by 1991. As we shall see, however, the nature of gender restructuring *within* the service class suggests that the underlying patterning of gender relations in employment has for the most part remained relatively stable despite these changes. Thus previous arguments to the effect that the internal cohesion of the class might be threatened by a female influx need to be re-evaluated.

In our discussion of the recent processes of gender structuring within the middle classes, we will use 1991 census data in order to examine variations in household structure between men and women in comparable occupational groups, defined in terms of SEGs.[4] Table 4.2 gives details derived from the 1991 UK census SARs.[5] The age group 30–50 has been selected because these are likely to be the crucial decades as far as both family formation and career development are concerned for both men and women. The bottom row of Table 4.2 illustrates, in broad outline, the family circumstances of men and women in employment. As would have been anticipated, women in employment are rather less likely to be living with a partner and dependent children (48%) than are men in employment (56%), and women are more likely to be lone parents (10%) than are men (4%).[6] However, the table reveals very striking occupational variations in family type amongst employed women, which are not paralleled by similar variations amongst employed men. The proportions of men living in families with children (dependent and non-dependent: column 3 plus column 4) averaged 68%, and the variation around this average is not extensive (from 76% [SEG 2.1] to 64% [SEG 6]). In contrast, there is a near 30% variation amongst the different occupational groups of women, from 41% (SEG 1) to 70% (SEG 2.1).

Table 4.2 Family circumstances of women and men aged 30–50 in employment, selected occupational groups (% by row).

| | 1 | | 2 | | 3 | | 4 | | 5 | | Numbers | |
| | Not in family | | Married/cohab: no children[2] | | Married/cohab: dependent children | | Married/cohab: non-dependent children[3] | | Lone parent[1] | | | |
Occupational group	F	M	F	M	F	M	F	M	F	M	F	M
Employers/managers, large establishments (SEG 1)	18	10	32 (50)	18 (28)	31	61	10 (41)	10 (71)	9	2	3,598	10,350
Employer, small establishments (SEG 2.1)	5	8	20 (25)	15 (23)	55	63	15 (70)	13 (76)	5	2	2,338	6,241
Manager, small establishments (SEG 2.2)	13	10	26 (39)	18 (28)	39	60	14 (53)	10 (70)	9	2	6,295	14,042
Professional, self-employed (SEG 3)	12	10	20 (32)	15 (25)	60	69	3 (63)	6 (75)	4	1	439	2,390
Professional, employee (SEG 4)	22	14	28 (50)	19 (33)	40	58	4 (44)	7 (65)	7	2	1,597	8,294
Non-manual supervisor (SEG 5.2)	10	9	28 (38)	18 (27)	35	58	17 (52)	13 (71)	11	2	1,475	1,100
Junior non-manual (SEG 6)	7	14	16 (23)	18 (32)	49	53	16 (65)	11 (64)	10	4	34,869	9155
Skilled manual (SEG 9)	8	13	22 (30)	16 (29)	39	55	20 (59)	15 (70)	11	4	2,472	24,853
All employees	9	12	19	17	48	56	15	12	10	4	10,3725	130,494

1. With dependent and non-dependent children.
2. Numbers in parentheses represent households without children (column 1 + column 2).
3. Numbers in parentheses represent households with children (column 3 + column 4).
Source: Census SARs (1991). *Note:* Percentages may not add to 100 because of rounding

The recorded variations in family type as between men and women, and women in different occupational groups, are in directions that might have been anticipated but they are nonetheless very striking. Women in senior managerial positions (SEG 1) are only half as likely to have dependent children (31%) as are men in these occupations (61%), and the pattern is repeated amongst other managerial and professional employees (but not the self-employed). Amongst women in different occupations, the greatest variation lies in the extent to which they are living in child-free households (column 1 plus column 2). A half of all female senior managers, and employed professionals live in households where there are no children, more than twice the proportion of female junior non-manual workers in this situation (23%).

More women may be entering service or middle-class occupations, therefore, but it is apparent that the combinations of work and family life characteristically experienced by women and men in the same occupational group are likely to be rather different, particularly amongst higher managerial and professional employees. Two-thirds of senior male managers (SEG 1) are living in households with dependent children, as compared with only one-third of senior female managers. This is indicative of the way that male "service-class" breadwinners have been able to rely on the domestic support of their wives, and also shows that, in contrast, a substantial proportion of the "career women" within the middle classes will need to avoid domestic commitments by having no or few children. However, it is not enough to examine the constraining impact of a woman's occupation upon her actual or potential family life. Women in these kinds of occupations *do* still tend to marry and have children, and indeed recent evidence demonstrates that rates of employment amongst mothers of young children are rising most rapidly in this occupational category (Harrop & Moss 1994). Increasingly, therefore, it becomes more relevant to put the question the other way round; i.e. what is the impact of family life – particularly the presence of children – upon a woman's service-class career?

There is a growing body of case-study evidence that suggests that women, even when they are professionally qualified and/or have gained service or middle-class jobs, tend to develop their careers rather differently from men, even if they remain constantly attached to employment. This has been identified as a distinction between "practitioners" and "careerists". In some occupations, this distinction is related to the pattern of intra-occupational segmentation by gender. For example, pharmacy is a degree-level occupation which is feminizing rapidly. However, whereas the majority of male pharmacists have built careers in organizations (such as Boots) and/or taken the entrepreneurial route through pharmacy ownership, most women pharmacists have worked as professional employees, often part time (Crompton & Sanderson 1990). Indeed, one reason why pharmacy has been regarded as such an attractive profession for women has been the extent of the availability of flexible work opportunities, particularly part-time work, at a professional level. However, this kind of flexibility has not, historically, been associated with bureaucratic careers in large organizations. The lack of such opportunities emerged as a criticism by women of early attempts to introduce career break schemes in organizations such as banks. It might have been anticipated that these

tensions will increase as more women move into occupations that have been associated with organizational careers, such as those associated with banking and other
large bureaucracies in the financial sector.[7]

However, empirical research suggests that, as women move into middle class
occupations, so a further process of gendered restructuring takes place, in particular
with regard to the different gender and family combinations in the "professional"
and "managerial" groupings. The distinction between "professional" and "managerial" occupations has provided the materials for an ongoing debate within what
amounts to a virtual sub-area within sociology (Crompton 1990a). It has been
argued that, as far as class analysis is concerned, the distinction is not, in fact,
particularly important, as there is in practice considerable movement between and
overlap within the two categories (see Mills, Ch. 6 this volume) – although others
have argued in a contrary fashion (see Savage et al. 1992). These debates will not be
directly engaged with here, but we will explore some gender differences between
"managerial" jobs, which are associated with positions of authority and control
within organizations, and "professional" jobs, in which the incumbents' position
rests upon the possession of specific expertise.[8]

A number of recent case studies have indicated that women have been moving
into managerial positions in which they are drawing upon specific expertise, rather
than exercising domination and control within an organizational context. For
example, Savage's (1992) research on banking indicates that, within one leading
bank, women managers were employed in specialist units alongside other employees of a similar status, and were only rarely in managerial jobs that involved the
exercise of direct control and/or authority. He suggests, therefore, that women
managers in banking are characterized by the possession of expertise rather than
organizational power, and "the increasing numbers of *expert* women in the labour
market should not be seen as evidence that women are moving into positions of
organizational authority and control, but rather that, as organizations restructure,
there is increased room for women to be employed in specialist niches" (1992: 147).
Similarly, Devine's work on professionally qualified women in engineering suggests
that women "will be eased into sex-differentiated managerial jobs in sales or personnel or towards the soft side of engineering such as computing where they can
manage other women rather than men"(1992a: 568). Other work on women in
engineering (Evetts 1994) has suggested that, as well as being "eased into" such
positions, professionally qualified women may be directing themselves towards
these organizational slots because of the conflicting demands of family life and an
organizational career. A number of Evetts' respondents were quite explicit: "If you
want a family, you are much better going up the professional ladder because you
can't really manage a department on reduced hours. You've got to put in all your
hours and some more. For most people who would prefer not to, they tend to go up
the professional ladder"(1994: 106).

This kind of evidence, therefore, suggests that, even when women are not actually
leaving employment with the advent of enhanced domestic responsibilities (and we
should remember, of course, that men have never done so), they nevertheless are

likely to follow the professional or expert, rather than the managerial, route within their employing organizations. However, it may be argued that this case-study evidence is merely suggestive, rather than conclusive. It may also be suggested that, in any case, the relatively recent increase of women in higher-level occupations means that it is as yet too early to draw any firm conclusions.

However, Table 4.3, which gives more detailed age breakdowns for women in employment, provides some aggregate-level support for the case-study evidence relating to the concentration of women, particularly those with family responsibilities, into gendered "professional niches". In the younger age group (30–40), the family circumstances of women senior managers and professional employees are very similar, and the proportions of professionals and senior managers living in childless households (column 1 plus column 2) are virtually identical (54% and 53%). However, in the 41–50 age group (where it is reasonably safe to assume that the die has been cast in respect of family formation as far as women are concerned), a marked gap has appeared, and 45% of senior managers, as compared with 37% of professionals, are living in childless households. Indeed, in respect of dependent children, the gap is very wide indeed, as 44% of professional employees, as compared with only 25% of senior managers, are living with dependent children. This difference is explained in part by the greater proportion of senior managers living with non-dependent (and presumably older) children. This suggests that managerial women might have had their children earlier and developed their careers subsequently, but it does not undermine the case being made here – i.e. that the presence of young children is remarkably low amongst senior managerial women as compared with other women in "middle-class" occupations.

It is also noteworthy that female employers and self-employed professionals are much more likely to be living with young children than are employed women in similar occupations, confirming the suggestion that, for women, self-employment may serve as a flexible alternative to organizational attachment (Scase & Goffee 1985). In general, flexible employment (including self-employment) is on the increase, and it may be anticipated that, as the level of skills and expertise rises amongst the female population, so will the opportunities for this kind of work (*Employment Gazette*).

There are a number of problems with the data in Table 4.3 as far as our purposes are concerned. As they are not longitudinal, they do not give direct evidence of occupational changes or interruptions in employment, and we cannot, therefore, be absolutely confident of the interpretation that has been offered above. Nevertheless, they do provide extensive empirical evidence of variation in family circumstances amongst middle-class women that is congruent with the evidence of case studies of women in these positions – that is, that gendered niches requiring expertise rather than authority, together with self-employment, would seem to be more compatible with the presence of children and the demands of family life than are positions directly associated with the power structures of large organizations. Again, it should be emphasized that these kinds of variations are *not* to be found amongst men in similar occupations. For example, 62% of male senior managers, and 55% of em-

Table 4.3 Family circumstances of women aged 30–40 and 41–50 in employment, professional and managerial occupations (% by row).

Occupational group	Not in family		Married/cohab: no children		Married/cohab: dependent children		Married/cohab: non-dependent children		Lone parent		Numbers	
	30–40	41–50	30–40	41–50	30–40	41–50	30–40	41–50	30–40	41–50	30–40	41–50
Employers/managers, large establishments	20	15	33	30	36	25	4	19	7	11	2,050	1,548
Managers, small establishments	15	10	26	25	46	31	5	25	8	9	3,373	2,922
Professionals, employees	24	16	30	21	39	44	2	9	5	10	1,109	488
Employers, small establishments	6	5	15	24	72	42	3	24	5	5	1,022	1,316
Professionals, self-employed	13	11	23	15	62	56	2	7	2	11	281	158
All employed women	10	8	17	21	60	36	5	26	9	10	53,141	50,584

Source: Census SARS (1991). *Note:* Percentages may not add to 100 because of rounding.

ployed professionals aged 30–40 are living in households with dependent children, as are 56% and 60% (respectively) of those in the 41–50 age group – that is, the relative proportions of "family men" show little variation by occupational category.

Both case-study evidence and aggregate-level data, therefore, suggest that extensive gender resegregation within the "service class" is already well under way, and that these emerging patterns are systematically linked to variations in family type. Small employers and self-employed professionals excepted, women in professional and managerial occupations are markedly less likely to be living with dependent children than are men in similar occupations. The presence of dependent children is proportionately greater amongst women in professional, rather than managerial, occupations, reinforcing case-study evidence of the tendency for women to specialize in expertise, rather than organizational power. Given that the middle or service classes continue to expand in number, these developments indicate that the suggestion (Crompton 1986) that improvements in women's career prospects and location within the organizational structure would threaten those of men was premature. There may be – as other papers in this volume argue – other factors associated with recession, restructuring, and organizational "downsizing" that have affected men's career prospects, but gender competition as such would appear not to be particularly important.

However, turning from class to gender relations *per se*, the improvement in women's occupational (and thus economic) position has had a discernible impact upon relationships between the sexes. Ermisch (1993) has conclusively demonstrated the very strong positive association between women's (full-time) employment levels and divorce rates. Census data (1991) show that, as might have been expected, the proportion divorced amongst employed women aged 30–50 (10.7%) is greater than that of employed men (7.3%). However, variations in the proportions divorced within different occupational groups are not large and show no consistent pattern – in contrast to the variations in the proportions of *single* women by occupational group (Tables 4.2 and 4.3). There is, however, another summary statistic that is perhaps even more revealing. The proportion of women (30–50) in employment cohabiting without children was approximately twice the average of that of working women in this age range – 7.6% of managers of large establishments and 6.7% of employed professionals, as against 3.2% overall. This suggests that the greater the level of economic independence amongst women, the more this is reflected in their household arrangements.[9]

4.4   Discussion and conclusion

The steady growth of female representation in middle or "service" class occupations has to be set against the broader background of industrial and occupational restructuring that has been taking place in Britain over the past decades. Deindustrialization and the growth of services (between 1971 and 1993, employment in manufacturing declined from 36.4% to 20.4%, while employment in services grew from 52.6% to 72.8%), together with the impact of recession and rising unemployment, have been accompanied by a growth of flexible or non-standard working. 9.7 million people (38% of all workers) were part-time temporary workers, self-employed, or on a government training scheme or unemployed family workers in 1993 – an increase of 1¼ million since 1986. The proportion of male flexible workers is rising, from 18% in 1981 to 27% in 1993. All of these changes are associated with the decline of the "male breadwinner" employment model of working husband and stay-at-home wife which was the gendered cornerstone of the initial development of the "service class". Today, in contrast, "Most two parent families are also dual earner families, more than three quarters of parents are now employed, and a third of male and female workers have dependent children" (Harrop & Moss 1994).

The generally higher earnings levels within the middle classes might possibly have sustained "male breadwinner" family behaviour for longer than in other social groups, but this does not seem to have been the case. Recent evidence suggests that employment rates amongst mothers of young children are rising most rapidly in precisely these occupational categories (Harrop & Moss 1994), and the projected increase in women's employment is anticipated to be concentrated in these groups (Lindley 1994).[10]

Other papers in this volume discuss the ongoing restructuring of the middle classes in relation to the trends described above. In this paper, we have charted its gradual shift from a predominantly masculine to a more heterogeneously gendered aggregation of occupations. The balance of evidence, however, points to internal resegregation by gender within different service-class positions. Given that adult households are predominantly heterosexual, this developing intra-class differentiation may on balance stabilize, rather than destabilize, middle-class solidarism.

However, this possibility rests upon the assumption that the relations between the sexes remain relatively stable – and, indeed, harmonious. In fact, divorce rates are rising in all industrialized countries, and Britain has one of the highest in Europe. As we have seen, it is well established that levels of divorce are correlated with increases in women's employment, and employed women in higher-level occupations are more likely to be cohabiting (without children) than are women in lower-level occupations. These kinds of trends give rise to some intriguing possibilities.

The sociological tradition from which the grouping of occupations and/or employment relations into "classes" is derived rests upon an assumption that the experience of employment, in a class society, is systematically associated with particular patterns of power, authority and subordination, material advantage and disadvantage and so on.[11] These patterns of power, material advantage, etc. associated with the "main breadwinner's" job have then been, within the "conventional view", mapped on to the household. Our empirical discussion, however, suggests that there is increasing segmentation by both gender and household type within the middle classes (it is true, of course, that the inevitable changes associated with the development of the family life-cycle mean that, in a very important sense, the latter has always been the case). However, if household type, gender and occupation vary together, then this might give rise to new possibilities of coalition and conflict centring on interpersonal as well as "class" relationships.

If (for the sake of this discussion) we exclude partnerships where there are no children, as well as single-person households, then the possible range of gender and middle or service-class household combinations may be summarized as follows: (i) the "traditional" pattern, with the man in a "service" or middle-class employment and his partner either not in employment or a secondary earner; (ii) the man and woman in "service-class" employment, but the woman in a "practitioner" or "expert managerial" rather than a mainstream managerial occupation; (iii) both partners in "practitioner" or "expert managerial" jobs; and (iv) both partners in middle or service-class employment, and the woman in a mainstream managerial job. In the case of family breakdown or divorce, then wives in the first category must be supported by their ex-husbands. As we have seen in recent years, government attempts to enforce this support and its level (through the Child Support Agency) have met with considerable opposition, particularly if the husband acquires a second family. Category (ii) might possibly be emerging as a potentially stable and prosperous element within the middle classes. The wife's earnings will approach the level of her husband's and, in cases of family breakdown, these will make a significant contribution to the maintenance of separate households. Category (iii) might be even more stable, as both partners are likely to be in (comparatively) "family-friendly" employment. Category (iv) is likely to be relatively small. However, it is within this group that there might be the greatest potential for interpersonal conflict along gender lines. Women in this group are vulnerable to the "backlash" against the successes of equality feminism – as in, for example, a recent high-profile case in the USA in which an ex-husband sought and won the custody of their children from his wife. The demands of the wife's job, it was argued, disqualified her from being the "primary carer".[12]

Our discussion of gender developments within the middle classes over the past decade, therefore, has briefly explored the consequences of women's entry at the occupational, organizational, and household levels. As more women move into middle-class occupations, so household types within the middle classes are likely to become increasingly diverse, leading to new sources of tension and conflict. In a situation dominated by the "male breadwinner" pattern, then, although the composition and nature of middle-class households would have changed and developed over the family life-cycle, there would nevertheless have been significant continuities within the 'service-class' as a whole. The growth of women's employment has brought forward a new range of possibilities of household advantage and disadvantage, together with associated gender conflicts. It may be argued that if anything it is more, rather than less, important to pay systematic attention to the gender/class (or employment) interface than it was when second-wave feminist criticisms were first articulated within the sociology of the 1970s.

This flexible approach to the understanding of the impact of gender (or, more specifically, women's employment) on middle or service-class formation has identified and described a very fluid and rapidly developing situation. This is in some contrast to the empirical approach developed by Erikson & Goldthorpe, who have stressed above all the remarkable *stability* of the service class in their terms. As we have seen, Erikson & Goldthorpe have explained this stability through a "social action" explanation of the development and reproduction of the service class, in which social actors (families) with access to power and material resources are able to arrange matters so as to maintain their favoured situation (1992b: 392, 394).

The family is obviously a central element in the perpetuation of advantage and disadvantage, and no attempt is being made to deny this fact here. However, the assumption that the family is the major agent in the reproduction of class inequalities rests upon the further assumption that the family is a relatively stable economic unit. It is an empirical fact that an enduring feature associated with this family stability has been the subordination of women within it. It is a matter of some interest, therefore, whether or not the changes in family patterns, as well as the extent of family stability, associated with the increasing economic independence of women will undermine the cohesiveness of significant elements within the "service class" and thus this capacity for the reproduction of material advantage.

Our discussion, therefore, has focused upon the outcomes of the interaction of "gender" and "class" (or employment) factors, rather than attempted to maintain their separateness. The position taken here would maintain that, as the boundaries between the "public" and the "private", together with their characteristic masculinities and femininities, are increasingly being eroded in the late twentieth century, so this should be reflected in our empirical sociology. This does not mean that we are witnessing "the end" of class analysis, as some have suggested (e.g. Hall & Jaques 1989, Pahl 1989). Rather, it is being argued that the best way forward is to embrace a more flexible approach to the topic as a whole.

Notes

1. It should be stressed that Table 4.1 is not intended to provide a set of watertight "boxes", and it is being used as a heuristic device only.
2. CASMIN = Comparative analysis of social mobility in industrial societies.
3. It should be noted that this criticism is more applicable to the earlier stages of Goldthorpe's research programme, in which the nature of the job assumed more significance in the allocation of occupations to classes, and no allowance was made for occupational segregation by gender.
4. The UK SEG (socio-economic group) classification has been employed. Separate details have been given for the following groups: SEG 1 = employers and managers, large establishments; SEG 2.1 = employers, small establishments; SEG 2.2 = managers, small establishments, SEG 3 = self-employed professionals; SEG 4 = professional employees; SEG 5.2 = non-manual supervisors; SEG 6 = junior non-manual workers; and SEG 9 = skilled manual workers.
5. The Sample of Anonymised Records (SAR). Grateful thanks are due to Professor Angela Dale, of the Census Microdata Unit, for her assistance in providing these analyses.
6. The actual proportion of female lone parents in the population is considerably greater

than this. However, female lone parents are amongst the women least likely to be in employment – see Harrop & Moss 1994.

7. Note that this point applies equally to firm internal labour markets (FILMs) as it does to occupational internal labour markets (OILMs) (see Halford & Savage in Ch. 7 of this volume), as both trajectories imply full-time, organizationally based, employment.

8. The SEG categories are admittedly broad, but suitable for this purpose. The definition of management refers to persons who "plan and supervise", whereas the definition of "profession" refers to "work normally requiring qualifications of university degree standard"; i.e. the bases of the classification reflect the assumptions being made here.

9. This might provide evidence for earlier feminist arguments relating to the role of occupational segregation in directing women into marriage (see Hartmann 1982).

10. Gregson and Lowe (Ch. 9 in this volume) have documented the growth of the new (female) servant class associated with these developments.

11. The extent of wealth and capital holdings would also be incorporated in a comprehensive analysis.

12. In particular the case of Sharon Prost. It should be emphasized that no evaluative stance is being taken on the case itself; rather, it is the discussion relating to the case that is of interest.

Chapter 5

Black middle-class formation in contemporary Britain

Deborah Phillips and Philip Sarre

5.1 Introduction

"Race" is as invisible in most discussions of middle-class formation in Britain as the middle classes are invisible in most discussions of the class position of ethnic minorities. However, we do not take this as a reason for avoiding analysis of race and middle-class formation. On the contrary, we interpret the common assumption that black people are nothing to do with the middle classes as a result of a past process of class formation that was intrinsically built on race: the middle class or classes, whatever else they might be, were in fact and theory indubitably white.

In recent years, it has increasingly been noted that some ethnic minorities have penetrated in substantial numbers into middle-class occupations. Ward et al. (1982) reported on "middle class Asians" and Robinson (1988) has described "the new Indian middle class in Britain". In our view, such titles oversimplify complex issues: even if Asians are in middle-class occupations, can they be regarded as simply middle class? How could we define a specifically Indian middle class? Such questions cannot be resolved without a fundamental reconsideration of the relations between race and class formation.

As early as 1975, Westergaard and Resler had noted that significant numbers of Asian immigrants to Britain were in middle-class occupations, but that did not prevent most analysts from regarding the ethnic minorities solely in relation to the working class. In part, this reflected the centrality of the white male working class to class theory, but, even when the new middle class became a central issue for class theorists and when gender had been recognized as a vital dimension, race rarely came on the agenda as an influence on middle-class formation. We would see this as a reflection of the social closure faced by ethnic minorities trying to get access to privileged positions previously monopolized by white people, and predominantly white men.

This paper examines race and class formation in post-war Britain, focusing on the emergence of black middle-class groups, but also indicating the effects of such groups on the white middle classes. If, following Savage et al. (1992), we take social classes to be social collectivities characterized by shared incomes, lifestyles, cultures and forms of exploitation, we cannot ignore the role of "race" and ethnicity in class formation. It is important to underline that we do not see "race" as simply a minority experience: in Britain, white people, especially middle-class white people, commonly gain privilege from their positions in a racialized labour process, whereas black people often find disadvantage. Thus, just as we cannot ignore the crucial role of gender relations in middle-class formation (Davidoff & Hall 1987, Witz 1992), so we must recognize the pervasive influence of "race" in conceptualizing and forming middle-class identities.

Our task is made more complex by the variability of economy and society over space and time. Ward (1985) has shown that ethnic minority settlement was predominantly as replacement labour in areas of moderate industrial prosperity but that a small business oriented minority were more apparent in declining industrial cities such as Manchester and Newcastle and in parts of the more prosperous south east. That initial geography has subsequently been transformed by de-industrialization and the shift to a service economy as well as by a degree of residential dispersal by the minorities. Now, after four decades of social, cultural, political and economic change in Britain, new structures of opportunity and constraint have emerged, and new responses have come from the black minorities themselves. The indications are that the emergence of a post-industrial economy has brought a greater polarization of experience for blacks and Asians (Sly 1994). On the one hand, black unemployment has grown disproportionately while, on the other hand, evidence of black socio-economic advancement comes to the fore. Thus, it appears that the class position of the black and Asian population in Britain has become increasingly heterogeneous over the decades. Analysis of the class position of the ethnic minorities has yet to reflect that growing complexity.

5.2 Theory

An attempt to theorize the relationships between black people and the British middle classes seems long overdue. In the absence of a substantial literature on the topic, such an attempt should take heed of developments in four related areas: class theory itself; analyses of black middle-class groups in other advanced countries; debates about black people and the lower classes; theories of class and gender. The relevance of the first three areas is obvious, but it is worth stressing why the fourth is relevant here. There are two reasons: first, debates about class and gender have tackled the recent move of substantial numbers of women into the previously male preserves of middle-class occupations; secondly, in our view the aim should be to develop towards theoretical positions that simultaneously handle the formation of class, race and gender identities.

Such an aim implies that our view of class theory must focus on the processes of class formation, though we would want to maintain a link to analytical work on class structure. Savage et al. (1992) have laid the foundations for such an approach with their development of the work of Erik Olin Wright to identify the bases of middle-class positions in property, organizational position and culture, plus their insistence that what matters are the historical effects in the formation of stable social collectivities. However, their work hardly mentions race and is somewhat equivocal about gender, discussing it as one of several "contingent conditions" in which class formation occurs, but then later noting that gender and race actually enter the definition of class positions. We would want to build on the latter view.

When seeking appropriate international cases of the formation of a black middle class, the USA appears particularly relevant. Its black population is much longer established and has had greater opportunities to reach middle-class positions. Fifteen years of privatization and the rolling back of the state have brought British society closer to the American model. In some respects the American experience is discouraging: even in a society that was built on mass immigration and upward mobility, black people have been much slower to reach middle-class positions and enter mainstream society than were white ethnic groups. As late as 1960, only 13% of blacks were middle class, compared with 44% of whites, and that "old" black middle class was largely composed of professionals serving the needs of black communities. The Civil Rights Act of 1964 removed the legal basis of discrimination and, combined with a period of economic growth, allowed a rapid growth of new black middle-class groups. Wilson (1980) has argued that race has ceased to be the primary determinant of life-chances for middle-class blacks and that they are in effect inside the mainstream class system. However, this is contested by Landry (1987), who argues that, although blacks have made some gains, they remain half as likely to be middle class as are whites, they are more likely to be in the lower parts of the middle class, and they are financially more precarious and dependent on a second income to maintain their status. College education was very important in gaining access to middle-class positions, but decreasing percentages of young blacks are now reaching college. Finally, slower economic growth and reduced commitment to affirmative action are slowing the growth of the black middle class. Collins (1993) confirmed the vulnerability of blacks in high-status jobs in white corporations in a detailed study that showed that many of their jobs were dependent on affirmative action programmes, which are politically vulnerable. Even with a longer history and much more determined legislation on equal opportunities, it seems that blacks in America remain disadvantaged and that the black middle classes are largely in ethnic niches rather than in the mainstream.

Much of the British work on race and class has been preoccupied with the position of black workers in relation to the working class. As discussed at greater length elsewhere (Sarre, 1989), both Marxists such as Castles & Kosack (1973) and Weberians such as Rex & Tomlinson (1979) concurred that black workers occupied a position below the British working class, though they used different terminology – a lower division as against an underclass. Both studies began to explore the interaction of citizenship rights, power and status with labour market position but neither could address the growing number of black people in middle-class positions.

Other theoretical approaches developed the analysis of the interactions of labour market position with racial identity and ideology. Miles saw black workers as working class but separated by ideological factors into a distinct class fraction. In his later work he recognizes the existence of a racialized class fraction of the petite bourgeoisie as well as of the working class (1982: 84). On the other hand, Parkin (1979), although perhaps belittling class, usefully focuses on struggles between groups, with established groups seeking closure while newer groups seek to usurp benefits previously closed to them. Such an approach anticipates Barbalet's (1986) concept of status as "enforceable norms" resulting from earlier struggles by groups differentiated by class, race and gender to strengthen their own positions at the expense of others. Such a view seems complementary to the approach, pioneered by Hall (1992) and developed by Gilroy (1987), that recognizes culture as the articulation between structure and action and that focuses on cultural struggles and new social movements as simultaneously race and class forming. Although emphasizing inner-city struggles, Gilroy explicitly recognizes the role of middle-class black people (in local government, the professions and the media) in contesting racism and redefining racial meanings as a basis for action. Our approach would seek to extend the consideration of cultural and political struggles to struggles to get access to economic positions, whether of ownership, occupation or credentials, that both yield immediate benefits in terms of income and offer strengthened resources for future struggles. However, in doing so we have to recognize the negative effects of past and present racism, which might be integrated into Savage et al.'s framework as "cultural liabilities".

Race and gender are categories with much in common and they have similar relations to class formation. Both start with biological differences that have been ideologically processed through racism and patriarchy to yield disadvantage and discrimination. In both cases, members of disadvantaged categories have been denied opportunities and even civil rights over very long periods of history. Under capitalism, both were used as part of the reserve army of labour, though women were also concentrated in the domestic sphere, either "in service" or as homemaker. Both have engaged in liberation struggles, both ideologically and through economic advancement, including migration. Both have made some progress in Britain in recent decades, though with significant differences. White women have been better placed to benefit from widened educational opportunities and have moved close to making up half of the labour force. However, they still suffer from clashes between domestic and work commitments, which continue to yield disadvantage in both. Black men have been either unaffected or advantaged by their domestic situations, but have faced strong discrimination in education and employment, and some groups have been more successful than others. Black women face disadvantage in both domestic and public spheres. The only consolation offered has been that black women are less disadvantaged in relation to white women than black men are in relation to white men, but even that has been contested by Anthias and Yuval-Davies (1992), who argue that official statistics omit the most disadvantaged women workers, many of them black, because they work within family businesses, in casual work or in illegal sweatshops. As regards the middle classes, perhaps the key implication for black class positions is the fact that, although women have been able to break into middle-class occupations in increasing numbers, it appears that they have been concentrated into niche occupations where rewards and prospects are less than those of men (Crompton & Sanderson, 1990). Indeed, Walby (1990) argues that the crucial issue is no longer the degree of access to middle-class occupations but the forms of discrimination that concentrate women into less favourable parts of those occupations.

This brief sketch of issues relevant to black people and the middle class suggests that there must ultimately be two levels of analysis. First, we should consider the evidence about the extent to which black people have been able to get access to middle-class occupations, qualifications and property. Evidence from the USA and comparison with the experience of women both suggest that access is likely to be to racialized niches rather than into the most privileged positions. We will argue that black people have faced serious discrimination in access to advantageous positions in mainstream organizations and have responded in two ways: they have pursued a high level of formal qualifications in an attempt to overcome their cultural liabilities: – this was noted earlier as a strategy which was important in the USA; that they have used property in a number of ways to avoid the problem of discrimination within organizations, only to suffer from disadvantage within markets. However, that evidence will tell us only whether black people are in middle-class positions. The second, and more difficult, level of analysis is to consider in what ways black people could be seen as belonging to a stable middle-class social collectivity. Here there is a range of possibilities. If their identification remains defined on the basis of race, they may not belong to any middle-class group. At the other extreme, if they identify with and are accepted by the broader middle class (if a single class exists), they could be said to be members of that class. Or there could be intervening positions in which they are part of one or more racialized fractions of the middle class(es).

5.3 Empirical evidence of the changing occupational class structure

The occupational structure of the ethnic minority population living in Britain has undergone a significant transformation over the past 30–40 years, although for some minority groups its character is still as distinctive as in the early days of mass migration and settlement. In the early post-war years, the economic migrants entered the country largely as a replacement labour force, settling in towns where the traditional labour-intensive industries were for a time to become dependent upon their cheap, manual labour. The explicit racialization and gendering of jobs at this time brought about a vertical and horizontal segregation of the immigrant and white British labour force. The immigrants' newcomer status, lack of marketable skills, language barriers and often blatant racial discrimination sealed their fate as a reserve army of labour, destined to suffer disproportionately from the social and economic consequences of the economic restructuring of the 1970s and 1980s.

In occupational class terms, most of the early black and Asian male migrants occupied the position of low-paid, low-statused workers, usually regardless of the skills and qualifications they brought with them upon migration (PEP 1974, Brown 1984). Early accounts report cases of doctors, who had qualified in the Indian sub-continent taking jobs in factories, unable to turn their skills (cultural capital) into organizational assets (Hiro 1973). Female migrant workers were also important contributors to the early post-war economy, with many forming part of the casualized, marginalized manual labour force of homeworkers (Phizacklea 1983). Many early migrant households supplemented low wages by becoming landlords, first renting out rooms in their own homes and then possibly acquiring a cheap, inner-city property for rental purposes and thereby embarking on the first rung of the propertied classes (Rex & Moore 1967). Upon arrival, the East African Asian refugees of the 1970s were the only migrant group to be distinguished by their cultural and economic assets. Commentators of the time readily differentiated them from the earlier influx of economic migrants from the Indian Sub-continent, referring to them as better educated, as of urban as opposed to peasant origins and more obviously "middle class" (Bristow & Adams 1977). They thus arrived with the skills and sometimes the financial resources to re-establish themselves as "middlemen" traders. As refugees, they also possessed another cultural asset in the form of public sympathy.

The racial divisions and inequalities within the post-war British labour market have been well documented (Brown 1984, Jones 1993). The statistics have depicted a general pattern of high unemployment (Labour Force Survey data for autumn 1993 indicate that, whereas the white unemployment rate was 9.5%, Pakistani unemployment was running at 30%) and an overrepresentation of black workers in the poorly paid, low-statused jobs of the secondary labour market. Black school leavers and black women are found to be particularly disadvantaged, although the pattern of unemployment and occupational structure varies geographically, with those living in manufacturing areas of restructuring and decline suffering disproportionately. All the indications are then that a labour market segmentation along racial and gender lines still exists, even when controlling for the impact of qualifications on occupational outcomes (Jones 1993). The evidence also suggests that minority workers earn less than similarly qualified whites in the same occupations (Ohri & Faruqi 1988).

The occupational structure of the black ethnic minorities in the 1990s, however, can no longer be seen simply in terms of racial disadvantage. It is clear that there is still a racial division of labour and, we will argue, closure still plays an important role in the labour market and in class formation; there is no doubt of the sustained effect of the cultural liabilities carried by the racialized workforce on their potential for advancement. Nevertheless, we can now see a far more complex picture of occupational structure emerging along the lines of "race" – one that is dependent upon family background, geographical location, gender, age, timing of entry into the job market and ethnic group. Most obviously, the experience of specific minority groups has started to diverge. By 1989, an analysis of Labour Force Survey data indicated that the position of African Asians and Indians within the occupational structure was converging with that of the white population, although Pakistanis and Bangladeshis were still in a very much poorer position (Jones 1993).

The empirical evidence on occupational class from the 1991 Census data indicates that some black groups are now well represented amongst the higher-statused occupations. Indian men show an occupational structure very similar to that of white men, with well-qualified workers just as likely to hold professional or managerial posts as whites. However, further scrutiny shows evidence of horizontal and vertical segregation within these broad occupational classes, with whites more likely to occupy managerial posts, especially within large organizations, and blacks more likely to be professionals or employers (see Table 5.1). Further evidence of horizontal divisions is to be found in the relatively high concentration of black minority males in the health professions compared with their low representation in teaching. As we explore below, black minorities' abilities to transform cultural capital in the form of skills and qualifications into organizational assets is hampered by social closure in many bureaucracies on the grounds of "race". The absence of the black minorities in senior management positions in large firms is particularly notable. The propensity of the black minorities to pursue professional work or become employers is clearly linked to the relatively high level of self-employment amongst these particular ethnic groups. For example, 15% of Indians are self-employed compared with 11.4% of the economically active white population (Labour Force Survey 1993), although very few are responsible for larger firms of 25 or more employees (Jones 1993). The pattern of black minority advancement through the occupational structure is, however, fragmented. As Table 5.1 indicates, Black Caribbean men are still significantly underrepresented in the higher occupational classes. Although this group is well represented amongst the skilled manual workers, about a third of Black Caribbean males are employed as machine operators or in unskilled occupations. Meanwhile, Pakistani and Bangladeshi men are significantly underrepresented in skilled manual jobs and in the professional occupations compared with the whites.

Table 5.1 Structure of male employment, 1991 (% by column).

Occupation	White	Black Caribbean	Indian	Pakistani	Bangladeshi
Corporate managers	12.3	4.7	7.4	4.9	3.2
Managers	7.0	3.2	14.6	14.4	16.5
Professionals	9.4	4.1	13.6	7.4	6.2
Associate professionals	7.9	7.5	6.2	3.6	2.0
Clerical/ secretarial	6.6	8.3	9.2	6.4	3.2
Skilled manual	23.4	26.2	16.4	13.1	8.6
Personal services	6.0	8.0	2.7	3.9	44.6
Sales	4.5	2.8	6.4	7.5	2.3
Machine operators	14.3	21.5	15.8	28.6	4.5
Unskilled manual	7.6	10.8	5.4	7.0	5.2
Other	1.0	2.9	2.2	3.3	3.6

Source: 1991 Census.

The smaller disparity between black and white female employment patterns is well established (Jones 1993). This is largely accounted for by the smaller proportion of women workers in the professional, managerial and employer category in general. The cultural assets associated with professional expertise and competence are defined in terms of patriarchal structures in the workplace, reflecting and reproducing the wider inequalities of gender relations in society. That gender relations are implicated in the formation of class relations is well known, the evidence suggesting that men's advancement in terms of their organizational and professional careers is often dependent upon the incorporation of their wife's/partner's labour (Finch 1983, Walby 1990). Black women, however, do occupy a distinctive position within this pattern of subordination (see Table 5.2). The Census statistics show that Indian and Pakistani women come close to the position of white women in gaining those coveted positions at the top of the organizational or professional structure, but that Black Caribbean women are underrepresented in the top jobs. If we disaggregate these occupational groupings further, other disparities surface. For example, over half of the Black Caribbean women falling within the associate professional category are in nursing (an occupation forecast to experience decline in the 1990s), whereas white women are more likely to be in administrative jobs (Phizacklea 1994). Recent work presents evidence of vertical segregation within the nursing profession along race lines, with a clear underrepresentation of ethnic minority staff at senior levels (Jewson et al. 1993). Furthermore, analysis within occupational sectors indicates that South Asian women are more likely to work as plant and machine operatives in craft and related occupations (especially manufacturing) than their white counterparts, a sector that is particularly vulnerable to job loss in the coming decade. Thus, racialized as well as gendered structures underpin class formation, with ethnic niches (to use Phizacklea's term) appearing particularly in traditional areas of "women's work".

The most recent and compelling evidence that ethnic minority women face "double discrimination" in the job market was provided by a study by the Equal Opportunities Commission in June 1994. The findings indicated that skilled and

Table 5.2 Structure of female employment, 1991 (% by column).

Occupation	White	Black Caribbean	Indian	Pakistani	Bangladeshi
Corporate managers	6.4	4.4	4.0	3.9	2.6
Managers	5.2	2.0	9.3	11.3	3.8
Professionals	7.6	4.9	7.3	7.8	12.9
Associate professionals	9.7	17.6	7.5	6.9	6.1
Clerical/ secretarial	28.2	28.5	25.5	21.7	19.1
Skilled manual	3.4	2.5	10.9	12.9	15.1
Personal services	13.0	16.6	4.7	7.3	13.6
Sales	10.6	4.2	9.0	11.6	10.4
Machine operators	5.0	6.0	14.5	9.1	5.2
Unskilled manual	10.0	10.9	5.2	3.3	3.8
Other	0.8	2.3	2.1	4.2	7.5

Source: 1991 Census.

experienced ethnic minority women were twice as likely as white women to be unemployed and, although better educated on average than white women (60% of Black African and over 40% of Indian women enter higher education compared with 25% of young white women), they tend to work longer hours, for poorer pay. There is also evidence that black women are far more likely to become unemployed than white women in periods of recession. Race and ethnicity fragment the experience of women both in the workplace and at home. The notion of "the middle-class family" is socially and culturally constructed and invariably conjures up images of white, suburbanized nuclear family life, and conformity to this will serve as a cultural asset (primarily for men) in terms of their organizational career. However, although the "middle-class" suburbs and the lifestyle associated with it may be a signifier of status for many white families, its meaning may be very different for the minority household, particularly its female members.

As Boys (1990) has argued, the notion of "home" as a "woman's place" is founded on conceptions of white middle-class domesticity. For Asian women in particular, separation from the ethnic community through suburban living may place them in a position where they become more dependent upon male members of their family, for mobility and socializing, especially if racial harassment is perceived to be a threat. It may also affect their chances of work, since women are even more likely than men to rely on information exchanged through social networks in their search for a job.

The experience of Asian women in particular may also be affected by their incorporation into the paid work of the male members of the household, as carers and workers. This is particularly true of the families of self-employed workers, amongst which Asians are disproportionately represented. For cultural reasons, 60% of Muslim women perform the role of domestic carers (Brah & Shaw 1993). Research by Brah & Shaw (1993) into young (16–24) Muslim women in Birmingham indicated that, despite a desire to enter the paid labour force, domestic responsibilities prevented not only mothers but also some single women living at home from taking a job. At the time of the research in 1989, this was generally found to be a more important constraint on their economic activities than family views on purdah and working outside the home. Their aspirations were influenced by the gendered divisions of the labour market, with most wanting jobs in the sectors where women predominate. Since, in a gendered labour market, much "women's work" is part-time, this constitutes a considerable disadvantage in terms of their own occupational advancement. It is also important to recognize that such women may not have the educational opportunities that might set them on a path of independence and individual achievement because their needs are subordinated to those of the family. Family status may improve their marriage chances but their lack of credentials is most likely to render them dependent upon their husband.

5.4 Cultural assets

The foregoing discussion has drawn an important distinction between professionals and managers in the formation of the black middle classes. The salience of this distinction between professionals and bureaucrats has been much discussed in the literature (Giddens 1973, Crompton 1990a, Savage et al. 1992), with particular attention having been focused on the construction and reproduction of certain types of "knowledge" through training and qualifications in the professions and the workplace. The overrepresentation of Indians in particular in professional occupations is linked to their eagerness to secure formal qualifications as a route into organizational career structures and serves to minimize the effects of cultural liabilities. As Larson (1977) has argued, professionalism constitutes a means of coupling high levels of formal education with highly prized occupational rewards, thereby transforming cultural assets through education into material gain. Such assets, unlike the organizational assets of managers, are easily transferable and may be used as a means of overcoming closure.

The statistics indicate that Afro-Caribbeans and Asians are more likely to stay on in post-compulsory education than are white people. For example, evidence from the Youth Cohort Study revealed that, whereas 40% of whites stay on in full-time education after 16, 50% of Afro-Caribbeans stay and 70% of Asians (Drew et al. 1992). These findings are consistent with a stronger desire for educational attainment amongst the black minorities than amongst whites, which is especially notable given the occupational background of many minority group parents. It is well known that parental attitudes to education and employment often serve to reproduce class positions over the generations, but research has shown that Asian ethnicity has a similar effect to middle-class status in white people in influencing attitudes towards education, training and employment (Penn & Scattergood 1992). Similarly, an analysis of variables influencing the decisions of 16 year olds to stay on at school revealed ethnic origin to be the single most important determinant (Drew et al. 1992). The propensity to then go on for professional qualifications is evident from data on university admissions by subject area, which reveal a strong preference for medicine and dentistry, and engineering and technology (Brennan & McGeevor 1990). This preference is strongly associated with a recognition of the exclusion facing black minorities from many areas of the job market and the need to secure transferable assets. There is nevertheless evidence that this drive for achievement does not translate easily into access to further education or jobs. Brah & Shaw (1993) found that stereotypes about Asian communities and their aspirations abounded amongst teachers, career advisers and YTS trainers (most of whom are white), disadvantaging in particular the women. Black minority students are still underrepresented in many of the old universities, although recruitment at the new universities has much improved. However, the opportunities open to new and old university students are not the same. For example, law firms prefer to recruit students from established universities into their legal practice courses, thus indirectly disadvantaging black students in their quest for places (*Guardian*, 13 April 1994).

Recent structural changes in higher education have included moves towards a mass higher education system and the search for new constituencies of students. This has brought initiatives for improved access to the old university system for ethnic minority students, although it is acknowledged that "much of the innovative work . . . has taken place at the margins rather than at the foundations of the University's structure" (University of Leeds 1992). Lack of financial support is also a major barrier to study for black people, especially given the disadvantages they experience in the job market.

Once in the higher education system, black students do not find themselves on an equal footing. A survey at the University of Leeds, for example, indicated that students from ethnic backgrounds tended to feel isolated and excluded, and are aware of cultural bias in the curriculum (University of Leeds 1992). Having to survive in a predominantly white environment can bring unusually high drop-out rates. Similarly, a recent enquiry into a significant discrepancy in failure rates between black and white law students at the Inns of Court School of Law (43% as opposed to 16%) referred of a "collapse of confidence" amongst black students, who said they felt isolated and socially and financially handicapped (*Guardian*, 13 April 1994). The Council for Legal Education, which until 1994 had a monopoly over training for barristers, has been accused of disadvantaging black students through its policies and procedures.

Racialized and gendered strategies of subordination have brought the exclusion and demarcation of black and female employees who have succeeded in entering the professions or the managerial structures of large organizations. Despite race relations legislation and despite the recent advances of a more credentialized black population, there is much evidence to suggest that racial minorities still face systematic discrimination in the job market and the workplace. Organizational assets and cultural power still largely reside with the white (male) population, who can use these assets to curb entry to higher-status occupations or to block promotion prospects, thereby securing their own privileges and rewards. Discrimination in the job market becomes most acute in areas of high unemployment and more generally in times of recession or other market swings. For example, in March 1994, the Banking, Insurance and Finance Union (BIFU) claimed that Barclays' Bank was targeting black staff in its programme of job cuts (*Runnymede Bulletin*, April 1994).

The problems of translating training and qualifications into organizational assets has been exposed in a study of ethnic pay differentials (Pirani et al. 1992). The evidence suggests that there is direct and indirect discrimination within institutions, which becomes manifest in the perception that ethnic minority employees are less suitable for promotion than their white counterparts. White workers are therefore more likely to get selected for training than black employees after a certain length of service, a closure strategy that in effect presents more opportunities for advancement to the white workforce. In addition to this, Pirani et al. demonstrate that, even when ethnic minority workers have higher education and training than whites doing the same job, they tend to be in lower grades and their wages tend to be less than the norm for their qualifications. The differential in hourly wages for male employees ranged from 30% in the teaching profession to 47% in private industry. The cultural asset inherent in educational qualifications may therefore be of dubious value in terms of material rewards for black minority workers.

The fracturing of the experience of well-educated black and white youngsters trying to embark upon a professional career can be illustrated with reference to the medical and legal professions. There is well-documented evidence that, although Indians in particular are well represented amongst the medical profession, they may be discriminated against in selection for medical school, they are less likely to be shortlisted for jobs when qualified (Everington and Esmail study quoted in the *Guardian* 22 March 1994) and, once practising, they tend to be overrepresented in the least popular, less prestigious specialisms, such as geriatrics and venereal diseases. This demarcation of work preserves the prestige and privilege accruing to white doctors. Recent findings indicate that the experience of ethnic minority doctors is also likely to be different from that of whites in the work environment, with six times as many black and Asian doctors facing disciplinary charges by the General Medical Council (GMC) compared with their white colleagues (*Guardian*, 22 March 1994). Whereas 18% of doctors practising are from ethnic minority groups, 58% of the doctors called before the GMC's conduct committee between 1981 and 1991 were from an ethnic minority group.

An analysis of ethnic minority experience in the legal profession reveals a racialization and a gendering of opportunities. A recent study by the Policy Studies Institute (*Guardian*, 13 April 1995) reported that solicitors' firms were actively discriminating against black students when recruiting trainees for articles from a surfeit of law finalists. Black women students were particularly disadvantaged compared with white men. Other research into the Bar's law school also concluded that barristers' chambers were discriminating against blacks in offering pupillages (*Guardian*, 20 April 1994). Blacks have established the Society of Black Lawyers to provide a system with its own organizational assets as a counterbalance to the established system, which is seen by many to perpetuate its own class, gender and race bias. There is also evidence of other strategies for advancement being set up by black minorities for the purpose of usurping resources and power from the white population. For example, in 1992, Britain's black churches, under the auspices of the Afro-Caribbean Evangelical Alliance and the Joint Council for Anglo-Caribbean Churches, announced that they were to launch a wealth-creation initiative, designed to promote the talents of religious leaders, community workers and professionals (*Independent*, 26 October 1992). Following their American counterparts, particular emphasis was placed on the need to nurture black business talent, to facilitate its development through black capital and to promote a "buy black" campaign through preaching from the pulpits. This political message was to be underlined by advocating protest strategies, such as black people withdrawing their capital from banks that were not seen to be supportive of black initiatives.

5.5   Property

Some racial minorities in Britain, notably those of Indian origin, have shown a long-term tendency to acquire and use property assets as a means of advancement. This was first reported in the 1960s in the form of residential landlordism, occurred also in a strong commitment to owner occupied housing and has more recently involved a move into self-employment or ownership of small businesses, especially in the retail sector.

One of the most seminal studies of immigrant communities in Britain (Rex & Moore 1967) was concerned with access to housing, and especially the role of the "lodging house". Recent migrants in low-paid jobs and suffering from overt discrimination faced a severe shortage of housing and soon turned to renting a room in houses in multiple occupation. By the mid-1960s many of these lodging houses were owned by members of minority groups, especially Pakistanis, and their plight is eloquently explained – caught between expensive loans and the demands of kin for shelter and support, torn between the need to increase the number of tenants and fear of raids by the Public Health Department, minority landlords seemed unlikely to make large profits and certainly gained little social esteem. However, this picture may fail to reflect circumstances in other parts of the country (Davies & Taylor 1970). More recently, the number of minority landlords is poorly documented: they do not appear in substantial numbers among minority self-employed, but ethnic minority landlords were numerous in a study of landlords in north London (Allen & McDowell 1989). Moreover, there are anecdotal indications that some landlords of homeless hostels used by local authorities are black, and also that black people were quick to take part in the expansion of private renting after the slump in the owner-occupied market in 1989. Although the former activity may be financially rewarding, private landlords seem to have recovered little status since the days of Rachmanism.

The shift of ethnic minority households into owner-occupied housing is, on the contrary, lavishly documented. As early as 1981 Indians had far outstripped the level of owner-occupation of the white British and by 1988 the same was true of Pakistanis and Bangladeshis (Skellington 1992). This would appear to have placed these groups in advantageous positions to benefit from the surge of house prices in the late 1980s. Saunders (1990) certainly argues this in his study of the gains from owner-occupation in three towns. However, there are some reasons for doubt. Minority homeowners still tend to own lower-value housing in less desirable areas – just the kind of housing that Savage et al. show to have made relatively low gains in the 1980s and that Gentle et al. (1994) showed to be particularly prone to negative equity in the 1990s. Minority homeowners may have been protected from negative equity if the tendencies to pay off mortgages early and to stay in the first owner-occupied home, which were identified in Bedford by Sarre et al. (1989), are true in other areas. Nevertheless, it is unlikely that many such households will have made the kind of gain that would transform their economic circumstances and hence their class position.

The third, and arguably the most effective, use of property as a means of advancement is through ownership of small businesses, as already identified in the discussion of employment and self-employment. The growth in numbers of Asian self-employed was apparent by the early 1980s, but again there are doubts about the causes and consequences. Jenkins (1984) recognized three interpretations: some authors regarding the move into self-employment simply as a response to economic opportunity, others as prompted by minority culture and others as a reaction to blocked aspirations in the labour market. We would argue that all three factors interact, and indeed that they do so differently in different places. Ward (1985) relates employment and self-employment to the geographic context when he points out the strong contrasts between cities in terms of replacement labour versus business-oriented black settlement. In so doing he reconciles the differences of view between Aldrich et al. (1984), who argue forcefully that most Asian shopkeepers in their survey work very long hours for low profits, and Werbner (1980), who documents a network of successful businesses in Manchester. The former pattern results from inexperienced and under-capitalized entrepreneurs starting businesses to serve an ethnic enclave market in declining industrial cities, whereas the latter reflects an experienced "middleman minority" (Bonacich 1973) developing businesses with a wider market. Patel (1988) demonstrates that shopkeepers with personal or family experience of business tend to have higher turnovers and more rapidly growing businesses than former migrant labourers with shops in ethnic enclaves. The indications are that some minority business owners are in the upper reaches of the petite bourgeoisie or even in the bourgeoisie proper, but that many more are more comparable to self-employed artisans. Even where businesses have grown, Ram (1992) shows that professional services face difficulties in attracting mainstream custom and that small manufacturers are forced to use white agents to secure contracts with British chainstores. Asian small business also has a gender bias as many such businesses use family labour, especially that of women, on an unpaid basis and subject to the decision-making of the male boss. Small businesses in manufacturing and services are notoriously dependent on contracts from larger firms seeking to reduce costs by subcontracting. Such relationships often involve short-term contracts that may be renewed only on more stringent terms. Ethnic entrepreneurs may often be required to drive down costs and margins as the price of survival. In such circumstances, the formal advantages of being self-employed or an employer may be very difficult to translate into economic benefits or status advances, let alone stored in a form that can be passed on to the next generation.

The effect of property on minority class formation seems to be contradictory. On the one hand, some businesses, and perhaps even some residential investments, offer substantial gains and take minority households into capitalist or solidly middle-class positions. On the other hand, experiences of business ownership and ownership of property are very heterogeneous and seem more likely to undermine the ability of black groups to see themselves as, or act as, stable social collectivities.

5.6 Conclusion

This paper has concentrated on the first level of analysis identified in the section on theory: the degree of access by black people to middle-class occupations, qualifications and property. The picture that emerges is remarkably similar in all three areas. Some groups, notably those of Indian origin, have penetrated in considerable numbers into previously white preserves. However, in every area, the real achievement has been less significant than it first appears. Black people have been successful in obtaining British qualifications, but these have been less effective in gaining access to prestigious employment than would be true for the white British. Many black people who have entered middle-class jobs have done so in less favoured occupations; this is especially true for Afro-Caribbean women, who are predominantly "associate health professionals", i.e. nurses. Even where they become doctors and lawyers, black people find themselves in the least prestigious niches and most liable to censure from their peers. Where employees have used owner-occupation of houses to boost their status, most have found themselves in less desirable property. Where they have turned to self-employment and business ownership, most Asians have been restricted to low-order retailing and labour-intensive manufacturing. For those who have developed successful businesses, Cashmore (1992) and Ram (1992) identify the ultimate paradox: they often have to conceal ethnic ownership and employ white people to deal with the public and with other businesses – in other words, they practise "racism by proxy". The overall picture is one not of unconditional entry to the middle class, but of reluctant admission to a variety of ethnic niches. In spite of efforts to obtain credentials, occupational position and property, black people still suffer from perceived "cultural liabilities" that set them apart from the white middle class.

One surprising feature of the British literature dealing with black people and the middle classes is that there is little systematic ethnographic work on the self-perceptions of black people in middle-class positions, or of white middle-class responses to them. In spite of the growing numbers of black middle-class people, including a significant number of social scientists, in spite of work and debates in other countries about blackness and class identity (e.g. Fanon 1980, Wilson 1980), and in spite of the suggestive argument that black Atlantic people experience double consciousness (Gilroy 1994), this question has hardly been addressed in the British literature. Husband (1982) suggested that, even in prestigious jobs like that of solicitor, blackness overrode occupation in everyday experience and identity. More recently, Hall (1992) argued that new ethnicities still tend to essentialize blackness. However, none of this gives any direct evidence about middle-class black identities.

Prima facie, given the ethnic and geographical variability of the British black population, there is little likelihood of a single self-conscious black middle class. The range of outcomes in terms of occupation, qualifications and property, plus the indications of the processes underlying those outcomes, suggest very strongly that racism and discrimination are just as pervasive, though perhaps less overt, in the white British middle classes as in the working class. Faced with ambitious and increasingly well-qualified black people, some ground has had to be given, but white resistance evidently continues. The whiteness of the British middle classes turns out to be not just an assumption or an oversight, but an implicit goal of British culture. If social science has any claims to be an emancipatory activity, it should challenge middle-class whiteness as a principle just as it refutes it as empirically outdated.

Part Three
Restructuring, employment and middle-class formation

The study of employment has always been at the heart of traditional class analysis and related studies of social mobility. Since both Marxists and Weberians see classes as arising out of various sorts of employment relationships and occupational positions, the study of the changing nature of employment has clear implications for the analysis of social class. The chapters in this section all consider various aspects of how current changes in the world of work and employment may affect our understanding of the middle classes.

The starting point is the fact that, as Mills shows in Chapter 6, there is no doubt that the numbers of people employed in "middle class" jobs, however defined, has expanded consistently throughout the 20th century. Even if a relatively restricted definition is adopted which only claims that professional and managerial employees are "middle class", it is still clear that around a third of the workforce is now part of the middle classes. However, there has been little consensus, hitherto, on what these broad aggregate trends imply for class relationships. One line of argument, endorsed by Daniel Bell (1973), was that figures indicated a "professionalizing" class structure, with an increasing proportion of middle class employees. Theorists of the service class, such as Goldthorpe and Urry also point to the numerical rise of professional and managerial occupations as testimony to the growing salience of the "service class", though they were both critical of Bell's view that as the middle classes expanded, so class conflict and division would become more muted.

Some writers were however more sceptical of the real significance of these numerical shifts. One line of critique came from radical professionalization theory (Johnson 1972; Larson 1977). Johnson (1972) took issue with the claim that occupations simply became professional because they took on some of the characteristics of the more traditional professionals such as law, architecture and medicine. Johnson dismissed this approach as "definition by attribution" and pointed out that not only were most of them located in the bureaucratic structures of the state but they also lacked the same control over entry to the professions as for instance exercised by doctors and lawyers. More fundamentally, Johnson and Larson argued that this ignored the question of power, which was at the heart of professionalism.

The key point is that it should not be assumed that the "newer" professions should necessarily be seen in the same terms as the "older", classic professions, and hence that the existence of a professional title may not in and of itself be of particular social significance.

This leads to a more fundamental line of critique, developed from a Marxist perspective by Braverman in *Labour and monopoly capital* (1974), which argued that as capital increased control over the labour process, this began to bite into not only the autonomy traditionally enjoyed by skilled manual workers, but also that of white collar workers. Whatever job titles might indicate, in reality white collar workers were in fact being downgraded in the content of their work tasks and skills. These issues bear clearly on the sorts of questions concerning the boundaries of the middle classes and their relationships with employers and other employees which have been rehearsed in Chapter 2.

Readers will see that although Chapters 6, 7, and 8 all contain material relevant to these themes (especially Chapter 8), none of these papers is specifically focused around questions of professionalization and proletarianization. These two themes can, in fact, be seen as products of an era of "organized capitalism" or "Fordism" and were a response to questions of how to regulate large organizations in large organizations. In recent years radical restructuring, "downsizing" and so forth have altered the nature of the debate and have posed new challenges to class theory. Notably Savage et al. (1992) argued that economic change had in fact radically weakened the relevance of bureaucratic position for the middle classes.

These developments have changed the nature of debate somewhat. In all the chapters except that by Gregson and Lowe, the main point at issue is how organizational restructuring is changing the nature of the middle classes. More specifically, does restructuring mean that traditional approaches to the middle classes that stress their bureaucratic basis are no longer valid? This question is approached in very different ways. Mills examines patterns of work-life mobility using survey data to assess how the ease of movements between various middle class occupations in the course of people's careers has changed in recent years; Carter & Fairbrother provide a case study of the Civil Service, and Halford & Savage one of banks and local authorities.

Chapter 9 by Gregson & Lowe raises similar issues in a very different way. It is concerned not with the middle class as employees – the classic focus of class theory – but with the middle classes as employers, in this case of domestic workers. Their paper suggests many ways in which orthodox class theory may seem problematic – in its treatment of gender, domestic work, and also of the multiple employment status of increasing numbers of the middle classes.

Chapter 6

Managerial and professional work-histories

Colin Mills

6.1 Introduction

In 1911 about 10% of the British work force held the sorts of occupations that indicate membership of the service class. In 1991 about 30% of the employed held nominally equivalent managerial or professional positions. The history of employment during the twentieth century is partly the tale of a shift from an economy where the vast majority of employees are directly engaged in the physical manipulation, transformation and transportation of things to one where a substantial number are engaged in the management, organization and dissemination of people, paper and ideas.

When did the growth of managerial and professional occupations become noticeable? Figure 6.1, based on Price & Bain's (1988) calculations from the decennial census, give us the best answer we are likely to get. Though the point has been

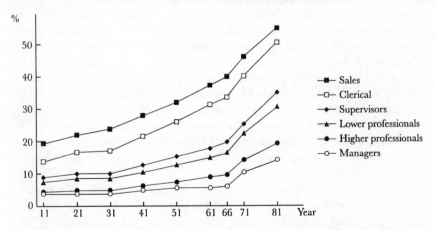

Figure 6.1 Percentage of workforce employed in "white-collar" occupations, 1911–81. *Source:* Price & Bain (1988).

95

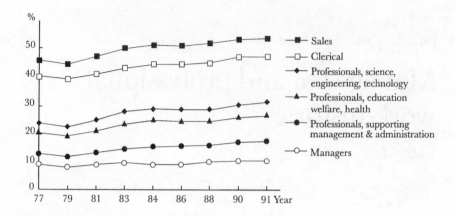

Figure 6.2 Percentage of employed in "white-collar" occupations, 1977–91. *Source:* Labour Force Survey.

made before (see Goldthorpe with Llewellyn & Payne 1987: Ch. 2, Table 2.3.), significant increases in the proportion of the workforce employed in managerial and professional occupations are largely a post Second World War phenomenon. The picture in the 1980s and early 1990s is one of continued but modest growth in the proportion of professionals and virtual stability in the proportion of managers (see Figure 6.2).

Goldthorpe on the service class

As Goldthorpe (1982) *inter alios* points out, the continued existence and indeed growth in the proportion of the workforce engaged in non-manual, professional and managerial occupations have posed a problem for "class theorists" of the left and right alike. Primarily concerned with the construction of conjectural prognoses about the future of "class action", the question they purport to answer is: when the ideological barricades are to be manned, on which side of the capital–labour divide will the higher white-collar workers line up? Though the intellectual agenda of radical 1960s sociology now looks rather ridiculous, it is possible to treat the question in slightly less dramatic terms. Prospective governing parties formulate policy packages that are explicitly targeted to appeal to particular social groups. The degree of congruence between these policy packages and both the naked interests and the political ideologies of groups within the electorate is a *prima facie* cause of electoral success.

How one identifies a naked interest or a political ideology is beyond the scope of this chapter. However, the core of Goldthorpe's argument is that "class theorists" often in practice do it in a rather mechanical way. In particular, he claims they ignore one rather crucial variable in their account of the ideological complexion of the service class: its degree of so-called "demographic identity". Though this might seem a somewhat mysterious macro-level property of a class, it can in fact be reduced to statements about individuals and their experiences. Goldthorpe singles out three factors for discussion: first, the extent to which service-class individuals are likely to have originated in non service-class homes: secondly the extent to which they have experience of non service-class employment during the course of their work career: thirdly, the extent to which their network of spare-time associates brings them into contact with other service-class employees. To the extent that work and life-course experience become increasingly circumscribed by exclusively service-class associations, the demographic foundations of ideological heterodoxy are likely to weaken, and as "class formation" proceeds apace service-class members are more likely to display a greater uniformity of interest and ideology. Though the specific content of interests and ideology cannot be deduced from the prediction of increased levels of demographic identity, Goldthorpe argues that it is likely to be in a broadly conservative direction. The reason for this lies in his conception of the employment relationship that characterizes service-class work. The numerical core of the service class consists of two broad occupational groups: professionals and managers. Professionals are "knowledge experts" and may work on their own account or be employed by public or private sector organizations. Managers are "organizational experts" and are, quite literally, the executives of public and private sector organizations. In the Goldthorpe scheme the service class is split into lower and higher portions but for a moment I will ignore this distinction and concentrate on his account of what differentiates the employment relation of the service class *in toto* from that of all other employees.

Above all else, members of the service class, as the name suggests, are the *agents* of individual and organizational *principals*. To a far greater degree than other employees their roles are difficult to specify completely in the form of an employment contract covering all possible contingencies. This means that the relationship between employer and employee is characterized, on both sides, by a high degree of trust. Managers and professionals are trusted to act in the best interests of the employing organization and in turn they trust that they will not be treated purely as wage labour. A crucial aspect of this implicit bargain is the provision by the employing organization of opportunities for human capital development and for career advancement. If a manager is routinely expected to advance the prospects of the organization, part of the employer's obligation is to create channels for promotion. It is clearly rational for an organization to do this if it enhances the productivity of employees in their current positions. The upshot of this should be that considerations of future personal organizational prospects weigh more heavily in the "action orientations" of service-class employees than in those of, say, manual employees. This is likely to be even more so if large portions of the service-class career are made within a single organization rather than by exposure to the vicissitudes of the labour market. In short, though the service class may appear differentiated by divisions of occupational *situs*, these, according to Goldthorpe, should not distract us from noting the distinct similarity of position shared by all those in high-trust, future-orientated service-class jobs. In essence, they have a stake in institutional continuity and are unlikely to favour changes that threaten their own prospects of advancement. Neither are they likely to favour redistributional policies that threaten the chances of their children attaining service-class positions. Nor will they be likely to favour democratization of the way they carry out their jobs. In the case of professionals, this threat is likely to lead to a defence of the traditional monopoly over specialist knowledge. In the case of managers, we should expect resistance to any threat to curtail traditional managerial prerogatives. Resistance may well take the form of legitimatory ideologies emphasizing, as appropriate, both the meritorious and efficient nature of current arrangements.

These then are the principal arguments for treating service-class occupations as being *in class terms* relatively homogeneous. There is also here a potentially fertile research hypothesis about variation within the service class, attributable to the causal impact of "demographic identity" on the propensity for individuals to hold class-related views and carry out class-related actions.

The challenge to Goldthorpe's views

A large amount of ink has been spilled expressing views *contra* Goldthorpe on the conceptualization of the service class and I am not going to rehearse them all here. However, it does seem in order to outline what needs to be demonstrated or at least convincingly argued if these anti-Goldthorpe views are to be given any credence. To do this I formulate two statements that seem to capture the intelligible essence of the "contras" argument, and follow each with a response.

Argument 1

The utility of combining professional and managerial occupations into one service class is not something that can be evaluated in the abstract. It can be judged only on a case-by-case basis in line with whatever the empirical evidence suggests is appropriate for a particular investigation. Professional and managerial occupations may appear very similar or very different depending on what features of remuneration, working conditions, perquisites, ideology or prospects one chooses to focus on. One should therefore choose whichever aggregation of occupations seems to work best in each application.

Reply 1

The question of the homogeneity of the service class does warrant attention and is amenable to empirical enquiry. The extent to which one should agglomerate occupations into "classes" is partly a practical issue and depends on whether one's explanatory project requires evidence at the level of broad impressionistic brush strokes or focused pointillism. In constructing his class scheme Goldthorpe has already conceded that we can often usefully distinguish between an upper and a lower service class. It seems in order then to ask whether a further distinction between managers and professionals might be helpful. A warrant for this distinction would be whether or not it had any explanatory power. *However, this should not be interpreted to mean that an increase in the amount of variation explained in a dependent variable of choice automatically requires the identification of two new social classes.* This would be only justified if the extra variation accounted for could be interpreted in a manner consistent with the way in which social class is conceptualized. In other words, it is necessary to show that there is something distinct about the employment relations of, say, managers *vis-à-vis* professionals that accounts for or, to put it more boldly, causes, the observed variation. If we cannot do this then we can justify our distinction on empirical grounds as an aid only to prediction rather than understanding.

Argument 2

But it can clearly be shown that the service class is internally differentiated along lines of sector, education, race and sex. Surely this means that Goldthorpe's conceptualization is deeply flawed?

Reply 2

As social scientists we should be wary of engaging in disputes about the mere usage of words. Class categorizations are only more or less useful ways of cutting up the world for a particular explanatory purpose. Nothing of consequence should hang on whether we use the word "class" or *situs* to designate a distinction between, say, managers and professionals. However, once having coined a concept, a minimum of consistency is required or we get confused and scientific communication breaks down. In particular we should avoid conflating different concepts, *even when in reality the empirical indicators of these concepts tend to be correlated.* To say that the coining of conceptual distinctions is a matter of convention is not to say that it is totally arbitrary. Criticism of "class analysis" because it "ignores" sexual, racial, educational and presumably many other plausible sources of systematic social differentiation is, at best, beside the point. Class is not race or sex or education; that is why we choose a different word to describe it. It is, at least in Goldthorpe's construal, about differential employment relations (see Mills 1994) and possibly about the causal effects of these on non-working members of conjugal households. Whether class or race or sex or education account for more or less of the variation in, say, welfare or political beliefs is entirely an empirical question and can be sensibly discussed only in the light of what the available empirical evidence suggests. However, this has no bearing on the question of how social class should be conceptualized and measured.

In summary, it is incoherent to reject Goldthorpe's notion of the service class simply on the grounds that on occasion we can usefully distinguish subgroups within it. For such a rejection to be tenable it would have to be demonstrated that the distinctions defining the subgroups were ones of social class. Nor can we reject Goldthorpe's concept by pointing to other partially overlapping causal variables.

Exercises along these lines cause a lot of sound and fury, but signify nothing apart from an inability to comprehend the issue at stake.

6.2   Empirical issues

Given what has gone before it would be inconsistent for me to purport to evaluate Goldthorpe's concept of the service class. I have no direct evidence on the nature of the employment relationships, whether they are changing over time or whether they are distinctive, in a relevant way, of subgroups within the group of service-class employees. What I shall do is present empirical evidence related to four issues concerning professional and managerial careers that in my view are of interest in their own right as well as indirectly bearing on the matters at stake. Some of this evidence is relevant to the question of the degree of demographic formation of each of the principle constituents of the service class and the degree of permeability of barriers between them. The rest of the evidence is pertinent to ascertaining the factual status of some widely cited claims about the occupational mobility experiences of service-class employees.

The work-life employment experience of managers and professionals

It seems plausible to claim that managers and professionals may have a propensity to act in different ways, hold different social and political beliefs and have different interests to the extent that the careers of the two groups tend over the course of the work life to unfold in distinctly different ways. Differences in career patterns may be a source of intra service-class heterogeneity. Common sense suggests two very different age–occupation profiles. Entry to the professions normally requires a period of full-time or part-time study, either coincident with or followed by a period of "internship" during which qualifying examinations are taken or some other form of accreditation is achieved. If qualifications or "internship" are not achieved during this window of opportunity the door may be closed to entry with few possibilities of working one's way up from the ranks.

By way of contrast, managerial jobs have not typically, at least in Britain, required as much in the way of formal qualifications. One consequence of this should be that on-the-job performance and possibly firm-specific human capital investments are more likely to be the key to entry into managerial positions. Thus promotion from the ranks should remain a possibility for a considerable portion of the career.

Professionals are likely to have undergone an educational experience in the company of other intending professionals that sets them apart and determines the direction of their work life from a rather early age. Managers are likely to be more heterogeneous in their work-life experiences, with the consequence that a proportion will enter managerial positions only after a considerable portion of their work history has elapsed. Thus it would seem reasonable to claim that entry into management or the professions represents two biographically distinct routes into the service class.

The professional and managerial careers of women

One of the most commonly cited "facts" concerning the careers of women in service-class occupations is that, after leaving employment to have children, on re-entry to the labour market they often take jobs that are markedly inferior to those they held before they started a family. This has been seized on in some quarters as evidence of female work-life déclassement or, less emotively, as an indication of systematic employer discrimination against women with children who are otherwise well qualified for service-class jobs. Even if one does not entirely accept these interpretations, if it is true that women with managerial and professional experience are forced to take jobs below the level of their capabilities it is clearly a waste of valuable and scarce human resources. Moreover it points to another cross-cutting line of division within the service class. If females with service-class jobs cannot look forward to the same sort of career advancement as their male colleagues, why, apart from the ties of marriage, children and cohabitation, should they line up with them ideologically or in any other way?

Work-life flows into and out of managerial and professional employment

The evaluation of hypotheses concerning intragenerational social mobility has been handicapped by the lack of good data on job transitions during the working life. Though the inadequacy of conventional first job to last job mobility tables is sometimes exaggerated (on this point see Erikson & Goldthorpe 1992b: Ch. 8), it seems clear enough that, if one wants to know about the relative permeability of the barriers between occupational positions over the life-course, one must use work-history data. Several issues have prompted discussion in this connection: first, the extent to which entry to service-class positions has, over the course of the century, become increasingly a matter of direct entry after leaving full-time education and less a matter of work-life mobility; secondly, the extent to which certain occupations, predominantly routine clerical jobs, serve as "feeders" into service-class work; thirdly, and of particular interest in the context of this chapter, the intensity of interchanges between the professional and managerial fractions of the service class. Especially important here is the degree of support for the claim of a gradual haemorrhaging of professionals into management as a natural part of "career development".

The organizational career

An emerging theme in the discussion of service-class careers is the allegedly changing way in which they are made. It has been claimed that, whereas in the past many managerial and professional careers were made within the confines of just one

101

organization, there is an increasing tendency for people to seek career advancement by moving between different organizations (Savage et al. 1992). Indeed there is a suggestion that increasingly there is an expectation that senior managerial and professional positions will go only to those who possess rather wide and varied inter-organizational experience. If this is true, it has rather fundamental implications for service-class employment relations. If careers must be made via inter-organizational job shifts, what motivational devices will replace the promise of good within-firm prospects to encourage professional and managerial agents to act in accordance with the interests of their principals?

6.3 Data and methods

In the following sections I use two data sources to address these empirical issues by tracing the occupational history of a number of birth cohorts of men and women from age 14 to age 40. The first of these is the data collected by the Government Social Survey in 1949 (hereafter referred to as the GSS49 data). Complete work-history information was collected for a large random sample of men and women in Great Britain (see Glass 1954: 94–7). The second source is the 1986 Social Change and Economic Life survey (SCEL86), which contains complete work-history information from a random sample of men and women residing in one of six towns or cities in either England or Scotland. With these two datasets we can trace the careers of men who entered the labour market between 1895 and 1961. For women, however, we are restricted to cohorts entering between 1940 and 1961.

The data from the two investigations are not comparable in a number of respects:

(a) The machine-readable data from GSS49 pertain only to a nationally representative sample of men resident in England and Wales in 1949, whereas SCEL86 contains information on men and women resident in 1986 in Aberdeen, Coventry, Kirkcaldy, Northampton, Rochdale and Swindon.

(b) In SCEL86 the retrospective work-history data took the month as the smallest time unit for which a job could be held. In GSS49 the smallest recorded duration is a year.

(c) The occupational classifications used are different in the two surveys. For the SCEL86 data I have used the well-known Goldthorpe class schema and split the service classes into professional and managerial subsections by using groups of occupations placed together in the same Hope–Goldthorpe scale categories. GSS49 uses an occupational coding devised by the GSS itself. The coding rules for this have not survived, though they do appear to distinguish between professional and managerial occupations (see Table 6.1).

(d) The GSS49 data were rescued and reconstructed some 20 years after the event and therefore detailed information about how they were originally collected and coded is lost. For want of anything better we have to take a number of things about them at face value, particularly the original coding of the occupational data.

Table 6.1 Occupational codings of professions and management in GSS49 and SCEL86.

GSS49	
Top professional & technical grades, plus minor professionals where professional training is normally essential (e.g. teachers, nurses, draughtsmen)	
Managerial, executives	

SCEL86	
Top professions	Doctors, lawyers, accountants, architects, surveyors, pharmacists, engineers, stock and insurance brokers, company secretaries, university teachers, airline pilots
Top management	Managers in large establishments and public utilities, senior civil servants, local authority senior officers, company directors
Lower professions	Work-study engineers, computer programmers, draughtsmen, laboratory technicians, clergy, journalists, primary and secondary school teachers, civil service executive officers, social workers, nurses, public health inspectors
Lower management	Managers in small enterprises, office managers, supervisors of clerical/sales employees

All of this means that, although I have access to the individual unit records, it is impossible to achieve as high a degree of comparability between the surveys as would normally be expected. However, as long as we are prepared to take the GSS49 data at face value and are duly cautious about the interpretation of comparisons with SCEL86, we can extract some useful information about the historical development of work-history processes. Using both datasets allows us a much longer historical perspective than would be available from, say, the simple comparison of birth cohorts within one survey.

In this chapter I will not be using any of the currently fashionable regression techniques for duration data. Instead I simply compare plots of birth cohort age– occupation profiles and contrast figures derived from a cumulative mobility table constructed from each set of data. As far as possible I distinguish five-year birth cohorts and plot the percentage holding a managerial or a professional occupation in each year from age 14 to age 40. I choose to censor the data for the older cohorts at age 40 so that the duration of the comparison is identical for all cohorts. By age 40 it is probably reasonable to assume that many of the major trends in the age– occupation profiles have unfolded. GSS49 gives us information on cohorts born: 1880–84, 1885–9, 1890–94, 1895–9, 1900–4, 1905–9. SCEL86 does the same for: 1926–9, 1930–34, 1935–9, 1940–44, 1945–6. Because at some ages the frequencies in the categories of interest are relatively small, the age–occupation profiles have in all cases bar one been graduated by taking five-year moving averages. The curves in Figure 6.6a (below) have been graduated by taking successively five- and three-year moving averages.

Unlike the traditional first-job to last-job intragenerational mobility table where we have no knowledge of intervening transitions between these two career points, the cumulative mobility table is a cross-tabulation of all transitions during the work life to age 40. The cumulative tables constructed here are somewhat different from those one normally sees in the mobility literature so it is worth saying a little about how they are constructed. Transitions occur between the various states that define the table and these are slightly different in GSS49 and SCEL86. In both, the majority of states are defined by occupational categories. However we also have a row in each table for transitions at the start of the career following the end of full-time education and a column to denote censored episodes that have not ended in a job transition. Transitions are defined as changes of job and need not imply a change of occupational category. Thus entries on the main diagonal indicate transitions between jobs within the same occupational category. The one exception to this is that we have ignored all transitions between out-of-employment states. Throughout I have ignored the distinction between part-time and full-time employment. This is of little importance for the data on men but glosses over an important feature of female work-life mobility that I do not have space to deal with here.

6.4 The age–occupation profiles of professional and managerial males

Figures 6.3a–6.5b show the estimated percentage of men in professional and managerial occupations at each age between 14 and 40 for 11 birth cohorts starting with men born 1880–84 and ending with men born 1945–6. In the GSS49 data I distinguish between men in "top professional and technical grades" and men in "management/executive jobs". In the SCEL86 data I distinguish between men in the Goldthorpe upper and lower service classes. These are further divided according to whether they have managerial or professional occupations.

There are several striking thing about these graphs. First, amongst the cohorts drawn from GSS49, born at the end of the nineteenth and beginning of the twentieth century, there is a marked contrast between the age–occupation profiles of professionals and managers. The percentage of professionals tends to increase quite steeply until men reach their mid-twenties and thereafter it remains quite stable, whereas the percentage of managers tends to increase at a fairly uniform rate throughout the whole age range.

There are several apparent anomalies in the GSS49 curves that deserve some comment. In Figure 6.3a the percentage of professionals in the 1895–9 birth cohort is noticeably lower than in the preceding three cohorts. In addition the curve is rather flat and does not appear to peak noticeably around the age of 25. This records the experience of men who would have been aged between 15 and 23 during 1914–18, prime ages for volunteering and conscription into the armed forces. Two conjectures about this cohort seem plausible. The first is that many of the "brightest and best" were killed in the war, possibly to the advantage of older and younger cohorts. However, this does not seem to have affected the 1895–9 cohort's success in attaining managerial jobs (see Fig. 6.3b). This suggests the second conjecture, which is in line with my earlier characterization of the typical professional career. The years between the ages of 15 and 23 are those in which men would typically be both qualifying and securing internships. They could not do this if they

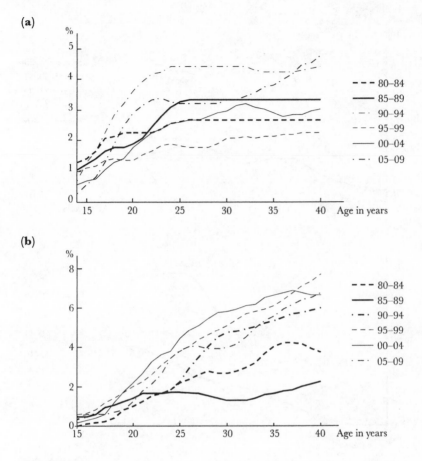

Figure 6.3 (a) Percentage in top professions by birth cohort to age 40. Men born 1880–1909. (b) Percentage in management by birth cohort to age 40. Men born 1880–1909. *Source:* GSS49.

were fighting in Flanders. When they returned to the land fit for heroes they might have been too old, too sick or too traumatized to gain a foothold in the professions. However, given the rather different tempo of the managerial career this would not debar them from entry.

It would be nice to corroborate this story with evidence on the impact of the 1939–45 war, but this is not possible as only a small fraction of the 1926–9 SCEL86 cohort would have seen war service. Let us look instead at whether the shape of the age profiles is maintained for these cohorts. By the time they were entering the labour market there were, of course, many more professional and managerial jobs. Focusing first on the top professionals and managers (Figs 6.4a, b), the broad picture looks quite similar. But if we turn to the figure for the lower professions (Fig. 6.5a) there seems to be a noticeable difference. Rather than peaking somewhere in

(a)

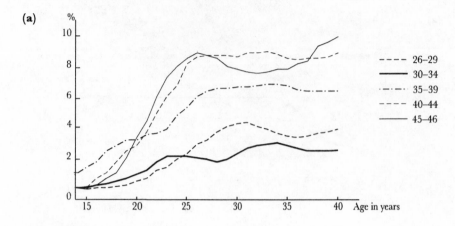

(b)

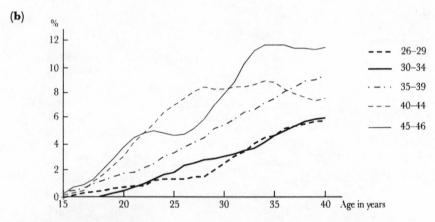

Figure 6.4 (a) Percentage in top professions by birth cohort to age 40. Men born 1926–46. (b) Percentage in top management by birth cohort to age 40. Men born 1926–46. *Source:* SCEL86.

the mid-twenties, the curves for cohorts born between 1926 and 1944 have a gently ascending gradient, rather like the curves for managers. The exception to this is the 1945–6 cohort, which witnessed tremendous growth and rather surprisingly subsequent decline (corresponding to the period circa 1975–86). It is not clear whether this pattern is an artefact of the relatively small sample numbers in the cohort. It could be due to an explosion in the availability of lower professional jobs during the 1960s followed by a comb-out during the recession of the late 1970s and early 1980s. But it would be necessary to look at the profiles of more recent cohorts before reaching even a tentative conclusion along these lines. However, the most interesting thing to come out of the comparison of Figures 6.4a and 6.5a is that the lower professions may not have the same barriers to work-life entry as the higher professions. The evidence is not conclusive because the profiles tell us only about

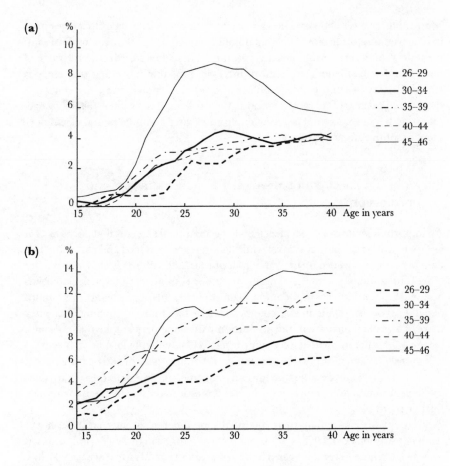

Figure 6.5 (a) Percentage in lower professions by birth cohort to age 40. Men born 1926–46. (b) Percentage in lower management by birth cohort to age 40. Men born 1926–46. *Source:* SCEL86.

the *stock* of professionals at each age and say nothing about *flows* into and out of professional positions. Nevertheless, the general picture is consistent with the commonsense observation that professions such as teaching, social work, the clergy and so on are more open to mature entrants than are, say, medicine, law and accountancy.

Figure 6.5b shows the percentage in lower management positions and the profiles take a rather similar shape to those for more senior managers in Figures 6.3b and 6.4b. There is some, though scarcely overwhelming, evidence that higher management profiles may be beginning to look more like those of the higher professionals (see Fig. 6.4b). This is most marked in the 1940–44 cohort, where the curve seems to flatten out in the late twenties. However, the curve for the 1945–6 cohort is much more difficult to interpret.

So what have we shown? The age–occupation profiles do seem to suggest that managerial and professional careers unfold at different tempos. For professionals the crucial period is during the early twenties. Thereafter a birth cohort's stock of higher professionals does not tend to increase, probably indicating that entry is closed. By way of contrast, the profiles for lower professionals are more similar to those for managers of all ranks. For both, the stock increases rather steadily by age, reflecting better opportunities for work-life entry after an initial period of employment in some other occupation.

6.5 The age–occupation profiles of female managers and professionals

An important feature of the typical female occupational career is that portions of it are spent out of the labour market while children are produced and cared for. The employment experience of the women in our SCEL86 cohorts is shown in Figure 6.6a. Female employment (full time and part time combined) peaks in the late teens and reaches a minimum in the mid to late twenties, the precise cohort minimum depending on age shifts in the commencement of family formation.Thereafter there is a gradual increase in the proportion with some paid employment, though by age 40 this has not reached the same levels as before family formation began.

Figures 6.6b and 6.6c plot the percentage of women (both in and out of employment) in the lower professions and lower management by birth cohort. There is not a sufficient number of women in the higher professions or management to produce reliable plots.

Starting with Figure 6.6b there are interesting differences between the cohorts. Amongst women born 1926–9 the proportion of women in the lower professions at ages 35+ is a little lower than when it peaked at about age 21. Moreover the decline after age 21 is relatively shallow, perhaps indicating that for this cohort women in the lower professions tended to have a career rather than a family. The same pattern holds for women born 1930–34, though the pre family formation peak is somewhat higher and a few years older. The key observation, however, concerns cohorts born after 1934. For these cohorts the proportion in lower professional employment at age 35+ is either as great as or, in the case of the cohorts born 1935–9 and 1940–44, greater than, the pre family formation maximum. The same story holds true for women in lower management. In all cases the proportion with this sort of job aged 35+ either returns to or clearly exceeds the proportion at the pre family formation maximum. In fact for the youngest cohort, born 1945–46, there is scarcely a fall in the proportion in the 25–30 age range at all, merely a plateau before tremendous growth in the 30–40 age range (though we should be aware that the number in this cohort is quite small).

Nothing in the foregoing is incompatible with the existence of the "downward" occupational mobility of formerly professional and managerial women when they return to the labour market. However, this appears to be only half of the story. As

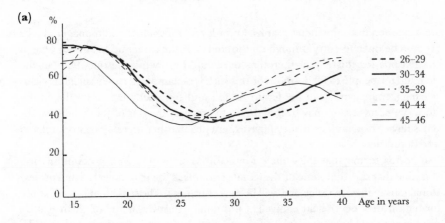

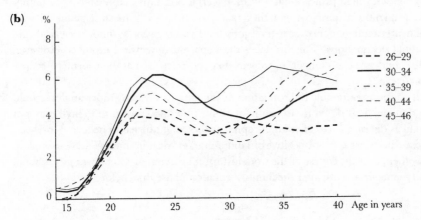

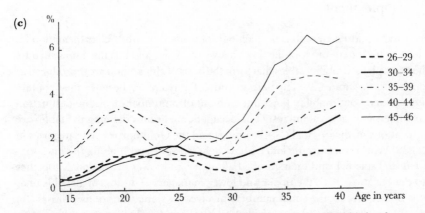

Figure 6.6 (a) Percentage of women born 1926–46 in employment by birth cohort to age 40. (b) Percentage in lower professions by birth cohort to age 40. Women born 1926–46. (c) Percentage in lower management by birth cohort to age 40. Women born 1926–46. *Source:* SCEL86.

we have seen from the men's graphs, lower-level professional and managerial jobs seem to be open to entry throughout the course of the career up to age 40. One of the reasons for this is that there has been rapid growth since the 1960s in the demand for people to fill positions of this sort, for example personal social services, teaching, management in the leisure sector, and somebody has to fill the empty slots. A second reason may be that these are precisely the sort of jobs where candidates have an advantage if they have experience in other areas, both work related and domestic.

It seems to me that the female graphs are compatible with a commonsense storyline that says that some of the female entrants to lower managerial and professional jobs in the age range 30+ will be new entrants, in the sense that before family formation they never held equivalent positions. However, many of them will be women who held professional and managerial positions before starting a family. On returning to employment they take part-time work because it fits in with childcare arrangements. Part-time jobs tend to be easier to find in clerical and manual occupations. This produces the apparent downward mobility. However, once childcare is no longer a problem they return to jobs at their former occupational level.

If this is a reasonable interpretation of the data (and clearly more analysis could be done to tie it down more firmly) it seems that "downward mobility" may not entail as decisive a loss of human capital as one might be led to believe. Moreover, those who cite it as proof positive of labour market "discrimination" have to explain why then, over the course of the work history, more women enter lower professional and managerial work after the family formation phase than before it?

6.6   Work-life flows into and out of managerial and professional employment

One way to address questions of "demographic identity" and "class formation" is to look at the extent of work-life flows between classes, and it is this I now turn to. The "complete" mobility tables that form the basis of this section are reproduced as Appendices 6.1 and 6.2. They are included for reference because they contain information about mobility flows into and out of a number of origin–destination pairs that are of general interest. The occupational groups defining the tables are aggregations of the original GSS49 codings and the Goldthorpe class categories in SCEL86. With respect to the latter I have split classes I and II along the lines suggested in Table 6.1 and then grouped all upper and lower professionals together and done likewise with the upper and lower managers. This loss of detail is unavoidable because of the small numbers involved in some transitions. Classes IIIa and IIIb are distinguished and labelled "clerical" and "sales" respectively. Classes IVa, IVb and IVc are grouped along with V and the large proprietors from class I into a residual "intermediate" class. The allocation of the large proprietors to this group is necessitated to produce some comparability between SCEL86 and GSS49, where this group is not distinguished from the self-employed, small shop-owners etc. Finally VI, VIIa and VIIb are placed in the "working class".

Table 6.2 presents information on transitions into professional and managerial occupations from various "origin" states (outflows) and information on where the transitions to professional and managerial positions come from (inflows). In the body of the table I give two percentage figures for each transition. The top row includes transitions between jobs in the same category (which are a large proportion of all transitions). The bottom row calculates the percentage of transitions *excluding* those between jobs in the same category. No figures are given for any origin–destination pair accounting for less than 1% of inflows or outflows. It is unfortunate but unavoidable that it is only for males that we can make the historical comparison between the GSS49 and SCEL86 data that are central to the substantive issues.

First, transitions to professional and managerial occupations are increasingly made at the very beginning of the career rather than during later phases of the work history. The bottom line of Table 6.2 tells us what we want to know. The outflow percentages indicate that, for men, a larger proportion of transitions from full-time education to work begin with professional or managerial jobs in SCEL86 than in GSS49. This increase is greatest for managerial jobs. However, the overwhelming proportion of transitions from school to work in both surveys do not lead immediately to service-class jobs. Turning to the inflow percentages, it is noticeable that there has been a considerable decline in the proportion of entry transitions amongst all transitions into professional jobs. In GSS49 almost 60% of transitions into the professions (not counting transitions from other professional jobs) came immediately after the end of full-time education. In SCEL86 this figure drops to about 20%. Looking at the same figures for managers, more than twice as many transitions into

Table 6.2 Outflow and inflow percentages for professional and managerial occupations, GSS49 and SCEL86, males.

| | Outflow | | | | Inflow | | | |
| | Professional | | Managerial | | Professional | | Managerial | |
	49	86	49	86	49	86	49	86
Professional	58	51	2	14	58	42	2	10
		4		29			2	17
Managerial	1	24	16	34	1	31	16	39
	1	37			3	53		
Clerical	3	6	3	18	4	5	4	13
	4	10	4	32	10	8	5	21
Sales	–	–	6	15	–	–	8	2
	–	1	8	18	2	–	10	4
Intermediate	–	2	6	6	–	3	12	9
	–	3	9	9	2	6	14	14
Working class	–	1	2	4	11	8	54	20
	2	4	8	11	26	14	64	33
Entry	3	7	–	5	25	11	4	7
	3	7	–	5	58	19	5	12

management are at the start of the career in SCEL86 than in GSS49. These figures should not be surprising. During the period covered by the two surveys the composition of the professions has changed, as has the way managers are recruited. After the Second World War the numbers in the lower professions increased dramatically, and we have already observed that these tend to be occupations that are open to entry for a significant proportion of the career. In GSS49 the bulk of professional jobs would probably be in the higher professions where early entry is crucial. With respect to management we are probably seeing a reflection of an increasing emphasis on graduate recruitment, which tends to make management increasingly a career started after the end of full-time education. However, it still seems to have a long way to go before reaching the degree of "career closure" enjoyed by the professions at the beginning of the century.

Though transitions from the working class into the professions and management (outflows) increased somewhat, though not remarkably, between GSS49 and SCEL86, the most startling fact concerns transitions from manual work as a proportion of all transitions into management and the professions (inflows). In GSS49 over a quarter of all transitions into the professions (excluding profession-to-profession transitions) and over three-fifths of transitions into management were from working-class origins. Though these proportions had declined considerably by SCEL86, manual origins are still the largest category of inflows into management. The second-largest category is from clerical jobs, and it is to these we now turn.

Entry into the professions from clerical positions is quite rare in GSS49, as is entry into management. In SCEL86, entry into professional jobs has roughly doubled but the big increase is in entry into managerial positions. Depending on how you count them, between about 20% and 30% of transitions from clerical jobs are to managerial positions. This picture of change amongst the managers is reinforced if one looks at inflows. The proportion of transitions into the professions from clerical work barely changes between the two surveys, but the proportion of transitions into management increases from about 5% to over 20%.

The key finding here relates not to the inflows but to the outflows. An influential argument in the social mobility literature is that much apparent social mobility from clerical work to higher white-collar positions does not deserve the name of social mobility at all (Stewart et al. 1980). This is because, it is argued, clerical jobs are mere staging posts on the sure and certain way to the top. Thus many clerical workers will experience a form of "anticipatory socialization" that makes it unhelpful to talk of subsequent social mobility consequent on occupational promotion.

The data presented here must bring this view into question. In GSS49 only 8% of transitions from clerical jobs end in higher white-collar positions. Though the chances are greater for the men in SCEL86, on the most favourable count still only just over 40% of transitions are to higher white-collar jobs (broadly defined); the majority are in fact to other locations in the class structure. If this is the sure and certain road to occupational mobility, many must be treading it with trepidation, fearing that their anticipatory socialization has been in vain.

A key issue in the context of this volume is the extent of exchange between management and professions. In fact Goldthorpe cites the extent of this, especially in the later stages of the professional career, as a reason for not turning a distinction of *situs* into a distinction of class. The data suggest that transitions between these two fractions of the service class are becoming increasingly common. In GSS49 they are rather rare but in SCEL86 they are much more common. Surprisingly, transitions from managerial to professional jobs are more common than transitions from the professions to management. We get a very similar story if we turn to the inflows. Whereas transitions from the professions make up less than 20% of all transitions into management, over 50% of transitions into the professions (over 30% if we include professional–professional transitions) come from managerial origins. I suspect that this result may stem from the merging of the lower and higher professionals, with the former being much more likely to receive inflows from lower management and administrative jobs. However, even if we accept this qualification, the magnitude of the flow between these two fractions of the service class has become impressively large and clearly they seem less demographically defined with respect to each other than they did at the beginning of the century.

6.7 The organizational career

It has been argued that professional and managerial careers are increasingly being made outside of a single organization. In order to assess this claim we cannot rely on the evidence of case studies alone and must turn to much larger micro-level datasets. Table 6.3 presents evidence relevant to the issue from the SCEL86 survey.

Table 6.3 Promotions within managerial and professional jobs, retaining same employer as a percentage of all promotions, by birth cohort. Men and women born 1926–46 to age 40.

	P. to P.	P. to M.	M. to P.	M. to M.
1926–29	50	57	50	61
1930–34	54	67	50	56
1935–39	53	44	48	47
1940–44	46	46	52	41
1944–46	57	36	50	45

These are data on transitions within and between the professions and management that are defined as promotions in virtue of the respondent claiming that the job shift led to an improvement in pay. The figures in the table give, by birth cohort, the percentage of such promotions that took place without a change of employer being recorded. For intra-professional transitions and moves from managerial to professional jobs there is little evidence of a shift into the external labour market. However, for moves from the professions into management and intra-management shifts there is clear evidence in support of the contention. Whereas for the oldest birth cohort almost 60% of these transitions took place within the same organization, for the youngest the figure is less than 50%. In the case of professional to management shifts, only just over one third of promotions were made via the internal labour market.

6.8 Conclusions

Let us start with the finding that those who wish to make a class distinction between managers and professionals should find most unpalatable. There is a substantial flow between professional and managerial occupations *and* vice versa. And according to our data, at least for men, *this interchange has become more rather than less marked during the century*. The frequency of career moves from the professions to management forms one plank of Goldthorpe's case against regarding professionals and managers as separate social classes. Expert knowledge needs to be refreshed and many who once possessed it eventually become the managers of those who currently have it, though, as our data suggest, this transition increasingly seems to involve a shift between organizations. It is plausible, though clearly I have not demonstrated it, that professional to managerial job shifts *per se* imply no differences in interests or, most importantly, in employment relations, and are a normal part of the natural history of a service-class career. However it is interesting that the amount of inter-organizational professional–management and management–management job shifts has increased. One interpretation of this, albeit highly speculative, is that *exit* is slowly replacing *loyalty* as a mode of ascent into middle management (it is worth remembering at this point that our career data are censored at age 40, before many of the most senior managerial positions will be attained). Trust and loyalty may only get you so far in an organizational hierarchy; thereafter, threats, bargaining and resort to the external labour market may become significant factors in turning career prospects into actual career advancement. This implies that a distinction between professionals and managers may be of less significance in terms of employment relations than one in terms of relative position in the career life-cycle.

What Goldthorpe did not anticipate, but in fact appears to strengthens his case, is the frequency of flows from management broadly defined into the professions broadly defined. Clearly, given the impossibility of coding the occupational data in a comparable way, this finding needs to be treated with circumspection. I know of no evidence to suggest that the older professions such as medicine, the law or architecture increasingly recruit their members from the ranks of management. However, in the period between the two surveys two important changes occurred in the composition of the professions. First, some new professions have been created. Secondly, some professions have undergone enormous growth. Take secondary school teaching. In 1949 there would be very few state secondary school teachers. In 1986 they account for a considerable number of the lower professionals. Or take social workers. Again, we would find very few in 1949 but many more in 1986. The growth of the professions is not just a result of the post-war growth of the public sector. Growth has also been strong in private sector accountancy, banking and finance. Professional growth may have had two important consequences for arguments about the integrity of the service class. First, since the Second World War the boundaries between professional and managerial activities have become quite blurred. In 1949 many professionals would have been self-employed selling a specialized service to a client. In 1986 most professionals are employees, with, I suspect, terms and conditions that differ very little from their immediate line managers'. Secondly, many of the new professions (social work, secondary school teaching) and some of the old (the clergy, for example) remain open to "late entrants". Many of these will have had work experience in managerial positions of some sort. Something like this must underlie the clear divergence between the career profiles of the lower and higher professions and the similarity between the profiles of managers and lower professionals. With perhaps the exception of the older professions, the division between what is a managerial activity and what is a professional activity seems to be becoming increasingly blurred and thus must raise some doubts, at least in this context, about its sociological significance.

In some ways, the SCEL86 data on female managers and professionals are the most intriguing. I should say at the outset that the major structural fact revealed is the continuing underrepresentation of women in the ranks of higher management and the higher professions. But this is scarcely revelatory. What is more unexpected, and I suspect somewhat unpalatable to so-called "feminist sociologists", is evidence that women are not restricted to menial occupations when they return to work after child-bearing. This is consistent with the accumulating evidence that a fundamental split is developing in the female population (Hakim 1991). On the one hand there is a minority, albeit a sizeable minority, who within the constraints imposed by family formation have much the same orientation to the labour market as their male counterparts. On the other, there is a majority who do not share this orientation. The implications of this for so-called "class analysis" are not clear to me. However, the welfare implications seem obvious. The number of dual-career service-class families is increasing, and, for the middle class, the key to a comfortable home, a private education for the children, two cars in the garage and a foreign holiday every year is whether or not the female conjugal partner has a professional or managerial job of roughly equal standing to that of her "husband". As we all become increasingly middle-class, it may well be the case that some households turn out to be more middle-class than others.

Acknowledgement

The data used in this paper were either supplied by the ESRC's Data Archive at the University of Essex or collected as part of the ESRC-funded Social Change and Economic Life Initiative.

Appendix 6.1 Complete turnover table. Frequencies, GSS49

	Professional	Managerial	Clerical	Sales	Intermediate	Working-class	Censor
Professionals	157	4	3	1	10	16	78
Managerial	3	41	5	2	9	42	152
Clerical	11	11	194	8	61	94	67
Sales	2	22	8	91	41	150	43
Intermediate	2	32	8	4	208	77	237
Working class	30	142	64	129	275	4,225	1,224
Entry	67	10	180	126	17	1574	11

Appendix 6.2 Complete turnover table. Frequencies, SCEL86, Men.

	Professionals	Managerial	Clerical	Sales	Intermediate	Working class	Censor
Professionals	279	290	17	1	18	42	114
Managerial	205	290	45	2	46	80	183
Clerical	30	94	223	6	47	70	49
Sales	1	16	13	18	14	38	9
Intermediate	21	63	36	9	351	379	163
Working class	53	149	101	33	524	2,809	482
Entry	74	53	93	37	47	771	0

Chapter 7

The bureaucratic career: demise or adaptation?

Susan Halford and Mike Savage

7.1 Introduction

It has long been thought that one of the distinguishing features of middle-class people is their reliance on bureaucratic, organizational careers that allow them to move through an internal labour market from junior to more senior jobs (e.g. Mills 1951, Whyte 1957, Goldthorpe 1980a). From the mid-1980s, however, there have been indications that this traditional picture has been overtaken by events, as some commentators have argued that bureaucratic organizational forms are on the wane. To give only a few examples, Lash & Urry (1987, 1994) suggest that a new era of "disorganized" capitalism has arisen; Clegg (1990) points to the rise of the "post-modern organization"; while others argue that the flexible firm has developed as a departure from bureaucratic norms (e.g. Atkinson 1984). If developments such as these are indeed occurring, it suggests that traditional conceptions of the middle classes may themselves be in need of overhaul. This paper offers a contribution to such an exercise by considering how organizational restructuring is redefining the nature of the middle-class career.

We begin by examining the different ways in which writers have explored the relationship between the bureaucratic career and the constitution of the middle classes and outline some recent accounts of current organizational and labour market changes that suggest possible departures from the traditional bureaucratic career. The bulk of the paper reports research carried out in banking and local authorities on the changing nature of career patterns and the implications these might have for understanding the relationship between organizations and their middle-class employees.

7.2 The middle classes and the bureaucratic career

There is a line of argument going back to Weber that suggests that white-collar bureaucratic employees occupy a middle-class position distinct from that of the self-employed middle classes, the employed working class, and the propertied upper classes. For Weber, there are two key, interlinked reasons for this. First, the bureaucratic official has a career in which "he expects to move from the lower, less important and less well paid, to the higher position" (1978: 963). This only became possible with the emergence of modern bureaucratic organizational forms, which were historically innovative in separating out officials from their offices – a precondition of career mobility. Indeed, for Weber, the technical efficiency of bureaucracies went hand in hand with job mobility: "a very strong development of the "right to office" naturally makes it more difficult to staff offices with an eye to technical efficiency" (Weber 1978: 962). Secondly, the bureaucratic career is vocational, requiring training and demanding fealty to the organization in return for security of employment and career prospects. This moral component of the bureaucratic career distinguishes the bureaucratic middle classes from other social classes.

This latter point can be traced to more recent accounts of the "service class" developed by Goldthorpe and others. Erikson & Goldthorpe (1992b) stress that the nature of service-class work makes it difficult for employers to supervise such employees directly. Instead, organizations attempt to secure the "moral" commitment of professional and managerial employees by constructing jobs and career ladders with prospective rewards. Erikson & Goldthorpe's account is worth quoting at some length here:

> Employment relationships regulated by a labour contract entail a relatively short-term and specific exchange of money for effort. Employees supply more or less discrete amounts of labour, under the supervision of the employer or of the employer's agents, in return for wages which are calculated on a "piece" or time basis. In contrast, employment relationships within a bureaucratic context involve a longer term and more generally diffuse exchange. Employees render service to their employing organization in return for "compensation" which takes the form not only of reward for work done, through a salary and various perquisites, but also comprises important *prospective* elements – for example, salary increments on an established scale, assurances of security both in employment and, through pension rights, after retirement, and, above all, well defined career opportunities. (Erikson & Goldthorpe 1992b: 41–2, our emphasis)

Another line of argument suggests that the bureaucratic career plays a vital role in shaping middle-class formation. Here the emphasis is on how the movement of people from junior posts to senior posts shapes class formation and identity, rather than on how the bureaucratic career is itself a defining feature of the middle classes (as above). Patterns of work-life mobility are seen as playing a crucial role in defining how the middle classes come to exist as social forces. Three main issues that bear on the general pattern of middle-class formation in advanced capitalist societies can be extracted from this literature. First, high rates of work life mobility in many white-collar jobs mean that many "middle-class" groups, especially clerical and junior white-collar jobs, never attain the sort of social stability necessary for them to form distinct social collectivities (e.g. Lockwood 1989, Stewart et al. 1980, Erikson & Goldthorpe 1992). Second, because there is little downward mobility within bureaucracies (Goldthorpe 1982), work-life mobility might slow as bureaucracies cease to expand, with the result that the service class might at some future date become a more cohesive entity (Goldthorpe 1982). Finally, there is the question of whether or not the movement of personnel from professional to managerial jobs means that these two elements of the service class should be regarded as one. Goldthorpe (1982) argues for the fusion of the two in the service class, whereas Savage et al. (1992) are more sceptical (see the further discussions of this point in the papers by Mills, Fielding, and Savage & Butler – Ch. 6, 10 and 20 respectively).

It is evident, therefore, that a number of reasons have been advanced to suggest that the bureaucratic career is central to (male) middle-class identities. However, there are problems in anchoring the analysis of the middle classes so firmly in the bureaucratic career. One difficulty is that the bureaucratic career has a gender, as well as a class, dimension (see, generally, Marshall 1988). Thus, Crompton (1986, and see also her discussion in Ch. 4 in this volume) argues that the "service class" career is dependent upon forms of gender demarcation and exclusion because it is premised upon the existence of a group of unpromotables, usually women. Further, she points to the domestic servicing role that women have performed, which has allowed men to pursue their careers unhindered by domestic responsibilities. The bureaucratic career is therefore "gendered" as well as "classed", and this may problematize any simple assumptions that it has its roots in class alone.

Another problem is that it is by no means clear that it is helpful to see all types of upward career mobility, or, more generally, mobility involving "middle-class" people, as quintessentially bureaucratic. Economic sociologists have explored a number of ways of conceptualizing work-life mobility that are anchored in labour market theory rather than Weberian organizational theory. Althauser & Kalleberg (1981), for instance, have emphasized the way that "firm internal labour markets" (FILMs) – where individuals are on job ladders within one organization – have different causes and consequences from "occupational internal labour markets" (OILMs) – where individuals move between firms in pursuit of a career where they specialize in an occupation. These may have important implications for class formation. Some writers have argued that FILMs are more conducive to employees' dependence on their employers, which may undermine their ability or motivation to engage in collective action (Edwards 1979, Gordon et al. 1982, Burawoy 1985), whereas it might be argued that OILMs are more conducive to professional loyalties because employees are less dependent on any one employer (Savage et al. 1992: Ch. 2). Thus workers in OILMs are less likely to feel the moral obligation to their employer that Erikson & Goldthorpe emphasize.

Leading on from this point, there is considerable debate concerning the extent to which current economic changes are affecting career patterns in the contemporary period. It has long been argued, in different ways, that internal labour markets are likely to become more closed. Traditionally, this view was endorsed by writers supporting the proletarianization thesis (Klingender 1935, Braverman 1974, Crompton & Jones 1984). Although strong claims for the proletarianization thesis have faded as it has become clear that the general rise in professional and managerial jobs allows considerable scope for promotion (see Mills, Ch. 6 in this volume), the idea that internal labour markets are being squeezed remains common. Thus Crompton & Jones (1984) suggested that, as women become more interested in developing their careers, so the increased competition for senior jobs will slow male patterns of promotion. Similar predictions are also made in more recent work. Cressey & Scott (1992: 91), for example, claim that in banking "a 'time bomb' is ticking away whereby clerical staff are becoming increasingly dissatisfied that their prospects of promotion to . . . managerial grades are drying up". Firm evidence on these matters is rarely produced, however, partly owing to the problems in extracting the sorts of reliable longitudinal data that would be necessary to evaluate such arguments.

Other writers actually claim that current patterns of economic restructuring are likely to consolidate the organizational career. A particularly strong example of this is Atkinson's model of the "flexible firm". The central claim here is that a growing polarization is taking place between "core" and "periphery" workers (see also Pollert 1988, MacInnes 1987, Bagguley et al. 1990). Core workers are required to be functionally flexible and, in exchange for learning new skills and being adaptable, they are cocooned from the external labour market by job security and good promotion prospects on the FILM. By contrast, peripheral workers are "numerically" flexible, employed casually and have little prospects for promotion. Thus, the model suggests a consolidation of organizational career prospects for some, but the marginalization of others from the FILM.

Conversely, there is a body of opinion that suggests that there is a growing trend for professional and managerial workers to rely upon *external* labour markets (OILMs) rather than developing organizational careers. Savage et al. (1992) argue that professionals and managers have become ever more likely to pursue entrepreneurial and occupational career strategies rather than organizational ones (to borrow Brown's 1984 terminology), since the assets of property and culture offer more potential for advantages to be stored and sustained. This contention is supported by recent surveys of managers showing that as few as 10% had worked just for one firm during their career. The implication is to put question marks over the significance of bureaucratic careers for the contemporary middle classes.

In short, there is considerable uncertainty as to the nature of current trends. Recent developments can be interpreted in two ways, as either reinforcing or undermining the organizational career. The difficulty arises in attempting to detect which is the dominant trend and providing firmer evidence on how job ladders and work-life mobility are being affected. It is this uncertainty that gives the research reported in this paper considerable pertinence. We now turn to specify the research design in more detail.

7.3 The case-study organizations

Our research is based on three organizations. These are (a) the regional and retail operations of one leading clearing bank (Sellbank) in two different areas, one a large industrial city in the English Midlands ("Midcity"), the other a prosperous new town in the South East of England ("Southtown"); (b) the large city council of Midcity; and (c) the smaller district authority of Southtown. In Sellbank, all activities within the spatial boundaries of Midtown and Southtown were examined, but in Midcity Council and Southtown Council we focused on two departments alone, finance and housing, because of the fragmentation of local authority labour markets (see below for further details).

Our analysis below focuses on distinctions between sectors (Sellbank on the one hand and the two local authorities on the other), because it is these broad sectoral comparisons that stand out as being important. Banking was chosen as a classic case of a FILM (Althauser & Kalleberg 1981), whereas local government included professional hierarchies more characteristic of OILMs. British banking has been the classic managerial hierarchy (which has historically demanded few pre-entry qualifications and in which job entrants could climb their way up an internal job ladder) together with weak professional structures. Local government, however, is characterized by specialized departmental structures, with a mixture of internal promotion and recruitment via professional labour markets within the various departments. In practice, the professionally qualified have tended to rise to managerial positions in their own specialist area (e.g. housing or finance).

Our research comprised a small postal survey in each of the sectors, providing extensive material on work-life history. The sampling was stratified in the proportion of 20% senior, 40% intermediate and 40% junior graded staff, and allowing 33% of the sample to be from Southtown and 67% from Midtown. The response rate was around 51%, producing 144 respondents from local government and 207 from banking (for more details of the research design, see Halford et al. 1996). This sample size is too small to permit statistically reliable data to be obtained, but nonetheless provides some important suggestions of general patterns. We also conducted around 30 in-depth interviews in each sector, examining (*inter alia*) respondent's work-life histories and their attitudes towards their employer. These were supplemented by interviews with key informants and documentary material provided by the organizations. Fieldwork took place in 1991 and 1992 at a time when all the organizations were undergoing considerable change, a point that should be borne in mind as we present our findings.

It should be emphasized that the research we report below is not designed to discover any general or aggregate changes taking place in middle-class labour markets. However, this does not mean that there may be no broader implications of our research. The organizations we have chosen are highly selective and atypical. But our suggestion is that because our case studies are from organizations that have traditionally been the heartland of the classic bureaucratic career, any evidence of change may have wider ramifications. If bureaucratic careers are in decline here, it is unlikely that they flourish elsewhere!

The analysis below selects material to reflect on three different issues that bear on the theoretical issues raised in the discussion above. First, we consider the arguments about the changing boundaries between "core" and "peripheral" labour markets brought about by the supposed development of "flexible working practices". Secondly, we examine the mobility of those workers clearly inside some sort of internal labour markets in order to examine whether patterns of career mobility are changing. Thirdly – perhaps most importantly of all for the issues tackled in this paper – we consider how changing career patterns are related to conceptions of vocation and trust.

7.4   Core and peripheral labour markets

On the face of it, there seemed good evidence from our research that peripheral labour markets have expanded in the 1980s. In the banking industry as a whole there was a massive increase in the use of part-time workers. Virtually unheard of until the later 1970s, by 1991 21% of all women bank workers were on part-time contracts (Cressey & Scott 1992: 85) and, in the parts of Sellbank which we studied, as many as 24% of women workers (but not a single man) worked part time. Sellbank has increasingly employed part-timers to staff branches during peak periods, and many are also now employed in new specialist units (for instance credit card departments, service centres for cheque processing, telephone banking operations) where many workers are outside the traditional job ladders on which job mobility was traditionally based.

However, two important caveats need to be entered. First, it should not be assumed that all part-time workers are outside internal labour markets. It is *possible* for full-time workers to move to part-time work, and back again. But does this happen? Sellbank encourages part-time work amongst those women who want to give up full-time employment, and, in the other direction, our postal survey shows that 4% of full-timers (and 7% of women workers) had previously worked part-time for Sellbank. However, part-time workers reveal two distinctive features. Traditionally, Sellbank does not poach workers from other banks, and rarely takes on any staff from other employers – 90% of our entire sample had only ever worked for Sellbank. But, 47% of part-time workers in our sample had previously worked for a different employer, and managers in Sellbank confirmed that it was less concerned that part-time workers should be internally recruited. A further important point is that, although it is possible for part-time workers to come back as full-timers, there is not a single case from our survey of any of these being promoted to more senior jobs afterwards.

This relates to the second caveat, which is that the expansion of part-time work might be seen as a reworking of the older gender divide, rather than as testimony to a particularly new development. Women did not enter banking until the 1930s and even then they were employed in gender-specific grades that made them ineligible for promotion to senior clerical or managerial jobs (see Llewellyn 1981, Crompton & Jones 1984, Crompton 1989, Savage 1993). The creation of this group of un-promotables allowed men to move out of the expanding routine clerical jobs without competition for the more senior posts. One male manager, reflecting on the 1970s, recalled the implications of this:

> I always remember [my first manager] saying to me, any young man join-ing the bank, two thirds of them make manager, nothing about young women joining the bank in those days. (Mr 3)

And, indeed, research on the work-life mobility of bank employees suggests that well over half of male bank clerks could expect to reach managerial status (Savage 1993). In the mid-1970s this traditional axis of exclusion was removed as Sellbank was forced by legislation to remove overtly discriminatory grading. Part-time work began soon afterwards, and in some respects this can be seen as an attempt to reconstitute the traditional female labour market: as we have seen it is entirely women who are employed part-time. In banking, therefore, it can be argued that recent developments are variations on a long-term theme of gender demarcation. However, this new form of division is less watertight than the old, since it is possible for women working part time to move into full-time work and, officially at least, re-enter the career hierarchy. Equally, women are not barred *as women* from career ladders, and it is possible for them to earn promotion to management (see Savage 1992).

It is much more difficult to define general patterns in local government because of its complexity. Part-time work was much more common in both councils than in banking, but is heavily concentrated in manual work. In Midtown Council, 86% of part-timers are in manual grades, and in the white-collar sectors only 7% of those in the finance department and 4% of those in the housing department were employed part-time. The only evidence of the use of temporary contracts is, surprisingly, amongst senior employees in Midcity Council, where managers work on fixed-term contracts (temporary contracts are not used in Sellbank.)

Another relevant development in local government is the introduction of compulsory competitive tendering (CCT) whereby services previously carried out "in house" have been opened for bids from external organizations. Opponents of CCT feared that it would create a fragmented peripheral workforce, and there is some evidence of this where contracts have been awarded externally, but it is important to point out that between 61% and 97% of contracts have been won by existing direct service organizations (Cochrane 1993). Furthermore, although there are plans to impose CCT on a wider range of local authority activities, it has not yet been applied to the white-collar sections we studied.

Thus, there is little evidence from either of our case studies that groups of workers who were previously inside internal labour markets are now outside them. This is not to say that nothing is changing; however, the notion of a core/peripheral division is too crude to capture the complexity of current developments. It would be unwise to suggest that significant numbers of workers who previously worked inside internal labour markets have now been forced to work outside them. The increase in part-time and temporary work is primarily directed to those workers who have *always* been excluded from, or disadvantaged within, internal labour markets. And, although part-time work is in many ways marginalized from internal labour markets, it would be mistaken to assume that it is hermetically sealed off from them, as might be implied by those supporting the "flexible firm" hypothesis. We are therefore sceptical of claims that within the organizations we studied a marked, new, polarization is taking place.

7.5 Job mobility

Let us now examine the career patterns of workers inside the internal labour markets in banking and local government. We will concentrate on (a) the amount of mobility to senior jobs via different internal labour markets; (b) the extent to which career routes are conducted on external or internal labour markets; and (c) whether job ladders are diversifying and/or fragmenting.

Mobility via internal labour markets

Broad aggregate figures suggest that levels of mobility continue to be high. In banking, 73% of men aged over 40 are in managerial jobs, all of whom have been promoted from below into these grades. This figure compares exceptionally well with earlier periods and undermines Crompton & Jones's (1984) prognosis of the imminent decline in male promotion prospects. However, only 10% of women over the age of 40 have reached management level. It seems that even in the 1990s (most) men continue to earn promotion at women's expense.

Local government displays a higher degree of gender equality: 36% of men over 40 and 29% of women over 40 have reached senior positions. However, men are much more likely to have moved into intermediate jobs than women. It is interesting to note that, in a sector where women's promotion prospects appear better than in banking, the prospects for men seem rather worse, suggesting that there are links between male career opportunities and women's subordination within bureaucracies. In general, figures from our survey suggest that apocalyptic accounts of declining promotion prospects in internal labour markets seem to be unfounded.

The distinction between FILMs and OILMs may affect the relationship between gender and career mobility, and between seniority and career mobility, because men appear to do better in banking, where careers are organized around FILMs, than in local government. Let us examine this issue further by considering the extent to which current developments have accentuated or undermined the distinction between these two types of internal labour markets.

Internal vs. external labour markets

Sellbank still relies overwhelmingly on internally promoted workers, and very rarely recruits from outside. Indeed, as the clerical and financial services labour market tightened following the 1980s financial deregulation and the subsequent emergence of smaller merchant banks that could pay higher salaries, Sellbank tried to *enhance* the attractions of careers on the internal labour market in order to compete with the better financial rewards offered by the newer institutions. By offering job security, career opportunities and a range of fringe benefits, it hoped to attract and retain staff who might otherwise be tempted by the greater financial rewards on offer elsewhere. This strategy was hit in the later 1980s, however, when Sellbank was forced to deliver the first large-scale wave of redundancies in its history as the financial services sector moved into serious recession.

Local government shows greater reliance on external labour markets. Although over 90% of all bank staff had made their last job move internally, this was the case for only 40% of local authority workers. Junior staff were more likely to have moved in from another employer. Over 70% of intermediate and senior staff had made their last move internally. Of the remainder, most had moved from another local authority, illustrating the career significance of the external labour markets. Here there is a considerable difference between the very large Midcity Council and the much smaller Southtown Council. In Midcity there are obviously more opportunities for senior staff to work their way up the internal job ladder, whereas in Southtown it is far more unusual: 28% of those in Midcity Council had previously worked for a different employer, compared with 57% in Southtown. Although recent organizational changes may impinge on this pattern in conflicting ways, respondents reported that the internal labour market has stabilized over recent years as pressure to cut jobs has often meant internal recruitment only in order to enable redeployment, and generally increased levels of unemployment have enhanced the attractions of remaining in local authority employment.

The general picture, then, is that there appears to be no marked decline of FILMs, within our two sectors. Of course, our research strategy does not enable us to consider whether these are typical findings, but it is at the very least interesting that these organizations have not abandoned notions of internal recruitment and mobility.

Job ladders

Having said this, there is evidence that job ladders are becoming more fragmented, specialized and internally heterogeneous, with the result that there is little awareness amongst our respondents of a "typical" career route. Instead, as the range of occupational specialisms increases, the number of possible career routes also expands and employees can piece together a number of specific jobs into more individualized and less routinized job ladders.

In Sellbank there was traditionally one clear job ladder (for men) following a single route through from remittance clerk (simple bookkeeping duties), to cashier and then on to more responsible forms of clerical work (e.g. securities or foreign business), clerical supervision, and then potentially branch management. Managers might then move to larger branches, or to regional or head office work. Thus, all managers followed a clear internal job ladder. Like its competitors, Sellbank has now diversified and become involved in more specialist activities, with the result that it is not feasible for employees to learn all these specialisms during their career development. Sellbank has demarcated two different types of jobs: those internal to the bank, dealing with systems and operations necessary for the smooth running of bank activities; and those external to the bank, primarily dealing with customers and selling financial services. This demarcation divides some clerical jobs but especially affects managerial jobs, cutting the traditional jurisdiction of the branch manager over both "internal" and "external" activities.

The crucial question, of course, is whether or not there are now different job ladders for these two types of "internal" and "external" jobs. Our research provides considerable evidence that some workers see their careers developing in one area or the other:

> I would like to go into lending . . . I find it more interesting. I don't fancy operations – it is such a stressful job . . . lending does give you more opportunities because you can loan to personal customers, you can loan to small businesses, the enterprise sector or you can lend to corporate customers . . . there are a lot more jobs in lending as well. (Ms 7)

From our small sample we cannot be conclusive, but it is striking that, of the 15 branch managers or operations managers, only one had moved in from a lending job. Conversely, 7 of 13 lending managers came from other lending jobs.

In the traditional banking labour market there were, officially, no jobs, except secretarial ones, from which upward mobility was not possible. Recently there have been suggestions that the development of "niche" jobs and "proletarianization" in banking are limiting upward mobility from some banking jobs (Crompton & Sanderson 1990, Cressey & Scott 1992). Our in-depth interviews indicate three areas of branch work from which upward mobility may be difficult: cashiering, securities and secretarial work. In the case of cashiering this applies mainly to part-time women workers, while others are employed in this area for only a few years and can still move on with relative ease. Securities work has become marginalized by the introduction of new technology and is increasingly being moved to regional service centres and thus dislocated completely from the traditional career routes based in branches. Mobility from secretarial work into management has always been difficult, and remains so. This partly reflects the continued tendency for secretarial employment to be defined in relation to a manager or group of managers (see, more generally, Pringle 1989). Also, until recently, secretaries were employed on different grading scales from other clerical staff. The case of secretaries is revealing because it throws the career prospects of clerical workers into clearer relief – none of them expressed anything like the same degree of dissatisfaction with their promotion prospects.

Local authority careers have always been more fragmented than in banking or nursing because the range of activities involved necessitates the employment of staff across a range of occupations and professions. Generally, these staff are structured into departments based on functional specialisms. Even today, departments work largely autonomously from each other and there are few promotion channels linking them. Traditionally, management of each department is recruited from the core professional group, compounding the organizational fragmentation created by functional specialism.

Current developments appear to be accentuating this pattern of fragmentation. In the past, the core career route involved studying for professional qualifications while working in a trainee post. Recently the significance of professional housing qualifications has declined (though this is more pronounced in Midcity Council than in Southtown) and new specialisms have emerged. In both departments, computing, personnel and management services functions offer alternative career paths to senior grades, and changes imposed by government legislation as well as the decentralization of services have created new posts offering new career opportunities. In finance, for example, the introduction of the community charge (poll tax) opened up a new job ladder. One officer in the community charge section told us:

> I'd been in the council so long that I didn't really know where I was going
> as far as a career was concerned . . . the last couple of years or so coincided
> with the poll tax coming in . . . and the opportunities that that brought
> [means] I've got to the stage where I'm managing a section. (Mr 19)

Like his colleagues, this man had reached a senior position without a professional qualification (or degree). In general, respondents emphasized the increasing variety of career possibilities:

> what happens is you . . . get some experience in one place and you transfer
> it to somewhere else; you work on the front line for a while; you might get
> seconded to do different things; you might get some training or you might
> not. I don't think there is one (classic career) anymore. (Key informant,
> Ms 6)

Rates of job mobility in local government are exceptionally high: 77% of the respondents had worked in their present job for less than four years (a figure higher than in banking), although there are some areas from which mobility may be difficult. This is especially true of benefits sections – both housing benefits and community charge benefits. It is almost exclusively women who work in these sectors, and the hierarchy is short, with a couple of supervisors and a section leader, and it is almost impossible to move from here to anywhere else. Experience in these sections is not usually regarded as a qualification for any other sort of work, although (similar to the cashier case in banking) there is some evidence that men are more able to move on than are women.

Across the two sectors there is therefore a trend for organizational careers to have diversified, with a greater range of job ladders opening up and less idea of there being a "normal" route. One result has been to sow doubt in respondents' minds about whether all the job ladders allow access to the most senior posts, and whether there are favoured routes or not. In banking, there is some evidence that "internal" managers, in operations management, find it difficult to move into senior management. In local authorities, the directors of departments continue to be recruited largely from professional ranks, whereas those employed in the new specialisms tend to stop at a lower – though still relatively senior – level.

What stands out is the way that this diversification can in some ways enhance the organizational career. There are only a few cases where jobs have been created by recruiting workers from outside the organization (IT-related jobs are the most unusual in relying on external recruitment). Furthermore, the same jobs that are backwaters for some people can also be staging posts for "high fliers". The possibility that this raises is that mobility is now defined less in terms of a distinct job ladder whereby people move from one job to another in a more or less clearly defined sequence, but more in terms of the personal qualities of specific sorts of individuals. Some individuals are earmarked for rapid progress and others are not, but they are all employed on the same sorts of job ladders. The propensity for upward mobility may become more an attribute of individuals rather than of specific jobs. In the following section we consider this and extend our discussion to the changing nature of the bureaucratic career more generally.

7.6 Bureaucratic or organizational careers?

From the discussion of our research so far it seems that the organizational career has retained considerable vitality, and that stories of its imminent demise may be unfounded. This seems to support Weber, Goldthorpe and Lockwood's stress on the relevance of bureaucratic careers to analysis of the middle class. In this last section, however, we explore two related elements that call into question whether the organizational career can continue to be characterized in traditional bureaucratic terms: first, the features of trust and vocation, so central to conventional conceptions of the bureaucratic career have been undermined and second, the separation of office from official, which lies at the heart of Weberian bureaucratic theory, is far from clear, especially now, as the central importance of personal qualities in the construction of organizational careers becomes more obvious.

In banking, notions of trust and loyalty have traditionally played a major role in career development. Bank workers were encouraged to commit themselves morally to the bank, not just through efficient work, but also through involvement in an active bank-based social life. In return, the "best" men were promised promotion, which was bestowed from above by senior managers. Jobs were filled not by advertisement and application, but by selection and notification from above, meaning that the aspiring had to wait until they were approached. Branch managers had considerable autonomy, particularly in credit decisions, and in return were offered excellent terms of employment.

However, a particularly pronounced element of organizational change in the 1980s was the dismantling of this traditional "bureaucratic" career based upon the exchange of "prospective rewards" for the conduct of trustworthy work. Credit scoring (and other devices) had reduced the need for "trust" and increased monitoring possibilities. More significantly, though, Sellbank has introduced performance-related pay based on managers' ability to meet targets set in annual appraisals. Also, Sellbank now advertises most managerial jobs, encouraging managers and would-be managers to plan their own careers rather than have them constructed from above.

These developments relate to a fundamental upheaval of the notion of career progress. In the past, *security* was one of the key benefits of a managerial career, acting as a reward for loyalty to the bank. By contrast, today it is only the clerical career that offers security and a reasonable degree of autonomy, whereas managerial careers, although potentially more rewarding in financial terms, are more risky and unpredictable. As a result some staff choose the safer clerical career rather than aspiring to climb further up into management. This deliberate choice of a non-managerial career has long been a feature of banking but, in the past, this choice would have entailed clearly lower rewards and certainly no extra job security. One senior male clerk described the new situation:

> The way that I look at work it is only, as I say, a means to an end to me . . .
> it has always seemed to me that if you aspire to the management side of it
> you have to devote more of your own time and personality to the bank,
> which I am not prepared to do . . . the package I get, I think is good for
> what I do, I find it sort of adequate really for what I do, it could be quite
> easy to, I think, to give more to the bank for basically less reward. (Mr 17:
> 4–5)

This package generally excluded the routine expectation of overtime, included pay for any overtime that *was* done and allowed this clerk to use his long work experience to negotiate considerable autonomy. In return, his salary was similar to that of junior managers. Similarly, a female clerk who had moved from a managerial appointment back into clerical employment confirmed that she had not suffered financially (Ms 11: 5). By contrast, managers are now eligible for performance-related pay and merit pay linked to targets and appraisal, indicating a growing tendency towards direct measurement of managerial performance (rather than trust) and more tangible and immediate rewards (rather than long-term security). Thus, it makes little economic sense for clerks to move into management unless it is part of a continued move to senior levels of management, where the financial rewards do increase considerably.

However, the transition into management remains a "risky" one. One junior manager, promoted late in his life, recalls that, when he was given his managerial post,

> I went for an appraisal with one of the area managers and he said "Tell me how you see your career going in the next five years" . . . and I just laughed, and he said "Did I say something funny?." I said, "Look John, I am fifty soon, I have just had my first managerial position, I am very happy about it, I am very excited about it, I have worked thirty years for this, how the devil can I tell you what I am going to be doing in the next five years, I haven't a clue, I hope I am still working for Sellbank . . . let me ask you a question, what do you think you will be doing in five years' time?" He said, "Hmm, I don't know." That gentleman was in one of the top positions in Midcity and was made redundant six months later. (Mr 1)

Indeed, at the time of our research a considerable number of managerial workers were made redundant. These changes suggest a rather different logic from that found in the Weberian notion of the bureaucratic career. In the new arrangements, although the organizational career remains, it is one that does not offer *prospective* rewards but ties rewards to measurable present performance. As we have argued elsewhere (Halford and Savage 1995), this is related to the redefinition of management in terms of its "pro-active", dynamic, "change-master" (Kanter 1987) qualities. Significantly these characteristics are defined through reference to the personal qualities of individual workers rather than – necessarily – the offices that they hold. This is most clear in the case of "tiered" entry in banking, whereby degree entrants move through the same jobs as other workers but are earmarked for rapid progression. However, the link between credentials and progression is far from perfect and there is clearly still room for the non-credentialed to reach the top if they demonstrate the right "personal" qualities.

The changes in local government are also marked. As in banking, local government used to be regarded as a secure job that provided a degree of status and stability (e.g. Byrne 1988). With the emergence of a "new managerialism" in local government there have been attempts to subordinate stable, clearly defined professional hierarchies to less clear managerial ones and to promote a new kind of management quality. One local government worker expressed it in the following way,

> Q: Who gets ahead here and why?
> A: Innovators, at the moment . . . The people we get here are the general management and they get the credit and get recognised and get taken seriously . . . the problem solving innovators are the people who get ahead at the moment.
> Q: And that's a change from the past?
> A: Very much so, yes. (Ms 27)

Whereas, in the past, rewards were based on length of service, stability and the successful reproduction of existing organizational norms, now the staff rewarded are those who can demonstrate the personal capacity for innovation, dynamism and creativity. At the same time, Midcity Council senior council staff have been moved onto fixed-term contracts, and they are clearly uncertain about their futures. The two most senior managers we interviewed mentioned this immediately when asked about their future prospects. These comments from one of these men are illustrative:

Q: Do you have a plan about what you would like to happen in the future?
A: . . . we were given a performance contract twelve months ago which brought us out of our permanent contracts . . . I would expect on the basis of the performance I've had this year, I have no doubt that over the next two years I can meet the performance contract, I will be offered another contract . . . I would like that contract to run from 55 . . . I mean that's my point [of view] though. The organization might look at it another way. With knocking around, whoever gets elected next election . . . maybe I ain't going to be offered a contract. (Mr 29)

In the past, both men would undoubtedly have had jobs for life, yet now their main plan is simply to stay in post. Southtown Council is also seriously considering introducing performance-related pay.

7.7 Conclusions

This paper is limited in many ways. It is a study of only three organizations in two sectors of employment, and the sample size of our postal questionnaire, as well as our sampling strategy, pose strict limits on what we can say for certain. Nonetheless, a number of potentially important findings do stand out.

First, we must not underestimate the adaptability of the organizational labour market. In both banking and local government there are very high rates of job mobility, and a high proportion of staff are not formally disbarred from internal labour market processes. The organizational career appears to remain a very important way by which social mobility can take place, and the vast majority of senior personnel continue to be recruited from below.

Secondly, models of "core and periphery", or of polarization, are really much too crude to be of any analytical value in understanding current changes within the organizations we have studied. The reality is that most workers are not part of a clearly demarcated core or periphery. What is especially important to note is the inadvisability of assuming that particular types of jobs are either core or peripheral.

However, although the organizational labour market remains vibrant, we have been rather more sceptical about seeing it in bureaucratic terms. In some ways it is hardly an original point to suggest limitations to the Weberian bureaucratic model.

Within the field of organizational theory, for instance, Weber is hardly referred to, and a number of approaches have been developed that attempt to find other ways of thinking about organizations other than as bureaucracies (e.g. Morgan 1986, Clegg 1990). What is striking, however, is that service-class theorists have not taken these developments on board and continue to work with notions that we would argue are of dubious contemporary value.

We would contend that the most important developments taking place within these organizational labour markets are concerned with the weakening of codified job ladders and the creation of more diversified jobs that offer a greater variety to job ladders. In such environments, however, it is less specific jobs and more the people who occupy such jobs who might be better seen as core or peripheral. Some cashiers are part-time women workers who might plausibly be seen as part of the peripheral labour market, whereas others might be graduate trainees being whisked up to more senior posts. But in many cases it is not formal qualifications, but other personal traits that may be significant. Gender continues to be an important factor in banking, but other personal characteristics, such as the role of "charismatic" qualities (see also Halford & Savage 1995), may also be important.

What implications, then, do these findings have for thinking about the contemporary middle classes? They suggest that the work-life patterns of the middle classes will exhibit rather greater volatility than in the past, but that this may take place within organizational labour markets rather than by removing them from the "cocoon" of bureaucratic shelters to be exposed to the rigours of occupational labour markets. The result is that it might be better to see the organizational labour market as a field in which different groups contest for position, power and status, and in which different sorts of assets are deployed.

Chapter 8

The remaking of the state middle class

Bob Carter and Peter Fairbrother

8.1 Introduction

Labour and class theory has largely ignored the state sector. Although there is no absence of political and sociological considerations of the state, there is scant consideration of the relationship between characterizations of the state and the class location of state employees (Holloway & Picciotto 1977, Jessop 1982, Clarke 1991a). Where labour and class theory has been addressed, it reflects the bias of studies towards manual worker occupations, incorporating paradigms of class appropriated from the study of the private sector (coal mining – Krieger 1983, Waddington et al. 1991, steel – Beynon et al. 1992, 1994). Nonetheless, with the massive restructuring and privatization of the public sector, this relative absence of studies is beginning to change (Taylor-Gooby & Lawson 1993, Farnham & Horton 1993). However, this new-found interest in the state sector has failed to give sufficient weight to the specificity of the labour process in the state sector or develop sufficiently a framework for the understanding of changing class relations within it.

The argument presented here is that the restructuring of the state sector has brought about not only the widely acknowledged changes in organization, but also changes in the labour process and class relations. During the 1980s, the core of the British state, the Civil Service, was transformed by a major restructuring and reorganization, from a traditional bureaucracy to a managerial employer (Fairbrother, 1994). Initially, in the 1980s, it was claimed that decentralization and devolution of managerial responsibilities could lead to the achievement of a cohesive and policy-responsive institution, pursued through a range of programmes concerned to reorganize department practices (*Financial management in government departments* 1983). By the late 1980s, the object was to restructure the Civil Service itself, with the implementation of what was termed the Next Steps programme. The aim was to improve management and to deliver better services within available resources, by establishing agencies and executive offices, semi-autonomous managerial structures, with discretion to provide services or goods according to proxy market criteria and indicators (Jenkins et al. 1988). By 1 April 1993, 80 agencies had been established covering 60% of Civil Service industrial and non-industrial staff.

Central to this programme was a range of policies aimed at challenging the established uniform and standardized conditions of Civil Service work and employment, not least to remove the basis for collective organization and action by Civil Service workers. The outcome is a restructured labour process together with a change in the dominant mode of control of labour, leading to a rearticulation of class relations within the Civil Service, and the creation of a more prominent new middle class from the former "supervisory" grades. Through a detailed examination of changes in a key section of the British Civil Service, the Benefits Agency, attention is thus drawn to the continued and growing significance of conflictual relations within state sector employment.

The data presented consist of a close reading of the reports and inquiries into the organization and operation of the British Civil Service, as well as the proposals for the Benefits Agency. Complementing this material, and providing detail of work and employment relations, case-study research was carried out, focusing on six union branches in the Benefits Agency. This resulted in 37 in-depth interviews with a selection of key informants in three sets of offices in the Benefits Agency. These interviews, gathered at annual intervals between 1990 and 1993, with four additional interviews dating back to 1986, are complemented by annual questionnaires of four union branch executives. In addition, three senior union officials, one senior manager, a Civil Service researcher, and a Member of Parliament have been interviewed at length. The research has involved limited observation, with attendance at five union meetings and at least three successive visits to six Civil Service office complexes.

8.2 Class and the civil service as employer

The modern Civil Service is very much a product of the reforms of the nineteenth century, particularly following the Northcote–Trevelyan recommendations of 1854 (reprinted 1968, Hennessy 1990: 5). These reforms reflected a general concern, particularly amongst the emergent bourgeoisie, with the principles of impersonal rational organization, and included the creation of a permanent and stable workforce, a concern with promotion on the grounds of ability and expertise, and the introduction of recruitment on the basis of merit. By 1870 a system of competitive examination had been established along with the reorganization of the Civil Service into a formalized division of labour, comprising high civil servants, principally recruited from the educational elite of Oxford and Cambridge, and a lower "class" of routine copyists or writers, refreshing in the honesty of the "class" reference. It was a Civil Service characterized until recently by universal grading structures, standardized rates of pay, and uniform conditions of employment.

One of the major political debates surrounding the modern state and the Civil Service concerns the question of neutrality. Traditionally, Marxists have insisted that the state was not a neutral instrument acting benignly on behalf of all citizens and interest groups. Hence Lenin, in the classical statement of Marxist theory of the state, *State And Revolution* ([1918] 1992), maintained that it was not possible for the working class simply to seize hold of the state and use it in its own interests; the state had to be smashed (on contemporary Marxist accounts, see Clarke 1991b). Both the state form and the content of its policies were fashioned by the interests of the bourgeoisie. However, this view was strongly contested by a social democratic theory and practice, based on the assumption of the autonomy and neutrality of the state. Policy aims would be achieved through macroeconomic measures and redistributional means. Hence, the state could be used to advance the interests of labour. It was exactly this contention – that there had been a "loss of power by the business class to the state" (Crosland 1956: 26) – that underpinned the claim that capitalism had been superseded. This loss of power was evident in three areas: increased economic regulation; nationalization of basic industries; and the growth of social welfare. Since the state was seen as neutral, state employees were above class. As the number of state personnel grew, the class basis of society simply atrophied.

There was a continuity to these debates, with the Communist parties throughout the 1970s, for example, advancing the theory of state monopoly capitalism in which the interests of monopoly capital were simply translated into state policy through its overwhelming economic power, through personal connections with the executive and the dominance of the executive over the legislature. Nonetheless, whatever the rhetoric that accompanied this theory, the practice of Communist parties was thoroughly reformist, being indistinguishable in its form from social democratic parties (Birchall 1974). The unambiguous role of the state under state monopoly capitalism should have predisposed theorists to see state employees as being either bourgeois or belonging to intermediate strata between the bourgeoisie and the proletariat. But as Communist parties were essentially reformist and pragmatic, the influence of these theories was minimal and they operated either with the assumption that the same orthodox, two-class model of the private sector (based on ownership and non-ownership of the means of production) existed in the public sector, or with a voluntaristic perspective that the structural position of employees was largely irrelevant, class being determined by political ideology and allegiance (on social workers and their managers, see Joyce et al. 1988).

Both sets of perspectives came under increasing scrutiny from the late 1960s. The growth of social welfare and corporatist political arrangements made the claimed fusion of monopoly capital and the state less and less credible. These arrangements in turn meant that the state was unable to adopt measures simply in the immediate interests of capital to stem growing economic instability. But if capital could not utilize the state in any simple fashion, nor could parties of the left. Faced with a slowing of growth in capitalist economies, they confronted severe constraints in their ability to continue on a reformist path, illustrated by the Callaghan Labour Government in Britain in the 1970s.

It was the conjuncture of the post-war settlement, economic expansion and a confident working class that allowed the transitional and ultimately unsustainable characteristic of the neutrality of the state to be taken by Weberian writers as essential. Claims for the neutral nature of bureaucracy were common (Crozier 1964, Blau 1966) and have also informed much organizational writing on the administration of the British state (Gray & Jenkins 1985). The argument can be sustained in its weak version – civil servants have no formal allegiance to either of the main political parties and remain in post when governments change – but the neutrality of senior members to politics and class strategies is open to structural and ideological challenge (Miliband 1969, Poulantzas 1973, see also accounts by various Labour ministers of problems they encountered – Sedgemore 1980, Benn 1989). Complementing these claims there has been much recent attention on the political, or at least electoral, orientation of employees (Edgell & Duke 1991, Savage et al. 1992). Where class analysis complements Weberian views of the state, state workers are attributed positions according to such indicators as market situation and work situation, rather than in terms of the social relationships of the capitalist state, both internally and as a consequence of operating its policies (Kelly 1980, Goldthorpe 1982, Lockwood 1989, for critical comments, Crompton & Gubbay 1977).

8.3   A theoretical lacuna?

The restructuring of the relations between managers and workers provides the starting point for an understanding of class relations within the Civil Service. During the 1970s there was a series of attempts by Marxists to give a more adequate characterization of the capitalist state (e.g. Poulantzas 1978). According to Clarke, these new approaches "rejected the traditional Marxist theory of State Monopoly Capitalism to retain the social democratic insistence on the *autonomy of the state* in order to insist on the *specificity* of the political and the *irreducibility* of the political to economic conflicts . . . they also emphatically rejected the social democratic illusion of the *neutrality of the state*, the class character of the state being determined ultimately by the *structural* relationship between the state and economy, embedded in the *form* of the state determined by its *function* within the system as a whole" (Clarke 1991a: 5, emphasis in original).

Although the theoretical advances in state theory were considerable, most threw little light on the class locations of state employees. Parallel to the advances in state theory, class theory was also being transformed by the rejection of orthodox Marxist models of class structure and the increasing significance given to the variously named new middle class, professional, managerial class or service class. Within these developments, Poulantzas (1978) was one of the few theorists to make explicit the class locations of state employees: all state employees outside certain nationalized industries and transport were considered bourgeois or petits bourgeois. Poulantzas' analysis of state employees stems not so much from the specific relations within the state as a consequence of its function but from an extension of his earlier considerations of class relations (Poulantzas 1975), considerations that have been subjected to effective critiques (Wright 1978, Clarke 1991b). The only other attempt to deal specifically with the class position of state employees, and arguably more effectively, also stemmed from an extension of general class theory. In an interesting but relatively neglected essay, Carchedi (1977), in a rereading of Marx, insisted on the continued relevance of the production and appropriation of surplus value to the determination of class. But he did so while recognizing the profound changes in societies that had reconfigured class relations since Marx's analysis. Carchedi argued that, although in the abstract the bourgeoisie and the proletariat have diametrically opposed relationships within the production process, the analysis of class must acknowledge the complexity of production relations and particularly the re-articulation of class relationships at the point of production.

As the capitalist production process proper was established, the mode of labour was revolutionized and less and less could an individual be said to be the direct producer. Products became the result of socialized collective labour. There occurs with this process an extension of the concept of productive labour and with it that of productive worker. The changes also signalled a transformation in the function of the capitalist within the production process. With the development of capitalism, the function of capital was also transformed from an individual one to a collective one, no longer embodied in the individual capitalist, who was replaced first by a manager and then by a managerial hierarchy. Central to this perspective is the idea that management of the enterprise has a double nature. As well as the function of capital, capitalists had always performed unifying and co-ordinating roles, roles that would be necessary under any system of social production. These latter roles did not arise because of the antagonism of classes under capitalism and were part of the labour process. The complex organization of modern production has increased rather than lessened the need to unify and co-ordinate the labour process.

These simultaneous changes – the growth of the collective worker and the growth of managerial hierarchies – have transformed the social structure of the workplace. Although it is still analytically possible to distinguish the function of capital and the function of labour, fewer occupations correspond with one function or the other in a pure way. An increasing number of people perform jobs whose composition is made up from both functions. Carchedi designated people in these locations the "new middle class".

Carchedi has the distinct merit of explicitly addressing the complex question of productive and unproductive labour, a question of direct relevance to an analysis of state sector employment. Although much state sector production is unproductive, it nevertheless takes place according to capitalist criteria, occurring as it does within a capitalist economic structure and dominated by it: "it produces use values just as capitalist commodities are produced, i.e. by the extraction of surplus labour" (Carchedi 1977: 133). State employees have surplus labour expropriated and are economically oppressed. Primary school teachers and clerical workers in the Civil Service, for example, are both non-owners of the means of production, are labourers performing the function of the collective worker, and are paid the equivalent of the value of their labour power. The extraction of surplus labour in the state sector, and the resistance to which this gives rise, necessitate, just as in the capitalist firm, a function of control and supervision. And, *pari passu*, a middle class also arises between the policy-makers and effective controllers, on the one hand, and those engaged in producing use-values, on the other. The functions of the state sector middle class are ones of non-strategic control or a combination of control and co-ordination, co-ordination being part of the labour process of service delivery.

Although Carchedi points to the internal relations of work and employment, developing an innovative account of the class position of state employees and thus laying the foundation for an analysis of the state middle class, his thesis awaits further refinement. First, in practice, class analysis of state employees is made more complex still by the wide variations in employment conditions and concrete tasks. The mode of control both by, and of, professional employees (teachers, doctors, social workers) has been traditionally very different from that of administrative workers in the Civil Service, and the police and army provide yet another model. The mode of control of the former has tended to be "personal" or "professional"; whereas the latter have been bureaucratic and coercive respectively. It should be stressed, however, that a dominant mode does not exclude the ready resort to others: social workers, for instance, work in parallel with bureaucratic rules on entitlement to benefits; psychiatrists with the ability legally to confine patients. Secondly, Carchedi provides a formalistic structural account of class relations that overlooks the way in which these relations are experienced and constructed in an ongoing way. This point is particularly important when considering the restructuring of the state sector and what this may mean for class recomposition. Indeed, it is our argument that the recent restructuring of the Civil Service, with the establishment of semi-autonomous management structures (agencies and executive offices), is part of a process whereby a state middle class is being refashioned. Not only are the internal relations of Civil Service work and employment being recast in the name of managerialism, but the new managerial incumbents are exposed to commercialized practices, making the value of labour power more transparent.

What makes analysis complicated in the state sector is that the class bias of state policy necessitates a perspective that goes beyond the internal relations of the work. The class nature of the state, and its subordination to the continuance of the accumulation of capital, place upon it dual roles of social control *and* the provision of services necessary in any complex society, such as education and public health. Although analytically separate, in practice these two roles are frequently combined in particular occupations. The dominance of one role or the other depends upon the nature of the service, the nature and degree of regulation of its performance by the state, and the strength and nature of working-class resistance and consciousness (London–Edinburgh Weekend Return Group 1980). To dwell only on the function of control would stamp relatively powerless state employees as middle-class. To concentrate only on positions within the state employment hierarchy would have social workers as unambiguously working-class, no matter how they interpreted and carried out their tasks (Callinicos 1987). The examination of the Benefits Agency below highlights the complexities of the role of the state and the relationship of the state functions to the roles and class position of its employees; these relationships are usually dislocated in theoretical discussions.

Looking at the process of class formation at office level in the Civil Service during the 1980s and into the 1990s there has been a decisive re-articulation of class relations. Central to this has been the reorganization of local offices so that a layer of staff are redefined as management, with responsibility for the organization of work, the budgeting of the office and the implementation of state policy. Managerial hierarchies have been recomposed, with the down-playing of unifying and co-ordinating roles and an emphasis on supervision and control. Initiatives have favoured neo-Taylorist solutions (Pollitt 1990) as opposed to those of new wave management (Wood 1989), thus running counter to the rhetoric in other sectors, particularly private manufacturing. In effect, this has meant redrawing the management–worker divide in these offices, as well as formalizing an already existing division that has often taken a sharply gendered form, men comprising management and women the workforce. Although the impetus for these changes came from outside the office, the way in which they were implemented depended crucially on the practices and commitments of the local management and workforce.

8.4 The management of benefits

During the 1980s the foundations for a recomposed set of class relationships were laid, first with an attempt to define a layer of staff in the offices as managers and then, when the limits of this approach became apparent, to fragment the Civil Service so that managers could manage and workers be managed. Crucially, this has involved shifting the emphasis in the organization of the Civil Service labour process from one where the senior office staff principally co-ordinated to one where direct staff control is emphasized. This has been neither straightforward nor uncontested by the new managers themselves or the workers. There is little evidence either that the restructuring was a result of a "service class" (Goldthorpe 1982) asserting its independence from government, or that it represented managers developing their organizational assets (Wright 1985); the reforms were very much externally, politically driven.

The first steps towards the clearer identification of a Civil Service middle class occurred in the early 1980s. Work procedures and financial accountability were tightened through computerizing the various areas of social security work. This was seen as a means of meeting the general strictures of public expenditure restrictions as well as modernizing the way this department and others were organized and operated. The core of these proposals delegated a range of budgetary tasks to local managers, thereby underwriting their authority in relation to other grades in the offices. This meant that, within a relatively limited framework, these managers had a responsibility for the allocation of staff, overtime and physical refurbishment of offices in ways that had not been the case in the past.

Alongside the decentralization of managerial responsibility, there was an attempt to refocus operations in the Department of Health and Social Security (DHSS) and then the Department of Social Security (DSS) so that staff dealt with claimants via an integrated computer system, rather than relying almost exclusively on clerical procedures. This initiative began in 1982 and continued throughout the 1980s and into the 1990s as part of a process of redesigning record-keeping and handling so that worker input could be measured and the output of benefit work targeted according to financial criteria. As noted elsewhere, simplification of the claiming process has been accompanied by the strengthening of administrative surveillance (Dean 1993).

Central to these initiatives therefore was the wider objective of reforming the labour process of benefit work. These were the necessary financial and work procedures that would permit the government to begin the fragmentation of the Civil Service. With the recognition of a diverse and inchoate managerial stratum in offices went a step-by-step and seemingly *ad hoc* granting of more authority and responsibility for person management to senior grades; the condition for breaking up the uniform terms and conditions of employment characteristic of the Civil Service was met. At the same time, however, comprehensive and highly centralized procedures for pay determination and employment conditions remained intact. Thus the exercise of managerial authority within the offices continued to be constrained by a centralized framework that covered the whole of the Civil Service.

The solution to this dilemma was to break up the Civil Service into semi-autonomous managerial units, each with the right to introduce specific terms and conditions of employment and to remould work procedures and organization so as to fit the requirements of each unit. The establishment of the Benefits Agency in 1991 created the opportunity for the explicit recognition of a Civil Service middle class in this sector of employment. First, the Benefits Agency was reorganized with a senior management, a board of management, that was empowered to flatten and decentralize the agency management structure. Secondly, and seemingly in contradiction to this, the offices were restructured with a centralized management organization at a local level. Thirdly, and only after these structures of control were in place, there was an attempt to legitimate to local managements and workforces the changed relationships that this entailed: work was reorganized and a new management ideology, emphasizing self-control, enthusiastically embraced.

In detail, these changes involved the removal of one complete tier of management, the delegation of further responsibilities to line management and a reduction of middle management by 20% (Benefits Agency 1992: 5). Accompanying this there was a major delegation of managerial responsibility to 159 district managers, who were previously senior managers in the local office units (Treasury and Civil Service Committee 1991: 28, para. 185). Nonetheless, as noted, one of the paradoxes of this reorganization was that, within a process of apparent managerial devolution, there has been a process of centralizing local management structures. The Benefits Agency is now organized on the basis of three territories rather than seven regions, and 500 offices have been grouped into 159 district management units (DMUs).

This centralization within the framework of managerial devolution is also evident in the offices. Previously, relatively large numbers of support staff were located at a regional level. Support responsibilities have now been shifted to the district level, with a consequent reorganization of district management structures. From the point of view of staff, the most significant part of this reorganization was that the single office, as an administrative and physical entity, no longer existed for managerial purposes; the former office manager (grade 7) was replaced by the district manager (grade 7), with support staff, now responsible for more than one office. In many cases it also meant some relocation of staff between offices because the district manager has the authority to reorganize and concentrate work, instead of providing the range of services in all offices.

Local offices were grouped together into districts, as the base organizational unit in the Benefits Agency. But, not only did these former office managers acquire the responsibility for two or more offices, they also had functions and responsibilities formerly exercised at a regional level devolved to them (Social Security Committee 1991: 35). As a result, there has been both an intensification of managerial work as well as the physical removal of managerial responsibility from the majority of local offices in the Agency; the processes of proletarianization and middle-class formation proceed as outcomes of the same movement (Braverman 1974, Carchedi 1977).

There has also been the beginning of a reorganization of work within the DMUs. On the one hand, offices were grouped together to create district offices, under the responsibility of a Principal Officer: on the other hand, senior staff (Senior Executive Officer – [SEO] and Higher Executive Officer – [HEO] levels) were given greater discretion and responsibility for both staff and financial issues. Changes in work, however, have not been uniform across the districts. Because managers have considerable discretion, as indicated above, some district managers have retained a traditional form of work organization while others have begun to reorganize work procedures and the related arrangements in the office. For example, in one office the work of checking and adjudication (previously organized as a separate unit) was devolved to Quality Control Command, involving 12 executive officer (EO) grade workers under an HEO. Alongside this, a Customer Service Command was created, gathering a range of difficult and previously independent functions together under the direction of a part-time EO, whose principal activity was to liaise with the public.

Each DMU was organized as a cost centre, laying the foundation for a degree of financial independence that has been unusual in the former department, while also creating the conditions for variation between districts. Initially this has been reflected in a distinction between districts where managers have been willing to exercise their increased discretion and those where managers have refused to accept responsibility for their own budget because they are unable to comply with its indicated requirements. This has led to a rather paradoxical development where the devolution of managerial responsibility has also led to increasing intervention from the area management as district managers look for guidance on a range of issues for which they have acquired new responsibilities. This variation in practice is highly visible and almost certainly these variations and disparities in costs will not be allowed to remain for long.

Qualifying standardized forms of employment and work routines

Specifying these structural changes is only the first step in the analysis of the developments in the Benefits Agency. Equally importantly, it is necessary to consider "work content, organization and control, along with relations with other work groups in the workplace" (Ramsay et al. 1991: 37), as well as the way particular groups identify themselves and act to realize these identities. A consideration of the nature and character of Civil Service work and employment as a labour process opens up the possibility of specifying the parameters of organization and activity by Civil Service workers in the context of restructuring and reorganization.

During the 1980s, as indicated above, the first steps were taken to introduce flexible patterns of working into social security work (Fairbrother 1991: 75–7). This was the beginning of a concerted attempt to devolve and redefine the remit of managerial authority and discretion at a local level. Managers found themselves in positions where they had opportunities to exploit the polyvalent nature of Civil Service jobs, particularly by initiating policies that underwrote the "flexible" use of labour resources. This was a period when changes in the calculation and administration of contributory benefit and subsequently supplementary benefit were introduced. These developments involved modifications to work routines, often involving an expectation that workers would acquire new skills, for example following the introduction of computerized work routines to facilitate the changes in benefit provision. The result was that, during this period, job mobility and the associated patterns of re-skilling became a feature of the work routines in these areas of employment.

As part of the reorganization in the then DHSS, local managements began to exploit the "flexible" margins of employment, illustrated by the use of temporary employment and increased overtime to clear backlogs of work. These forms of employment took on a new significance during this period when local managements began to exercise their discretion to relax staff-in-post targets, vary grading mixes, and move funds within staff budget headings. As the pressure for staff savings increased there was a move to achieve such economies by converting full-time posts into temporary ones. In general, these temporary workers were employed as clerical assistants, doing largely unskilled, extremely routine and often physically arduous work. They were usually young women, employed for fewer than 51 weeks on the lower pay bands of the clerical assistant scales. This practice of employing temporary workers in the benefit offices has been maintained and even extended in the 1990s. In one DMU in 1992, temporary workers had been employed in reasonably large numbers for the previous two and a half years. They were employed on fixed-term contracts that were often extended on a year-to-year basis, thereby introducing a qualified notion of regular employment. Thirty-five workers out of the 280 (12.5%) were employed on such contracts. This confirmed the continuity of the trends identified by Potter (1987) five years earlier.

The use of temporary workers was complemented by an increased use of overtime working in these offices. In the early 1980s, office managers were assigned a complement for the office, as well as an allocation for a specified number of hours of overtime. Offices were organized on the basis of "manpower" budgeting, with office managers being given two budgets: (1) a budget that was the amount of the cash equivalent of the staff complement and (2) a "manpower" substitutes account, which could be spent on overtime, casual or full-time staff, subject to staff number ceilings. During the 1980s and into the 1990s, local managers exploited the opportunities that these changes presented to vary the mix of hours worked in local offices.

It is within this prism that the consideration of individualized pay and grading arrangements needs to be understood (Treasury and Civil Service Committee 1991: 36, Q.259). The Benefits Agency has placed a priority on considering the possibility of introducing flexible pay arrangements and related conditions. In particular, the senior management of the agency have investigated a group bonus scheme (ibid.: xiii, Q. 259) as part of a wider examination of the relationship between pay and performance. This consideration has involved the Treasury as well as the DSS. It would appear to be part of a general move to establish a Civil Service with department- and agency-specific conditions of employment.

The other side of these moves toward managerial devolution was the exercise of new-found discretions in what were very novel areas of decision-making in the Civil Service. This is illustrated by seemingly small items to do with office conditions, including the purchasing of office equipment, discussing plans for relocation with staff, and the consideration of more varied work routines. Management have used their increased discretion over the use of budgets to move away from the previous practices, which were reliant on central authorization, and instead have begun to take independent decisions about the terms and conditions of office work.

8.5 The revival of unionism

The reorganization of the 1980s and 1990s, and the recomposition of class relations in the Civil Service, occurred against the backdrop of increasingly restive trade unions in the 1970s. These unions emerged out of highly centralized and consensual bargaining structures that had promoted the creation of an administratively controlled Civil Service organized on the basis of standardized terms and conditions of employment. With deteriorating terms and conditions of employment, relative to equivalent workers in the private sector, Civil Service unionists began to question government policy towards the Civil Service, particularly on wages. In the late 1970s and into the 1980s, these unions embraced a form of economic militancy that created problems for governments concerned to maintain control over income levels.

What was notable about the unionism of the late 1970s was the lack of an indication within it of class differences at the level of the workplace. As a result, it was not unusual for the so-called office management staff to identify with and support the wage struggles of this period. Although they may have had individual concerns about promotion and managerial favour when they supported union action, they did not see themselves as managers; rather they were senior grade staff located in a broadly consensual set of work and employment relations. In the 1980s, with the reconstitution of class relations in the workplace, divisions began to appear within offices, with many managers pursuing anti-union policies although formally remaining union members.

Restructuring was utilized to change the culture and relations within the Benefits Agency:

> They have restructured the management set-up. Whereas before each of-
> fice was a separate entity, with its own manager . . . and its own Whitley,
> they grouped the offices into so-called districts. So each district comprises
> several local offices and has only one manager . . . doing several times the
> work for the same money and in fact what they did was to weed out the
> older less enthusiastic elements. They all had to re-apply for their jobs . . .
> So they ended up with basically the harder, tougher, leaner, younger, more
> committed elements as the managers of these districts. (Office secretary,
> Social Security, 1992)

Nevertheless, the changes were far from even. Managers still pursued different managerial approaches towards their staff and unions, ranging from the co-operative and consensual to the provocatively conflictual.

> So much more of what goes on depends on their approach and personal-
> ity. For example the Manager of [Countryside] a very clever capable
> woman . . . after initially appearing to be a bit of a dragon . . . has actually
> been as nice as pie to the unions in [Countryside] whereas we have had a
> hand-picked evil bastard really in [Car Town] and it has taken us since
> April to cut him down to size. He nearly cut us down to size on a few occa-
> sions. (Office Secretary, Social Security, 1992).

The establishment of the Benefits Agency, in April 1991, threatened the unions that organized workers in the former department; these unions faced a new and in some cases aggressively confident management concerned to undermine what they saw as privileged and difficult local union leaderships. Facility time was restricted, managers were less forthcoming in their dealings with local union leaders, and the regional level of the Whitley structure was abolished, on the grounds that most, if not all, locally based problems would be settled at a local level. The decentralization of managerial authority, aimed at undermining the basis of national action by Civil Service trade unions, has had the consequence of laying the foundation for more active forms of unionism in workplaces. In the face of these challenges, unions at a local level reorganized, often in novel ways, reflecting their diverse experiences as non-manual workers, women and men, who could no longer rely on past procedures and forms of organization (Fairbrother 1994).

The creation of the Benefits Agency signalled a shift in the frontier of control between workers and management (Goodrich [1920] 1975). Previously, the offices were organized in a bureaucratic form that meant that at a local or office level there were relatively few grievances or problems that could be or indeed were settled at this level. As a consequence, the union form of organization in the DSS (and its fore-runners) was also centralized and relatively remote for most members. There were exceptions to these arrangements, particularly where a small number of active union members in offices attempted to force a shift in decision-making from regional or national levels on at least some issues, such as overtime working during the mid-1980s. This, however, was very limited and notable because of its relative infrequency.

With the shift to agency status, and the authorization of devolved and decentralized managerial structures, the frontier of control both shifted in favour of management and was policed much more overtly as newly empowered managers attempted to impose new procedures and practices on an often reluctant and uneasy workforce. It was in these circumstances that unions at a local level, with limited support from their national leadership, began to look anew at their forms of organization and practice at this level. The contradiction in these developments was that, for both management and the unions nationally, there remained strong pressures to retain control over the developments that were taking place. As a result, in the face of managerial devolution and local union renewal, there are still strong pressures towards control and centralization.

8.6 The remaking of class relations

These changes in organization and practice amount not to the introduction of class relations into the Civil Service, but to their re-articulation. Increasing difficulties with capital accumulation in Britain and other capitalist economies, coupled with an increasingly restive Civil Service working class, questioning the traditional policies of consensus and co-operation, provide the background to these changes. In these circumstances governments have been impelled to re-examine the basis of financial and social control in the state sector, and the Civil Service in particular. This re-examination has displayed a growing concern to restructure the control of the Civil Service work process in order to increase work intensity and the appropriation of surplus labour. In order to achieve these ends it has been necessary to re-make and subordinate the Civil Service middle class, ensuring that it represents government policy and is prepared to manage with authority.

The first step in this process, which involved the encouragement of senior office grades to take on the responsibilities of office management, was the beginning of an attempt to consolidate a Civil Service middle class from within existing organizational structures. There clearly was a recognition that these staff occupied structurally ambiguous positions, combining the tasks of collective labourer and controller in one person. The problem for successive governments was how to shift the balance towards the task of control and away from the collective worker. Initially, there was a rather naive belief that this could be done without breaking up the Civil Service.

Nonetheless, this initial step was partly successful – successful enough to prompt Civil Service workers to begin to look more closely towards their local union organization to represent them on a range of local issues, including personal grievances, appraisals, and the allocation of work. Unions with highly centralized pasts, mirroring in an organizational form the passing structure of the Civil Service as a whole, were slow to react. Workers experiencing the significance of the changes taking place began to question the relatively inappropriate union structures representing them in the changing setting of Civil Service work and employment.

With the introduction of the Next Steps programme, the government began to fragment the Civil Service, thus providing the conditions for drawing a line between a Civil Service working class and middle class much more clearly. The establishment of agencies and their equivalents allowed employment to be organized so that middle and junior managers would be forced to accept their responsibilities as controllers in the new emerging Civil Service. Like their private sector counterparts, these are now employees who will not be allowed to overlook the fact that a key part of their remit is the control of labour. They have been forced into this situation in two ways: first by having direct responsibility for the deployment of labour and secondly by assessing and appraising the performance of labour. In the process of performing these functions, their own failures will be highly visible.

The creation of a Civil Service middle class has involved a shift from the relatively comfortable anonymity of the centralized and hierarchical Civil Service of the past to the naked relationships of authority and control of the present. Of course, this is not to suggest that these layers of staff were not involved in control activities in the past. Rather it is to point out that such relations were obscured and relatively invisible in the labyrinthine procedures and arrangements of a centralized Civil Service. Moreover, although implicated in past control relations, the extent of their control and the degree of their performance of the labour function have changed. Nor have these changes been universally welcomed by managers, and the government has been well aware that resistance to the restructuring was possible, with middle management consistently seen as a particular problem in the Civil Service, opposed to many of the new initiatives (Metcalfe & Richards, cited in Tonge 1989: 89). There is still an unevenness of practice, but the service as a whole is now more policy driven and there has been a move away from custodial management concerned with the protection of the service (Ackroyd et al. 1989). Although strategic aims continue to be centrally controlled, control of local workforces is more overt. It is in this respect that managers are being exposed as controllers and supervisors of the work of others.

These arrangements are somewhat irreversible, at least in the short run. The structural fragmentation of the Civil Service will not readily allow a return to the invisibilities of the past, not least because the basis of central control is the structural fragmentation that is taking place. Nonetheless, there is another side to these developments, which also may be a sign for the future. With the exposure of the relationships in the Civil Service labour process there is a clear social and political division between the Civil Service middle class and working class. It is in this context that workers are more likely to look to their unions for immediate and direct solutions to their problems and worries. This brings them into direct conflict with their local managers, also members of the same unions. What may now develop is a clarification of the class interests of different sections of the Civil Service within their unions and the beginning of a sharper appreciation of the nature of the social divisions within the work process than has been the case in the past. Perspectives on class stressing determination of the working class by non-ownership and the status of wage labour are thus revealed as increasingly formalistic (Carter 1995). It is in this respect that the class struggle within the Civil Service may be a harbinger of a clearer understanding of the character of class interests in this crucial sector of work and employment.

Chapter 9

"Too much work?" Class, gender and the reconstitution of middle-class domestic labour

Nicky Gregson and Michelle Lowe

9.1 Introduction

In this chapter we consider the nature of domestic labour within a significant proportion of middle-class households in contemporary Britain, focusing particularly on the growing tendency through the 1980s and into the 1990s for such households to use *waged* domestic labour for at least certain of their daily reproductive tasks. The empirical work we present here draws heavily on our much fuller exploration of waged domestic labour in middle-class Britain (Gregson & Lowe 1994b). However, in reworking this material for this volume our objective is to consider the implications of the resurgence in waged domestic labour within middle-class households for class analysis. Briefly stated, our position with respect to class analysis in this context is one that, while acknowledging the continued importance of class, maintains that class provides by no means the only explanatory framework for analyzing the nature of day-to-day social reproduction within middle-class households in contemporary Britain. Thus, although we see merit, for example, in both service class and performative versions of class for an examination of the use of waged domestic labour by the middle classes, at the same time we maintain that such perspectives do not allow us to see why certain middle-class households in Britain (but not all) use waged domestic labour. Moreover, although class analysis enables us to account for how and why middle-class British households have been able to satisfy their increasing levels of demand for waged domestic labour, it cannot account for why it is *waged* domestic labour that is being used by such households, rather than other (unwaged) forms of domestic labour. As we emphasize in this chapter therefore, other frameworks of analysis, most notably those of gender, are vital to the analysis of middle-class day-to-day social reproduction. As a consequence, our general position in relation to class analysis can be summarized as twofold. First, although we certainly do not want to dispense with a class framework of analysis, and indeed urge its continued importance (Emmison & Western 1990, Devine 1992b, cf. Pahl 1989, Saunders 1990), at the same time we feel it is important to stress the need to move beyond versions of class rooted in the labour market.

Secondly, however, we take the view that class is never the sole determinant of social phenomena. Correspondingly, and counter to at least recent tradition, we maintain that class should not be accorded analytical privilege by social scientists. Rather, and as our empirical analysis here shows, we prefer a position that emphasizes the simultaneous and interwoven constitution of class with gender (and for that matter with race, ethnicity and sexuality). For us, therefore, gender relations are central to the constitution of the contemporary middle classes in Britain, to middle-class identities and to middle-class formation (Savage et al. 1992, Savage 1994). Much of this chapter is devoted to providing support for this position. However, in the final sections of the chapter we examine the political implications of the resurgence of waged domestic labour amongst the middle classes (highlighting the conservative gender politics that this tendency undoubtedly reveals) before moving on finally to consider the implications of our research for middle-class formation.

9.2   Class frameworks of analysis and middle-class domestic labour

In thinking about the utility of class analysis for interpreting middle-class domestic labour, it is pertinent to point out that the recent history of class analysis in the field of domestic labour is not auspicious. Twenty years ago, for example, the domestic labour debate became locked in the conundrum of whether domestic work can be constituted as "productive work" (Seccombe 1974, Gardiner 1975). Meantime other feminists, notably Christine Delphy, were arguing that women, by virtue of their performance of domestic labour, comprised a class exploited by men. More recently, the feminist critique of class analysis has moved away from domestic labour. Focusing on the gender limitations of the dominant versions of mainstream (malestream) class analysis (be these Marxist, neo-Marxist or Weberian), this work pointed initially to the limitations of conventional class analyses, which define class purely in terms of labour market positions and derive women's class position from male heads of household (Acker 1973, Delphy 1981, Britten & Heath 1983, Stanworth 1984, Crompton & Jones 1984, Crompton & Mann 1986). Such analyses, however, have since moved on, to argue not only that social classes are gendered but that the processes of class formation are themselves gendered (Crompton 1986, Crompton & Sanderson 1990, Savage & Witz 1991, 1992, Witz 1992). Thus, Rosemary Crompton, for example, has argued that the service class is a gendered class, not just in terms of its dependency on female white-collar workers but in terms too of its reliance on domestic servicing offered by wives and kin (and see, too, Bell 1968, Edgell 1980). Domestic labour, then, and its importance to class formation, is once more being acknowledged. Such arguments, and Crompton's in particular, provide the start point for our analysis here. However, our work exposes the limitations inherent in this homogeneous representation of the service class and its mode of domestic servicing. Indeed, as we show here, a significant proportion of contemporary middle-class households not only differ from the conventional middle-class family structure, but differ too in their mode of domestic servicing. The households that we are concerned with here are dual-career households, many of which use their (considerable) household financial assets to purchase waged domestic labour.[1]

In contrast to feminist work, the only contemporary framework of class analysis to make reference to the place of domestic labour in middle-class formation is provided by André Gorz in his *Critique of economic reason* (1989). Broadly stated, Gorz's argument goes like this. He maintains that the class structure of the advanced capitalist nations is characterized by two groups. The first comprises those who have "too much work". Employed in demanding, career-structured occupations, such individuals are argued to have insufficient time to perform domestic labour. Their households therefore can be said to be experiencing a crisis in day-to-day social reproduction. In contrast, a second group is composed of those whom Gorz labels as having "too little work". These are the victims of the collapse of skilled working-class employment within the advanced capitalist economies. Such individuals (Gorz neglects to mention that these are for the most part men!) are the long-term unemployed and, so Gorz maintains, have little option but to work in the homes of those who have "too much work".

There is plenty that can be criticized in Gorz's arguments, notably the complete disregard for gender in these schematic remarks. As volumes of feminist scholarship have shown, domestic labour itself is highly gendered (see, for example, Oakley 1974, Yeandle 1984). Moreover, those with "too little work" in the advanced capitalist societies are mostly working-class men. There is therefore something of a gender mismatch in Gorz's analysis. Those with too little work (men) working in the homes of the middle classes, performing their reproductive labour? Maybe as gardeners and decorators, but as cleaners and childcarers . . . not very likely! A second problem with Gorz's arguments is the lack of evidence behind his contentions about the hours worked by particular classes. In the British context at least, such absences start to look a little suspicious, particularly given the contraction in average weekly working hours for those in full-time employment from 40.9 hours in 1984 to 37.9 in 1993.[2] Moreover, in identifying those with "too much work" as the middle classes, Gorz misses the point that the working class itself has fragmented into those households in work (many of whom are involved in multiple employment strategies; see Pahl 1984) and those dependent on state benefits. Finding the time for daily reproductive work is as much a problem for the first group of working-class households as it is for the middle classes, but for these households it is for the most part self-provisioning and/or kin substitution (rather than waged labour substitution) that is used to perform domestic labour.[3] Gorz's analysis, however, does not enable him to develop such points.

Although these criticisms are important, there is nonetheless an appealing quality to Gorz's arguments concerning the crisis in day-to-day social reproduction within middle-class households. Much of this is to do with the way in which these arguments accord with the self-perceptions and rhetoric of middle-class employment – we see and frequently present ourselves as having "too much work"! This coincidence, together with the fact that Gorz's arguments provide the only framework of class analysis to engage with the importance of waged domestic labour to the day-to-day reconstitution of the middle classes, and the concerns of this volume with class analysis, means that we "hang" this chapter around an evaluation of Gorz's arguments. We begin, however, by outlining the growth of waged domestic labour in Britain through the 1980s, identifying this with the middle classes and commenting briefly on its salient class and gender characteristics.

9.3   The return of waged domestic labour in middle-class Britain

The growth of waged domestic labour in middle-class Britain

Charting the resurgence of waged domestic labour within middle-class households in contemporary Britain is no straightforward task. Official employment statistics amalgamate a number of "domestic" occupations, making it impossible to differentiate between those employed privately within households and those employed by firms and/or institutions (for instance in schools and hospitals), and between "domestic" occupations as diverse as housekeepers and play attendants. A further complication is provided by the informal, "off the cards" nature of certain forms of waged domestic labour, notably household cleaning. In the face of such difficulties we have used alternative data sources, specifically advertisement data and household questionnaire surveys, to estimate the extent of the resurgence in the employment of waged domestic labour in contemporary Britain.[4]

As can be seen from Table 9.1, advertised demand from households for waged domestic labour escalated rapidly in Britain through the 1980s, and is particularly associated with domestic labour relating to childcare. In the early 1980s the mother's help (someone who assists a full-time housewife/mother) was the most important childcare-related waged domestic labour category. However, as the decade progressed it was the nanny (someone who cares for children within their own home and in the absence of the parent(s)) who came to assume primary importance – a change that reflects clearly the increasing tendency for women to return to full-time employment after childbirth. Figure 9.1 shows the distinctive geography of this advertised demand, one that manifests the spatial distribution of the middle classes. Demand for waged domestic labour nationally through the 1980s can be seen to be concentrated in London and the South east region. Within conurbations, too, the geography of advertised demand for waged domestic labour duplicates that of middle-class housing areas. In London for example, not only is advertised demand concentrated strongly in the NW and SW postcode areas, but it was the south-west area (an area strongly identified with gentrification through the 1980s) that became progressively more important as a source of demand for nannies through the 1980s, leaving the older, established middle-class housing areas of the north-west as the primary source of demand in the housekeeper category.

Advertisement data then suggest a strong association between the geography of advertised demand for waged domestic labour and the geography of middle-class Britain. This association is confirmed by questionnaire surveys of middle-class households.

Table 9.1 Recorded and estimated advertised demand for waged domestic labour in Britain, July 1981–June 1991.

Advertisements	July 1981[1]	1982	1983	1984	1985	1986	1987	1988	1989	1990	1991[1]	June Total
Recorded	577	1,201	1,374	1,709	1,742	1,922	1,949	2,176	2,187	1,848	649	17,334
Estimated totals	–	9,608	10,992	13,672	13,936	15,376	15,592	17,408	17,496	14,784	–	128,864

1. Estimates have not been produced for 1981 and 1991, given the half-year samples. *Source*: Gregson & Lowe (1994b: table 2.1) based on *The Lady* (12.5% sample)

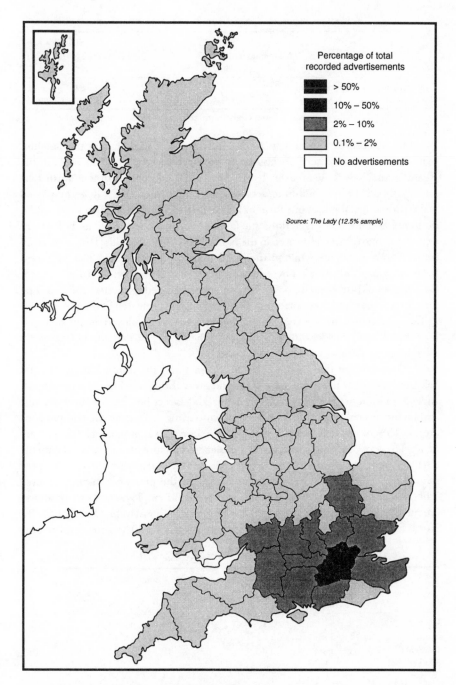

Figure 9.1 Spatial distribution of recorded advertised demand for waged domestic labour, 1982–91. *Source:* Gregson & Lowe (1994b: Fig. 2.2).

Table 9.2 Incidence of employment of waged domestic labour.

	North East		South East	
	No of households		No of households	
	(N=268)	%	(N=274)	%
Employing waged domestic labour	97	36.2	91	33.2
Not employing waged domestic labour	171	63.8	183	66.8

Source: Field research 1991.

Table 9.2 records the findings from a survey of 542 dual-career partnerships (with both partners in service-class occupations) conducted simultaneously in the Reading and Newcastle areas in 1991. Of the 268 households in the North East with both partners in full-time service-class employment, 97 (36%) employed waged domestic labour in one form or another. In the South East, 91 (33%) of 274 households employed waged domestic labour.[5] For the most part households were employing one person. However, in the North East, 17 households (18%) employed more than one person, while in the South East 20 households (22%) employed more than one individual. These findings suggest that over one-third of service-class households in contemporary Britain employ waged domestic labour in one form or another, and they correspond well with market research findings.[6]

Table 9.3 shows the forms of waged domestic labour employed by our surveyed households and provides a useful counter to the picture of demand portrayed by advertisement data.

Here we can see that in both the North East and the South East it was the "cleaner" category that proved to be far and away the most commonly employed. Indeed, in both areas well over 60% of the dual-career households surveyed and employing waged domestic labour were employing a cleaner. In comparison, around 15% of these households employed a nanny and approximately 12% a gardener. However, such figures provide a misleading picture of nanny employment. The vast majority of dual-career households employ a nanny only to care for pre-school-age children. When we take into account the presence/absence of pre-school-age children within households surveyed and employing waged domestic labour, the incidence of nanny employment increases considerably. Thus, of the 97 North East households employing waged domestic labour, 30 had one or more pre-

Table 9.3 Incidence of employment categories of waged domestic labour in case-study areas.

	North East		South East	
	No employed		No employed	
	(N=103)	%	(N=104)	%
Cleaner	67	65.1	67	64.4
Nanny	15	14.6	18	17.3
Gardener	14	13.6	12	11.5
Mother's help	4	3.9	1	1.0
Au pair	1	1.0	4	3.9
Other	2	1.9	2	1.9

Source: Gregson & Lowe (1994b: Table 2.10), based on field research, 1991.

school child and, of these, 14 (47%) employed a nanny. In the South East, of the 91 employing households, 38 had one or more children in this age range, 14 (37%) of whom employed a nanny. Such findings lead us to suggest that approaching three-quarters of all dual-career households employing waged domestic labour in contemporary Britain employ a cleaner, and that between a third and a half of such households with preschool-age children employ a nanny. They also suggest that the cleaner and the nanny are the major forms of waged domestic labour used by the middle classes in contemporary Britain.

So far, then, the arguments made by Gorz look to have at least a degree of substance to them. That over one-third of middle-class households employ waged domestic labour in some form or another seems to testify both to a crisis in daily social reproduction within middle-class households in Britain and to the reconstitution of domestic work within such households. But is this really the reconstitution of domestic work on class lines? On whom are the middle classes drawing to satisfy their demand for waged domestic labour?

9.4   Who works in the homes of the new middle classes?

As we saw above, the two main forms of waged domestic labour employed by middle-class households in contemporary Britain are the cleaner and the nanny. But who works as cleaners and nannies? And can we label these occupations as class specific?

On the basis of our research the answer to the second of these questions would have to be "yes". Household cleaning in our research was shown to be the preserve of older, usually married, working-class and white women, many of them from households dependent on state benefits (invalidity, unemployment/income support and the minimum state pension).[7] In contrast, nannying emerged as an occupation characterized by young women from intermediate status households, typically with a father working in lower management and a mother in secretarial/clerical employment. In addition, the majority of these women had a professional qualification relating either exclusively or partially to childcare (either the National Nursery Examination Board certificate [NNEB] or the Preliminary Certificate in Social Care [PCSC]). Such findings suggest that, although the waged domestic labour force in contemporary Britain may be homogeneous in its gendering, in class terms it is not a homogeneous entity. Rather, what we have here is evidence for a *class differentiated* labour force, in which class is articulating with domestic work to produce forms of domestic work that are identified with women from particular class backgrounds. Thus, much as in a previous historical epoch in Britain, the dirtiest, heaviest and most physically demanding facets of domestic labour in middle-class homes seemingly are being transferred to working-class women, while the more valued tasks of daily childcare are transferred to younger women whose class background is closer to that of their employers.[8]

Such findings are important, not just for what they tell us about the class specificity of waged domestic labour, but for what they reveal about the limitations of Gorz's assertions regarding those who have little choice but to labour for those who have "too much work". If Gorz's arguments touch base anywhere here, they do so with household cleaners. Although household cleaning has, almost certainly, always been characterized by working-class women supplementing household incomes, it is the benefit-dependent nature of this particular form of waged domestic labour that we take to be symptomatic of Britain in the 1980s. As other research has shown, the economic restructuring of the 1980s hit working-class households particularly hard. Household cleaning is one of the few sources of informal sector earnings for women, and in the majority of cases we encountered it was benefit dependence (and the limitations that this places on female earnings) that accounted for a move into this form of work in the 1980s. With the nanny, however, the "no choice" arguments stem not from labour force position but from state policy with respect to childcare provision. Albeit that the gendering of the youth labour market means that the employment options for young girls leaving school with minimal educational qualifications are not immense, such girls do have a (limited) choice of occupations open to them. However, for those who opt for childcare training, the lack of widespread "collective" affordable daycare in Britain means that employment as a nanny frequently represents the only childcare option available to newly qualified childcare workers. In comparison with the situation with household cleaners, the labour upon which middle-class households have drawn to satisfy their need for childcare services is predominantly a pool of displaced professional workers.

The cracks in Gorz's arguments, then, are starting to appear. Yes, domestic labour within middle-class households is being reconstituted, and yes, class is "in there" influencing who does waged domestic labour, but there is more to all this than a straightforward class transfer in reproductive work. As we show in the following section, the resurgence in waged domestic labour is more appropriately tackled through a framework that focuses on the articulation of gender, class and waged domestic labour *within* middle-class households.

9.5 The reconstitution of domestic work within middle-class households

As we showed in the previous section, waged domestic labour became an increasingly common feature within middle-class households in Britain through the 1980s. But in making this generalization it is vitally important that we do not lose sight of two points. The first is that, although widespread, the use of waged domestic labour within middle-class households does not characterize the middle classes en masse. The second is that waged labour is being substituted for *particular* domestic tasks, and not all domestic tasks. In this section we explore this reconstitution, focusing particularly on why certain middle-class households substitute specific forms of waged domestic labour for their own unwaged labour, and on the social relations of waged domestic labour employment. As will become clear, Gorz's framework of class analysis is by no means the most useful or indeed the only class framework through which we can examine waged labour substitution.

Why substitute?

Time–space impossibilities and service-class employment

As well as the most straightforward of the reasons encountered for substitution, lack of time and space in which to perform domestic tasks is also the reason most closely associated with service-class employment. Indeed, for dual-career middle-class households with young, preschool-age children, waged labour substitution in relation to childcare is essential if they are to maintain this pattern of employment. However, notwithstanding the demands made by service-class occupations structured on masculinist careerist principles, middle-class households still have the time–space in which to perform other domestic tasks (notably cleaning, washing, ironing and cooking) if they so wish – evenings and weekends for example. Why then do some of these households argue that they do not have this time–space? One answer to this question is provided when we examine domestic divisions of labour within dual-career households.

Domestic labour coping crises and domestic divisions of labour within middle-class households

We have discussed elsewhere the associations between particular forms of the domestic division of labour within middle-class households and the use of specific categories of waged domestic labour (Gregson & Lowe 1994a). The nub of our argument, however, is that, whereas dual-career middle-class households with traditional forms of the domestic division of labour (around 40% of our survey) are highly likely to substitute waged domestic labour for the unwaged labour of the female partner, those with shared forms of the domestic division of labour are much less likely to do so, except in the case of childcare services. Moreover, our investigations revealed consistently that, whereas traditional forms of the domestic division of labour proved to be workable domestic labour coping strategies for dual-career partnerships without children, the advent of childcare responsibilities, or even pregnancy, generated a domestic labour coping crisis for such households. Faced with a situation in which "spare time" has to provide the time–space for all domestic tasks and childcare activities, female partners in middle-class households with traditional domestic divisions of labour find themselves confronted by a domestic labour coping crisis. In contrast, households with shared domestic divisions of labour simply assimilate childcare tasks and activities within the shared division of labour. But why is it that households encountering domestic labour coping crises choose to resolve these crises by using waged labour substitution? Why don't these households switch to using a shared form of the domestic division of labour?

The answer to this last question is that to do so would require a fundamental reappraisal of the relationship of the male partner in such households to domestic labour, something that many of our respondents made clear was tantamount to living in fantasy land! Indeed, in a number of the middle-class households we encountered, the choice posed by male partners to their partners was as clear cut as either to flog themselves day and night or to "get someone in to do the work". Our research revealed, then, that waged domestic labour substitution in many middle-class households is frequently a manifestation of middle-class men's unwillingness to do more than the bare minimum in the way of domestic labour, as well as being often about men's inability to "see" the tasks of domestic labour.

We need to recognize that waged domestic labour substitution by middle-class households says a very great deal about both the gendering of domestic labour and the place of domestic labour in the identities of middle-class men and women. For the majority of middle-class men, domestic labour – and particularly cleaning-related domestic labour – is an irrelevance, insignificant and time consuming. For their female partners, however, it is something that, however tiresome, cannot be ignored. Domestic work has to be performed to socially acceptable standards and this means that homes have to be kept clean and tidy. In the face of such gender conflict, waged labour substitution is one of the few paths forward for certain middle-class households, as well as the only means by which female partners within such households can resolve "their" domestic labour coping crises.

Quality time

In contrast to the circumstances discussed above, our research identified another group of middle-class households substituting waged for unwaged domestic labour – this time to enable them to do something other (and more pleasurable) than domestic work. The following two extracts typify the arguments made by these households:

> Ruth Frazer: And then we both developed definite interests – hobbies. It became, *"This is how I want to spend my time. I want to do this"* [her emphasis]. Time became more valuable. And Mike said, "Let's get someone in to do the cleaning." And I said, "No, we're two adults. If we can't keep this place clean it's a pretty poor show." And this went on for a couple of months. And by then I was virtually convinced. Because Mike was saying, "If you rationalize it, what you're doing is not buying a slave. You're buying time. Because you are paying someone else to do these jobs; jobs which you'd have to do otherwise. So if you want to have your weekend free to do what you want to do then you're going to have to find somebody else to do the dirty work." And that's what we did.

> Ann Harris: It started to be that I was working longer and longer hours. And it meant a certain amount of work over the weekend. So we just thought that we needed time to switch off and just do things together. I was also travelling away from home quite a lot. So the time together became more important. And we wanted to be doing better things with it than brandishing a hoover!!

Faced with perceived pressures on time beyond employment, imposed either by the demands of service-class employment itself or by the development of new hobbies/leisure activities, both the above households are using the concept of "quality time" to shape their constructs of time spent outside paid employment. Time beyond paid employment is seen as a scarcity, to be valued and to be given over to activities that themselves are seen as valuable pursuits. Such activities might include certain domestic tasks (childcare activities – play, outings, reading, etc. – were seen in this light, and so too was cooking, particularly for entertainment), but they just as frequently include other leisure activities, sports and hobbies. Interestingly, and as the above extracts both make clear, cleaning activities – although acknowledged to be important and necessary – are not seen as activities worthy of prime leisure time. Labelled as "dirty" and as work, such activities are constructed as conflicting with middle-class ideas of how time beyond employment ought to be spent.

What's going on here is rather different from the gender conflicts over domestic labour outlined previously. In these middle-class households it is the proliferation in consumption and leisure activities through the 1980s, and the increasing importance of such activities within middle-class identities, that have led to the substitution of waged for unwaged labour (and see, too, Urry in Ch. 12 in this volume). However, it is important to note that substitution is occurring only in relation to specific domestic tasks. These are those tasks deemed to be dirty, time consuming and/or heavy in their labour demands, i.e. cleaning and ironing. In contrast, other domestic tasks are seen as valued, pleasurable activities. Such observations suggest that we may be witnessing the collapse of the post-war association in Britain between *all* women and *all* domestic tasks. Indeed, our research provides evidence for the identification of the more pleasurable domestic tasks with middle-class women (and to some degree their male partners) and the transfer of the dirtiest, heaviest and most physically demanding and/or labour-intensive tasks to working-class women. Apparently, within certain middle-class households in contemporary Britain, a class-mediated hierarchy of domestic tasks is once more being constructed.

In this section on the reconstitution of domestic work within middle-class households, we turn next to look at the social relations of waged domestic employment, using as our example some of the key features of nanny employment within middle-class households.

The social relations of waged domestic labour employment

Although by definition a waged form of domestic labour, and therefore defined through class relations, the social relations of nanny employment are constructed by and shaped through both wage and false kinship relations. Moreover, it is the latter that dominate the day-to-day practices of nanny employment. These false kinship relations involve the families of both employers and employees, and centre around the nanny and the child(ren) being cared for. Thus, nannies were frequently represented to us as "part of the family", while the child(ren) being cared for were frequently seen as pseudo-grandchildren by mothers of nannies (for a full discussion of this, see Gregson & Lowe 1994b).

Why, then, do the social relations of nanny employment take this form? Why is it that such relations are not just class relations, but overlain so heavily by the relations of false kinship? Our explanation rests on two key relations, those between the nanny and child(ren) and those between the nanny and the female partner within the dual-career middle-class household.

To take the nanny–child(ren) relation first. There is little doubt that this relationship is one of deep attachment. Thus, although the nannies we spoke to were well able to articulate in theory the dangers of over-attachment to their employers' child(ren), the bond between the two was manifestly apparent, in terms of both what was said and what was done with children in our presence. Here, for example, are the comments of "Rebecca" and "Louise" on this theme. They are by no means unusual.

> Rebecca: You get really attached to the children. It doesn't matter how hard you try not to, you can't. And even with Neil – I mean I didn't have Neil from a baby, I had him from one – even now I would hate to think of someone else looking after him. And that's what I was thinking when I was due to leave in September. That was on my mind. And I used to think, "Oh, I wouldn't like to see him running up to some other nanny." You know. 'Cause they are just like your own in a sense.

> Louise: It's a weird job. You get so close to them. Like in my first year working here it was horrible when I took holidays. I just didn't want to take any holidays. You know what I mean? I'm alright now. Like I don't mind taking them but in the three weeks when I went away in the summer I really missed them.

In seeing themselves as the specific carers of specific "others", nannies come to see their charges as needing, as being dependent on, themselves, as well as themselves defined in relation to the needs of their charges. As a consequence, the relations that assume importance within nanny employment are those of emotional support and practical care – forms of support that traditionally characterize kin relations.

The second key relation within nanny employment is that between the female partner (mother) and the nanny, and this is also generative of false kinship relations. The key to what is going on here is the construct of the working mother. Given the identification of childcare in contemporary Britain with mothering (rather than with fathering and parenting), forms of childcare that go beyond normative guidelines (mother at home with children) are conceptualized in terms of mother substitution. Many of the female partners we interviewed internalized this construct. They felt that the employment of a nanny enabled them (and not their partners) to work, and in many cases such feelings were cemented by the financial organization of nanny employment (in which it was frequently the female partner's salary that was used to pay the nanny). It is important to be clear about the implications of this for nanny employment. What enablement points to is that the nanny – and specifically one or two particular nannies – come(s) to be seen by women within dual-career middle-class households as the means through which they negotiate working motherhood. As a result, a clear set of "debts" appears to be established, some of which form the basis for the development of feelings of obligation by the female partner towards "her" nanny. As we now show, these feelings of obligation work to produce social relations overlain by false kinship.

As a form of waged labour, part of the debts involved in nanny employment are repaid through the wage relation. Others, however, are emotional. It is here that the feelings of the female partner start to intersect with the relations between the nanny and the child(ren) outlined above. Indeed, we maintain that it is precisely the bond of attachment between the nanny and the child(ren) that works to create feelings of obligation in female partners. Thus, in providing quality childcare, the nanny enables the female partner (at least at the personal level) to negotiate the moral burden (and frequent guilt) heaped on the working mother. For many of the women whom we spoke to, therefore, it became necessary to repay this emotional debt. We consider the false kinship relations that characterized the representation of nanny employment by our female employers to be both a manifestation of this emotional debt and their way of repaying it. Constructing nanny employment on these lines was their way of showing how much they cared about the work their nanny was performing.

If we are to account for how and why the social relations of nanny employment within contemporary Britain come to be constructed in terms of both wage labour and false kinship, but dominated by the latter, we have to recognize the way in which social relations within this occupation are produced by and through the ideology of childcare. The ideology of childcare provides the framework that ensures that nanny employment assumes the form of mother substitution and hence becomes permeated by feelings of attachment and obligation between women. We consider false kinship relations between women to be an almost inevitable consequence. Moreover, this same construction lies behind the marginalization of male partners within the social practices of nanny employment. Conceptualized in terms of mother substitution (rather than parental substitution), nanny employment for men in dual-career households carries none of the connotations of emotional "debt" and obligation discussed above. Instead, for them, the relation is simply one of waged labour – albeit located within their own home and albeit in relation to their child(ren).

The utility of class analysis

So, where does this investigation of the reconstitution of domestic labour within British middle-class households leave us in terms of the utility of class analysis and more particularly the arguments of Gorz? Without doubt, a sensitivity to class

analysis is important to an examination of the waged domestic labour phenomenon within middle-class households in Britain. The expansion in the professional
division of labour, coupled with the growth in women's participation in service-class
occupations, has generated a crisis in day-to-day social reproduction within middle-class households, particularly with respect to childcare. Dual-career middle-
class households simply do not have the time-space to combine full-time parenting
with the demands of (masculinist) career-structured occupations and, as such, they
provide a degree of support for Gorz's thesis that the demands of "work" for the
middle classes are such that they are unable to perform reproductive labour. Moreover, there is little doubt too that reproductive work within the homes of the middle
classes represents one of the few forms of paid employment open to certain (and
particularly benefit-dependent) working-class women. The changing nature of
"work" through the 1980s in Britain, then, has brought with it a fundamental
reworking of the form of middle-class domestic servicing. But, as our research has
shown, there is far more to this reconfiguration than Gorz's arguments about
changes in the occupational class structure, and the demands of careerist employment within the service class. Indeed, as our analysis within British middle-class
households has shown, Gorz's arguments are flawed and partial. Certainly, as our
discussions of quality time reveal, more "performative" versions of class are to be
found amongst middle-class interpretations of domestic labour. As with "performative" readings of gender (Butler 1990), performative accounts of class see class as
something one does, rather than something one is, and as things that are done in
interaction with others. In utilizing the concept of quality time to label certain
domestic tasks as an inappropriate use of their time and to legitimate using part of
their (high) disposable incomes to pay someone else to do this "dirty work", the
middle classes are clearly defining certain facets of domestic labour as outside their
vision of self – for them, doing the cleaning is not part of acting middle-class,
whereas activities such as playing golf or cooking for a dinner party are. If we are
fully to comprehend the increasing incidence of waged domestic labour amongst
the middle classes then, we need a form of class analysis that is sensitive to both
material and performative readings of class. In this respect Gorz's analysis is found
wanting.

But, at the same time, and regardless of the class framework adopted, the substitution of waged domestic labour in middle-class households is not entirely explica-
ble through or reducible to a class lens. As we emphasized above, part of the
resurgence in waged domestic labour in middle-class households – and a very large
part of it at that – is about gender conflict, about middle-class men's inability and
unwillingness to do their full share of all forms of domestic labour and the coping
crises that such attitudes precipitate for their partners, particularly with the onset of
childcare responsibilities. Moreover, when we examine the nature of the social relations of employment within waged domestic labour in middle-class Britain, it is
apparent that a class framework is a very long way from appropriate. Here the
gendering of childcare works to produce relations of employment between women,
and relations that are heavily overlain by those of false kinship rather than those of

class. Rather than interpret the resurgence of waged domestic labour in middle-class households in terms of either a class framework or a gender framework, we prefer an approach that acknowledges the importance of both but that privileges neither. Indeed, to attempt to say that class is more important than gender, or gender more important than class, would be to miss the point that the form of domestic labour within middle-class households is constituted simultaneously by and through class and gender relations and identities, as well as something that is negotiated by partners within specific households.

9.6   Implications for middle-class politics and middle-class formation

Moving on, what about the politics that infuse and shape the resurgence of waged domestic labour within middle-class households? At one level it is important to stress that the waged domestic labour solution to the crisis in day-to-day social reproduction within middle-class households is one that is firmly embedded in the politics of Thatcherism. This is a market solution to domestic servicing and an individual solution, in that it is individual middle-class households (rather than the state or employers) who are constructing this particular solution to the general need for household domestic servicing. Moreover, waged domestic labour itself is totally unregulated (employers are able to determine wages and conditions of employment and employees have no recourse to collective bargaining). But to label the politics of those employing waged domestic labour as "Thatcherite" would be ingenuous. Rather, what we encountered in the course of our research was a diverse range of middle-class households, some positioned in accordance with the values of the New Right, others very much opposed to these. For the former group, the market solution was something they very much favoured. The latter group, however, articulated their situation (and particularly their situation in relation to childcare) as one of no political choice: they found themselves compelled to employ waged domestic labour in order to reproduce the dual-career pattern of employment. At a more general level, such comments testify to the gender politics of service-class employment through the 1980s in Britain. Women can participate within service-class employment, but they can do so only as honorary men, with household domestic labour needs and requirements (be these childcare related or other) remaining invisible, unarticulated and unacknowledged.

We remain convinced that the careerist forms of employment found within service-class occupations are in the interests of neither women nor men and that restructuring the nature of service-class employment is a political project of the utmost importance. However, to explain the resurgence in waged domestic labour entirely in terms of the nature of service-class employment would be misplaced. As we have stressed here, the resurgence of waged domestic labour in middle-class Britain also reflects middle-class men's unwillingness to perform a sizeable share of domestic labour. It is therefore the gender politics of domestic labour that we feel need addressing. And it is here, unfortunately, that we came up with some of the most depressing of our research findings. Thus, rather than identify their partners as central to their household's domestic labour crisis, most of the middle-class women we spoke to presented the situation in terms of *their* failings and the employment of waged domestic labour as the means of enabling *themselves* to cope with full-time service-class employment and the social reproduction of the household. Rather than expressing progressive views on the gender division of labour then, many of the middle-class women who currently employ waged domestic labour (and their male partners) seem to hold extremely traditional views on the gender politics of domestic work. Moreover, women who did not hold such views and who were prepared to criticize men in general (and specific men at that) were extremely pessimistic: men could be identified as the problem, but getting them to change was an entirely different proposition. Ultimately, what the resurgence in waged domestic labour amongst the middle classes of contemporary Britain signifies is: the extent to which many middle-class men continue to hold on to very traditional constructs of domestic labour; the degree to which many middle-class women collude in this; and the pervasiveness of the traditional form of the domestic division of labour amongst the middle classes. Employment of waged domestic labour is but one variant of all of this. Such findings provide a useful counter to those arguments that stress the radical (anti-capitalist) nature of middle-class politics (Ehrenreich & Ehrenreich 1979).

Finally, what are the implications of this research for debates on middle-class formation? Following Davidoff & Hall (1987), Savage et al. (1992) argue that gender relations were central to the constitution of middle-class identities and middle-class culture in the nineteenth century. Moreover, they go on to suggest that shared gender practices (notably the identification of the "public" and "private" with middle-class men and women respectively) potentially enabled middle-class formation through the nineteenth century – serving to counter the parallel tendency for differing middle-class male career patterns and identities based on cultural and organizational assets to emerge. Commonality, the basis for social collectivity and for class formation, is seen by Savage et al. to be created as much in the middle-class home as in the labour market. We endorse such remarks wholeheartedly, as well as Savage et al.'s extension of these arguments to the middle class in immediate post-war Britain, in which, despite the difference between organizational and occupational careers, dependency on female kin for domestic and career servicing was a common feature of middle-class formation (Kanter 1993, Finch 1983). However, whether it is as appropriate to see the same degree of commonality in contemporary middle-class formation is more doubtful. Indeed, different middle-class strategies are currently as much in evidence within the home as they are in the labour market, with commonality in middle-class domestic servicing seemingly having disappeared. With increasing levels of full-time female labour force participation in middle-class occupations and the associated proliferation in middle-class household forms, so diverse middle-class strategies regarding domestic servicing have emerged. Indeed, as we have shown here, a sizeable fraction of the contemporary middle class use their considerable financial assets to purchase waged domestic labour, particularly in relation to childcare and labour-intensive domestic tasks. Others, meanwhile, continue to service themselves. Taken with the suggested increasing differentiation between professional and managerial sections of the contemporary British middle class, such tendencies point towards a dissolution in middle-*class* formation, growing divisions amongst the middle *classes* within Britain, and the forestalling of service-class formation.

Acknowledgements

The empirical research on which this chapter draws was funded by the Economic and Social Research Council (Grant number 000232817) between 1991 and 1993. Thanks to all the Danbury Park participants, and particularly to Mike Savage and Doreen Massey for their comments. The usual disclaimers apply.

Notes

1. As a result of women's increasing levels of participation in service-class occupations, such households are now more prevalent than in the period during which earlier research on the "dual-career family" was conducted (Rapoport & Rapoport 1971, Hunt & Hunt 1977, 1982, Bailyn 1978).
2. Labour Force Survey (1993: Table 7). Although not disaggregated by socio-economic group, these data reveal reductions in the hours of men and women in full-time and part-time work, as well as in the working hours of the self-employed.
3. Pahl (1984) shows instances of the various domestic labour strategies used by working-class households with multiple forms of employment. Further confirmation of the limited use of waged domestic labour by working-class households came in the pilot stages of our research, in which survey work revealed dual-career households with both partners in full-time service-class employment, households with both partners in service-class employment but with the female partner working part-time; and professional single-parent households as the "users" of waged domestic labour. Of these it is the first category of household that predominates.
4. It is important to emphasize that advertisement data are subject to the problem of variable turnover.
5. Households employing waged domestic labour span the various sections within the middle class and include those working in professional and managerial occupations within both the public and private sectors.
6. See, for example, research conducted by Gallup in 1990 (*Guardian*, 6 February 1990).
7. It should not be inferred from these findings that we regard the household cleaning labour force as exclusively this; in certain areas of Britain for example, notably parts of London, anecdotal evidence points to women of colour working as household cleaners.
8. For research on nineteenth-century domestic service in Britain, see Davidoff (1974, 1983), Higgs (1983, 1986), Jamieson (1990), Peterson (1972), Roberts (1984, 1988).

Part Four

Place, space and class

The study of the relationship between class and place has undergone something of a revivial in recent years after a long period of neglect. Increasingly, in the years after the Second World War, research on social class tended not to be based upon case studies of particular places, but increasingly shifted towards random national sample surveys which tended to lose sight of any possible significance of "locale". This is especially true of studies of social mobility, such as Glass (1954) and Goldthorpe (1980a), neither of which were interested in patterns of migration or the influence of local factors in social mobility.

The dominance of national sample surveys went hand in hand with the idea that class structures were primarily "national" in character, an idea that was championed by C. Wright Mills (1959) and has more recently been justified theoretically by Michael Mann (1993) who has explored the way that class and national identities are intertwined. However, from the early 1980s a number of social geographers began to suggest that class formation need not necessarily take place at the level of the nation. The Marxist geographer Doreen Massey (1984) played a large part in developing this interest. She coined the phrase of a "spatial division of labour" within Britain and argued that economic restructuring involved the use of space to reorder the division of labour in manufacturing and services. Some of the old industrial areas (such as the north-east of England, Scotland and Wales) had become the centres simply of assembly line production, whereas by contrast there had been a concentration of research and development activities around London and the Home Counties. Massey argued that this geography of production played an important role in defining distinct geographies of class.

Furthermore, a number of writers began to suggest that class identities were not always national but could be defined at different spatial scales. The idea of the "working class community" had always suggested that working class identities could be based on local ties (see Gilbert 1992). The middle classes, by contrast, were frequently regarded as more mobile, and hence less localized, though Watson & Bell suggested one central division within the middle classes was between "burgesses" and "spiralists". A number of questions were raised by these observations.

The extent to which common patterns of spatial mobility tend to unify or fragment the middle classes compared to other social classes is discussed by Fielding, who examines the inter-regional migration of various groups of middle class individuals. Butler examines the way in which inner-city residence can be linked to a particular form of middle-class culture. The extent to which middle-class identification is based on common appreciation of particular places is taken up by Urry and by Cloke et al. They consider the question of the middle classes and the countryside. The British middle classes tend to be strongly identified with a countryside tradition which endorses rural living, active outdoor pursuits, and so forth. As Urry discusses, the influential work of Howard Newby even argued that the middle classes were the key agents in transforming the countryside in recent years. Both these papers critically examine these arguments, and in the process make some important observations about the relevance of class itself. Some of the general issues are also taken up by Massey in Chapter 19.

Chapter 10

Migration and middle-class formation in England and Wales, 1981–91

Tony Fielding

10.1 Introduction

This chapter draws heavily upon recently available information from the Longitudinal Study for 1981–91 of the Office of Population Censuses and Surveys (OPCS). Its prime focus is to explore the nature of the "missing link" between social mobility and geographical mobility (Savage 1988) in the 1980s. More specifically, it examines the role that interregional migration plays in the intragenerational social mobilities of men and women in contemporary Britain. This has been a surprisingly difficult area to investigate in the past. The reasons for this include, first, the academic division of labour whereby sociologists have studied social mobility and geographers and demographers have studied geographical mobility, and, secondly, the lack of suitable data for the whole population at a national level. Empirical studies have been either very local, and have therefore raised doubts about the validity of the results for other places, or cohort-specific, and have therefore raised doubts about the validity of the results for other times and other generations.

It has recently been recognized that data from the Longitudinal Study (LS) can provide valuable answers to these questions, and section 10.2 of this paper explains why. Section 10.3 explores in some detail the LS data for 1981–91 and offers evidence on key relationships and processes linking social mobility and spatial mobility, class and region. Section 10.4 compares the results for 1981–91 with those obtained previously for 1971–81, to see whether or not the 1980s were as socially distinctive as they are so often claimed to be. The final section reflects upon the significance of the results obtained here for the wider debates about the nature of the middle classes in contemporary Britain.

10.2 The Longitudinal Study

The general issue investigated by this paper – what is the role of interregional migration in the intragenerational social mobilities of men and women in contemporary Britain? – can be broken down into a number of researchable issues relevant to the main theme of this book. These are:

(a) Is there a relationship between intragenerational social mobility on the one hand and interregional geographical mobility on the other? Are those who are more geographically mobile likely also to be more socially mobile?

(b) How are the middle classes formed? For example, where (socially and geographically) in 1981 were those people who were members of the three middle classes (professionals, managers and petits bourgeois) in 1991?

(c) Once formed, how geographically mobile are the members of the three middle classes? Are professionals more or less mobile than managers? And how does middle-class spatial mobility compare with working-class spatial mobility?

(d) How stable are middle-class memberships? Where (socially and geographically) do people go when they cease to be professionals, managers and petits bourgeois?

(e) Are certain places more important in middle-class formation than others? Specifically, does the South East region (roughly equivalent to the extended city-region of London) play a special role in the construction of middle-class careers?

(f) Do men and women face similar "geographies of opportunity" or are there gender differences in the spatial patterns of social mobility? If the patterns are different, how does this affect the benefits from migration for men and women?

The answers to these questions can be obtained through analyses of the OPCS's Longitudinal Study dataset. The LS is a 1% sample of the whole population of England and Wales. One becomes a member of the LS sample by having a birthday on one of four specific days in the year (thus the sample is slightly over 1% – 1.096% to be exact). The census records for these LS members are linked. This means that (although full confidentiality is maintained throughout) we can know all that the census tells us about a person at one census, and all that the census tells us about that same person at the next census. The LS is not, therefore, a true longitudinal study; it is rather a linked census–record study. The LS numbers are maintained between censuses by adding babies born on those four birth dates, and by subtracting the deaths that occur among the population of LS members.

What this means for studies of the middle classes is that we can know where, in terms of both class and region, the members of the middle classes at the time of the latest census were located at the time of the previous census (or where the members of the middle classes at the time of the previous census were located at the time of the latest census). We do not, of course, know what happened to these LS members in the interval between the censuses, and for this reason we do not know how closely connected in time are the recorded changes in social class and changes in region of residence. Nevertheless, for the first time in Britain (and possibly in the world) we have data drawn from a very large sample (about 500,000 individuals) that allow us to explore in very great detail the associations between social mobility on the one hand and geographical mobility on the other.

10.3 Migration and middle-class formation in England and Wales 1981–91

The relationship between social mobility and spatial mobility

Our first task is to establish whether there is evidence of an association between migration and social mobility in England and Wales for the period 1981–91. To carry out this task we need to examine transitions between social classes for the whole population (Tables 10.1a, b), and transitions between social classes for interregional migrants only (not reproduced here). Table 10.1a gives the raw data for LS member social class transitions between 1981 and 1991. Table 10.1b shows, as a percentage of each origin class in 1981, the distribution of destination classes in 1991 (labour market destinations only). Each percentage can, of course, be interpreted as a likelihood or probability. Thus there is a 69% chance that someone who was a professional in 1981, would (if he or she were still in the labour market) be a professional also in 1991.

Table 10.1 tells us a great deal about social change in England and Wales. Notice,

Table 10.1 Social class transitions for the total population of England and Wales, 1981–91 (1.096% sample).

	Social class in 1991						
Social class in 1981	PRO	MAN	PB	PWC	PBC	UE	TLM
(a) absolute numbers							
Professionals	14,868	2,930	733	1,244	1,177	595	21,547
Managers	2,132	7,575	1,634	1,655	1,151	683	14,830
Petite bourgeoisie	445	738	7,272	614	1,192	554	10,815
White collar	3,346	5,340	2,083	21,086	4,796	1,728	38,379
Blue collar	2,466	3,131	5,446	4,063	35,875	4,859	55,840
Unemployed	809	611	1,366	1,467	3,780	3,366	11,399
Education	8,971	4,949	2,483	18,431	15,477	9,960	60,271
Other	2,328	1,175	1,531	8,603	5,335	1,364	20,336
Total	35,365	26,449	22,548	57,163	68,783	23,109	233,417
(b) percentages							
Professionals	69.00	13.60	3.40	5.77	5.46	2.76	100.00
Managers	14.38	51.08	11.02	11.16	7.76	4.61	100.00
Petite bourgeoisie	4.11	6.82	67.24	5.68	11.02	5.12	100.00
White collar	8.72	13.91	5.43	54.94	12.50	4.50	100.00
Blue collar	4.42	5.61	9.75	7.28	64.25	8.70	100.00
Unemployed	7.10	5.36	11.98	12.87	33.16	29.53	100.00
Education	14.88	8.21	4.12	30.58	25.68	16.53	100.00
Other	11.45	5.78	7.53	42.30	26.23	6.71	100.00
Total	15.15	11.33	9.66	24.49	29.47	9.90	100.00

Source: OPCS Longitudinal Study 1991 (Crown Copyright Reserved).

Abbreviations used in Tables

PRO = professionals (SEGs 3, 4 and 5.1 plus 1.1); MAN = managers (SEGs 1.2 and 2.2); PB = petite bourgeoisie (SEGs 2.1, 12, 13 and 14); PWC = low-level white-collar workers (SEGs 5.2, 6 and 7); PBC = blue collar workers (SEGs 8, 9, 10, 11 and 15 plus 17); UE = unemployed; TLM = total in labour market; TOT = total (labour market and non-labour market); ED = education; OT = other (including armed forces); RT = retired; DD = dead.

for example, the relatively high stability of the professional and petite bourgeoisie classes compared with that of the managerial middle class. It is also interesting to see how the managerial middle class recruits more from low-level white-collar workers than does the professional middle class, and that managers are much more subject to downward mobility into working-class occupations and into unemployment than are professionals. Most distinctive of all is the difference between managers and professionals when it comes to switching into the petite bourgeoisie. Managers are more than three times as likely to make this move than professionals. Finally, the older average ages of managers and the petite bourgeoisie compared with professionals can be seen from the lower entry rates from education.

Table 10.2 indicates the interregional migration rates of different social groups. If all the values in Table 10.2 were 100 or thereabouts, it would indicate that there was no relationship between social mobility and spatial mobility. As it is, the values are far from being consistently around 100. It can be seen that the values in the diagonals (93, 102, 63, 76, 64 and 82) are mostly below, indeed well below, 100. In contrast, most of the values away from the diagonals are well above 100. It is difficult to overstate the significance of this result; it means that those who remained in the same class (the social class stayers) were less geographically mobile than the average for that class, while those who were inter-class movers were more mobile than the average for that class. Thus social mobility and geographical mobility *are* positively related to one another: those who change their class locations are also likely to change their geographical locations.

Table 10.2 Interregional migration rates for each social class transition (standardized to class of origin in 1981 = 100),

| Social class in 1981 | Social class in 1991 | | | | | | |
	PRO	MAN	PB	PWC	PBC	UE	TLM
Professionals	93	131	125	107	67	128	100
Managers	114	102	100	82	75	122	100
Petite bourgeoisie	173	171	63	208	144	215	100
White collar	146	145	161	76	76	162	100
Blue collar	249	208	155	133	64	131	100
Unemployed	207	163	99	129	72	82	100

Source: OPCS Longitudinal Study 1991 (Crown Copyright reserved). *Abbreviations:* see Table 10.1.

The social and geographical origins of middle class members

The next step in this analysis is to enquire into middle-class formation. The LS can provide us with evidence relating to the social and geographical origins in 1981 of those people who were members of one of the three middle classes in 1991. To obtain the data, all one needs to do is to express each cell value in Table 10.1a as a percentage of its column total (this table is not presented here) and then calculate the proportion of people making that transition who were also interregional migrants. The principal results of this exercise are as follows.

Professionals

Professionals in 1991 were drawn from two main groups, those who were professionals also in 1981 (42%) and those who were in education in 1981 (25%). Of much less significance as origins were the white-collar working class (9%), and the blue-collar working class, others and managers (all at 6–7%). The geographical mobility of those who were professionals in 1991 was exceptionally high at 17%, but one figure stands head and shoulders above the rest: 30% of those who entered professional jobs from education had migrated interregionally since 1981. Thus professional people tend to be social class "stayers" and include in their number a very high proportion of spatially mobile young adults.

Managers

Managers in 1991 were drawn from a much wider range of groups than were professionals. Only 29% of them were also managers in 1981, 20% had been promoted from the white-collar working class, 19% from education, 12% from the blue-collar working class, and 11% from professionals. Thus both upwards mobility from the working class and sideways mobility from the other half of the "service class" contributed to the making of the managerial population in 1991. The spatial mobility of managers (14%) was lower than that of professionals but still high in comparison with the rest of the population. Those coming from education were the most geographically mobile (22%), but those moving from professional jobs to managerial ones were also highly mobile (17%).

Petits bourgeois

Members of the petite bourgeoisie were drawn from two main groups, the petite bourgeoisie themselves (32%) and the blue collar working class (24%). This latter figure was much higher than I expected, and contrasts with the situation in the 1971–81 period (see below). The petite bourgeoisie always was a highly diverse group, but the evidence from the 1991 LS suggests that its working-class component has become so great in the recent period that it may now be necessary to question its status as a middle class category. The spatial mobility of those in the petite bourgeoisie in 1991 was much lower than that of professionals and managers, and, at 8%, was even slightly below that for all those in the labour market. Those who were also in the petite bourgeoisie in 1981 were exceptionally immobile at under 4%. In this respect petits bourgeois are unlike either professionals or managers since both of the latter had spatial mobilities of their social class "stayers" that were only slightly lower than their averages. Conversely, the spatial mobility of those who entered the petite bourgeoisie was high at 11–12% for managers, white-collar workers and others, and at 17% for professionals.

The spatial mobility of the three middle classes in context

The analysis of spatial mobility begun in the last section can be extended using Table 10.3. This shows the interregional migration rates for all six social classes

Table 10.3 Interregional migration rates by social class (England and Wales = 100) (1.096% sample).

| | Population No. | Interregional migration rates | | |
		Population %	In LM in 1991	In LM in '81 and '91	In LM in same class
Professionals	35,365	15.15	185	162	204
Managers	26,449	11.33	151	159	195
Petite bourgeoisie	22,548	9.66	85	94	59
White collar	57,163	24.49	89	89	96
Blue collar	68,783	29.47	52	50	46
Unemployed	23,109	9.90	95	112	121
Total	233,417	100.00	100	100	100

Source: OPCS Longitudinal Study 1991 (Crown Copyright reserved). *Abbreviations*: see Table 10.1.

used in this work. But it calculates these rates for three different, but overlapping, groups. The largest consists of all those in the six classes at the time of the 1991 census. The next largest excludes those who were out of the labour market (LM) in 1981. The smallest excludes, in addition to this, those who were inter-class movers between 1981 and 1991. All rates are relative to the England and Wales average (=100).

The figures in Table 10.3 are highly revealing. The data in the third column show that the members of the "service class" of professionals and managers are much more spatially mobile than are other groups in the population. The mobility of the unemployed is (to the frustration and even disbelief of the neoclassical economists) below the average, the low-level white-collar employees and the members of the petite bourgeoisie are rather immobile, and the blue-collar working class are highly immobile. The data in column four (which, unlike those from column 3, are not derivable from ordinary census data) show that, for those who were in the labour market in both 1981 and 1991, the interregional migration rates are slightly different. Professionals and managers are now much more alike in their mobilities, and the value for the unemployed now exceeds the average. The reasons for this shift are that the professional occupations are supplied by large numbers of highly spatially mobile youngsters (as discussed in the previous section), and that interregional migration is also associated with downward social mobility into unemployment as well as upwards social mobility into the middle classes (as is shown, for example, in column six of Table 10.3).

It is the final column of Table 10.3, however, that is the most novel and the most significant. This shows the spatial mobility of those who were social class stayers, that is, those who were in the same class in 1981 as in 1991. This is, one could say, a "true" measure of class-specific geographical mobility. The spatial mobilities of the professionals and the managers remain very similar to each other but are now much higher than before at around twice the average interregional mobility. At the other extreme, blue-collar working-class mobility decreases to less than half the average. The figure for the unemployed is now distinctly higher than the average, but the mobility of the petite bourgeoisie becomes very low at 59% of the average. This last figure, taken together with those in the other two columns, can be interpreted to mean that people are geographically mobile into the petite bourgeoisie but are immobile within it. These figures are conformable with early work on the contrasts within the membership of the middle classes between burgesses or "locals", on the one hand, and cosmopolitans or "spiralists" on the other (see, for example, Bell 1968).

The social and geographical destinations of middle class members

From data already presented in this chapter we have seen that the three middle classes differ in the stability of their memberships. The most stable in terms of class stability are professionals, followed by the petits bourgeois, with the managers as the least stable. In terms of geographical mobility, it is the petite bourgeoisie who are the most stable, followed at a distance by the managers and professionals. We can now use the LS to discover what happens to the members of these classes after the passage of 10 years. The main results are as follows.

Professionals

Professionals predominantly stay as professionals (52%), but if they change they move either into retirement (17%) or into management (10%). Very few move to unemployment, to the petite bourgeoisie, or to the white-collar or blue-collar sections of the working class. They are highly geographically mobile both as social class stayers and as movers, but, in particular, they migrate between regions when they change to become managers, members of the petite bourgeoisie or unemployed (all at around 17%), or when they retire (12%). Highly significant, however, is the high migration rate (22%) for those who enter the category "other". This refers largely to women who in 1981 were professionals but who in 1991 were in full-time domestic work. It appears that women often migrate interregionally as they leave the labour force to look after children or elderly relatives.

Managers

Only just over one third (36%) of the managers in 1981 were still managers in 1991. The remainder distributed themselves widely between retirement (21%), professional occupations (10%), and the white-collar working class and petite bourgeoisie (both 8%). The category "others" also figures prominently for the percentage of interregional migrants among the managers (16%), but so too do the transitions to unemployment (14%), to professional occupations (13%), and to retirement and the petite bourgeoisie (both 12%). So, once again, the managers and professionals have a lot in common in their social and geographical mobility regimes, but the managers are a little less spatially mobile and much less stable – their sideways and downward mobility rates are considerably greater than those of professionals.

Petite bourgeoisie

The social and geographical destinations of the petite bourgeoisie are highly distinctive. Almost half of them (49%) remain in the same class and are highly geographically immobile. The principal alternative destinations are retirement (17%), the blue-collar working class (8%) and death (7%). In both of the latter cases the rates are much higher than for the service class members, as is the movement to unemployment. Members of the petite bourgeoisie are especially unlikely to become professionals, white-collar workers or managers (all below 5%). As for spatial mobility, petits bourgeois are distinctive in having high migration rates only for transitions into working-class categories; the rates for transitions to unemployment and to the white-collar working class are the highest figures at around 12%.

Some of the differences between the middle classes listed above are interpretable as reflections of the differing age and gender compositions of these classes, but most of the differences can be explained only in terms of contrasts in the nature and security of employment within those classes.

South East England as an "escalator" region

So far the analysis presented here has been couched in terms of structures and relationships. Now it is time to speculate about some of the processes that lie behind these statistics. This subsection explores the role of regional context in middle-class formation, while the next subsection investigates the difference that gender makes.

The idea that the South East is an "escalator" region involves examining the following conditions (see Fielding 1992a for a full development of this concept): (a) the South-East must attract, through interregional migration, a large number of potentially upwardly mobile young people at the time when they are entering the labour market; (b) these in-migrants, along with the long-term residents of the region, must be promoted at rates that are distinctly above those for England and Wales as a whole; and (c) the South East must lose a significant proportion of those so promoted through out-migration to other regions at later stages of their working lives, or at, or near to, retirement. These three conditions represent the three stages within the "up" escalator metaphor – stepping on the escalator, being taken up to a higher level by the escalator, and stepping off the escalator.

On the first of these points, Table 10.4 provides evidence on the social composition of the in-migration stream. It was constructed in the following way: (1) each social class transition in the in-migration stream to the South East region was expressed as a percentage of the whole in-migration stream; (2) each social class transition in the matrix of all interregional migrants in England and Wales was expressed as a percentage of the total interregional migrants; and (3) the former percentages were expressed as ratios of the latter. Thus, where a ratio (or dyadic location quotient) of 1.00 occurs, the social composition of the in-migration stream to the South East is the same as for all interregional migrants; a figure above 1.00 indicates a stronger presence of this transition in the stream to the South East; a figure of less than 1.00 indicates a weaker presence.

Table 10.4 The social composition of in-migrants to the South East region from elsewhere in England and Wales (standardized to all interregional migrants, i.e. location quotients).

Social class in 1981	Social class in 1991									
	PRO	MAN	PB	PWC	PBC	UE	TLM	RT	OT	TOT
PRO	0.98	1.18	0.57	1.02	0.94	1.10	1.01	0.32	0.84	0.89
MAN	1.17	1.03	0.37	0.91	0.77	0.34	0.91	0.31	0.78	0.78
PB	0.75	0.97	0.50	1.07	1.13	1.03	0.80	0.45	0.61	0.70
PWC	1.20	1.15	0.75	1.05	0.82	0.92	1.03	0.26	0.76	0.83
PBC	1.26	1.16	0.78	1.24	0.78	0.82	0.93	0.24	0.58	0.72
UE	1.69	1.64	1.38	1.51	1.39	1.18	1.43	0.50	0.79	1.15
TLM	1.09	1.12	0.70	1.10	0.90	0.92	1.01	0.31	0.74	0.83
ED	1.69	2.05	1.40	1.63	1.28	1.17	1.61	0.78	1.35	1.26
OT	1.02	1.09	0.72	0.90	0.80	0.84	0.89	0.61	0.85	0.80
TOT	1.35	1.39	0.80	1.29	1.00	1.02	1.21	0.60	0.94	1.00

Source: OPCS Longitudinal Study 1991 (Crown Copyright reserved). *Abbreviations:* see Table 10.1.

By inspecting the final column of Table 10.4 we can see the social origins of the migrants to the South East region. They were to be found amongst those in education in 1981 (26% above the England and Wales average) and amongst those who were unemployed in 1981 (15% above the average). Thus, the migrants towards the South East are indeed biased towards young people and towards those trying to enter the labour market (the location quotient for the total labour market was 0.83, showing that the migrants were biased towards those who were not already in the labour market). So much for their social origins outside the South East, but what about their social class destinations within the South East? The figures in the bottom row of the table provide this information. It can be seen that these young migrants to the South East were predominantly going into the labour market (1.21), and especially into managerial, professional and lower-level white-collar jobs. The three highest figures in the whole table are for those moving from education to managerial occupations (2.05), and from education and unemployment to professional occupations (1.69). The picture presented by these data is very clear: the migrants to the South East are precisely those expected on the basis of the escalator concept.

We can therefore turn to the second requirement, which is that the social mobility rates for non-migrants be distinctly more favourable to upward social mobility in the South East than elsewhere in the country. The evidence for this is provided by Table 10.5. The data in this table were generated by dividing the transition probabilities for the South East region by those for England and Wales. So, as before, a figure of 1.00 means no difference; above 1.00 means that the South East is biased in that direction; below 1.00 means away from that direction. The most obvious feature of Table 10.5 is the clustering of the values that are over 1.00 on the left-hand side of the table, and of those less than 1.00 on the right. This expresses the general bias in the South East towards higher than average rates of social mobility into the middle-class categories and lower than average rates of mobility into the working-class categories.

Table 10.5 The social mobility of non-migrants in South East England (standardized to non-migrants in England and Wales, i.e. location quotients).

Social class in 1981	Social class in 1991						
	PRO	MAN	PB	PWC	PBC	UE	TLM
Professionals	0.97	1.17	1.04	1.04	0.90	1.17	1.00
Managers	1.03	1.02	1.01	0.98	0.84	1.01	1.00
Petite bourgeoisie	1.22	1.23	0.94	1.13	0.95	1.30	1.00
White collar	1.07	1.15	1.01	0.98	0.84	1.07	1.00
Blue collar	1.15	1.26	1.17	1.16	0.93	0.97	1.00
Unemployed	1.44	1.34	1.19	1.19	0.84	0.88	1.00
Education	1.23	1.40	1.08	1.09	0.78	0.83	1.00
Other	1.15	1.27	0.95	1.08	0.80	0.92	1.00

Source: OPCS Longitudinal Study 1991 (Crown Copyright reserved). *Abbreviations*: see Table 10.1.

In the case of professionals, it is only the social class stayers who are less represented in the South East than in England and Wales. It is tempting to speculate that this is due to the fact that public sector professionals can make their nationally negotiated incomes stretch further outside the South East than within it (notwithstanding the London weighting) (see Mohan 1989). Those who were in working-class categories in 1981, or in education, or even in "others" all experienced higher rates of upward social mobility into professional occupations than the average for England and Wales. The rates were particularly high for those coming from unemployment (1.44, but a small category), and from education (1.23 and a very large category).

For managers, all of the values are greater than 1.00; so the intra-regional movement into managerial occupations is greater in the South East than in England and Wales for all origin social class categories. It is significant that the highest rate of all (1.40) is for the large group of people making the transition from education in 1981 to a managerial job in 1991.

The situation for the petits bourgeois is quite different. Most of the figures are around 1.00, but the value for petite bourgeoisie stayers is less than 1.00, and the two cases where the values are distinctly above 1.00 are the "working-class" categories of blue-collar workers and the unemployed. It seems as though the "proletarianization" of the petite bourgeoisie might be even more pronounced in the South East region than elsewhere in the country. This result probably reflects differences in work cultures, but the significant number of Asian households may also be a contributing factor (Fielding 1995).

The evidence from Table 10.5 supports the view that the South East region is particularly privileged when it comes to upward social mobility into "service class" occupations. It is also a region of "sideways" mobility between the middle classes, and especially so from professional jobs to managerial ones. Thus, the second requirement of the "escalator" concept is met: people tend to achieve more rapid social promotion in the South East than elsewhere in England and Wales.

The final stage in the escalator process refers to out-migration. Does the South

Table 10.6 The social composition of out-migrants from the South East region to elsewhere in England and Wales (standardized to all interregional migrants, i.e. location quotients).

Social class in 1981	Social class in 1991									
	PRO	MAN	PB	PWC	PBC	UE	TLM	RT	OT	TOT
PRO	0.98	0.95	1.39	1.17	1.06	1.01	1.00	1.66	1.22	1.12
MAN	1.16	1.02	1.38	1.23	1.46	1.46	1.15	1.75	1.27	1.28
PB	1.26	0.73	1.22	0.76	1.01	1.22	1.08	1.35	0.85	1.13
PWC	0.96	0.99	1.49	0.95	1.29	1.30	1.06	1.93	1.34	1.29
PBC	0.81	0.85	1.16	0.71	0.95	1.00	0.94	1.74	1.09	1.16
UE	0.47	0.68	0.91	0.65	0.60	0.82	0.69	1.24	0.73	0.81
TLM	0.96	0.95	1.27	0.93	0.99	1.08	1.00	1.71	1.18	1.17
ED	0.52	0.40	0.67	0.58	0.77	0.83	0.59	1.06	0.65	0.78
OT	0.99	0.94	1.05	0.92	0.98	0.82	0.95	1.30	1.06	1.09
TOT	0.76	0.79	1.16	0.78	0.92	0.95	0.85	1.30	0.99	1.00

Source: OPCS Longitudinal Study 1991 (Crown Copyright reserved). *Abbreviations*: see Table 10.1.

East region show the expected properties of middle-class out-migration to retirement and to other middle-class jobs, in other regions of England and Wales? To help us decide on this issue we can turn to Table 10.6. This table has exactly the same form as Table 10.4. It records the class-transition specificity of the migration flow from the South East in comparison with all interregional migrants in England and Wales. The data in the final column tell us from which class categories in the South East region the out-migrants are drawn. It can be seen that they come from all parts of the labour market except unemployment, and that the rates for white-collar workers and managers are particularly high. The bottom row indicates which categories the migrants enter as they settle in regions outside the South East. Retirement figures prominently, as was expected, but the other figure that is greater than 1.00 is the petite bourgeoisie. If we look up this column we notice that it is people leaving white-collar jobs, the professions and managerial jobs who are particularly likely to enter the petite bourgeoisie after they leave the South East region.

Other interesting features of Table 10.6 are the low total destination rates for professionals and managers. On closer inspection, however, it can be seen that this arises not because of any lack of out-migration of professional and managerial "stayers" but because of the very low incidence of entry into the professions or management from education. In fact, the preponderance of low figures for exits from education is a strong indication of the older average ages of those leaving the South East region. Given the differentials in promotion prospects discussed above, it would, of course, be generally disadvantageous for a young person to leave the South East at the time when he or she was entering the labour market.

The picture is now complete. In every respect, the data from the LS support the view that the South East region acted as an (upward) social class escalator region in the 1980s.

Gender differences in social and spatial mobility

A full regional analysis of gender-specific social mobility rates (equivalent to that reported in Fielding & Halford 1993) has not yet been undertaken. So this section concentrates on just three aspects of the topic: (a) the general situation, in which the social mobility rates for men and women for the whole of England and Wales will be compared; (b) the situation in South East England, to see if the upward social mobility regime there is the same for men and for women; and (c) the social mobility that accompanies migration to and from the South East, to see if such migrations imply different career prospects for men and for women.

Table 10.7 is equivalent to Table 10.1b. The data show the probability of a man or a woman making specific social class transitions over the 1981–91 period. There are some striking differences between the sexes. Notice, for example, the much higher rate of promotion of men from the low-level white-collar jobs to the service class of professionals and managers, the much higher rate of promotion of men from the three working-class categories to the petite bourgeoisie, and the much higher rate of "sideways" movement of men into managerial positions from the professions (usually considered to be associated with a promotion). On the other hand, the table also shows the higher rate of movement of women from working-class jobs into the professions, and lower rates of movement into unemployment (though there are problems of definition here). The figures show the higher stability of middle-class membership of men, the higher stability of working-class membership of women, the higher upward mobility from the working class to the middle

Table 10.7   Social class transitions for men and women, England and Wales 1981–91 (equivalent to Table 10.1b).

Social class in 1981	Social class in 1991						
	PRO	MAN	PB	PWC	PBC	UE	TLM
(a) Males							
Professionals	63.45	18.63	4.01	4.04	6.56	3.31	100.00
Managers	13.91	54.16	11.58	7.41	8.12	4.82	100.00
Petite bourgeoisie	3.58	6.70	70.67	2.27	11.15	5.63	100.00
White collar	12.09	23.67	7.96	38.12	12.39	5.76	100.00
Blue collar	4.39	6.17	11.23	3.73	65.23	9.26	100.00
Unemployed	5.52	5.25	14.43	5.16	35.91	33.72	100.00
Education	13.90	8.30	6.08	16.50	35.90	19.32	100.00
Other	12.13	10.99	11.11	14.34	33.33	18.10	100.00
(b) Females							
Professionals	77.40	5.99	2.48	8.39	3.80	1.93	100.00
Managers	16.52	36.83	8.41	28.50	6.10	3.64	100.00
Petite bourgeoisie	7.03	7.51	48.41	24.38	10.33	2.34	100.00
White collar	7.24	9.65	4.32	62.30	12.54	3.95	100.00
Blue collar	4.55	3.18	3.35	22.66	60.00	6.26	100.00
Unemployed	11.78	5.68	4.70	35.78	24.98	17.07	100.00
Education	16.06	8.10	1.80	47.28	13.55	13.21	100.00
Other	11.39	5.31	7.21	44.81	25.60	5.69	100.00

Source: OPCS Longitudinal Study 1991 (Crown Copyright reserved). *Abbreviations*: see Table 10.1.

class for men, and the higher downward mobility from the middle class to the working class for women. It also shows the slight bias towards higher male upward mobility rates from education. In short, it confirms much of what we know from other sources about gender segregation in the labour market and about the effects of constraints on the upward social mobility of women.

Data for men and women who were in the South East region in both 1981 and 1991 ("non-migrants") can be compared with the data in Table 10.7 to see whether or not the gender differences in this region match those for the country as a whole (this table is not reproduced here). The results are highly revealing. As would be expected (on the basis of data discussed in the previous section), the figures for the South East region are biased for both men and women in the direction of upward social mobility (typically by about two percentage points). But other differences also appear. For example, the stability of class membership is almost always lower in the South East region than in England and Wales, and especially so for women. However, there is a significant exception – women in managerial occupations are more stable in the South East (40.0% compared with 36.8%) than in England and Wales. And indeed, more generally, it is the better performance of women in managerial jobs that distinguishes the South East from England and Wales as a whole. This does not mean that, in general, the upward mobility rates into managerial posts are higher for women than for men, only that women are relatively advantaged in this region. However, the effect of this is to push the upward mobility rate of women from working-class origins into managerial occupations in the South East region to a level that is higher than the equivalent rate for men in England and Wales. Furthermore, the transition from education to manager in the South East is slightly higher for women (10.4%) than for men (10.2%). There is, however, a downside to this. The rates of promotion into the professions are relatively low for women in the South East, and, as far as the petite bourgeoisie is concerned, while men are generally more likely to enter this class in the South East than elsewhere, women are less likely to do so.

Finally, we can explore the gender differences in the social compositions of the migration streams to the South East region from the rest of England and Wales, and from the South East to the rest of England and Wales. Data equivalent to those presented in Tables 10.4 and 10.6 were produced for men and for women (not reproduced here). In the case of in-migrants to the South East, the differences in origins were small but the differences in destinations were very marked. Women were much more likely than men to enter the service class categories, and especially managerial jobs (1.62 for women, 1.29 for men). What pushed this figure up was not so much the propensity for women to move from education outside the South East to a managerial job in the South East (both figures were very high at 2.09 for women and 2.01 for men), but rather the high level of promotion to managerial positions in the South East of women already in the labour market outside the South East (notably in the professions and in working-class categories). In the case of professionals, it is interesting to note that the probability of a woman in-migrant to the South East being a professional "stayer" is significantly higher than that for men (1.11 compared with 0.89).

In the case of out-migration, the social origins for men and women were again fairly similar, but also again it was the destination rates that were different. Women tended to move into professional and managerial posts outside the South East at rates that were somewhat lower than those for men (0.72 vs. 0.80 for professionals and 0.70 vs. 0.84 for managers). This was, however, compensated not by higher rates of movement into the working-class categories, but instead by movement into the category "other". This means that women were leaving employment in the South East and becoming full-time domestic workers in the regions outside the South East. For those in the labour market in 1981 this flow was 20% above the England and Wales average, but it was even higher for those leaving professional, managerial and low-level white-collar jobs. Either by choice or by constraint, women tend to leave the labour market as they migrate away from the South East.

From these results we can say that there are clear signs that migration to the South East implies upward mobility for both men and women, but is especially favourable to the development of women's careers, whereas out-migration from the South East implies sideways (for example, into the petite bourgeoisie) or (sometimes) downward mobility for men but downward mobility or termination of career for women. (For both men and women the rate of movement into retirement is high – 1.31 and 1.30 respectively.)

This concludes the analyses of social and spatial mobility based upon the newly available data from the LS. Although the picture that has been presented is fully dynamic in the sense that we are allowed to see all the social class and interregional transitions that lie behind the structures with which we are familiar, it is not yet an analysis of social change. To study contemporary social change, migration and the middle classes we need to compare the results for the 1980s with those for the 1970s. Because the LS covers the period 1971–81 as well as 1981–91, it can be used to explore these changes in social and geographical mobility.

10.4 Contrasts in social and geographical mobility between the 1970s and 1980s

Social mobility, 1971–81 and 1981–91

Table 10.8 compares the social class transitions of the 1981–91 period with those for 1971–81. A positive value means that that particular transition was more important in the 1980s than in the 1970s; a negative value means that it was less important. Table 10.8 shows that for men the rapid decline of the manual working class was brought about partly through a lower stability of blue-collar membership (−7.28), but also from the extreme downturn in the rate of entry from education (−11.17). The higher rate of flow from education to unemployment is also significant. But it is the transitions affecting the middle classes that are the centre of our interest. The rate of flow into the professions was generally slightly higher in the 1980s than in the 1970s, but the figures are especially high for those coming from low-level white-collar jobs (1.88), and above all for those coming from management (6.31). The pattern for those becoming managers is very curious. There is a large negative value for manager "stayers" (−5.43), indicating a much reduced stability of managerial employment, but mostly positive values elsewhere, and high positive values for those coming from low level white-collar work and from education. But far and away the most remarkable are the shifts in the transition rates into the petite bourgeoisie. In all cases the rates are higher in the 1980s than in the 1970s, but the highest increases are to be found first for the petite bourgeoisie "stayers" (9.61) and secondly for those transferring in from the blue-collar section of the working class (5.38, and 5.93 for unemployed). Here is firm evidence of the social class content of the rapid growth of the male section of the petite bourgeoisie in the 1980s.

Table 10.8 A comparison of the structures of gender-specific social class transition matrices for 1971–81 and 1981–91 (standardized to class of origin; % point differences).

	PRO	MAN	PB	PWC	PBC	UE	TLM
(a) Males							
Professionals	0.24	0.83	1.35	−1.38	−1.64	0.59	0.00
Managers	6.31	−5.43	3.11	−3.02	−2.01	1.04	0.00
Petite bourgeoisie	0.66	−1.71	9.61	−0.96	−7.63	0.03	0.00
White collar	1.88	2.18	2.66	−2.43	−5.08	0.79	0.00
Blue collar	1.11	1.47	5.38	−0.41	−7.28	−0.28	0.00
Unemployed	0.76	0.46	5.93	−0.59	−7.90	1.35	0.00
Education	0.35	2.18	2.65	1.22	−11.17	4.76	0.00
Other	3.02	1.93	4.78	0.60	−13.35	3.02	0.00
b) Females							
Professionals	4.73	−1.62	0.64	−3.28	−0.31	−0.16	0.00
Managers	4.77	−3.05	2.46	−3.87	−1.79	1.48	0.00
Petite bourgeoisie	1.97	−0.25	2.62	−3.33	−1.13	0.12	0.00
White collar	2.27	3.63	1.35	−8.16	0.51	0.41	0.00
Blue collar	1.27	1.30	1.27	−2.99	−1.48	0.64	0.00
Unemployed	−1.99	1.15	0.96	−8.29	3.21	4.97	0.00
Education	−0.51	4.62	0.88	−5.64	−1.26	1.91	0.00
Other	1.80	1.34	2.76	−5.60	−2.30	2.00	0.00

Source: OPCS Longitudinal Study 1981 and 1991 (Crown Copyright reserved). *Abbreviations*: see Table 10.1.

For women the pattern is quite different. It is, of course, the white-collar section of the working class rather than the blue-collar that has seen the main downturn, notably white-collar "stayers" (−8.16). (Some of the transitions into the blue-collar working class are actually higher in the later period, notably that from unemployment.) There is also a sharp rise in the stability of female unemployment. But, once again, it is the changes in the middle-class transitions that are the main concern here. It is clear that the female section of the professional middle class has become significantly more stable over time, and that (as with men) women were more likely in the 1980s to transfer from managerial jobs into the professions than in the 1970s. The petite bourgeoisie also shows higher rates of entry in the 1980s, but this time there is no clear bias towards a growth of entry from working-class origins. It is the managerial group that is most distinctive. Once again, the stability of membership of this class has gone down, but the mobility rates from the white-collar working class and from education into managerial jobs were much higher in the 1980s than they were in the 1970s, and this upward trend was higher for women than for men. On the other hand, the trend for transfers from professional to manager was downward, (whereas it was upward for men).

Spatial mobility, 1971–81 and 1981–91

Studies of interregional migration in Britain (for example, Fielding 1992b) have used the National Health Service Central Register data to show that there has been little change in the numbers migrating between regions over the past 20 years, except, that is, for the major shifts that could be shown to be related to the business cycle. On the basis of this it was argued that, since the class structure was shifting towards high-mobility groups and away from low-mobility ones, intra-class spatial mobilities must in some cases, or maybe in all cases, be declining. The LS tells a rather different story. For those in, entering and leaving the labour market, there was an increase in interregional migration between the 1971–81 and 1981–91 periods of 13% for men and 11% for women. A comparison of the figures for those in the labour market in 1991 with those in 1981 gives a total growth rate of 17%.

This is a considerable growth. On closer examination, however, it becomes clear that this growth arises not from changes in the class-specific migration rates (in fact, the class-specific rates are remarkably similar between the two decades) but from that "compositional" effect, that is, from the situation in which the share of those classes that have high spatial mobility has increased, relative to the total population. Insofar as there are shifts between 1971–81 and 1981–91 they seem to be in the direction of slightly higher rates of interregional migration for young working-class men and women, while managerial spatial mobility has gone up slightly (especially for women) and professional mobility has gone down slightly.

The links between social and geographical mobility, 1971–81 and 1981–91

As with class-specific migration rates, the links between social mobility and spatial mobility seem to have changed very little over the recent period. For example, if one compares the findings of this chapter with their equivalents for the 1971–81 period, the differences are largely explained by two factors: (a) the differential growth of the social classes over the two decades (notably the growth of the petite bourgeoisie in the 1980s); and (b) the downward adjustment to the rates that results from the average mobility being increased by the growth in size of high-mobility classes. However, certain changes are not accounted for by these factors. For example, the interregional migration rates for the 1970s equivalent to those in Table 10.2 show a surprising increase in the rates into and within unemployment (the rate for unemployed "stayers" in the 1970s was 70, whereas in the 1980s it was 82). And this rise in the spatial mobility of the unemployed is confirmed by the figure for unemployed "stayers" in the final column of Table 10.3 (an increase from 104 in the 1970s to 121 in the 1980s).

It is, however, in the migration rates to and from the South East region that one begins to see interesting differences. For in-migrants to the South East there is (a) an increase in the importance of unemployment as an origin category – more people are leaving unemployment outside the South East to enter blue-collar and white-collar working-class jobs in the South East; (b) an increase in the attractiveness of the petite bourgeoisie in the South East as a destination category, especially from working-class origins and from education – this might be due in part to the migration of second-generation Asians from northern and midland industrial cities (as suggested in Robinson 1992); and (c) an increase in the importance of the labour market as a whole in the South East (the location quotient increases from 1.12 in the 1970s to 1.21 in the 1980s). For out-migrants from the South East the main changes are: (a) an increase in the importance of the working classes as origins of out-migration flows (it is tempting to see this as evidence of the "squeezing out" of the working classes as the South East region becomes more bourgeois in its social composition); (b) a growing importance of the petite bourgeoisie as a destination category, especially for those leaving working-class jobs in the South East region; and (c) a slight decrease in the significance of the labour market as a whole in the destination regions outside the South East.

10.5 Conclusions

Let me conclude by considering what these figures imply for the concept of the "service class". My judgement is that, in relation to debates about social and spatial mobility, the service class concept retains a good part of its salience for the following reasons:

(a) Similarities in recruitment, spatial mobility, exit and growth trends support the notion that professionals and managers have much more in common with each other than either group has with the petite bourgeoisie or with working-class groups. Both groups recruit young upwardly mobile people either straight from education or from the white-collar section of the working class. These people often migrate to the South East region at the start of their professional and managerial careers.

(b) Managers and professionals experience high spatial mobility as part of their work histories. The rates of interregional migration for these groups are far higher than for other groups in the labour market, even for the unemployed.

(c) Managers and professionals show a high propensity to migrate away from the South East region at, or before, retirement age. Many stay in their own social class, but some transfer into the ownership of small or medium-sized businesses.

(d) Managers and professionals differ from the petite bourgeoisie in almost all aspects – social and geographical origins, migration, social and geographical destinations, and steadiness of growth over the 20-year period.

However, the differences between professionals and managers, though some-times subtle, are many, and they often relate to the gender composition of the middle classes and to the much higher stability of professionals than managers. Furthermore, some recent trends seem to have exacerbated rather than diminished these differences. In particular:

(a) The instability of managers compared with professionals results in many former managers working in the petite bourgeoisie, but it also implies downward mobility into the working class. It is surely significant that this difference between managers and professionals increased in the 1980s compared with the 1970s.

(b) Professional positions have far more women in them than managerial ones, which are still strongly male dominated. However, the growth in the number of women managers over the two decades is remarkable (assuming, that is, that what it means to be a manager has remained the same over this period).

(c) The transition from professional work to manager remains, however, largely a male phenomenon.

(d) Professionals recruit more directly from education than do managers, while the latter recruit more directly from working-class groups than do professionals.

(e) The South East region is even more the location for the building of managerial careers than it is for professional ones (and especially so for women).

The other principal conclusions are:

(a) The geography of opportunity in Britain is deep-rooted and relatively unchanging. The South East region acted just as much as a social class "escalator" region in the 1980s as it did in the 1970s (but not significantly more so as one might have thought, given the "serious money" that was offered by City of London employers to capable and ambitious young people in the heady days of the late 1980s' boom).

(b) Social mobility and spatial mobility are intimately related. The LS dataset demonstrates this again and again. Different kinds of work histories imply different rates of both social *and* spatial mobility. A professional or managerial career (even in the 1980s) seems to involve a high degree of spatial mobility both in the process by which entry into these jobs is achieved but also within these forms of employment.

(c) Linked with this is the awareness that migration is of crucial importance in the formation of the three middle classes, and in shaping their characteristics as political and cultural entities: 17.2% of those who were professionals in 1991 had been interregionally mobile in the previous ten years; the figure for managers was only slightly lower at 14%. The equivalent figure for the blue-collar working class was 4.8%. Not only does this have implications for social cohesiveness and class consciousness, it also influences the nature of regional social and cultural relations. Although he was referring to a different context (that of immigrant communities in European cities), the recent comment by Castells (draft version of 1993) that "the fundamental . . . dualism of our time [is the cosmopolitanism of the elite versus the tribalism of local communities" seems very relevant to the results reported here.

Acknowledgement

I would like to express my thanks to Simon Gleave at the Social Statistics Research Unit at the City University for the way he helped me obtain the LS data on which this paper is based. Without his quick responses to my queries and requests this paper would not have been completed on time.

Chapter 11

Gentrification and the urban middle classes

Tim Butler

11.1 Preamble

Gentrification has been with us as a concept since Ruth Glass coined the term in the early 1960s to describe the process whereby some young middle-class people – mainly singles and childless couples – were repopulating areas of inner London instead of heading for the suburbs. This chapter is based on a study of the wave of

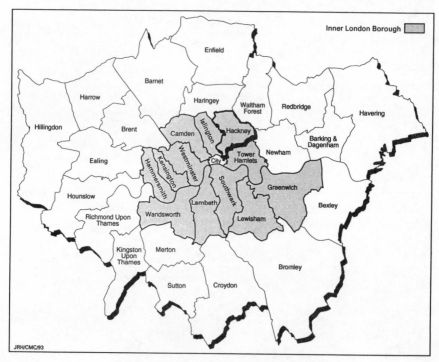

Figure 11.1 Map of London showing study area.

gentrification that embraced parts of the London Borough of Hackney (see Fig 11.1) in the 1980s.

Although some consensus has emerged about what gentrification is and what its causes might be (Hamnett 1991a), agreement does not extend much beyond this. There is considerable disagreement about what its consequences and effects have been. Bourne (1993a), for example, has argued persuasively that gentrification has been no more than one particular episode in the ebb and flow of urban development and that in many Canadian cities, despite gentrification, the income of the inner city has continued to decline. He argues (Bourne 1993b) that the main conditions that generated gentrification during the 1980s will not be present to anything like the same extent in the 1990s. The potential pool of gentrifiers will be smaller and the supply of inner-city areas and dwellings suitable for gentrification will decline:

> Much of the literature on gentrification was written during what now appears to have been a unique period in post war urban development in North America – a period that combined the baby boom, rising educational levels, rapid growth in service employment and real income, high rates of household formation, housing stock appreciation, public sector largesse, widespread (and speculative) private investment in the built environment and high levels of foreign immigration. This set of circumstances, except for the latter no longer prevails. (Bourne 1993b: 106)

This view, needless to say, has been challenged on a number of grounds but mainly around the issues of what defines gentrification and what particular parts of which particular cities one takes as the unit of analysis. Warde (1991) usefully distinguishes between two different forms of gentrification — by big capital and by individual households – and argues that they need to be explained with reference to different approaches. Given that much of Bourne's argument about the inner city is concerned with luxury condominium development, this is a helpful distinction.

Badcock (1993) has taken Bourne to task for basing his analysis on the whole of the metropolitan area, as opposed to those inner areas where one might expect to find evidence of the consequences of gentrification. Badcock himself (1992) has argued, on the basis of an intensive study of Adelaide, that gentrification has played an important role in regenerating the city's inner core. Nevertheless, it is hard to dispute Bourne's assertion that:

> No single theoretical paradigm or model and no simplistic social or ecological dichotomy, adequately addresses the changing geography of income and well-being in our cities. (Bourne 1993a: 1294)

What is clear though from the various research studies is that the household formation of families has changed considerably with an increase in single-person households through non-marriage, divorce and old age and, at the same time, there has been an increase in multi earner households. Whatever the detailed empirical

189

data on differences between and within urban and suburban areas show, the problem is a complex one of continuing, and perhaps growing, social inequality. It is for this reason that the focus of gentrification research has widened again to one of urban development and deprivation.

> The conundrum is one of a persistent if not a deepening level of social deprivation and poverty, co-existing with but worlds apart from areas of extensive revitalization and gentrification in the inner city. The result is also not new, but its explanation attests to the complex chemistry of social (ethnicity, demographic, and lifestyle), labour market (occupational), economic (sectoral) and housing (living arrangement) changes as well as policy shifts. (Bourne 1993a: 1313)

This chapter looks at some of these changes amongst a small group of middle-class gentrifiers in Hackney in order to make some assessment about the nature of change that is occurring amongst the middle classes in Britain.

11.2 Gentrification, cities and the middle classes

Although gentrification has been observed in many disparate cities, it has largely been an anglophone phenomenon, with the main sightings being in the USA, the UK, Canada and Australia. This could be partly an outcome of the biases of social geographers but more probably has to do with the way that these societies suburbanized in the post-war decades as compared with southern European and Latin cultures more generally, where the middle classes clung to the urban core for longer. The main issue, however, is to do with cities: in what kinds of cities has gentrification taken place and what, if anything, do they have in common? This is a major source of confusion in the literature and, although not doubting the importance of gentrification in Adelaide over recent decades, does it have the same social meaning as that in London and New York or even Toronto, Vancouver or Sydney?[1] The most coherent attempt to untangle this problem is to be found in the debate over global cities and, in particular, in the work of Sassen (1991, 1994). Sassen has argued that, as cities have moved away from their traditional role of being the servicing centres for their industrial hinterland within national boundaries, they have developed new roles. These new roles, for those cities that have survived the transition, have included beoming corporate "command and control" centres for transnational corporations; providing business services (accountancy, advertising, legal services, general consultancy, etc.); and, becoming centres of "financial production". In this "global economy", finance has moved on from being the medium of exchange for commodities to becoming a commodity itself for which new instruments of production are continually being dreamed up (for example, the securitization of debt in the 1980s). These cities' relations are with each other rather than with their national hinterlands. Exemplary of global cities are the three nodes of the new global economy, London, New York and Tokyo (Sassen 1991), with a supporting cast of regional cities such as Miami, Toronto, Sydney and São Paulo (Sassen 1994). Examples of cities that have declined over the same period include Marseilles and Liverpool, Melbourne and Rio de Janeiro. The strength of this analysis is that it identifies a role for these global cities that in turn, according to Sassen, provides the basis for gentrification. The gentrifiers are those who service the new international economy and, who, although very well paid, are not independently wealthy in the sense of a traditional ruling class or national bourgeoisie. The other side of globalization is the marginalization of the urban working class, whose consumption provided the motor for the post-war economies, and its replacement by a servicing class to cater for the needs of the new economy (as messengers, office cleaners, fast food vendors and copy shop operators) and for the *new* service class (as domestic workers, nannies, restaurant workers).[2] Gentrification is thus a relative concept and is partially responsible for the creation of a new subclass recruited from migrants, refugees, women and others forced into working antisocial hours for low wages. Sassen's work has been criticized, mainly around her claims that the urban social structure has become polarized between the gentrifiers and those who service them at work and play (Hamnett 1994).

Although this debate awaits further empirical investigation, the main thrust of the argument should not be lost: namely that certain cities have acquired a dominant economic role in the post-Fordist global economy. In particular, it provides a basis for understanding the attraction that the middle class and "world cities" have for each other. A central tenet of the "world cities" argument is that it requires the human agents of the "creative" aspects of financial accounting and business services to be in close spatial and social contact with each other. Financial districts in these cities have been getting more, not less, concentrated and the need to work longer hours and to coincide with at least part of the working day in other global nodes increases the importance of minimizing the distance between home and work. There have therefore been important changes in some sections of the middle class, whose centre of gravity has begun to shift away from the suburbs back to the inner city. This has coincided with shifts in the skills required for many middle-class occupations and their gender compositions (Savage et al. 1992). Global cities, however, are not just business and financial centres but are often capitals of nation-states, cultural centres and "metropolises". These latter functions are under emphasized in Sassen's accounts which is overdetermined by the economics of global production. It is within this political, economic and cultural conceptualization of the city that a significant restructuring of middle-class life appears to have taken place during the 1980s.

Gentrification has thus been used as a metaphor for the changes that have taken place in societies, classes, economies and cities. This chapter attempts to unravel the empirical basis for this through a study of the gentrification of Hackney in the late 1980s. Bringing together these agents of gentrification allows us to study people working in a variety of employment sectors and to make some tentative generalizations about the structure and formation of the contemporary urban middle classes.

11.3 Gentrification

As indicated above, gentrification had its academic genesis in North London in the 1960s and Ruth Glass's (1963) observation that what had been termed the great game of "urban leapfrog" from the centre to the suburbs was being reversed by some members of the middle class. In fact, as research quickly indicated, gentrification was not about people moving back to the city from the suburbs but about how some of the new cohort of young middle-class singles and childless couples were not leaving the city for the suburbs (for example, Gale 1984). Gentrification was quickly and empirically established as taking place in the major cities of the anglophone world (Smith 1979b, Hamnett 1984b, Ley 1988). In London, gentrification occurred in inner-city districts to the north of the centre such as Islington (Williams 1976) and Camden by the early 1970s and later in the west and southwest such as in Fulham and Battersea (Munt 1987) (see Fig 11.1). Only in the 1980s did it establish itself in the northeast and southeast of inner London in areas such as Hackney, Greenwich and Lambeth. The gentrification of inner London needs to be distinguished from the long-standing colonization of areas of central London such as Mayfair, Belgravia and Chelsea by the upper and upper middle classes, who had never left (except for their country houses during parts of the social calendar). Similar movements can be mapped for New York City and other anglophone metropolitan centres (for example, Zukin 1988).

Although gentrification was established as an empirical fact by the late 1970s, its significance and causation were much debated (see Hamnett 1991a for a discussion). Warde (1991) has argued, following Rose (1984), that gentrification is a "chaotic conception" in that it conflates a number of different processes.

> From a social scientific point of view there is an enormous difference between the collective action of individuals who construct in a piecemeal way an environment with a particular aesthetic unity and large corporations that invest in land and buildings in major construction projects. The first is amenable to analysis in terms of a theory of collective action, the latter in terms of the logic of capital. Their mutual influence on each other seems comparatively minor. (Warde 1991: 230)

The gentrification of Hackney very much comes under the first heading: as an episode of collective action by a number of disparate individuals. This is where the issue of the middle class becomes important, although, in Warde's view "attempts to establish theoretically the links between fractions of the middle classes and gentrification have proved inconclusive" (Warde 1991: 226). His basis for arguing this is that the existing accounts given by Jager (1986) on Melbourne, Rose (1988) on Montreal, Mills (1988) on Vancouver and others all give different answers to the questions "Who are the gentrifiers?" and "Who consumes gentrified housing?" Jager considers them an "in-between class" who disguise their lack of class self-confidence by adopting a highly stylized form of domestic consumption. Rose identifies a somewhat different group, which consists of relatively highly credentialed but lowly paid technical, managerial and professional workers, mainly from the public sector, who are, to an extent, forced into gentrification because it offers relatively cheap, but potentially attractive, housing. Mills, on the other hand, identifies an emergent, affluent group that uses its financial power to create an appropriate infrastructure for its desired lifestyle in new condo developments in Vancouver. There is however, as Warde points out, a world of difference between the large-scale gentrification of Fairview Slopes, Vancouver, and the restoration of Victorian houses in Stoke Newington, East London (Warde 1991: 224). The remainder of this chapter will consider some empirical data about the gentrification of Hackney – including Stoke Newington – in the light of these considerations.

11.4 The gentrification of Hackney

Hackney is a local government district of inner London located to the northeast of "the City" (see Fig 11.1). Gentrification in Hackney "took off" only in the 1980s, although during the 1970s there were quite extensive pockets of what Rose (1984) has termed marginal gentrification, often by those wishing to make political statements about living amongst the dispossessed or more simply who were unable to afford the costs of gentrified areas to the west and were prepared to take a risk on Hackney. Smith's (1986) notion of "pioneer" gentrifiers pushing forward the "frontier" and opening the area up to more mainstream gentrifiers would be an apt description of the middle-class forays into the Hackney housing market from the early 1970s. All of this made it attractive as a place to live for the middle-class youth who had come of age around the events of 1968, had some capital and wanted to live in the inner city (Ley 1994b). It was in part therefore the counter-culture, radicals and others who were prepared to put up with the lack of boutiques and to negotiate the difficulties in getting housing finance who began the process of pioneering the gentrification of Hackney in the 1970s.

The study was undertaken in two of the most gentrified areas in Hackney: De Beauvoir Town and Stoke Newington (see Fig 11.2). De Beauvoir Town is, in many respects, "Islington exiled in Hackney". Not only does it neighbour Islington geographically but it also shares the symbolically significant N1 postcode. De Beauvoir Town's housing differs from that of much of gentrified north London in that many of its houses are semi-detached and set in quite large plots. Its streets form a most un-English gridplan, having been developed by one developer in the mid-nineteenth century to provide housing for City workers (shades of Mr Pooter). Many of the houses are still owned by the family of the original developer, who have also retained the leasehold of many others. It looks different from Islington and it has few shops and fewer public spaces: almost all the space is private. What perhaps counts most is that the houses are somewhat cheaper than those elsewhere in Islington and that it is very near to the City – many offices can be walked to in half an hour and cycled to in considerably less – which, given the lengthening of the middle-class working day, is an important consideration in deciding where to live.

Stoke Newington differs from De Beauvoir Town in most respects. Architecturally, it is "North London terrace", with an almost postmodern mixture of style as a result of its piecemeal development in the late nineteenth century. Whereas in De Beauvoir Town there is little public space and relatively generous private space, in Stoke Newington the private houses seem more cramped but there is a lot of public space and plenty of shops. It is centred around Stoke Newington High Street, and estate agents market it as Stoke Newington "Village", stressing the park, the High Street and the general conviviality. Stoke Newington was the centre of much of the "counterculture" of the early 1970s (the "Angry Brigade" – Britain's answer to the Baader Meinhof gang – were allegedly based there). Alternative liv-

Figure 11.2 The London Borough of Hackney, showing ward boundaries. *Note*: Stoke Newington comprises three wards: Clissold, North Defoe and South Defoe.

ing seemed overrepresented there (for example squats, communes or collective houses), which corresponds well to the notions of "pioneers" or "marginal gentrification" found in the literature (Rose 1984, Smith 1986). By the 1980s, however, gentrification was in full swing, with prices rising rapidly, and Stoke Newington was losing its "alternativey" nature and was becoming somewhere, in the mind of David Lodge at least, a foreign exchange dealer could happily live.

11.5 The gentry of De Beauvoir Town and Stoke Newington

In this section I describe the social backgrounds of the survey population and their socio-economic formation.[3]

Demographics: cohorts, life-cycles and lifestyles

The sample for the survey was drawn from the electoral registers in two wards (the basic electoral area) in Hackney – one in De Beauvoir Town and one in Stoke Newington (see Fig. 11.2). The criteria for inclusion were that the house was in owner-occupation and that the name on the electoral register had changed over the previous seven years. This generated approximately 250 interviews (split almost exactly between the two areas), which were carried out over six months in 1988, and a smaller number of follow-up interviews, which were undertaken a year later.

Of the 245 people interviewed, 131 were males and 114 females; the mean age was just under 37, with a standard deviation of 8.4 years. This points to a highly "focused" cohort of people raised during a similar period in Britain's post-war history and at a similar stage in their life-cycle, even if they did not all share the same lifestyle. A rather greater number in Stoke Newington lived together with a partner or in some other (usually communal) arrangement as opposed to marriage (Table 11.1). The percentage of single-person households was three times the 1987 national average of 9% for persons below pensionable age (Central Statistical Office 1989: 35).

Compared with a national figure of 32% of households with dependent children (Central Statistical Office 1989: 35) 42% of households in the sample had children, which suggests that inner-city gentrification is by no means confined to single people or childless couples. Of the 169 respondents who were living in households with

Table 11.1 Household structure.

Household structure	De Beauvoir Town		Stoke Newington		Total	
	No.	%	No.	%	No.	%
Husband/wife	63	50	43	36	106	43
Partner	26	21	33	28	59	24
Other	5	4	9	8	14	6
Single	33	26	33	28	66	27
Total	127	100	118	100	245	100

partners, 149 of those partners also had paid employment; in other words, 88% of two-person households were dual-earner households. There was a variation here, with 84% of two-person households in De Beauvoir Town having two incomes and 93% in Stoke Newington. Almost all of the women who were interviewed in Hackney worked full time in paid employment.

Backgrounds

Only 15% of respondents had moved in to Hackney from outside London, which confirms that gentrification is not a "back to the city movement" but a process of resettlement of those already there (Smith 1979a, Gale 1984). Few of the studies on gentrification, however, tell us much about the social and spatial origins of those who gentrify the inner city, although Williams (1986) asserts that they tend to be drawn from suburban childhoods and Warde (1991: 226) makes reference to the suggestion that they are upwardly socially mobile. The data from Hackney tend to confirm the first claim but to deny the second. Goldthorpe (1982: 173) indicates that two-thirds of those who constitute what he terms the service class (his social classes 1 and 2) have been upwardly mobile into it. Using the same definitions, two-thirds of the Hackney respondents came from service class backgrounds. Almost all the rest came from the self-employed or other non-manual groups – only 11% came from the manual working class. Two-thirds of those *not* from a service class background came from a home–owning one. Admittedly, Goldthorpe's data refer to the early 1970s, but nevertheless the contrast is sharp and I would argue significant. Savage et al. (1992: 147) demonstrate that the *professional* (as opposed to managerial or petit bourgeois) middle class is drawn disproportionately from a middle-class background. It is not surprising, given the suburbanization of the middle classes in the 1950s and 1960s, that a majority of respondents were brought up in the suburbs. What this all suggests is that there is a process of elite recruitment into the middle class of Hackney, or perhaps that the middle class is recomposing as a mainly urban grouping, drawing its membership from the sons *and daughters* of the suburban middle class of the post-war decades.

Since the end of the Second World War, education and particularly higher educational qualifications have held the key to entry into the professional middle class, and the middle classes have jealously guarded their privileged access to, and benefit from, the education system. The means of achieving this in Britain has primarily been through elite forms of secondary education in the guise of fee-paying or selective-entry schools, ("public" and grammar schools respectively). The middle-class residents of Hackney appear to have been beneficiaries of both these systems (Table 11.2).

Among the Hackney respondents, 28% had been to an independent school, a further 11% attended a Direct Grant school (many of which have subsequently become fee paying) and 34% went to grammar school. Approximately 5% of school children nationally attended independent schools in the 1960s and 1970s (Central Statistical Office 1989). Given the middle-class nature of their family back-

Table 11.2 Type of secondary school attended.

Secondary school	De Beauvoir Town		Stoke Newington		Total	
	No.	%	No.	%	No.	%
Grammar	47	37	37	32	84	34
Independent	40	32	28	24	68	28
Comprehensive	13	10	28	24	41	17
Direct Grant	14	11	12	10	26	11
Secondary modern	5	4	4	3	9	4
Other	8	6	8	7	16	7
Total	127	100	117	100	244	100

Missing data = 1

grounds and their age, the percentage going to grammar school is perhaps not surprising, but the number going to private schools is remarkable. This underpins the suggestion that we are discussing a subgroup of the middle class who share a highly privileged educational background – either through the ability of their parents to pay and/or by their own ability to pass competitive examinations. This elitism is carried through into higher education; over 80% had entered higher education, but what is perhaps of more significance is the type of institution they went to and what they studied when they got there (Tables 11.3 and 11.4).

Table 11.3 Place of higher education (first degree).

Institution of higher education	De Beauvoir Town		Stoke Newington		Total	
	No.	%	No.	%	No.	%
Oxbridge	26	25	13	14	39	20
Other university	48	47	49	52	97	49
Polytechnic & college of education	13	13	18	19	31	16
Art college	8	8	4	4	12	6
Other	9	9	11	12	20	10
Total	104	100	95	100	199	100

Missing data = 46 (i.e. respondents not receiving a higher education)

Table 11.4 Discipline studied.

Discipline	De Beauvoir Town		Stoke Newington		Total	
	No.	%	No.	%	No.	%
Arts and humanities	38	37	32	34	70	35
Social sciences	18	17	29	31	47	24
Science & technology	14	14	10	11	24	12
Business	3	3	1	1	4	2
Law & accountancy	12	12	2	2	14	7
Art & design	10	10	7	7	17	9
Other/failed to complete	9	9	14	14	23	12
Total	104	100	95	100	199	100

Missing data = 46

Taking into account respondents' family background and the smaller higher education system of 20 years ago, an above-average higher education participation ratio might be expected. The 1986 General Household Survey shows that, of those in professional employment (i.e. a rather more selective group than used here), 62% of respondents had attained a degree or equivalent, of whom 40% had been to university and a further 27% had attended a polytechnic or college of further education (Central Statistical Office 1989). Not only had 80% been to university amongst the Hackney respondents but a quarter of graduates had been to "Oxbridge". The discipline of respondents' first degree reveals a bias towards arts, humanities and social science subjects and away from science and technology.

The restricted range of disciplines and of institutions at which they studied suggests a very particular higher educational bias towards elite institutions and non-business/commercial subjects. The lack of scientific and technological disciplines is in striking contrast to Savage et al.'s (1988) study of middle-class respondents in Berkshire, who were either professional managers or skilled high-level technicians and, presumably, had a more technical or business-oriented education. It conforms to Lash & Urry's (1994: 97) idea of a "discursive reflexivity" amongst the expanding service class in Anglo-American societies; Gouldner (1979) refers to this group as a speech community whose common background in higher education was based on what he terms a "careful and critical discourse". The number of respondents with an art and design training is also of interest given the claim that symbols and images are becoming one of the dominant modes of communication in the new post-industrial economies (Lash & Urry 1994: 4).

Work and income

It is difficult to summarize the range of respondents' occupations because of their diversity. Also, the classifications developed by OPCS do not easily incorporate many middle-class occupations. A range of approaches therefore needs to be adopted to indicate not only the diversity of occupations but also some of their basic similarities. Taking social class as the first indicator, respondents were overwhelmingly members of the middle class: 87% of those interviewed were, by their own (i.e. not by their husband's in the case of females) occupational classification, members of the middle class, i.e. in social classes 1 and 2 (by Goldthorpe's classification). Approximately one-third of those interviewed were in social class 1, i.e. senior administrative and professional occupations, as compared with social class 2, which Goldthorpe rather dismissively refers to as the "cadet" section of the service class and includes more routine professionals such as teachers and social workers. There was a massive difference between the two areas in the distribution of respondents in social class 1 and also in their gender composition. Nearly half the respondents in De Beauvoir Town, compared with less than one-sixth in Stoke Newington, were in social class 1, whereas nearly three-quarters of respondents in Stoke Newington were in social class 2. Turning to the gender composition, there were nearly twice as many men as women in social class 1 (41% compared with 22%); on the other hand, nearly two-thirds (65%) of women were in social class 2, as compared with just under half of all male respondents (47%). Looking at the gender and area distribution together is illuminating: in both areas there were fewer women than men in social class 1, but there were three times as many women in social class 1 in De Beauvoir Town as in Stoke Newington (32% compared with 10%). Gender and space therefore seem to be important in making comparisons not only between gentrified and non-gentrified areas but also within gentrified areas. This is not to suggest that in De Beauvoir Town there was greater equality between the sexes – data on income distribution clearly show there isn't – but that there does appear to be a spatial gradient in women's occupational attainment. There does not, however, appear to be any evidence that this has led to any greater equality within households.

Within households, the differences between the social class of partners and their respondents is gendered. Nearly half of the (female) partners of male respondents in social class 1 were in social class 2 and only 15% in social class 1, whereas only one male respondent in social class 2 had a partner in social class 1. The position for female respondents is rather different: of those in social class 1, 44% had partners in social class 1, and of those in social class 2, 15% had social class 1 partners. Gender differences within relationships therefore correspond to the broader pattern of gender inequality; it was relatively rare that women had a higher class position than men. There were three major divisions in respondents' class relations, first between social class 1 and social class 2, secondly between men and women, and thirdly between the two areas.

The majority of the middle class in Hackney, as Table 11.5 shows, were employed in what might be termed the market sector (i.e. the private and self-employed sector taken together) as opposed to the public/voluntary sector.

More men worked in the private sector and more women in the public, and, although the association between gender and employment sector was not *statistically* significant, there may be some sociological significance in the findings. There was a strong association between partners working in the same sector. Two-thirds of those working in the public sector, had partners working in the public sector with no significant variation between the sexes. The (female) partners of men working in the private sector were evenly distributed across the sectors, whereas the (male) partners of women working in the private sector were much more likely themselves to be

Table 11.5 Employment sector.

Employment sector	De Beauvoir Town		Stoke Newington		Total	
	No.	%	No.	%	No.	%
Private sector	51	42	39	35	90	39
Public sector	24	20	45	40	69	30
Self-employed	44	36	24	21	68	29
Voluntary sector	3	3	4	4	7	3
Total	122	100	112	100	234	100

Missing data = 11

working in the private sector or to be self-employed; nearly two-thirds of women who were self-employed had self-employed partners. In other words, women working in the private sector were less likely to have public sector partners (cf. the discussion of cross-sectoral relationships in Savage et al. 1992: 154–7, which broadly confirms this trend).

This emerging pattern of gender and spatial differentiation is repeated for salary. As a group, respondents were better paid than the middle class nationally (this is illustrated in Table 11.6 by comparison with the 1987 General Household Survey data for people with degrees). Those living in De Beauvoir were considerably better paid than those in living in Stoke Newington and men were considerably better paid than women. Although women may benefit from gentrification in terms of occupational status and salary, this is in relation only with women in general; compared with middle-class men there appears to be a consistent gender disadvantage in terms of status and salary. High salaries are restricted to the private sector and, to a lesser extent, the self-employed. Nobody working in the public or voluntary sector earned more than £30,000 per annum.

Table 11.6 Salary comparisons for respondents.

| | De Beauvoir Town | | Stoke Newington | | General Household Survey (1987) | |
	Male	Female	Male	Female	Male	Female
Average salary (£)	30,625	19,768	19,956	14,915	NA	NA
Earning over £20,000 (%)	68	34	32	14	18	4
Earning over £40,000 (%)	29	8	9	4	NA	NA
Household income over £50,000 (%)	28		6		NA	

NA = not available

I believe that there is some significance in these complex findings for the overall argument about the class structure and formation of the contemporary middle class, which is that, although the employment status of both members of the household is important, it remains structured by dominant gender relations and that, generally, men are likely to have the higher status and higher-paid jobs. Two-income households may be the norm but nevertheless within households there seems to be evidence of continued gender inequality.

The politics of the middle class in gentrified Hackney

Compared with the middle class nationally, respondents generally were better educated, better paid and more likely to be in professional or administrative employment. They were also more likely to have come from a similar social background to their current one than the middle class as a whole. Their expressed sympathy for the Labour Party, shown in Table 11.7, is therefore, on the face of it, surprising (respondents were asked, "If there were to be a general election tomorrow, which party would you vote for?").

Table 11.7 Voting intention (%).

Voting intention	De Beauvoir Town	Stoke Newington	All
Labour	33	70	51
Conservative	26	9	18
Liberal/SDP	18	7	13
Other	22	14	19

Among the respondents 22% were members of a political party, two-thirds being members of the Labour Party, (in Stoke Newington, 21 out of 24). The political views of respondents were, on the whole, long-standing. Three-quarters of those who voted in the 1987 general election had voted the same way in 1983, and those who had switched had generally done so from Conservative to Alliance. Two main reasons emerged to justify their voting intention. First there was an ideological loyalty to their chosen party and antipathy to the other main party or parties (in the case of Alliance voters). The second main reason depended on which party respondents supported: Labour Party supporters cited support for the party's position on social justice, whereas Conservative supporters focused either on the party's management of the economy or on Mrs Thatcher's "leadership" qualities. Perhaps the single clearest indicator of "who" these people are is given by the daily paper they read: 70% of those who read a daily paper in Stoke Newington and 49% in De Beauvoir Town take the *Guardian*, which is by any account regarded as the paper of the "liberal intelligentsia".

Although the propensity to support the Labour Party contrasts strikingly with the voting intentions of the middle class nationally, it has been noted previously that the professional sections of the service class are more likely to support the Labour Party than are those in managerial and technical sections (Savage 1991a: 40–2). Nevertheless, the contrast with the service class as a whole is stark when illustrated by comparing the voting intentions of the sample with a similar group from Crewe's (1987) general election data and Marshall et al.'s (1988) data (Table 11.8).

It is immediately apparent that the Hackney respondents are far more disposed to vote Labour and less for either the Conservative or Alliance parties. Although this is less the case in De Beauvoir Town, the Conservative vote there is still well below the national figure and the Labour vote higher. These figures should, of course, be treated with caution because we are dealing with smaller numbers and data that

Table 11.8 Voting intentions for service class.

Voting intention	De Beauvoir Town %	Stoke Newington %	Hackney All %	Marshall Service class %	Crewe Prof/manager %
Conservative	34	6	20	52	59
Labour	43	88	65	22	14
Liberal/SDP	23	7	15	26	27
N	88	88	176	361	4886

are statistically less representative than in either of the other two surveys; nevertheless they point to a trend identified by Bagguley in Chapter 17 in this volume.

11.6 Discussion

The findings reported here from Hackney do not support the idea of a single service class in the manner suggested by Goldthorpe (1982) or Abercrombie & Urry (1983), neither does a hard-edged picture of gentrification emerge such as the one painted by Sassen (1991) and encapsulated in Tom Wolfe's novel *The bonfire of the vanities*. Gentrification in Hackney has on the whole been gentle and understated. The data support the idea that gentrification is associated with the concept of a "cultural new class", which Ley defines as: "tertiary educated professionals in the arts, media, teaching and academic positions as well as public sector managers in regulatory and welfare activities – a subgroup I shall identify as the *cultural new class*" (Ley 1994a: 56).

Ley demonstrates that in Canada this group is strongly associated with gentrification and what he terms "reform politics". The importance of higher education and the emphasis on discursive as opposed to traditional professional or technical skills are also supported, as is Gouldner's (1979) notion of a "speech community" based around a "careful and critical discourse", which is helpful in characterizing the sense of "community" to which many of the respondents in Stoke Newington refer. Although the range of occupations is so wide as to defy categorization, what is interesting is both their diversity and their convergence. Respondents were working in very different areas, often in sectors of the economy with what had in the recent past been regarded as mutually antipathetic goals, yet this did not seem to divide respondents ideologically or culturally. It was often difficult to distinguish between the attitudes of those working in the private and public sectors (cf. Lash & Urry 1987). In other words, the range of occupations seems to have multiplied yet the differences between those occupying them seems to be relatively minimal. For example, it was not possible to find consistent differences in terms of voting behaviour amongst respondents except in terms of the area in which they lived.

There is, however, another continuity/discontinuity, and that is between the middle class of Hackney in the late 1980s and the "traditional" middle class of the postwar decades. Occupationally, socially and spatially they could not be further apart – suburban versus urban; single versus multiple earners – but taken as a whole their lives demonstrated a remarkable continuity and stability. Unlike the members of the service class living in Berkshire and working in "high tech" industries investigated by Savage et al. (1988), respondents did not swop jobs often – most had worked for the same employer for more than five years. There was little evidence of the increased instability of the middle-class career identified by Sassen (1991: 283–4), although, given that the research was undertaken at the beginning of the recession in 1988/9, this may now have changed. The recession may also have affected rather more directly those working in the marketing and development of financial services, who are probably underrepresented in Hackney but will be found in areas of new "condo" development such as Docklands, which appears to have suffered much more directly than Hackney from the effects of the post-1987 slump in the City.

There are two key findings from this work that, if found by subsequent research to be representative, would be of considerable importance in explaining how the middle classes have adapted to a changing social and economic environment. The first finding concerns the extent to which respondents came from middle-class families. The second finding is the extent to which gender plays a role in gentrification and middle-class life. These two findings may be linked, in that it would appear to be largely the daughters of middle-class families who benefited from the expansion of educational opportunities during the post-war decades, which may account for gentrifiers in an area such as Hackney being drawn disproportionately from those with middle-class family backgrounds (Butler & Hamnett 1994). Warde and others (e.g. Bondi 1991) are correct to draw attention to the role that gender plays in gentrification, but it may well be that this is itself a class-influenced process. Whether this is also a cohort specific phenomenon remains to be seen but there certainly seems some justification for claiming that the middle classes have ridden the crest of the social and economic restructuring that was meant to have undermined the basis for their privileged position – at least if you believe the rhetoric of Thatcherism. It also remains to be seen whether or not this is a life-cycle effect and whether or not there will be a subsequent move from Hackney, with its inadequate infrastructure for "social reproduction". Anecdotal evidence would suggest that many middle-class Hackney residents with young children are contemplating moves to other boroughs with a more malleable education system that will allow them to pass on the "cultural capital" from which they have been such beneficiaries. The other option, which flies directly in the face of their expressed political values, has been to turn to private provision, particularly as far as education is concerned. What this may suggest is that a professionalized elite is emerging within the middle classes who are disproportionately drawn from middle-class families, and that it has maintained and even improved its economic wellbeing by becoming formed around a two-income household – albeit with a clear gender hierarchy of earning and occupational status within the household.

There is thus considerable support in these findings for the "assets" model of the contemporary middle classes developed by Savage et al. (1992). Almost all respondents had accumulated large amounts of "cultural capital" from their family backgrounds or the formal education system, which they were realizing either through an organizational career or else through self-employment. There appears to be rather less support in this research for the model of the service class proposed by Goldthorpe (1982). The research that I have reported on here provides strong support for Warde's (1991) contention that gender is of equal or greater importance than class in understanding gentrification, while arguing that it is strongly influenced by class background.

What we find in Hackney is a new middle class – highly educated, internally differentiated and politically liberal, but also one that demonstrates considerable continuities with the "old middle class", which may well be because in large part this was from where it emerged. This is not to suggest that this group is homogeneous; the data show that although, as a whole, the Hackney middle class stands apart from the middle class, nationally, there are, even within Hackney, consistent differences between the two areas studied. This suggests that spatial differentiation is an important aspect of middle-class formation and that people make choices about where to live that are informed by their sense of "who they are", which, in turn, confers an identity on them. This raises questions about the continued value of a class analysis, in the sense of understanding classes as collectivities with a particular relation to the means of production. This has always been problematic in relation to the middle classes but it would now appear that middle-class life has become much more individualistic, and, to an extent, individuals are able to shape an image of their class situation through their engagement in work and with other people in a similar situation. Gentrification is one such outcome.

Notes

1. Badcock (1992: 1170) makes the interesting, but largely unsubstantiated, claim that a city's degree of "primateness" is likely to have a bearing on its predisposition towards inner–city gentrification, presumably because of the concentration of state and state-related activities that will be concentrated there. This might be the case in Australia but certainly is not in Peru, where Lima is a primate city par excellence and the centre has more or less been abandoned by the middle classes, both residentially and commercially.

2. It might of course be argued that this is just the reappearance of domestic service in a new uniform after a gap of half a century; although, as Gregson & Lowe in Chapter 9 in this volume and elsewhere demonstrate, much of this domestic labour is now hired to replace time spent by women in paid professional employment, which was not the case previously.

3. The results of this survey and other findings on the research undertaken in Hackney are fully reported in Butler (1992).

Chapter 12
A middle-class countryside?

John Urry

12.1 Revisiting the countryside

Since Newby's classic studies of rural Suffolk burst onto the academic scene in the later 1970s a certain interpretation of the role of the middle class in the countryside has become relatively commonplace. I shall begin with Newby's account before turning to the various limitations that it possesses as an analysis of *contemporary* rural relations in Britain. Two particular claims will be advanced. First, there are important divisions within the "middle class" and it should not be presumed that such a class has a unitary or unambiguous relationship with the countryside. Second, it is necessary to analyze not just work and residence patterns but also the consequences of changing leisure and travel practices for rural social relations in Britain, particularly with the way the countryside is implicated in the production not just of food but also of leisure sites and of deeply held and contested meanings.

First, then, Newby argued that, as job opportunities in agriculture had declined in many lowland rural areas, so middle-class urban newcomers move into such areas instead (1979: Ch. 6). Such commuters, retired couples and second-homers are attracted by cheaper housing and especially by what Pahl (1965) termed "the village in the mind". For these urban newcomers the village is not the only focus of their activities. As a result people no longer know everyone else. A new social division develops between the locals and these newcomers; the former, consisting of both farmers and labourers, constitute an "encapsulated community" organized around farming activities and defined in opposition to the middle class in-migrants (see Wiener 1981 on the parallel nineteenth-century migration of the bourgeoisie to the English countryside).

Social conflict particularly occurs over two issues. First, local people want cheap local housing but this is increasingly hard to find because newcomers are normally able to buy or to rent property at higher prices. Newcomers often try to prevent the building of public or even low-cost private housing in "their" village. Secondly, newcomers hold stereotyped images of village life – they seek to preserve quaint and inappropriate aspects of rural charm. Newby argued that the "village in the mind" "leads them to be aggressively protective against any changes in the village that threaten their image. Hence, typically, it is the newcomers who form village amenity societies, complain about uprooted hedges or diverted footpaths, and who . . . protest against any plans to build more houses in the village" (1979: 331–2). The newcomers also expect the locals to have certain "rustic" charms but not to intrude too heavily upon the rural vision that the newcomers have bought into when moving into the countryside from town or city.

One consequence of this influx is to unite the farmers and their workers against such middle class newcomers. Thus farmers want to ensure there is low-cost housing for their employees; all those involved in agriculture believe that the newcomers do not understand why, for instance, hedgerows have to be removed or modern fertilizers are necessary; and farmers and their workers often participate together in countryside sports.

However, whether or not this was an accurate account of lowland England in the 1970s, it is clear that by the 1990s rural social relations have become much more diverse and affected by a strikingly wider set of economic, political and cultural processes (see Cloke et al. 1994). First, this means that the very association of "newcomer" with "middle class" is itself unhelpful. These are not interchangeable terms because:

> Recent work on the middle class suggests that there exists a series of complex intra-class divisions that tend to cut across traditional occupational class divides. It therefore seems extremely unlikely that just one distinctive middle class group will have evolved in rural areas. Instead we should expect to encounter different fractions of middle-class presence. (Cloke & Thrift 1990: 166)

Moreover, the socio-cultural effects of such fractions are highly diverse and one cannot easily identify a "middle-class making of the countryside". This is particularly the case if we go on to consider the varied leisure activities of different class fractions. It is a lacuna in Newby's account that he mostly neglects the countryside as a site for travel, leisure and tourism. But the socio-historical development of certain rural areas is incomprehensible without taking into account such leisure practices, and these have grown enormously in the past 20 years.

In the next section I consider some of the ways in which various social classes have historically helped to produce what we have come to know as the English countryside. In the third section I demonstrate that there are increasingly diverse social activities and cultural constructions to be found in and of the "countryside". These activities and constructions stand in complex connections with the "middle class". There is a brief conclusion.

12.2 Class and the countryside

The most obvious point to make about the countryside is that its character has been predominantly shaped by landowners. Any effects that other classes might have had have been substantially less significant than those of the large and medium-scale owners of the mass of rural land. This power of the landowning class can be seen in the forms in which access to land is highly regulated; in the ways in which the state has been able to play a rather limited role in transforming rural ownership and access has usually been opposed by private landowners; and in the very appearance that the countryside has taken through the development of a "countryside aesthetic". These relations of domination have been secured over a long time, certainly from the eighteenth century with the widespread building of stately houses and landscaped gardens. Up to the last third of the nineteenth century the ownership of land was exceptionally concentrated so that, by 1873, four-fifths of the land in the UK outside London was owned by fewer than 7,000 people (Walton 1989: 21–6). In England such land was mainly farmed by tenant farmers who employed large numbers of landless labourers.

Since then there has been a revolution in landownership. Rural land in England is now predominantly under the control of owner-occupying farmers. Many of the large houses built by previous generations have been sold off to those who have made their money away from the land or have been turned into hotels or other kinds of leisure complex. Other houses have become tourist sites owned by the National Trust and English Heritage, often with the "family" retaining a portion for residence. And yet the English countryside, particularly the area of the "home counties" surrounding London, has stubbornly remained especially emblematic of Englishness (Urry 1995: Ch. 13).

The last of these developments represents a curious kind of class compromise, which has been playing itself out in the English countryside for the past two centuries. Just as in a sense the landed class was making the countryside in its image from the eighteenth-century onwards, so there has been a continuing struggle against this by the middle class so as to acquire some access and influence over that landlord-dominated countryside (see Harrison 1991). This class struggle emerges in the later eighteenth century when the notion of "scenic tourism" first develops within the English "middle class". There are a number of key moments in the development of this "class struggle" between the owners of land and those who increasingly wished to live in or visit the countryside: the eighteenth century shift in the nature of the Grand Tour, from "discourse" to the "eye", from education to visual consumption (see Adler 1989); the "discovery" of certain ruins and landscapes as being either sublime or picturesque (see Ousby 1990); the emergence of Romanticism, especially within the English Lake District, and the consequential reassessment of its previously inhospitable scenery (see Bunce 1994, Urry 1995); the development of the railway in the mid-nineteenth century and its enormous effect in opening up much of the English countryside to commuters and visitors; the discovery of the coastline as a site to visit and often to retire to (see Walton 1983); the formation of the first conservation organization, the Commons, Open Spaces and Footpaths Preservation Society, in 1865 and many subsequent developments (Sharpley 1993); and the emergence in the nineteenth century of walking and climbing as appropriate leisurely activities for the (mainly) male middle class (Wallace 1993).

This middle-class movement also sought to impose habitus upon the urban poor. This was part of the "rational recreation" movement, to provide not only parks, museums and libraries within towns and cities, but also to acquire countryside sites close to such cities for the moral enjoyment of the urban poor (Harrison 1991: 9–10). The extent of this was limited however. Harrison argues that, "countryside recreation . . . remains severely constrained and influenced by private property rights" (1991: 13). Thus public access to common land outside the major urban areas is not a right; there is no general right to roam in the countryside; access negotiated by the state involves land that is already settled and farmed; there are no real "national" parks owned by the state; farming and agriculture have been in effect exempt from planning controls; and land owned by the Forestry Commission and the water companies has recently been partially or wholly "privatized".

There are three key points to emphasize about the history of class struggle in the countryside. First, there have been enormous changes in who actually owns land since the late nineteenth century with the marked reduction in the scale and earning capacity of many large estates. Cannadine (1990) has analyzed the "decline and fall of the British aristocracy", especially from the First World War onwards when tenant farmers were able to purchase their rented land and become owner-occupiers. Other changes, especially in England and Wales, have involved the buying of land by agribusinesses and more recently by large leisure companies to build theme parks, golf courses, holiday centres, heritage sites and so on (Clark et al. 1994b).

Secondly, the issue of conservation plays a complex role in this history. Following the formation of the first conservation organization in the world in 1865, the National Trust was formed in 1895. In its development of a particular "countryside aesthetic" in the twentieth century, the National Trust conserves buildings and landscapes in ways that do not significantly disturb the existing relations of landownership. The countryside has come to be regarded as principally suitable for "considerate recreational use of the countryside" and later for "quiet recreation". The National Trust has thus brought about a class compromise. The middle class could obtain access to engage in certain quiet activities within rural areas but this has been on terms structured by the existing proprietorial rights over land and property (Walton 1989, Harrison 1991).

Thirdly, there are two hidden classes in this history. On the one hand, there are the agricultural workers and their families, who have dramatically declined in numbers. They are absent from most accounts of rural life and little recognition is given to their leisure needs (see Williams 1973 on how "landscapes" are un-peopled). On the other hand there is the urban working-class. Because of limited means of access and considerations of taste it has been largely absent from the countryside, except within certain very particular countryside "honeypots" (such as Cheddar Gorge, Stonehenge, Bowness) or places chosen not for aesthetic appreciation but for active use (as in the Kinder Scout mass trespass or the socialist cycling clubs of the inter-war period). The concept of "quiet recreation" tends to exclude such collective working-class activities (also see Aygeman 1989 on "black people [and the] white landscape").

Thus the English countryside has reflected a class struggle in which the interests of landowners have been paramount. However, landownership patterns have themselves dramatically changed. Also, landowners have had to adapt to powerful movements for rural conservation articulated by the mostly professional middle class and instantiated in various pieces of legislation, especially the 1949 National Parks and Access to the Countryside Act. The notion of "quiet recreation" as reflected in that legislation has consecrated the leisure activities that that class favours and represents a class compromise with the interests of landowners and farmers. In the next section I consider the contemporary situation and suggest that this historic compromise will not easily survive current changes in British society.

12.3 The middle class and the countryside

I will begin with the thesis that it is the service class that is currently remaking the contemporary English countryside. On the basis of research on rural migration in north Lancashire, Halfacre (1992) takes the service class to be characterized by rapid numerical growth, high levels of educational credentials, a considerable degree of autonomy and discretion at work, reasonably high incomes (but lower than its cultural capital), opportunities for promotion within or between enterprises, and relative residential freedom. These characteristics enable this class to create space in its own image, to impose its habitus upon particular places (see Cloke & Thrift 1987, Thrift 1989). Halfacre (1992) suggests that service class growth depends upon appropriate employment opportunities, existing and potential commuting patterns, the provision of suitable housing, and the availability of appropriate consumption nodes. The last of these is the most significant and stems from the vulnerability of the service class's credentials to devaluation. Hence he suggests that place-based consumption is of great importance to the reproduction of the service class, which seeks to advance and legitimate its position in society through the deployment of symbolic capital (Bourdieu 1984). Such a focus upon symbolic capital is closed to much of the working class (for cost and taste reasons), and is unnecessary for the bourgeois and landed classes because they already possess high levels of economic capital (see Halfacre 1992: 159–60).

Halfacre links such symbolic capital with the apparent growing attraction of the countryside. Within the general pattern of counter-urbanization, service class residential growth between 1971 and 1981 was particularly concentrated in more rural areas (Cloke & Thrift 1987, Halfacre 1992: 161–3). More generally, over half the new houses starting to be built in 1988 in England were in rural or semi-rural areas (McGhie 1988).

Thrift argues that it is the service class that "seems to be social group that has taken the countryside and heritage traditions most to heart" (1989: 31). And Halfacre (1992) argues that "pastoralism" provided the habitus of the emergent service class in the 1970s and 1980s. This habitus consists of the following features: the rapid manipulation of images through the development of the "symbolic professions", which help to produce new leisure spaces; the elaboration and circulation of a "countryside aesthetic"; the positive cultural emphasis upon "nature" and "natural products and activities" and a resistance to the apparently contrived (imported health foods as natural – local beef as unnatural!); the attraction of being seen in the countryside and obtaining souvenirs of a rural tastefulness; the use of rural images in marketing and in the media more generally; an emphasis upon countryside pursuits and locations that involve relatively little economic capital (walking, climbing); an extensive discourse in books and magazines in which the service class can demonstrate rural knowledge and skills; the purchase of consumer goods with apparent rural origins or associations (Barbour jackets, Range Rovers, Laura Ashley fashions); and a modest "environmentalism" in which the environment is equated with the particular "designer-places" that people live in, or have second-homes in, or like to visit and "appropriate" (see *inter alia* Cloke & Thrift 1987, Thrift 1989, Halfacre 1992, and especially Phillips 1993b, on rural gentrification). Thrift talks of the "service-class character of places replete with manicured countryside" (1989: 34). Thus: "the service class lives in a series of milieux bent towards tasteful consumption. These are designer civil societies, the consumption cultures. In them, the consumption-cum-reproduction preferences of the service class are made particularly clear" (Thrift 1987a: 242).

This is a dynamic process because designer-places constituted as positional goods (for residence or for visiting) can become rapidly unfashionable. Also, the service class's image of the countryside is a fundamentally constructed one; a "bucolic vision of an ordered, comforting, peaceful and, above all, deferential past" does little justice to the back-breaking hard work undertaken by men and women who have historically worked in the countryside (Thrift 1989: 26). Such a vision is comprised of elements that never existed together within a single historical period.

Although this is an illuminating thesis (the service class's remaking of the English countryside), it does suffer from some deficiencies (see McCrone 1992 on some contrasts in Scotland, and Phillips 1993b on Wales). First, it is difficult to show that its habitus is literally being imposed on other classes because many within such classes have enjoyed a lasting relationship to the countryside. As Thomas argues, historically "[w]hether or not the preoccupation with nature and rural life is in reality peculiarly English, it is certainly something which the English townsman [sic] has for a long time liked to think of as such; and much of the country's literature has displayed an anti-urban bias" (1973: 14, Williams 1973). This feeling for the country is found in sections of the urban working class and is best exemplified in the large and growing contemporary membership of the Ramblers Association (70,000 members in 1990 with 330 local groups, Halfacre 1992: 171).

Secondly, a significant proportion of the service class does not participate in countryside activities (in any year about one-third of those in categories AB). Thus there is not a single habitus possessed by the emergent service class.

Thirdly, the widespread availability of the car (now found in over 70% of households) means that many leisure activities take place at a considerable distance from one's place of residence. Many are in the countryside (Alton Towers) or may involve a long journey through the countryside (Wigan Pier Heritage Centre). However, there may not be much commitment to "pastoralism" from those who drive fast along rural motorways, whatever their social class.

Finally, Halfacre empirically investigated rural migration patterns to north Lancashire in the light of this service class thesis (1992: 620–5, see more generally Cloke et al. 1994). He notes that about 40% of those moving into rural areas between 1970 and 1988 came from the service class, this proportion being about twice as high as those respondents who had lived in such areas for all the period 1970–88. Moreover, the more rural the settlement, the higher the service class proportion amongst those who moved in. Many of these service class in-migrants were long-distance migrants who moved because of job changes. Other classes did not engage in such long-distance employment migration to the same extent and they therefore had less inducement to "counter-urbanize". Working-class moves to rural areas were overwhelmingly retirement related rather than employment related.

Halfacre argues that "members of the service class are undoubtedly tailoring rural areas to their interests" and he cites the high quality and tastefulness of new housebuilding (estates described as villages, the use of vernacular or rustic style, and so on); the increasingly middle-class character of village leisure activities; and the somewhat fuller and more academic representation of their conception of rurality (1992: 624). However, he interestingly concludes that the differences between social groups living in rural areas in terms of attitudes and activities are not marked. They all express a strong pro-ruralism. It is not possible to ascertain whether this pro-ruralism is because there have never been significant class differences or because the service class habitus has been imposed *upon* other classes.

It is now necessary to widen this debate and consider what has been generally ignored in the literature, namely the significance of the countryside as a place of travel and leisure, given that such leisure activities are particularly important for identity-formation. It should be noted that most of the empirical data on leisure and the countryside suffer from a number of deficiencies: class is categorized in terms of categories that do not relate to contemporary class theory; there is little or no research on the gender and ethnic composition of visitors; the data do not reveal the ways in which people combine the consumption of certain *goods* with the consumption of particular leisure *services*; there is little opportunity to break down patterns into different geographical areas; and countryside activities are characterized in ways that do scant justice to the variation in meaning that such experiences may entail (one person's walk is another person's solitudinous contemplation of nature).

Nevertheless, the following are the main features of our existing knowledge of countryside recreation patterns (see Blunden & Curry 1988, Harrison 1991, Sharpley 1993, Clark et al.1994a, b):

- Three-quarters of the population of England visit the countryside at least

once a year (1990); about one-quarter of the population are frequent visitors, one-half occasional visitors, and one-quarter rarely or never visit.
- Those with professional/managerial jobs are twice as likely as those with semi-skilled or unskilled jobs to visit the countryside, and they are more likely to be frequent visitors; this is shown both in national surveys and in studies of particular countryside sites.
- People with cars are much more likely to visit the countryside – 70% of households now have a car and 45% of car journeys are for leisure purposes. These proportions will continue to grow, with the result that traffic on rural roads is expected to increase by between 125% and 267% by 2025.
- The counter-urbanization of the population means that the increasingly rural population seek to engage in and indeed influence the forms of countryside-based recreation.
- There has been a sharp growth in the proportion of the population with non-manual jobs that require further or higher education qualifications – and those with such qualifications are more likely to visit the countryside.
- Policies pursued up to the 1980s were designed to restrict rural leisure developments whereas those followed since then, especially in the context of the perceived "over-supply" of agricultural land and the development of a post-productionist countryside, have sought to promote and market rural leisure to many new markets.
- Those without cars, those with manual jobs, women, the disabled, the elderly, members of ethnic minorities and single-parent households tend to visit the countryside less frequently.

Some further survey data on middle-class leisure practices are presented by Savage et al. (1992: Ch. 6). They argue that, in terms of the consumption practices of 11,000 respondents surveyed in the late 1980s, three relatively clear groupings can be identified *within* the "service class" (those in categories AB). First, there is what they playfully term the "post-moderns" (1992). These are professionally qualified workers in the private sector who participate in an eclectic mixture of high and low cultural forms, including combining a healthy lifestyle with a high consumption of good food and wine (the health-with-champagne lifestyle!). Secondly, there are the "ascetics", mainly employed in welfare and related public services, who have a high concern for health and exercise, especially conducted outdoors, so as to preserve their cultural/bodily assets. They have low consumption of alcohol but high consumption of arts events. Thirdly, there are the "indistincts" or "organization-persons", managers and administrators employed in government and private sector bureaucracies, who appear to exemplify relatively few distinctive cultural practices. They seek advancement *within* their organization, not through cultural wars conducted vis-à-vis other social groups (Bourdieu 1984 fails to see the significance of such "organization-men", see Whyte 1957). These three loose social groupings are cross-cut by gender, educational attainment, age and region.

In relationship to the countryside, these arguments about health and exercise need further examination. The ascetic lifestyle particularly characterizes those employed in "education, health and welfare" public services, those who stayed on in education until their twenties, and women. For example, the first of these groups are particularly high consumers of opera, plays, climbing, skating, tennis, classical concerts, table tennis, contemporary dance, camping, rambling, yoga, museums and galleries; and low consumers of vodka, whisky, gin, golf, sea and coarse fishing, champagne, snooker, and Spanish holidays. Service class women are high consumers of yoga, keep/fit, dancing, health clubs, ballet, horse riding, skating and vermouth; and low consumers of cricket, snooker, golf, fishing, whisky, chess, squash, sailing, jogging, climbing, wind-surfing, brandy and bowls.

There are three points to make about the growth of such an ascetic lifestyle. First, this interest in the "body culture" stems from a reflexivity about the self and a concern to preserve bodily rather than financial assets (since the latter are not particularly high; on reflexivity, see Lash & Urry 1994). Glassner maintains that fitness programmes "suggest that by exercising and eating correctly, one will achieve professional-quality mastery, not just of one's appearance and health, but of one's position in the labour and mate markets" (1989: 186).

Secondly, the countryside plays a particularly significant role in relationship to many of these activities. The ascetics are major users of the countryside and are members of organizations concerned to conserve and protect it (as I will discuss further below). Their commitment is often to a holistic concept of "nature" that embraces both the body and the countryside. Their countryside practices normally involve activities that appear to them as "natural", such as climbing, camping, rambling and simply being in the countryside. These activities are not of course simply "natural", as the history of leisure walking shows very clearly (Wallace 1993, Urry 1995: Ch. 13). Particularly striking, moreover, is the contrast between the "ascetics" and the "indistincts" (or managers). It is the latter "who indulge in the more staid and conventional sports such as shooting . . . , fishing, sailing and golf", activities that typically involve large-scale resources, considerable expense and particularly obvious "interventions" in nature (Savage et al. 1992: 116). They "seem more prone . . . to seek 'escape' in the form of modified versions of country pursuits earlier adopted by the landed aristocracy. For the managers at least the pursuit of a cleaned-up version of the 'heritage' or 'countryside' tradition seems apposite" (Savage et al. 1992: 116).

Thirdly, it is argued that this "ascetic lifestyle" developed by what Bourdieu would term "intellectuals" (intellectuals as the vanguard of the ascetic) has in turn affected other social groups and helped in particular to provide further conditions that form the habitus of the "postmodern". Savage et al. maintain:

> What were once the practices of an "alternative" middle-class minority resisting materialism and the dictates of professionalized medicine have now been adopted on a large scale by those with much greater economic resources. However, in the process it has not replaced other cultural practices but sits alongside them as another one to "sample". (1992: 113)

The "post-moderns" appear to combine a body culture with many of the character-istics of non-healthy living. The development of such pastiched and eclectic lifestyles demonstrates the demise of certain traditions of taste and how in the 1980s cultural practices could be sampled and juxtaposed in novel and heterodox patterns.

In relationship to the countryside, Thrift (1989) particularly emphasized how the purchase of a substantial country house in the southern half of England became a reasonably common element of a postmodern lifestyle practised by the private sec-tor young(ish) professional in the later 1980s. Harrison (1991) more generally sug-gests that such postmoderns have affected the countryside through their willingness to transgress the cultural norms of "group", whether this be age group, class, gen-der, ethnicity or neighbourhood (and see Urry 1990). Harrison proceeds to argue that such "post-moderns" experience a decentring of identity:

> [This can be seen] in the transgression of boundaries through play, the casting on and off of identities and the opportunities to engage vicariously in other people's lives. Theme parks, medieval fayres and feasts, pop festi-vals and "living" museums provide the opportunities to temporarily adopt identities which have new [temporary] meanings for their participants ...[T]his dismemberment of group norms allows people to lead eclectic lives unshackled by the legacy of tradition or collective expectation and to respond freely to the market place. (1991: 159)

These distinctions between the ascetics, the postmoderns and the indistincts take us as far as survey data allow. I now turn to a number of other sources of argument and information relating to a possible service class remaking of the English coun-tryside, a remaking that would challenge existing landed and agricultural interests. These further analyses involve changes in the nature of "work" and "leisure", and in the politics of rural resistance and conservation.

It is something of a truism to suggest that there have been striking changes in the nature of work and leisure over the past two or three decades. The following are some of the more important developments relating to the countryside.

First, for at least a decade and a half there has been a large and persistent level of unemployment and underemployment. This has helped to produce a significant number of people who do not expect to undertake regular paid employment of the sort that was common in much of the post-war period. And, as such "work" has dis-appeared for some people, so too has its opposite, "leisure". The two are opposite sides of the same coin.

However, there is an increase in the range of activities in which people engage outside so-called "work". In his survey of the relations between time and money, Cross concludes that there are "increasing signs of non-commercial and active uses of free time in the 1970s and 1980s" (1993: 201). In relationship to the countryside the decline in paid work has led many, especially young people, to lose their oppor-tunities to engage in the kinds of regular "leisured" visits to the countryside that would have occurred in the past. And yet the countryside has become the kind of place that many young people do in fact regularly "travel" through for festivals, raves and informal camps. Such practices are in part based upon the rejection of the very distinction between work and leisure and hence provoke great antipathy from much rural (and urban!) society. At the extreme, the so-called "travellers" seek to travel through and to camp temporarily in the "countryside", often on their way to certain rural sites that are endowed with "natural" or "spiritual" significance. The itinerary of the young traveller consists of a quite different travel map from that possessed by the middle-aged car driver, although both are engaging in similar kinds of pilgrimage to certain sacred sites within the countryside. And on occasions, as with Glastonbury, the objects of their pilgrimage can in a sense coincide (Bowman 1993, Clark et al. 1994a, b).

Such social practices, of which travelling is perhaps the extreme form, cannot be conveniently viewed as simply "leisure", let alone as mere "hobbies". And yet those are the two terms by which such non-work practices are normally understood. As we have written elsewhere:

> . . . such activities and affiliations may now frequently be playing an existentially more significant role, in that they help to constitute the very identity of the individuals in question . . . This throws light on the forces of opposition and advocacy that can be unlocked when these activities are threatened. Leisure is no longer to be understood as the trivial use of "spare time". Instead it is becoming a key element of meaning in people's lives in providing the context in which new social groupings may develop and be sustained. (Clark et al. 1994a: 31, 1994b: 44–8).

These "new sociations" relevant to the countryside include bird watchers, communes, groups of travellers, religious retreats, war games, allotment associations, railway preservation societies, Greenham Common peace camps, historical enactment societies, mountainbikers, civic amenity societies, road protestors, and so on. There are a number of characteristics of such "bund"-like sociations: they are joined out of choice and people are free to leave; they are self-organized and relatively unbureaucratized; there is a high degree of mutual aid reinforced by "norms of reciprocity"; people remain members in part because of emotional satisfaction rather than the achievement of goals; they provide sites for identity-formation and the acquiring of skills; and many of the products (written, artistic, spoken, visual and so on) are consumed by the membership itself (Hoggett & Bishop 1986, Hetherington 1993, 1994, Urry 1995: Ch. 14, on "enthusiasms"). We have become familiar with these movements or organizations within the urban context – they are often characterized as "urban movements" or "new social movements". My claim here is that, in the renegotiation of the work–leisure relationship in the late twentieth century, a similar transformation is taking place within rural areas, transformations that are certainly *related to* changes in the wider society, including the striking growth of a service class, but that cannot be literally described as the service class remaking of rural localities.

I will now turn to the most obvious context for the activities of such new sociations, namely the politics of resistance and conservation. The first point to note is how agriculture is now subject to much closer scrutiny than in the past, a scrutiny resulting from the changes in the social composition of rural localities. The National Farmers' Union reports the unease that farmers experience in many parts of the country at such threats to their autonomy (see Clark et al. 1994a: 43, on the following). In a recent study it has been shown that the emergence of farm waste pollution as an issue has been as much a function of social change in the countryside, arising from the monitoring and documenting practices of new rural residents, as of any apparently objective environmental change. Thus what we may characterize as the "non-work" values and activities of new residents in rural localities – their amenity, aesthetic and leisure interests increasingly surround and constrain well-established farming practices. Harrison summarizes: "it is new residents, untutored in the ways of the countryside but vociferous in the protection of their newly acquired 'rights', who farmers and rural landowners regard as most problematic" (1991: 158).

Such conflicts will become even more pronounced with the newer proposals for farm diversification, which will result in farmland or buildings being turned into golf courses, accommodation, sites for war games, small-scale theme parks, cafés and so on. Many local residents are likely to resist such developments ("not why they moved to the countryside"!). They may also be better informed about how to use the statutory planning system to prevent such developments from occurring, especially in view of the extra traffic volumes that such initiatives will undoubtedly generate. Indeed, Harrison goes on to argue:

> It is clear . . . the members of a service class are likely to play an important role in the resolution of land-use conflicts, particularly when these new residents become involved directly in the institutions responsible for planning and protecting the countryside that they have worked hard to secure and enjoy (1991: 158)

In Rutland, Duckers & Davies report on how farming in "environmentally sensitive areas" is being absorbed into the heritage industry and farmers might be best thought of as scene-shifters in a living museum (1990: 160).

The significance of conservation is supported by research on patterns of environmental politics. Lowe & Goyder note: "The membership statistics of [environmental] groups, however, show no dramatic increase until the early 1970s, when most groups experienced rapid growth and there was a large crop of new groups" (1983: 17). There was high amenity society membership in the home counties surrounding London and in Devon, north Yorkshire and Cumbria; and low membership in all the conurbations outside London, Scotland and the Midlands (ibid. 28, and see Harrison 1991: 161–2 on the 1980s). Short et al. similarly show that there had been a national increase in the number of amenity societies in Britain from fewer than 100 in 1957 to about 1,500 in 1982 (1986: 204), while in central Berkshire, where they conducted their research, there were 149 such groups/societies in the early 1980s, almost all of which had been formed in the 1960s and 1970s (ibid. 206–7). Such residents' groups had a combined membership equivalent to 12% of the population of central Berkshire. Short et al. divide such groups into the stoppers (43%) and the getters (37% of new developments). The core activists in *both* groups were either housewives or white-collar workers, with 47% being professional or managerial workers. Over 80% of members were owner-occupiers. However, the "stoppers" were overwhelmingly professional or managerial employees owning their own homes, whereas the social composition of the "getters" was more varied, although professional employees were still the largest group.

From this research there is little doubt that the pattern of countryside development in Berkshire was significantly structured by conflicts *within* the service class. This was also seen in research conducted in Lancaster where we distinguished between the material, ideal and aesthetic interests of different sectors of the service class in order to explain social and cultural conflict over a new shopping development (see Bagguley, et al. 1990: Ch. 5).

However, such approaches are partial because they fail to consider the manner in which certain rural areas have been subject to relatively new forms of politics in the past few years. This has been most visible in relationship to the new anti-road movement, described by Lean (1994) as "the most vigorous new force in British environmentalism". Much of the campaigning is in fact focused in rural areas and is concerned with the protection of certain valued landscapes against new road-building. Such campaigns often involve a rather strange combination of the public sector service class and "travellers". The latter often use a range of unconventional tactics, a spectacle-ization of protest including humour, music, fashion and the aesthetic, which deliberately plays on the "otherness" and marginality of such groups. Part of what is involved here is their rejection of the "professional" service class's conception of the environment and environmentalism. They seek to replace it with a non-expert cultural mode of protest where the objective is relatively straightforward and visible (and where the loss can be easily visualized and graphically conveyed). Berens (1993) describes these new sociations as contributing to a new tribal underground, composed of collectives, squats and tribes, and where people find a common identity through the creation of their own music, fashion, employment and "direct" environmental protest. However, we know little about the scale of such direct protest, its likely effects and its relations with existing amenity societies with their service class membership. We also do not know how the "otherness" of such groups within rural areas will undermine, negate or alienate the service class efforts to remake the countryside in its various images.

Finally, it is appropriate to consider here the contemporary significance of enhanced reflexivity. Two instantiations of this can be seen to be of increasing importance within the countryside (Lash & Urry 1994, Urry 1995: Ch. 14). First, heightened consciousness of the environment has now begun to affect people when engaging in travel and tourism. Many of the TV programmes concerned with mass tourism have special features or prizes for good examples of sustainable tourism.

There are a number of organizations that attempt to induce a heightened consciousness of the environmental effects of particular travel choices. Such a consciousness can refer to the environmental costs of getting to the destination, the aesthetics of the hotel or the resort, the consequences for water and other resources, the social/moral consequences of "inauthentic" developments, the inappropriate scale of development, and the use or not of local products, services and so on (see Wood & House 1991 on the "ethical tourist"). To some extent this is a replaying of the tourist–traveller distinction, which has been a culturally significant distinction of taste for the past century and a half (see Buzard 1993). It leads certain visitors to go only to certain places that appear to be relatively unravaged by mass tourism (places that are supposedly "authentic"), and to view other places as so environmentally damaged that they will not make them worse by also visiting. This reflexivity even about one's holiday choices is most pronounced amongst those with high levels of educational credentials but there is little evidence yet about how it is affecting rural places in Britain (unlike Majorca, where it is already having marked environmental effects).

Secondly, we are familiar with people travelling to certain places for organized sport, such as golf at St Andrews, water-skiing in Cornwall, and bowls at south coast seaside resorts. However, what is now developing is more complex connections between body, travel and therapy. This is in a way to return to one of the origins of modern travel, that is, the development of the upper and middle-class spa towns of Europe in the eighteenth century. In the case of Glastonbury this is given a particular contemporary twist (see Bowman 1993). This place has been the object of pilgrimage for many centuries. It is believed to be the cradle of English Christianity and many saints have visited; as the supposed Isle of Avalon it is associated with the legend of King Arthur; its abbey drew many pilgrims to it even after dissolution; the healing waters are found in the Chalice Well; and it is hailed as a significant centre of ley lines and has become the focus of New Age and related contemporary pilgrimage. It is a place associated with an enormous array of myths and legends, a kind of magical zone that diverse religious and spiritual groups have endowed with enormous and overlapping significance, including that of healing. Nearly all such visitors refer to the very special atmosphere of the place, which is said to transcend even the large number of such visitors. This is paradoxically a place made for and by visitors.

Bowman (1993) brings out the range and growth of an extraordinarily complex "new age" service industry that has developed to provide for the large numbers of visitors, many of whom describe themselves and are described by the service-providers as "pilgrims" or "seekers", as opposed to mere "spiritual tourists". These services include those associated with the Glastonbury Festival, various religious and other retreats, Zodiac picnics, vegan cafés, mystical tours, psychic readings, the Unicorn Light Centre bed and breakfast, Gothic Image, the Glastonbury experience, and over 100 healers providing every imaginable alternative health treatment.

12.4 Conclusion

The development of these two "leisure" phenomena within the countryside – sustainable tourism and alternative health and spiritual centres – reinforces the general argument that the countryside is being remade in surprisingly complex and partly novel ways. It is by no means a simple service-class or even a more general middle-class remaking.

I have shown that the historic compromise between landed interests and the professional service class, which had been organized around the concept of "quiet recreation", is dissolving because of the following: changes in the nature of agriculture and its special significance for the look of the English countryside; the large-scale temporary and permanent movement into rural areas of the service class with extremely diverse lifestyles and politics, including that of "pastoralism"; the effects upon rural activities of "post-modern" culture; the increased importance of a relatively novel "body culture"; changes in the significance and nature of "leisure" and "hobbying"; the appeal and use of the countryside as a special place for youthful "travelling"; and the location within rural areas of many diverse "new sociations", some of which stem from a strikingly enhanced "reflexivity".

Can the English countryside survive this onslaught? Can it cope with such a diverse set of groupings all trying to impose their sense of "countryside", what Bender in her analysis of the ultimate contested site of Stonehenge refers to as "a cacophony of voices and landscapes through time, mobilizing different histories, differentially empowered" (1993: 275).

Chapter 13

The new middle classes and the social constructs of rural living

Paul Cloke, Martin Phillips and Nigel Thrift

13.1 Introduction

Class formation has all but disappeared from the mainstream of intellectual attention. All the attention now focuses on social divides such as gender and sexuality, ethnicity and ecological consumption, of which the "cultural turn" in so many subjects in the social sciences and humanities is both a cause and a symptom. In a world of AIDS, Bosnia and Chernobyl, the study of class formation seems to be something anachronistic, best left to a few loony quantifiers and some sad, old social critics.

To write of class formation as though it is a large beached whale, gasping for intellectual air, may seem premature, but it is clear that the importance of class can no longer automatically be assumed. In this paper we will consider whether the concept of class formation retains any utility by reporting on results from an Economic and Social Research Council sponsored research project, "Local impacts of the middle class in rural areas" (R000231209), which studied villages in Gower, the Cotswolds and rural Berkshire. In this work we interviewed people in order to understand the impacts of in-migrating middle classes on different rural areas. We use this research in this paper to examine the "colonization" of particular rural places by different fractions of the middle class (Cloke & Thrift 1990, Phillips 1993b). Here we explore how visions of rural life are currently socially constructed in Britain, and particularly how some villages offer in-migrants not only the idealistic features of community, environment and aesthetic quality, but also the opportunity to colonize what were constructed as risk-free environments. In addition, we look at lifestyle strategies in these colonized rural places. Here, while noting that some visions of the rural may cleave to particular class fractions, we also find that others are highly dispersed amongst class fractions to such an extent that any one person's lifestyle may be a poor marker of their class position, at least when class is understood in terms of structural relations of production. So, our goal in this paper is to explore how these cultures of the rural, informed by processes of cultural formation as well as conditioned by the structuring relations of class, are highly

220

significant in establishing collective actions in rural action spaces.

This paper starts by setting out the general arguments for the decline of class formation as a significant structuring principle. We then develop our argument that the determinants of middle-class formation in Britain have become more cultural and, specifically, more attuned to rural discourses and life-spaces. In the third section of the paper we approach and fill out this argument through the work of Eder (1993). The fourth section then moves on to our empirical material to consider the colonization of the countryside and examines the range of different strategies by which the middle classes are gaining access to rural life-spaces. In the fifth section the relationships between class, middle-class rural discourses and life-spaces are explored by reference to Eder's model.

13.2 Middle-class formation in Britain

"Detraditionalization" processes (see Beck 1992) have had a particularly devastating effect on traditional notions of class formation. Ideas of class as a kind of straightjacket, unambiguously positioning subjects in particular occupations and, by extension, in particular lifestyles have become more and more difficult to hold, suggesting that notions of class formation need to be revised. In Britain, we can identify four "detraditionalization" processes that have affected the middle classes – always the most ambiguous of classes – and have weakened the ties between class and necessary outcomes.

The first of these processes has been the decline of large organizational forms, in both the public sector and the private sector. Market testing, contracting out, flattened hierarchies, subcontracting – these are all synonyms for an unsettling of middle-class lives and liaisons. Supposed to work to the advantage of the middle class as "consumers", they work to the disadvantage of the middle class as "producers". They point to a future of less settled careers and greater difficulty in accumulating organizational assets (Savage et al. 1992).

A second process has been the decline in the effectiveness of credentials. As higher education has expanded, so there has been an inflation in educational credentials, and a consequent devaluation. This decline in the effectiveness of credentials extends also to the institutions of taste (Bourdieu 1984). Here, the democratization of so many previously elite objects and institutions (e.g. the transmutation of museums into part of a heritage industry) leaves the middle class with fewer exclusive objects and institutions on which to fix as generators of symbolic capital. Further, many of the non-material values to which the middle class used to cleave have been increasingly marketized, with unpredictable consequences.

> The middle classes have always enjoyed a complex relationship with market and non-market values. High levels of remuneration have ensured a superior lifestyle, but that lifestyle has traditionally placed a high premium on non-material values: schooling, breeding, knowledge, paternalism,

221

> politeness, manners, hierarchy, background, style, accent . . . But the transformation of large areas of cultural activity into a marketable commodity – not least with the erosion of the traditional distinction between high and low culture – is leading to the growing commercialization of traditional middle class institutions and a marked change in their value systems. There is a quite new emphasis on the market, efficiency and value for money. (Jacques 1994: 9)

A third process has been the change in the nature of the household. The rise of dual-career households points to the greater significance of women as formal wage-earners. This rise has been accompanied by the growth of single-person households, which also has a significant gender dimension. In both cases, the significance of class has changed, not least because "women tend to draw considerably stronger cultural boundaries, weaker socio-economic boundaries, and slightly stronger moral boundaries than men" (Lamont 1991: 133).

Changes in the nature of the household point to a fourth process, that is the rise of difference. New social movements, based on sexuality, ethnicity, ecology, and so on, have come into being which are not only new representations of the world but are actively used by people to represent themselves. This process, forced by the various media institutions, has massively elaborated the importance of the "cultural texture" (Eder 1993) of values, identities and minor knowledges as a crucial determinant of class. At the same time, and in related vein, the traditional determinants of middle-class cultural texture – for example, notions of Englishness based on institutions such as the House of Windsor, the BBC, the judiciary and Westminster – have suffered a loss of respect and identification.

Other processes might also be pointed to, though we do not develop them here. These might include: the rise in spatial mobility, a generalized fear of crime, and the changing relationships between time (delay) and consumption, as revealed in new forms of credit relation (see Brennan 1993). What all these processes point to is that class formation has declined in importance as a structuring principle in modern societies. Yet we want to suggest that this conclusion requires some degree of qualification. There are a number of related ways in which class formation may have changed.

First, it is clear that the theoretical representation of class has changed. Thus, conventionally, class is now read as co-determinant with gender, race and so on: gender, race and so on no longer just produce variations on the basic theme of class – that is, "fractionize class" (see Cloke & Thrift 1990) – but are seen as inextricably involved in class formation. Secondly, it might be argued that class has become "more cultural" for reasons we develop below. Thirdly, given this latter point, the determinants of class may have changed to such a degree that we no longer recognize them. Eder argues, for instance, that features of social life that spell problematic cases for "traditional class theory" may well be "the unproblematic centre of a new class relationship" (Eder 1993: 183). In this paper we are interested in exploring how the "rural" may play such a role for the contemporary middle classes.

In order to register the significance of culture for class formation it is necessary to avoid taking a false turn at the outset. Recently, attempts to examine the interrelationship between class and culture have turned to Bourdieu's (1984) work (e.g. Savage et al. 1992). Bourdieu sees the relation between class and culture as a set of strategies of accumulation of symbolic capital in different but related social fields mediated by the habitus. Although we strongly agree with Bourdieu's notion of the habitus as a means of characterizing the embodied improvisations through which everyday life is carried forward, we are much more sceptical of Bourdieu's reciprocal mapping of the habitus on to social fields that are each of them the arenas for a competition of symbolic advantage with the aim of maximizing symbolic capital. What are the reasons for our scepticism?

First, Bourdieu's work radically downgrades cultural complexity by recoding culture as simply part of the pursuit of symbolic advantage. "Everything from accumulating monetary capital to praise for being burned at the stake automatically counts as symbolic capital. To say that whatever people do they do for social profit does not tell us anything if profit is defined as whatever people pursue in a given society" (Dreyfus & Rabinow 1993: 42). This does not mean that we are denying the pursuit of symbolic advantage, rather it is to assert that this pursuit cannot become a totalizing principle, because "then (1) it conceals what it does not fit, or else (2) it requires a repression of exceptions; and (3) the resulting demystifying methodology can never take actors' self-understanding at face value" (Dreyfus & Rabinow 1993: 42). Secondly, too often, as de Certeau (1984) and Rigby (1991) have pointed out, Bourdieu's accounts become, through their emphasis on symbolic advantage, little more than social reproduction models that take little or no notice of the "tactics" that de Certeau and others regard as a cultural *sine qua non*. Thirdly, and following on from the previous two points, it is debatable whether Bourdieu actually has a strong theory of class and culture at all. Most particularly

> . . . there does not appear to be a way to explain how society can produce individuals who, operating in a specific field (especially science and art), produce forms of thought that expose and threaten the reproduction of the class structure. Such thought is possible only when the symbolic order and linked fields have a structure and dynamic which is not reducible to, or a function of, the social system. (LiPuma 1993: 24)

Of course, Bourdieu would deny all these charges (see, for example, Bourdieu & Wacquant 1992, 115, 131, Bourdieu 1993). But they make us wary and not least because it seems to us that Bourdieu's work has been (mistakenly) used in some of the contemporary literature on class to justify a reductionism of culture to class that is insupportable. It is noteworthy that Lamont's (1991) study of American and French middle-class cultures broadened out her focus to emphasize that moral distinctions could not be collapsed into symbolic or socio-economic ones. We have therefore chosen to look elsewhere for inspiration, towards discussions of class and culture, which may well appear "vague" or "indefinite" (but see Bourdieu's comments, in Bourdieu & Wacquant 1992, on the positive value of the vague and indefinite in studying culture), but which at least in our view may avoid accusations of reductionism.

13.3 Klaus Eder: the cultural texture between class and collective action

If Bourdieu is of limited value for registering the significance of culture and class, where should we turn? We believe that the recent work of Klaus Eder offers important pointers. In *The new politics of class* (1993) Eder suggests that class theorists have been asking the wrong questions and formulating inappropriate assumptions about modern class(less)ness. He argues that our assumption should not be that classes no longer exist in modern societies, but rather that recognizable forms of collective action tend to differentiate relatively independently of class structuring as defined by the social distribution of resources such as power, wealth and even cultural capital. His response, therefore, is not to abandon class as a useful conceptual device, but instead to propose what he calls "a culturalist concept of class" (Eder 1993: 1). Previously, the importance of culture to class has been acknowledged most often by recognizing culture as some kind of direct bridge between class and action and as dependent on them for its significance. Eder sees that culture has become much more than an intervening variable; actions are embedded in "culturally defined action spaces" or "public spheres" (cf. Phillips 1994) and so the impacts of class on action are mediated by the "cultural texture" of that class. Eder focuses specifically on the constitution of collective action and proposes a three-layer model:

Layer 1: CLASS – class is a structural variable made accessible through probabilistic constructs of aggregates of social positions.

Layer 2: CULTURAL TEXTURE – the cultural texture of values, identities and knowledge gives meaning to the structural variable of class.

Layer 3: COLLECTIVE ACTION – collective action, denoted by preference structures and nominative orientations, occurs within the context of cultural textures.

Whereas traditionally the concept of class privileged layer 1, Eder's interesting reformulation of the question is "How does collective action constitute and reproduce a symbolically defined action space that is both the condition and the outcome of collective action?" According to Eder's model, collective action events are always situated in culturally defined action spaces. Thereby, collective action is embedded in a cultural texture that represents a form of reality that consists of a specifically organized discourse that provides the setting for the motivations of actors to act together, and even overrides those motivations on some occasions. It is cultural texture, according to this view, that represents those cultural life-forms (Thompson et al. 1990) that allow individuals to act collectively. These life-forms are action spaces that are symbolically organized and that co-ordinate the subjective motivations of people. They can be said to be subject to a cultural logic (or a series of such logics) and it is the understanding of these logic(s) that Eder sees as the key to the analysis of cultural texture in research on collective mobilization and action.

A number of claims follow from this interpretation of class, culture and action. First, class impacts on action through cultural constructions that are produced and reproduced as part of historically specific life-forms. Eder (1993: 2) argues that culture develops through its own logics and suggests that contemporary modern societies have the "paradoxical development" of class structures that develop "more and more along complex but clear cut lines" and cultures that have "developed independently of class and have complex and fluid boundaries". Secondly, Eder retains an emphasis on class structure, while arguing for its integration with life-forms and actions. For Eder, class analysis can be seen as "a 'funnel' model of explanation . . . [C]lass comes last: it is the most restrictive variable; it reduces the variability of events that explain what is going on" (Eder 1993: 10). It is, however, an important – arguably the "critical" (Thompson 1984, 1990) – moment of interpretation. Eder claims that class structures generate positions that stand for opportunities (or lack of them). Thirdly, Eder argues that class structures do not have to operate through conscious relations. Class structures are the creation of the social observer and may therefore exist only for such an observer. On the other hand, they can figure in the discourses occurring within particular action spaces; indeed, Eder argues that equality and inequality of life-chances are central "development logics" in culture. A fourth claim made by Eder is that we need to discard hierarchical notions of relations between classes and instead follow a network model of class relationships (see Callon & Latour 1981, Knorr-Cetina 1988, Clegg 1989,) in which one set of actors attempt to engage another set of actors in a stable set of relations. Fifthly, Eder argues that social structure and power should be seen as the outcomes of these actions. In Latour's (1986) phrase, social structure is "not what holds us together, it is what is held together" (Latour 1986: 276). Similarly, Eder argues that "class is a social construction which puts together social categories in order to form a more encompassing whole" (Eder 1993: 183).

Thus Eder adopts a constructionist and culturalist concept of class, in which networks of constitutive and reproductive iterations between structure and agency generate opportunity positions, impact on social action through cultural construction, and are (re)generated by the outcomes of social action. In Eder's view, class is

> a structure that translates inequality and power into different life-chances for categories of individuals. It is therefore a structural determination of life-chances, a structure which distributes chances to act, and de-limits action spaces, which are often highly resistant to the attempts of social actors to change them. We can then add cultural and socio-psychological variables, which explain the choice of options that is opened up by a structurally determined and culturally textured action space. (Eder 1993: 12)

Clearly the construction of these cultural classes is historically specific. Eder suggests that life-chances have increasingly been related to conditions of existence that are moulded by collective goods borne of collective decision-making processes. This dependence on collective goods has shaped the emerging class structures of the post-industrial era, which are increasingly characterized by, for example, "risk-laden" processes of reproduction. Eder notes that middle-class life has long been peculiarly risk laden because of the contradictory positions the middle classes hold in capitalist economies and argues that the rise in concern over the environmental risks and degradation has become of moral concern to the middle classes because "they are exactly those things that most threaten the physical and increasingly the psychic world" (1993: 187). Thus Eder claims that class can be seen as an empirical class of people at risk, cultural texture as a socio-cultural system that allows for the representation of risk, and collective action as a propensity to mobilize action for or against that risk, thereby reproducing a public representation of a class of people at risk (or not at risk).

Social groups, and inequalities between them, are interpretative schemes of social reality, and cognitive representations of social position will take account of a range of competencies. Eder's argument is that the interdependence both of income and qualifications and of moral and aesthetic competencies allows us to identify the social distribution of the quantities of competence that represent the class structure as it develops as networks in advanced industrial societies. Again, cultural mediation is crucial in this process:

> An actor's occupation is insufficient as a class marker. (S)he also needs culture . . . Nowadays to have culture means to have opinions . . . [O]pinions related to politics and morals or to art and technology now tend to be the marker replacing the classical indicator of distance from the sophisticated high culture. We can distinguish between those with opinions, to approve of those who know what opinions to have, and to pity those who do not. (Eder 1993: 87)

A final significant contribution of Eder's work to our discussion of the importance of morality to the middle classes is his identification of three schemata that can be used to justify social class positions. In Table 13.1, Eder links a particular interpretative schema of identity and ethos with a particular cognitive representation of the cultural texture of class and with a particular arena of life-world. In the first schema, social inequality is seen as the result of differential individual achievements. This interpretative strategy will be common amongst those whose economic and cultural wealth allows them to afford the ethos that it is necessary to ensure that the "best" people enter the higher social positions. Cultural competence is thus embedded in this notion of "best" people, and cultural texture is represented predominantly in life-worlds that reflect interests in the cultural, political and public spheres. In the second schema, material inequality is seen as the outcome of differential cognitive competence. Here the emphasis is on achievement, and the best positions are reflected by the culture that can be achieved. Hence the predominant life-worlds are those that reflect interests in the private sphere, often the family arena. In the

Table 13.1 Types of class-specific cultures.

Interpretative schema	Cognitive form	Type of life-world
1. Individualistic ethos of personal identity and of the potential equality among men	Idealistic fallacy: what counts is the culture one has	Predominance of life interests in the cultural, political and public spheres
2. The ethos of achievement, recognition of inequality between men	Ecological fallacy: what counts is the culture one has achieved	Predominance of life interests in the private sphere (family)
3. The ethos of maximizing the chances of consumption, recognition of the division of society into social classes	Materialistic fallacy: what counts as culture is the goods one has	Predominance of life interests in the sphere of work, especially the workplace

Source: Eder (1993: 98).

third schema, social position is interpreted in terms of consumption. Here, the representations of status positions in society are reduced to the particular material resources they are tied to, and the predominant life-worlds reflect interests in work areas.

Let us now see how Eder's insights can be applied to our study of the middle classes and their rural cultures.

13.4 Class colonizations of the countryside

The colonization of the countryside has become a significant feature of contemporary modern societies. In England, for example, the number of people living in areas classified as being "remote rural" grew by 6.4% between 1981 and 1991 while the population of metropolitan areas fell by 5.2% over the same period (Rural Development Commission 1992). Furthermore, it has been argued that the social make-up of these areas is "disproportionally biased towards those who, in terms of their wealth, power and influence, are influential in deciding national policy and public opinion" (Rogers 1992). The reasons for the movement of the affluent middle class into the countryside has been a subject of long-standing debate (see Urry's discussion in Ch. 12 in this volume). More recently a series of works (Cloke & Thrift 1987, 1990, Thrift 1987, 1989) have discussed the significance of "the new middle classes" in the growth of the rural middle class and have made some suggestions about how notions of an "idyllic rurality" have figured both as a motive for colonizing the countryside and in the constitution of the "service class".

Both "rural idyll" and "service class" have been applied increasingly to an understanding of rural social change, and each requires some cautionary comments. First, the "rural idyll" is a problematic and rather chaotic conception that has been used to draw together a number of ideas about how rurality is socially constructed to represent a string of mythical imagined communities and landscapes in which problem-free, bucolic and "close-to-nature" lifestyles may be lived out. It is important to note in this context that the cultural prompts to any such idyll will vary in both time and space (Cloke & Milbourne 1992, Cloke 1995) and that, rather than talk of the idyll, we should clearly be thinking in terms of a large number of different idylls and different imaginations of rural communities in order to make sense of the differentiation in lay discourses of rurality (Halfacre 1993). Secondly, the notion of service classes also requires some examination. Marsden & Flynn (1993), for example, identify "the heterogeneous 'service class'" as one of the four "contested transitions" restructuring the contemporary British countryside. Indeed, it has been argued that rural restructuring led by the service class has become the emergent orthodoxy of rural social studies (Phillips 1993a). There have, however, been some more critical examinations. In an earlier paper based on this research project it was argued that changes in housing policies in the Gower Peninsula reflected not so much the preferences of service-class residents, but rather more an attempt by central government to attract "senior managers from externally based private-sector firms" (Cloke et al. 1991: 52) to settle in Gower. Murdoch & Marsden (1991) examined whether the notion of a "service-class culture" could be applied to rural Buckinghamshire. They concluded that "there is not one 'culture' associated with the middle class in the rural areas of Buckinghamshire, although we would agree that these 'cultures' are becoming 'hegemonic'" (Murdoch & Marsden 1991, 45).

Murdoch & Marsden do not document these cultures in any depth and they rather misread the original arguments. It was never claimed that the service class equals the middle class, or that all rural areas were becoming dominated by the service class; rather it was claimed that the service class is an increasingly important "fraction" of middle-class residents within selected rural areas.

The results of our studies in Gower, the Cotswolds and rural Berkshire certainly reinforce the need for a cautionary approach to applying the notion of service class led rural restructuring. One of the most immediate problems is the thorny issue of how to "measure" class. When using the system of class classification produced by Erik Olin Wright (1978) it appears that rural residents come from nearly all classes, but that the working class was the largest single class grouping in all three of our case-study areas. Analysis using the Nuffield class schema, however, shows that no less that 65% of residents in our case-study areas were from the "service class", a figure that supports the contention that it is becoming an "historic and hegemonic block" in the countryside (see Cloke & Goodwin 1992). Figure 13.1 also shows that this service-class dominance includes not just new residents but those who have lived at their current addresses for over 20 years.

There is also the difficult question of whether class should be measured individually or by some sort of household measure. There has been a tendency in discussions over the service-class led rural restructuring to talk about individuals – to talk about in-migration leading to a rising number of "service-class members". However, most rural in-migration involves not single individuals but households; that is, people tend to migrate with partners, with children, with relatives of some form. In

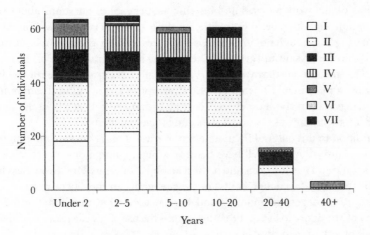

Figure 13.1 Goldthorpe classes by length of residence.

an earlier piece of work from the project (Phillips 1993b) it was suggested that there may be a high degree of class asymmetry within households moving to the country-side, with women generally being classified as working in more proletarianized jobs than their male partners (according to Wright's class schema). A hitherto neglected facet of service-class led restructuring may well be that a largely female working class is being drawn into the countryside through being partners in highly class-asymmetrical households.

The issue of classification certainly raises some questions about the size of the service class in rural areas. It is, however, important to recognize that the signifi-cance of the service class may reflect much more its general powers to restructure rurality than its numerical significance in colonizing particular rural spaces. It has, for instance, been argued that members of the service class have both a particular concern for the state of the countryside and the capacity to do something about that predilection (Thrift 1989).

This last argument has recently come in for some criticism. Savage et al. (1992) have suggested that there are significant cultural divisions within the service class, and in particular that an interest in the rural is much more a preference among managers and government bureaucrats than it is among private sector profession-als and service workers. Our surveys would suggest that there may be some value in their arguments. For example, when we asked some questions about peoples' con-ceptions of the countryside and their views on contemporary rural change we found that 70% of men from the managerial middle-class fractions wanted plan-ning controls in the countryside strengthened, compared with less than 20% of pro-fessionals. Nonetheless, the general picture does not neatly map onto occupational group. When asked about whether visitor numbers should be restricted, profession-als were the most enthusiastic (nearly 80% agreeing that they should be). The asso-ciation between cultural texture and class fraction was far from clear cut, and responses of the working class and intermediate classes to questions about rural conservation were in general little different those of the service class. One of the most striking – although not unexpected – features was the association of attitudes towards the countryside and gender. When talking of the rural culture of the managerial class fraction one may well be very specifically talking about the rural culture of "organizational men". There were also clearly processes of cultural communication and negotiation about the rural occurring within and between households that further fragment any links between class and individual lifestyle.

In addition to this cultural fragmentation of class, it also became apparent to us that the countryside may well have become a highly ubiquitous object of desire across a range of class fractions and not just an object of desire for narrow class fractions, be these the "need merchants" of private service or the "inconspicuous consumers" of managers in industry and bureaucracy. One manifestation of the ubiquity of the desire to live in the countryside is the use of a wide range of different channels of entry into a rural lifestyle.

The mechanics of the colonization of the countryside by the middle classes have become well rehearsed: "restrictive planning policies cause an upward spiral in house prices; occupancy of houses thereby becomes restricted to those social groups who can afford the new prices[;] . . . the new rural middle class are immediately engaged in conflict with the 'working-class locals'; and political power gradually accrues to newcomers" (Cloke et al. 1991: 39). Colonization of the countryside is seen to be reliant on the accumulation of sufficient income to be able to bid successfully in the competitive rural housing markets. This is usually associated with a well-paid occupation, successful business ventures or accumulated savings at the end of reasonably paid career. Hence rural colonization is associated with gentrification (the replacement of a population with working-class jobs by people in the private and public sector middle classes) and geriatrification (involving the movement of people at or near to retirement age).

Such processes of class colonization are clearly still highly significant. Our research revealed the importance of high-paid occupations and accumulated savings over a lengthy career in establishing an ability to bid successfully in the rural housing market. The research also highlighted the continuing influence of occupation in determining locational decision-making, although there was also a variety of other influential factors including changing household composition and, quite noticeably, the wish to raise children in the countryside (Fig. 13.2). On the other hand, our research has also indicated a variety of other strategies for gaining access to the countryside. Here we will just indicate three such strategies.

The purchase of a house in the country is often seen as personal and, increasingly, as "positional" consumption (see Cloke & Thrift 1990, Cloke et al. 1991, Savage et al. 1992, Phillips 1993b). It is important to recognize, however, that housing can also act as a very important financial asset and that it may provide a more lucrative mechanism of economic accumulation for many middle-class people than does employment. The spiralling cost of rural housing in the 1980s made it a particularly attractive investment. In our survey, over 65% of the respondents had "traded

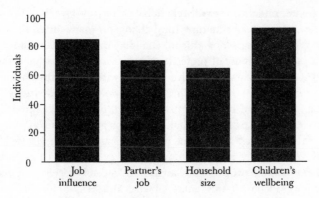

Figure 13.2 Reasons for moving to villages.

up" in the housing market and, although only 22% stated that they had purchased their residence with an eye to its resale value, over 86% considered that housing was a good investment in their area. Although it is important to recognize that, as Lash (1990: 49) puts it, houses have exchange, use and sign values and therefore may not be used exclusively as a capital asset for a petty property-dealing middle class, our results would suggest that such activity may be a factor fuelling some middle-class colonization of the countryside. A passage from one interview portrays quite graphically this channel of entry into the countryside:

> The previous house . . . was a 4 bedroomed very nice house . . . and I had moved around a lot to get that . . . Took me eleven years to get that one . . . [Moved] for the money, because I wasn't earning much money doing what I did. The only way I could do it – for the things I wanted to do – was to move. And so, some of the houses I have had, I really loved . . . but we moved . . . to something cheaper but which had the potential to go up again.

Housing was hence a capital asset to be invested in and realized to support the desired rural lifestyle. Although the current house was an important component of that lifestyle, if the value of the house in that lifestyle was threatened, then there was always the "choice" of returning to the housing market to purchase a new house with the required exclusivity and desired rurality. When asked about how they would react to new housing development in the village, the respondent answered: "To be honest with you, I hope I would call my house 'Main entrance' and try and say 'take the lot' and I'll bugger off somewhere else."

Trading in houses was one important channel of entry into a country lifestyle. It was particularly important for those of moderate income but who still aimed to reside in the countryside. Our surveys have found, however, that accumulation of value through dealings in the housing market was not the only way of gaining entry into the rural housing market. An earlier paper (Phillips 1993b) suggested that "gentrification" – understood as the rehabilitation of run-down housing stock – was of great relevance in understanding rural change in many areas. Examples were given of people spending a long time in rebuilding dilapidated buildings or in constructing houses without use of professional builders. In one instance, the building work lasted over eight years and involved a family with two children living in a caravan in the garden of the new dwelling because they could otherwise "only have bought a small detached house in Port Talbot" (quoted in Phillips 1993b: 135). Here was a clear instance of a household forgoing a great deal in order to be able to live in a rural dwelling; they were, in the words of Rose (1984), "marginal gentrifiers". Interestingly, a recent study of rural parishes in 12 English counties concluded that a number of its study areas had "recently received significant proportions of lower income in-migrants" (Cloke et al. 1994: 95–6).

Often such cases of gentrification can be seen as a strategy of capital accumulation by petit property owners in which people invest their personal labour power, or "sweat equity" (Smith 1979a), to raise the value of a property. It is closely associated with the strategy of dealing in houses, and people "gentrifying" their houses in Gower generally stood "to make significant clear financial gains from selling their improved properties" (Phillips 1993b: 129). It is important to recognize that there may well be a variety of other motives for gentrifying houses, including changing household structure (see Phillips 1993b).

As well as suggesting the need to recognize the colonization of the countryside by marginal gentrifiers, our research also revealed a large number of what may be termed "marginalized rural dwellers". These were people who lived in the countryside, often in far from idyllic conditions and generally with no desire and/or scope for material investment to improve their situation. One of the most socially exclusive villages studied in our research, for example, had a permanent caravan site attached to it. Caravans here cost up to £70,000 plus a monthly ground rent and, although located on the margins, both physically and socially, of the village, were apparently desirable because they were located in "peaceful" and "lovely" countryside. Although many of these mobile homes were extended, it was frequently stated that they were not a good investment because, whatever you did to them, "mobile homes do not go up in value". Other cases of marginal rural dwellers included young people "trapped" in the homes of their parents by the high prices of rural housing, and households in tied or council housing. One should add to these "marginalized rural dwellers" the various "illegal dwellers" in the countryside, including "New Age travellers".

Our research suggests that such marginalized dwellers, the marginal gentrifiers and the petit property dealer should be added to the list of significant rural colonizers alongside the more classical middle-class occupationally sustained rural colonist. It is in the interrelations between such groups that the symbolic boundaries outlined by Lamont (1991) will be so important in the reproduction of inequality in the rural setting. Much more needs to be understood about the symbolic moral boundaries in these settings. The range of class fractions colonizing the countryside seems to us to raise important questions that resonate with some of Eder's ideas discussed earlier. First and foremost it seems to suggest the significance of rurality as an intervening variable between class and action. During the course of conducting interviews it became very apparent that people from a whole range of class fractions – including some that were well outside the traditional boundaries of the middle class – were expressing strong concerns about the countryside (see Table 13.2).

Following on from this we began to consider why a dwelling in the countryside should be so appealing to people from such a wide range of class backgrounds. One reason may certainly be the widespread peddling of the image of countryside as some bucolic idyll (see Thrift 1989, Cloke & Milbourne 1992). Some of the descriptions of the countryside given by rural dwellers read like those of a place marketer: "[the village] is a dream place to live in – beautiful environment, great for the kids, so sunny . . . and a thriving community." It is not only on the television (Youngs 1985) or in the glossy advertisements that the sun always shines! Here certainly is one possible iteration of class, culture and rurality: the image makers in the service class produce images that express an idyllic cultural texture of the rural that is then disseminated by the mass media and marketing agencies; this image of the countryside is bought and accepted by people from a wide range of class backgrounds; the culture (and arguably thereby power) of the service class has become hegemonic. There may well, however, be problems with this interpretation, not least in that the rural idyll may have a far deeper history than does the service class (see Thomas 1973, Williams 1973, Mingay 1989, Short 1991, Cloke et al. 1995).

A second feature that became apparent during our interviews was that people across a wide range of class fractions were investing not only economically but also culturally and psychologically in the countryside. One illustrative example of what might be interpreted as socio-economic investment in rurality is provided by the following remarks made by an interviewee minutes after the initiation of an interview:

> This morning, funny enough, I was going to have you down at the sheep dip
> 'cause I had planned to go dipping sheep this morning with a mate of mine
> . . . I had sheep here but with the job commitment I had to give them up.

This interviewee was also heavily into rural pursuits such as clay shooting – which was "all part of the game" of living in the countryside – and leisure appeared to have played an important part in his decision to move into the country, he having apparently moved "simply" for his wife's horses. Overall, one can suggest that there is more than a slight hint of a "conspicuous display of rurality" in his remarks, and evidence of a conscious attempt to purchase commodities to construct a leisured rural lifestyle. More generally, this kind of text from rural colonizers echoes Eder's ideas of class structures both being the creation of the social observer but also figuring in the discourses occurring within particular action spaces.

However, as mentioned earlier, it seems to us that much of the contemporary discussion of the relationships between culture and class relies too exclusively on the notion of cultural capital and positional consumption. Our research suggested that there are other "cultural textures" at play in the desire to live in the countryside

Table 13.2 Attachments to rurality across class boundaries.

Valued aspects of village[1]	Goldthorpe class position		Wright class position
"A well mixed community of people . . . different age groups . . . real locals and also enthusiasm of newcomers . . . very nice place to live . . . very friendly"	I	Higher grade professional	Capitalist
"It does not really feel like a village – no real community, not that we want to be part of it. We like living here because we can see for miles and feel freer and it can be quiet"	I	Higher grade professional	Capitalist
"The standard of the properties is high – beautiful houses and still a village feel . . . still a lot of green space . . . area not too built up . . . village is quite small, quite tidy and a pleasant area	I	Higher grade professional	Top manager
"Relatively small . . . good class of people . . . education good . . . sufficient amenities . . . well located for airports"	II	Lower grade professional	Middle manager
"Attractive . . . community atmosphere . . . good for children . . . convenient location"	II	Lower grade professional	Line supervisor
"Its location relative to Ascot, Windsor and London . . . It is in the Green Belt . . . It is quiet but not dead"	IIIa	Routine non-manual	Proletariat
"Friendliness and the concentration of services"	IIIa	Routine non-manual	Proletariat
"The community as a whole . . . the lovely countryside ara"	IIIA	Routine non-manual	Proletariat
"The closeness here . . . community centre and school . . . I didn't realize I would feel so strongly about it . . . I would not move away from the village"	IVa	Small employer	Small employer
"It is countryside – that's it . . . fields, trees, peace and quiet"	IVa	Small employer	Top manager
"Peaceful and friendly"	IVb	Self-employed	Petit-bourgeois
"Very friendly . . . quiet, very safe feel about it, you can walk to shops, play-grounds, etc."	V	Low grade technicians	Technocrat
"The local community is very strong . . . the general area is an AONB"	V	Lower grade technician	Line supervisor
"Friendly . . . people ready to help . . . close groups . . . church activities"	VIIb	Agricultural work	Semi-autonomous employee

1. Respondents were also asked about aspects of the village that they did not like. All the respondents quoted in this table answered that they did not think there were any negative aspects of their villages.

than simply a desire to live in some idyllic world – indeed there was a general acceptance that no such world existed – or to live in an environment displaced from work, or to make some statement about socio-economic position. For example, for some people the movement to the countryside seemed to be a realization of personal ambition. One respondent in Gower, for instance, stated: "I wanted to live in the country . . . the move was a realization of my ambition, although it did coincide with a change in my husband's job."

Her husband expressed another seemingly widespread motive for living in the countryside when he explained that he wanted to move because he felt that "London was not suitable to bring up children". As Figure 13.2 illustrates, the wellbeing of children was frequently cited as a reason for moving to the countryside. Explanations of the relationship between the countryside and the raising of children frequently drew upon notions of "a caring village community", of a "natural, healthy environment", and, perhaps most dominantly, of a "peaceful", or at least "less violent, less crime ridden" society (see Phillips 1993b).

These arguments reveal sharply the concern over risk in perceptions of the countryside and how living in the countryside is often seen both as a means of escaping risks and also as a form of life very much under threat. These arguments also clearly draw upon specific gender (see Little 1987, Phillips 1993b) and sexual identities (see Valentine 1995), and also constructions of ethnicity. Murdoch & Marsden, for example, have argued that: "The yearning for the rural corresponds in many ways to . . . . 'Anglo-centricity'. Within this . . . space identities are fixed within a white, family centred, increasingly middle class domain" (Murdoch & Marsden 1991: 47). They note that one of the reasons a rural school they studied was popular was that there were no ethnic minority children there.

As well as a clear racial dimension in some people's desire to live in the countryside, there are also interesting refractions of national identities. Even in rural Wales, for example, one can witness the imaginary power of the notion of an "English Village": a nucleated village located in a rolling and cultivated landscape and often described with reference to "the Cotswolds, the Sussex Downland and parts of Suffolk" (Matless 1994: 78). Asked to describe the positive aspects of their Gower village one respondent answered:

> I like the sense of community . . . and it has some visual interest, although it also has some misfits . . . It has no unity, such as in a Cotswold village, although it is nice around the village green . . . has two village pubs, quite a good village hall and a nice community spirit.

Another respondent explained that they chose to settle in their Gower village because:

> It looked like an English village to us, rather than many ribbon-like villages north of Swansea . . . I suppose it's our preconception of what a village should look like.

235

Gower historically has been an English-speaking area, but even here there were some clear expressions of resistance to the construction of English rurality. Many of the people colonizing the Gower villages we studied appear to have been born in Wales and many of them were clearly constructing their migration to Gower as a return to their homeland after many years working in another country.

13.5 Middle-class lifestyle strategies in rural areas

Our interviews with residents of three rural areas therefore suggest to us that there are a number of differences in the ways in which middle-class households gain access to a rural residence and in their reasons for wishing to colonize the countryside. We also want to suggest that there are important differences in the way in which middle-class individuals and households react to different cultural expectations of life and lifestyle in these villages. In effect, these different embodied dispositions will iteratively reproduce many different cultural textures in the same village. In our surveys we found that there was a large range of differences in the manner in which our interviewees interpreted the way they acted in the countryside. For example, length of residence, age, gender, previous place of residence, income, mobility and, where appropriate, ethnicity seem to interconnect with varying cultural and moral competencies to result in a variety of different accounts of what is important about rural life as experienced in their particular place of residence. We were, however, able to interpret some significant differences in and amongst these factors. These might be generalized as:

(a) *A local gentry*. Individuals and households whose presence in the village was, or was represented to be, intergenerational, prized the links between heritage, belonging, intimate knowledge of life in the place and a secure position within their own construction of local community. Community organizations, political representation and the constitution of the "common good" in the village tend to be cherished life-world arenas for these people, even though in terms of occupation and profession they may not now have the significant links with the agricultural economies and cultures that are often assumed of them.

(b) *Village regulators*. Many people in the village took a keen interest in the regulation of the village, particularly in terms of planning controls. These people saw themselves less as community leaders, as did the local gentry, and much more as protectors of an often abstracted notion of village space. This group tended to be quite legalistic and concerned that regulations and policies were implemented both efficiently and comprehensively.

(c) *Move in and join in*. We interviewed several individuals and households for whom the prospect of a rural lifestyle was significantly bound up with being able to take part in village community life. Frequently, their view of the village revolved around aspects of the friendliness, inclusiveness and close-knit nature of rural life. In order to live out this interpretation they would join village-based activities, such as the local pub, cricket team, golf club, or church, charity or political activities. These

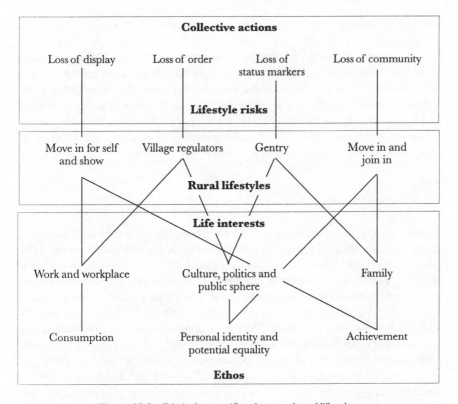

Figure 13.3 Eder's class-specific cultures and rural lifestyles.

strategies were all outward looking from the dwelling or land the individual or household had built into.

(d) *Move in for self and show.* An alternative strategy was that their imagination of the culture of the rural had been restricted to ideas of a quality dwelling in a quality environment. Here the village was only an aesthetic backdrop, and the emphasis upon lifestyle strategy was centred on the house and garden.

These four lifestyle strategies can be seen in the terms developed by Eder (see Fig. 13.3). The "move in and join in" households, for example, although drawing upon the ethos of achievement, also seemed to draw upon the ethos of personal identity and to strive to be in the same life-worlds as the village gentry. The "move in for self and show" households, although displaying the ethos of maximizing consumption chances, also seemed to respond to the idea of an ethos of achievement, in that their rural status involved a recognition of social inequality. Such households also represent a mix of cognitive forms, resting partly on achieving a cultural niche, but perhaps more significantly on buying commodities of house, garden or land and view or backdrop, which count as cultural credentials. For each lifestyle type, the cultural texture of the rural is important in affecting action, including collective action. Risks to the village arena threaten each lifestyle strategy (by posing threats to display, order, status and communality) and can therefore mobilize action across different groups.

These lifestyle types are related, in diverse ways, to various occupational locations and to the deployment of different middle-class assets. Thus one of the "village regulators" was a senior manager who, with his experience of regulations and organizational planning, may well have felt most comfortable in acting within the public activity space of the village through planning mechanisms. However, there is no simple link between such lifestyles and occupational positions, and for many of those we talked to occupation itself was of marginal significance.

13.6 Conclusions

Conventionally, the rural, seen as a set of specifically organized discourses and activity spaces, has been regarded as one more middle-class identifier, as one of the ways in which the middle classes identify themselves. In this paper we have shown that "the rural" has now become more important than this. The affective investment made by middle-class people in rural activities has become greater than simply a set of "leisure activities" or even a form of "cultural capital". Thus, analysts such as Giddens (1991) and Beck (1992) have pointed to the way in which the elements of the modern self have to be more consciously adopted through choosing affiliations and goods that often incorporate moral concerns (Clark et al. 1994a, b). In turn, this work on the self produces new allegiances and structures of feeling. Linked to this, "the rural" has become ever more important as a site of middle-class collective action. Precisely as rural activities have been surrounded with emotional investments arising from work on the self, so threats to the continuation of these activities (understood in both a locally specific and a more existential sense) become heartfelt, leading to a rise in protests and membership of rural pressure groups. Moreover, "the rural" has expanded its orbit because of the rise of the cultural industries that remorselessly circulate rural imagery (Lash & Urry 1994).

The rural may have become critical to the constitution of the middle class to the point where the relation between class and "the rural" has been almost reversed: whereas in the past middle class signified rural, it might now be claimed that the cultural texture associated with the rural has expanded to a point where "rural" signifies the middle class. In other words, the middle class is now discursively constructed to a much greater degree than previously, and "the rural", as activity spaces and as a set of organized discourses, may be playing key roles in this construction.

Part Five

Consumption and the middle classes

The sociology of consumption is one of the fastest growing areas within sociology, and also poses some of the most exciting and original issues for class analysis itself. Until the 1970s the sociology of stratification was rooted in a "productivist" framework, which placed prime emphasis upon the employment relationship as the crucible of class, and, insofar as it considered consumption at all, tended to see it as a simple reflex of class itself.

This position began to change in the 1970s when a number of writers began to stress that consumption should be seen as a signficant social proces in its own right. Within urban studies the writings of Manuel Castells played a key role in alerting researchers to the way that struggles over "collective consumption" (by which he meant publicly provided collective services such as housing, education, health, etc.) were a chronic feature of modern capitalist urban life. Castells himself wavered on whether such struggles could be rooted in class or not (compare Castells 1977 with Castells 1983). Subsequent writers were less hesitant. Peter Saunders (1986) emphasized the emergence of what he termed "consumption cleavages" at the expense of class. Saunders argued that those relying on public provision of services were located in a different social situation to those who could afford private services, and that conflict between these two groups could be anticipated as the former tried to maximize public subsidy of services to reduce their costs whilst the latter tried to minimize their taxes (and hence maximize their disposable income) by cutting public services. The long debate that these arguments spawned need not concern us here (see Savage & Warde 1993 for one discussion), but what it relevant is the extent to which divisions arising out of housing relate to those of class.

Hamnett's paper (Chapter 15) comes directly out of these debates over the relative importance of class and consumption, using home-ownership as the specific vehicle of inquiry and can be seen as an attempt to explore the interplay between class and housing without trying to assert the theoretical primacy of one over the other. Warde's paper (Chapter 14) can be seen as part of a more recent trend whereby the sociology of consumption has shifted from well rehearsed areas such as housing to consider issues of "taste" and fashion. This, in part, links into class theory through

Bourdieu's work, and his emphasis of the grounding of taste in different class habitus. Warde's paper is one of the first to investigate seriously the impact of class divisions on diet, and offers an unusual way of reflecting on the different theoretical approaches to the middle classes discussed in this book.

Chapter 14

Taste among the middle classes, 1968–88

Alan Warde and Mark Tomlinson

14.1 Preamble

Much recent sociology has argued that there has been a radical diminution in the impact of class on other aspects of social behaviour both in the United Kingdom and in the rest of Europe. The basis for such an argument has often been reflection on cultural practice and consumer behaviour. Most forcible has been the frequent assertion of the prevailing wisdom among new cultural intermediaries, such as advertisers and market researchers, that lifestyle has become autonomous from the constraints of class because individual taste has become the primary basis of any sense of group attachment. The most influential riposte to the argument about the decline of class has been the article by Goldthorpe & Marshall (1992). They argued that there was little reliable evidence to support the argument that class has become less determinant of important social outcomes (such as social mobility and voting) in recent decades. They therefore outlined a research programme in class analysis, the "modest programme", to encourage empirical investigation of the association between occupational class positions and social practice.

This paper is written in the spirit of the modest research programme and sets out to provide some empirical data about expenditure on food, in order to evaluate aspects of these general claims. Ours is a case study, directed ultimately towards understanding the connections between class and lifestyle, using food preferences as an indicator of the latter. Food remains an important element of British consumption behaviour, on average absorbing around one-sixth of all household expenditure. It is also one means to exhibit distinction, as Bourdieu's (1984: 175–200) classic dissection of class differences in eating habits in France so convincingly demonstrated.

Using discriminant analysis, we examine the relationship between class position and expenditure in single-person households on a large number of food items in 1968 and 1988. Subject to the limitations of the statistical sources and techniques, this permits the evaluation of a number of hypotheses about the class structuring of consumption behaviour and changes over time, thus helping to adjudicate between different accounts of the character of the contemporary middle classes.

14.2 Three contested theses

The data are directed towards the evaluation of three contested theses about class structure and change. The first concerns whether or not patterns of class difference have diminished in recent years. To demonstrate the existence of classes requires that we show internal homogeneity among people within a class, and differences from those in other classes. The strength and the persistence of the similarities and differences between and within classes, although often difficult to measure, are the principal grounds for determining whether class is in decline. By comparing the statistical correlation between class position and patterns of expenditure over two decades, further light is shed on the empirical claims of Goldthorpe & Marshall. The period examined is strategic in the sense that most accounts, both of class decline and of the rise of lifestyle differences, would consider the relevant changes to have begun after 1968 and to have been markedly visible by 1988.

A second thesis concerns the structure and development of the middle classes. We evaluate the recent arguments of Savage et al. (1992), who chart the existence, and anticipate the perpetuation, of internal cultural differentiation within the upper reaches of the class structure. They challenge the view, advanced explicitly by Goldthorpe (1982), that the consolidation of a service class might be anticipated in the current period. According to Goldthorpe, although it is as yet less homogeneous than the manual working class, it might be expected that service-class members (i.e. employers, managers and professionals) would come to develop a common style of life that would distinguish them clearly from intermediate and working classes. Savage et al. identify distinctive fractions within what Goldthorpe calls the service class, based on their possession of different types of "assets" (property, organizational and cultural assets), and different ways of transmitting assets between generations. In the manner of Bourdieu (1984), they argue that cultural or consumption practices are central to the creation and reproduction of the three key fractions. To the extent that food purchase is a part of lifestyle and is typical of, or associated with, other elements of lifestyles, we evaluate the adequacy of these competing views of the middle class.

A third thesis, which is less easy to specify precisely, is that social divisions other than class have grown in importance in recent years. Thus, studies of stratification have come to pay more attention to gender, ethnicity, age-groupings, etc. Our data about middle-class food practice indicate differences between men and women. Although it is neither possible nor sensible to make a claim that one division is more important than another, it is enlightening to speculate about how simultaneous shifts in the occupational structure and the gendering of occupational positions impact upon the cultural formation of the middle classes.

Much of the paper is concerned with the detailed examination of the statistical results of our discriminant analyses. In section 14.3 we outline the research design and statistical techniques employed. Section 14.4 describes and discusses some findings. Section 14.5 summarizes the evidence concerning the three theses outlined above and speculates about the implications of the findings for understanding change in the British middle classes.

14.3 Method: Family Expenditure Survey and discriminant analysis

Patterns of class differentiation in food habits in the UK were explored by applying discriminant analysis to data from the Family Expenditure Surveys (FES) of 1968 and 1988.[1] This source has the advantage of a large sample size, over 7,000 households in each year. It also contains a substantial amount of information of a socio-economic nature (such as income, demographic characteristics, socio-economic group). The data on food expenditure are broken down into food categories, for example, different types of meat, milk products, take-aways, etc. Unfortunately, however, the expenditure categories for 1968 are not the same as those for 1988 and so to get a precise comparison some categories have to be merged, thus inevitably losing some detail.

Discriminant analysis is a multivariate technique that can be used to create a system of equations (similar in some respects to regression equations), which are used to discriminate between different groups of cases within the sample, the groups usually already having been ascertained. The method can also be used to see which variables serve to discriminate most efficiently between groups. The best summary expression of the results of a discriminant analysis is to show how effectively the class model predicted the group to which an individual household belonged on the basis of its food-purchasing patterns. The summary statistic shows the level to which the variables (food items) allocate households to class groupings and is useful for comparing the power of different class models. If patterns exist then we should expect the number of correctly classified cases to be greater than would be expected by chance. So, for a four-class system, we would expect more than 25% of cases correctly classified by the functions if the analysis is working. It is possible to make inferences from the patterns revealed by the misallocation of households to class groupings. It is also possible to identify some of the key food items that distinguish one grouping from another.

In this paper we examine only households containing a single person in employment (see Table 14.1 for the gender and socio-economic composition of this subsample). The analytic cost of analyzing single-person households is a substantial reduction in the size of the sample. However, better models are achieved because food patterns are more class distinctive for individuals (i.e. one-person households) than they are for households allocated to classes on the basis of the occupation of the head of household. This avoids problems of deciding who among household member(s) should be considered head, a matter of disquiet in feminist critiques of class analysis. It also allows us to appreciate how men and women behave when their household does not include a partner or children. Potentially we can distinguish gendered tastes, and thus throw some light on the argument that women would eat differently if they were not impelled to choose and prepare foods preferred by their co-residents (Charles & Kerr 1988: 73–4).

Table 14.1 Numbers of men and women in single-person households in various middle-class groups, economically active.

Socio-economic group	Men	Women
2 Managers, large establishments	30	28
3 Employers, small establishments	7	1
4 Managers, small establishments	21	9
5 Professional, self-employed	8	1
6 Professional, employee	41	14
7 Ancillary or artist	44	68
8 Non-manual supervisory	12	15
9 Junior non-manual	33	79
15 Own account workers	23	3
16 Farmers, employers	3	2
17 Farmers, own account	1	1
Total	223	221

Source: Family Expenditure Survey, 1988.

14.4 Findings

Employed people, 1968–88

In the course of our research using the FES, we experimented with many different models of the class structure. Generally, those that included employers, employees and the unoccupied generated the most successful predictions. Such models tended to show little difference in predictive power between the two surveys of 1968 and 1988. Indeed, they often increased slightly in predictive power, exhibiting some evidence of polarization between the occupied and the unoccupied and of growing distance between owners and employees (see Tomlinson & Warde 1993).

Nevertheless, models that dealt solely with employees, while indicating statistically acceptable evidence of continuing class differentiation, indicated some fragmentation over the 20-year period in question. We give evidence here of just one such model in order to indicate patterns of class differentiation among all employees. Examining employees only, there is a clear drop in the power of models predicting class membership at the two dates (see Tables 14.2 and 14.3). Table 14.2 shows that, in 1968, 56% of all cases were correctly allocated, but this was primarily the result of very effective discrimination between the blue-collar workers and all others. The majority of employees living alone were in the manual working class (256 cases) and they clearly ate differently from the white-collar groups (as successful prediction of 63.3% of the cases proves). But the difference between the professional and clerical households was not statistically significant, with as many professionals (37%) being misallocated to the clerical category as were accurately identified as professionals. This suggests a certain homogeneity both within the working class and among white-collar workers in 1968.

The closest comparable model for 1988 gave a somewhat weaker prediction, with 48% of cases correctly allocated (Table 14.3). The pattern of allocation was

Table 14.2 Single-person households, all employees; discriminant analyses, 1968 (% by row). Percentage of "grouped" cases correctly classified: 56.4%

	Actual group	N	Predicted group membership			
			1	2	3	4
1	Professional	57	36.8	17.5	36.8	8.8
2	Managerial	16	12.5	62.5	18.8	6.3
3	Clerical	75	18.7	8.0	46.7	26.7
4	Working class	256	9.4	5.5	21.9	63.3

Classes: 1, professionals and teachers; 2, managers; 3, clerical workers; 4, working class (skilled, semi-skilled and unskilled manual workers).

Table 14.3 Single-person households, all employees; discriminant analyses, 1988 (% by row). Percentage of "grouped" cases correctly classified: 47.7%

	Actual group	N	Predicted group membership			
			1	2	3	4
1	Professional	64	39.1	28.1	17.2	15.6
2	Managerial	88	20.5	37.5	20.5	21.6
3	Other white collar	278	20.1	19.8	41.7	18.3
4	Working class	162	10.5	7.4	16.0	66.0

Classes: 1, SEGs 5 and 6; 2, SEGs 2 and 4; 3, SEGs 7–10; 4, SEGs 11–14 and 18.

not, however, much different. Blue-collar workers were even more distinctive, 66% being correctly allocated compared with 63% in 1968. The food items that distinguished working-class people were very similar in both years: expenditure was comparatively high on bread, sausages, cooked meats, beer, fish and chips, sugar, tea and canned vegetables, and relatively low on fresh vegetables, processed fruit, wine, meals out and fresh fruit. The only item that was typically middle-class in 1968 that became common in all household budgets 20 years later was coffee.[2] In general, this parallels Heath et al.'s (1985, 1991) findings from the British Election Surveys that the working class itself has not changed much since the 1960s, except that it has decreased in size. The overall strength of the model was reduced because the proportion of manual workers among single-person households was much smaller (only 27% by 1988). Nevertheless, the 1988 model was less good at discriminating among middle-class occupational groups.

The impression given by this and other general models of the employed population generated by our research is that the distance between the working and the middle classes has altered relatively little, but that there is some evidence of change within the middle class.

Change within the middle classes

As always, it is difficult to deploy the occupational categories of official statistics to explore the more theoretically sophisticated sociological accounts of the class structure. Occupation is only an approximate indication of the concepts of class specified in sociological theory. In the light of the debate about the most appropriate way to understand internal divisions within the middle class, we did attempt to compare a model approximating to the Nuffield scheme (e.g. Goldthorpe 1980a) with an alternative (the "assets model") suggested by Savage et al. (1992). The comparison was severely limited by the necessity of reconstructing the competing class schemes from the socio-economic group classification used by the Family Expenditure Survey and because the occupational categories used by the FES altered between the two dates. On our approximate statistical evidence there was nothing to choose, empirically, between the two alternative models.[3] In the subsequent analysis we therefore follow our initial theoretical preference for the conceptualization of Savage et al., because it explicitly takes into account the distribution of "cultural assets", which might be anticipated to handle an issue such as food choice better than a classification system theoretically based on the market and work situations of household heads. We take a distinction between owners, managers, professionals and other white-collar workers as the best set of categories to operationalize the model on which Savage et al.'s argument about the distribution of assets among fractions of the middle class was based.

For 1968, a discriminant analysis successfully classified 53% of occupied, single-person, middle-class households (see Table 14.4). Professionals were identified in 60% of cases. Analysis of the discriminant functions indicated that they spent disproportionately highly on coffee, ice cream, pork, canned vegetables, fresh vegetables and potato products. Overall, there was quite strong differentiation within the

Table 14.4 Single-person households, middle-class occupations; discriminant analysis, 1968 (% by row). Percentage of "grouped" cases correctly classified: 53.2%.

	Actual group	N	Predicted group membership			
			1	2	3	4
1	Self-employed	45	55.6	6.7	8.9	28.9
2	Professional	57	12.3	59.6	7.0	21.1
3	Managerial	16	12.5	12.5	56.3	18.8
4	Other white collar	87	24.1	19.5	9.2	47.1

Classes: 1, self employed (white and blue collar; 2, professionals and teachers; 3, managers; 4, other white collar (clerical and shopworkers).

Table 14.5 Single-person households, middle-class occupations; discriminant analysis, 1988 (% by row). Percentage of "grouped" cases correctly classified: 44.2%

	Actual groups	N	Predicted group membership			
			1	2	3	4
1	Self-employed	41	56.1	9.8	19.5	14.6
2	Professional	64	15.6	39.1	17.2	28.1
3	Managerial	88	13.6	23.9	35.2	27.3
4	Other white collar	278	12.6	17.6	23.4	46.4

Classes: 1, SEGs 1, 13, 15, 16, 17; 2, SEGs 5 and 6; 3, SEGs 2 and 4; 4, SEGs 7–10).

middle class. The tendency for misallocation to be into the routine white-collar group again suggests that there might have been some common elements of middle-class taste in 1968, with routine white-collar styles as the common denominator. However, such a finding is complicated, if not confounded, by the gender distribution of taste within middle-class occupations (see below).

A broadly comparable set of class categories in 1988 produced a model with a 44% success rate (Table 14.5). The self-employed and the lower grades of white-collar workers were accurately predicted to the same degree as in 1968, but the professional and managerial workers were harder to isolate: 39% of professionals were correctly identified and 28% were misallocated to the routine white-collar grouping; only 35% of managers were accurately diagnosed. These findings are not inconsistent with the Savage thesis insofar as Savage et al. see the managerial fraction as the least coherent, while owners and professionals do exhibit mutually exclusive signs of distinction. However, whether or not managers, despite possessing organizational assets, ought to be deemed a coherent grouping is debatable. In all the models we ever ran it was enormously difficult to identify who held managerial positions. Managers are a most heterogeneous group. In several models they were allocated randomly across the categories. Either they are "inconspicuous consumers" (Savage et al. 1992) in food purchasing as well as other areas, or they are internally differentiated in such a way as to distribute themselves rather evenly to the styles of other, "core", fractions of the middle class. Probably the main reasons are both the vagueness of the occupational title "manager" and the heterogeneous social origins of people who become managers. The circumstances in which managers learn and practise taste are very variable (see Crompton & Jones 1984, Stewart et al. 1980, Scase & Goffee 1989).

The evidence of this section, then, certainly gives little support to the thesis that either the middle class as a whole or its salaried upper echelons are becoming more homogeneous. If anything, it suggests the opposite, that people in service class occupations have become more internally heterogeneous in their purchasing preferences. The extent of such change is not sufficient to conclude that class-related patterns of food behaviour have atrophied sharply, as would be consistent with postmodernist or anomic projections about the individualization of taste. Nor is the change sufficient to accept that there has been a significant sharpening of the boundaries between different fractions of the middle class, sometimes described as niche consumption in post-Fordist economies.

Middle classes elaborated: differentiation in 1988

Even with systematically comparable data for 1968 and 1988, difficulties arise in interpreting change. One problem is that the way of classifying the items of food and drink recorded in the household budget diaries altered. This presumably reflected an awareness that the indicators of distinction between households change over time. For instance, in 1968 "meals out" was a single recording category; by 1988, some 20 different heads of expenditure on eating were distinguished, it becoming possible to identify canteen meals, take-aways, street foods, etc. Alcoholic drinks similarly were broken down in greater detail in 1988. These items were particularly good at distinguishing between classes in 1988. In 1968, the most discriminating items included exotic or luxury, as opposed to "ordinary", fruit and vegetables, but these were not separately classified in 1988. Hence, collapsing items together to produce precise comparability at both dates actually loses some of the most distinctive items identifying taste. Using instead the most elaborate set of items available in 1988 indicates considerably greater systematic differentiation within the middle class. Expenditures on alcohol and eating out most powerfully indicate structured taste within the middle class, even suggesting increasing differentiation.

This pattern was apparent when the "assets model" was run using all the items recorded in the 1988 FES. The success rate for the model was 52%, an 8% improvement on the same class model using the "collapsed" categories. The improvement was most marked in its prediction of membership of the professional groups, 59% being correctly allocated on this occasion, compared with 39% before. This implies that it is through their patterns of eating out and alcohol consumption that professionals exhibit distinctiveness. Indeed, they spent disproportionately large amounts on eating at work, restaurant meals, and drinking wine and beer outside the home, while avoiding biscuits, sugar and bread. Professionals are rarely misclassified as owners or managers, but shared some of their tastes with routine white-collar workers, as did managers. Once again managers were particularly heterogeneous, but also were the group least like the owners. Owners spent relatively more of their food budgets on beer drunk away from home, beef, bacon, sausages, take-away meals, street foods and sugar.

Gender differences within the middle classes

There are systematic differences in the food expenditures of men and women. This is hardly surprising, because it might be expected that many aspects of gender difference would be reflected in purchasing and eating habits. Income from employment, access to public places, bodily disciplines and culinary skills are among relevant and unequally distributed attributes. To examine gender divisions within the fractions of the middle class, we analyzed separately the single-person households of men and women to see how strong a model could be derived for each. We again used the categories of the "assets model", and the results are detailed for men and women separately in both 1968 (Tables 14.6 and 14.7) and 1988 (Tables 14.8 and 14.9). The findings from the discriminant analysis for the genders separately can be compared with the model for all single-person households (i.e. men and women together) in Tables 14.2 and 14.3. Since gender differences exist, improvement in the fit of class models might be anticipated.

An improved fit is suggested for 1968. As Tables 14.6 and 14.7 show, admittedly on the basis of small numbers of cases, 71% of single men and 65% of single women were accurately identified. Middle-class men rarely lived alone in the late 1960s,

Table 14.6 Single-person households, men only, middle-class occupations; discriminant analysis, 1968 (% by row).

			Predicted group membership		
Actual group	N	1	2	3	4
1 Self-employed	24	79	8	0	13
2 Professional	16	6	69	6	19
3 Managerial	4	25	0	75	0
4 Routine white collar	20	20	15	0	65

Percentage of "grouped" cases correctly classified: 71.2%. *Classes:* see Table 14.4.

Table 14.7 Single-person household, women only, middle-class occupations; discriminant analysis, 1968 (% by row).

			Predicted group membership		
Actual group	N	1	2	3	4
1 Self-employed	21	76	10	0	14
2 Professional	41	5	68	0	27
3 Managerial	12	0	8	75	17
4 Routine white collar	67	13	21	8	58

Percentage of "grouped cases" correctly classified: 65.3%. *Classes:* see Table 14.4.

but those who did belonged to well-defined class fractions. Each of the four groupings were internally homogeneous, with marked differences between them: 79% of the self-employed, 75% of managers, 69% of professionals and 65% of white-collar workers were correctly allocated. The same model for women was also very powerful and exhibited considerable differences between occupational classes. Thus 76% of the self-employed, 75% of managers, 68% of professionals and 58% of routine white-collar women were accurately identified.

The same model, applied to the 1988 data, showed that the distinctiveness of middle-class women had changed very little (see Tables 14.8 and 14.9). The number of women in higher-order occupations living alone had fallen considerably by 1988. It was harder to identify statistically the self-employed and the managerial workers, but the large group of routine white-collar workers had become more distinct, as had the professionals, who were correctly allocated in 80% of cases. The equivalent model for men was, however, very much weaker, with only 42% of cases correctly classified. Both managerial and routine white-collar workers proved very difficult to identify, and professionals were successfully allocated in only 47% of instances. The difference between male professionals, managers and routine workers declined, though the self-employed exhibited strong preferences for beer, fish and chips, bacon and sugar.

The weakness of the model for men confirms again the indistinctiveness of the holders of managerial positions and implies something similar about male clerical workers. In both cases, the job label covers many different work and market positions and differential career paths. The indistinctiveness of the professionals is less easy to explain, since this is a group that might be expected to exhibit shared cul-

Table 14.8 Single-person households, men only, middle-class occupations; discriminant analysis, 1988 (% by row). Percentage of "grouped" cases correctly classified: 42.0%.

			Predicted group membership		
Actual group	N	1	2	3	4
1 Self-employed	34	62	12	18	9
2 Professional	49	8	47	18	27
3 Managerial	51	24	24	31	22
4 Routine white collar	97	22	26	14	38

Classes: see Table 14.5.

Table 14.9 Single-person households, women only, middle-class occupations; discriminant analysis, 1988 (% by row). Percentage of "grouped" cases correctly classified: 62.9%.

			Predicted group membership		
Actual group	N	1	2	3	4
1 Self-employed	7	43	0	14	43
2 Professional	15	0	80	7	13
3 Managerial	37	0	14	57	30
4 Routine white collar	181	1	13	22	64

Classes: see Table 14.5.

tural capital as a result of their educational experiences and because they can be expected to remain in similar occupations throughout their working lives. In fact, their food tastes were most indistinct: close examination of what they spent their money on showed no distinguishing traits.

By contrast, professional single women, though there were few in the sample, were much more distinctive, and tended to spend comparatively heavily on products popularly associated with healthy and stylish diets – poultry, margarine, vegetables and wine. Routine white-collar workers particularly liked cooked meats, sugar and bacon, while the self-employed consumed a disproportionate amount of beef, eggs, cooked ham and tea.

In 1968, men and women separately were much more strongly differentiated than when put together. That is to say, in 1968 the models for men and women separately were successful in 71% and 65% of cases respectively, while the same model for all single persons was 53%. This suggests that men and women in the same occupational classes had different tastes, for, had they had shared tastes, the model for men and women combined would probably have been more successful. Placing men and women in the same classificatory group, in other words, made the class culturally more heterogeneous.

In 1988, the model for men was reduced to 42% success rate, while that for women held up at 63%. The model for all together registered 44% success. This suggests that, for women within the middle class, tastes remained quite strongly differentiated and perhaps that taste, style and status distinctions within the middle classes are, indeed, more effectively preserved by women than by men. Thus, whereas the women professionals have a quite marked diet, male professionals are undistinguished. Among men, it was the managers who exhibited the most distinctively "late modern" patterns of consumption, spending heavily on meals out, fruit, coffee and wine. The items consumed most heavily by their female counterparts (compared with other middle-class women) were quite different, including sweets, biscuits, bakery products, beer, spirits and fresh vegetables. The indications are that men and women belonging to the same occupational groups have in some instances significantly different tastes.

Thus, considering men and women separately tends to confirm the view that there has been some dilution of class-based taste among employed people in the period since 1968. Misallocation of cases becomes slightly more random over the 20 years. This might be taken as some evidence of the "massification" of middle-class taste. This is not, however, a "middle mass" that flows over the boundary between blue- and white-collar work. Rather, it indicates a slight tendency for fractions of the middle class, and especially men, to lose their occupational identity, though not to the degree that would suggest their imminent unification. The evidence for women is, though weakly, in the opposite direction. The slight sharpening of the boundary around female routine white-collar workers between 1968 and 1988 is the most compelling evidence of a service class becoming more differentiated from the intermediate classes. However, the coherence and distinctiveness of taste among professional women do not suggest commonality with owners and managers. Employed single men are losing their class distinctions and becoming more heterogeneous.

Assuming the existence of a general and systematic connection between occupational class and food taste, we would speculate that the evidence of gender differences might be explained by a number of factors. First, persistently high levels of occupational segregation by gender mean that, despite sharing the same occupational title, men and women will really experience different work and market situations and also, therefore, are likely to have exclusive networks of associates. Secondly, women and men in higher-order jobs are likely to be at different points on a career trajectory, because the opportunities for women's access to professional and managerial positions have improved only very recently. Thirdly, women and men in similar occupational positions are likely to have come from different social origins. Thus, we might explain the greater heterogeneity of male middle-class fractions in terms of their having experienced extensive upward mobility into the middle classes earlier than women, such that the effects of their social class backgrounds have been diluted to a greater extent. This would imply that the persistence of status or class consciousness, as it is expressed through food tastes, is more apparent among women than among men. While this might merely indicate that women have a better understanding of the meanings of food, it could have more general significance and perhaps solve some of the anomalies in the empirical findings about class and gender.

Ethnographic and in-depth interview studies of women's attitudes towards class seem to suggest that, in discussion, some women are indifferent to class and are unable to attribute people to social classes, that a second group of women are consciously hostile to the use of the language of class and are unwilling to talk about it, and that the remainder exhibit highly developed senses of class difference (e.g. Charles 1990). It has also been shown that, among young women, those from the middle class are far more class conscious than their working-class counterparts (Frazer 1988). *If* the latter finding were generalizable to older women, it might be argued that it is women who express and sustain class-related differences through visible and interpretable consumption patterns. If, in addition, those women hostile to discussions of class were also capable of managing class discriminations, then we might glimpse the origins of the high levels of class identification reported by Marshall et al. (1988). We might also appreciate some of the paradoxical effects of marriage on women's consciousness of class. One remarkable feature of opinion poll data is that there has been a substantial and steady increase in the number of people who say that there is a class struggle in Britain: 79% said so in July 1991, compared with 48% in July 1964 (Abercrombie & Warde et al. 1994: 169). This figure must include most women and most of the middle class. Survey evidence shows that married women vote in accordance with their husband's class location and that they operate with a definition of their own class position as one conferred by marriage. Single women presumably express their *own* class position, one presumably also usually influenced by the position of their family of origin. Single women, especially of the middle class, are able to exhibit class identity more strongly than their married sisters, and they do. Middle-class single women, more than men, use food consumption to signify and relay class differences.

14.5 Concluding discussion

Many of the lessons to be learned from our investigations concern the difficulties encountered in trying systematically to compare statistical data over different time periods. Changes in the categories of food items and in the occupational classification make the kind of systematic comparison called for by Goldthorpe & Marshall (1992) extremely difficult. Even if more precise comparison were achieved, there would still be considerable problems of interpretation, partly because our technique is unable to weight the relative importance of different social variables (the multivariate element in the analysis concerned the food items, not the sociodemographic variables), partly because of difficulties of turning occupational titles into class categories, and partly because spending patterns are a problematic proxy for taste, at least as it is understood in analyses of cultural distinction.

The possible range of motivations behind differential food expenditure is large. It could be a result of concern with status or health, or it might be a matter of style and fashion, or one literally of taste, or it might be a consequence of long-learned and deeply entrenched preferences developed in childhood. Given this range of possible bases of preference, it probably is remarkable how *strong* are the patterns divulged on the basis of simple expenditure data. The level of the capacity to predict a person's class position on the evidence of highly aggregated grocery bills does suggest the persistence of very powerful influences from class milieux. That the measure of milieux is merely current occupation makes the power of the models even more remarkable.

Our analysis cannot isolate which aspect of occupational class milieux acts as the mechanism for shared taste in food. There are several possibilities, for instance: occupational community and communication between colleagues; level of education, a process wherein obtaining credentials coincides with the learning of other cultural practices; the nature of differential scheduling of the working day between different occupations, involving eating out during working hours; or levels of class self-recruitment, which would account for the frequency with which our various models showed the working class especially to have quite distinctive food expenditure patterns.

As regards our initial theses, their evaluation is complicated by the methodological and technical–interpretive difficulties so far described. Nevertheless, we have reported some findings that offer valuable clues towards discriminating among competing general arguments.

First, class distances in general did not reduce very significantly between 1968 and 1988. The evidence for change within and between classes identifies, with confidence, little more than trendless fluctuation (to use a phrase of Heath et al. 1991) around a generally persistent pattern of class differentiation. We have found that the working class remains as homogeneous as ever, and indeed, on almost all measures, is becoming more, rather than less, easy to differentiate from workers in white-collar occupations. This offers some support to Goldthorpe's explanation of the effects of class self-recruitment. The working class might be expected to be more homogeneous and culturally coherent than the middle class, because it is more self-recruiting. Goldthorpe (1980a) reasoned that, because rates of absolute upward mobility into the service class had been high in post-war years, the opportunity for the creation of socio-cultural identity among such men would have been limited. By contrast, as the manual working class declined in size owing to shifts in the occupational structure, and because rates of downward mobility were low, the current generation of manual workers was likely to be second or third generation and thus culturally stable and homogeneous. The claim that similarity of disposition is greater among long-established and well-formed classes than among others is supported by our data.

The second thesis concerned the homogeneity of the higher echelons of the middle class. Within the middle class there is some evidence of the fragmentation of taste. In those calculations where we tried to ensure strict comparability on categories of food items, a number of patterns emerged. Taken as a whole, the employed middle class, compared with other large groupings, became less easy to identify. Distinctions between the intermediate and the service classes remained quite stable. Some quite strong differences between fractions of the "service class", apparent in 1968, seemed to dissolve in subsequent years. This did not, however, have the effect of creating a more homogeneous and distinguished service class, as was anticipated by Goldthorpe (1982). There was no compelling evidence for such a trend. Rather, most apparent was the increasing heterogeneity among managerial workers: by 1988, managerial workers seemed to have almost nothing in common as regards taste, a finding that can be explained by their lack of shared cultural capital, the varied jobs that pass under the label, and their multiplicitous career trajectories. Nevertheless, the evidence does not suggest a fast dilution of class-based consumption patterns and their simple replacement by unregulated individual choice, as would be anticipated by some accounts of the informalization and individualization of consumption. Class differentiation has certainly not yet disappeared to a degree sufficient to warrant such a conclusion. More important, one part of our evidence tends to suggest the opposite.

When we used a full range of categories for itemizing food expenditure in 1988, we obtained some very strong indications of well-developed and significant internal differentiation within the middle classes. Apart from managers, other middle-class fractions maintained their distinctiveness. In one other model that we generated (reported in Tomlinson & Warde 1993), which excluded managers and instead contrasted employers, the self-employed, professionals and routine white-collar workers, we were able correctly to predict 67% of single-person households in 1988. It was the incorporation of detailed evidence about expenditure on eating out and on alcohol (distinguishing both type and location of consumption) that permitted a really strong sense of internal striations within the middle class. Differentiating items were also interpretable in terms of concerns for healthy diets. This suggested the existence of some "core" styles of food consumption and gave some genuine support to Savage et al.'s view of internal differentiation within what others call the service class. It also provided evidence of a meaningful boundary between such workers and different sections of the Nuffield scheme's intermediate class.

It might seem, then, that we do need a model of the class structure that divides the upper reaches of the middle class in terms of their primary assets, rather than envisaging a horizontal division between upper and lower echelons of the service class as in the Nuffield scheme. However, the heterogeneous food tastes of managerial workers suggest that Savage et al.'s notion of organizational assets might be unsatisfactory. Their own evidence suggested that there were few cultural corollaries of an elevated position in a bureaucratic hierarchy, which, if shared cultural traits are critical to class formation, might suggest that organizational assets do not, at least at present, provide a basis for class formation. Indeed, Savage et al.'s account fits our 1968 data better.

The third area we hoped to illuminate concerned the interrelationship between gender and class. Analysis is further complicated by taking account of gender differences in behaviour. There is evidence that gender does operate independently of occupational class with respect to taste within the middle class. Perhaps most remarkable is the apparent coherence of taste among professional women workers. It may be that, taken overall, it is women who are the principal inheritors of class taste (and of the shopping skills to display taste) and it is their behaviour that most strongly underpins class-based patterns of consumption (compare Warde 1991).

We would speculate that the persistently strong class differences among women in middle-class occupations is a function of their comparatively recent incorporation into these sections of the labour market and of their having had fewer opportunities for social mobility than men because improved access to higher education is still very recent. It would be consistent with the limited available evidence (McRae 1990, Goldthorpe with Llewellyn & Payne 1987) to imagine that women currently in professional positions are particularly likely to have originated from professional households. By comparison, the much larger group of female routine white-collar workers, whose tastes, although still very distinct, are less homogeneous, will have more diverse class backgrounds. This might begin to explain some puzzles in recent findings about women's attitudes to class, politics and social orientation.

Finally, this research, for all its difficulties, does suggest that the continuation of the research programme in class is worthwhile. It suggests that an "assets approach" might be particularly valuable, because variations in taste within the service class are less easily attributable to employment and work situations than to aspects of the possession of cultural capital deriving from education, social networks, openness to government propaganda, awareness of women's issues and so forth. In that sense, approaches like that of Bourdieu (1984, 1987) that incorporate the cultural into their understanding of hierarchy and distinction seem theoretically appropriate.

Acknowledgements

The research was conducted at Manchester University where Mark Tomlinson was a Research Associate and Alan Warde a Hallsworth Research Fellow in 1991–2. Many thanks to Manchester University for its support. Material from the Family Expenditure Survey was made available by the Central Statistical Office through the Economic and Social Research Council Data Archive and has been used with the permission of the Controller of HMSO. Neither the CSO nor the ESRC Data Archive bears any responsibility for the analysis or interpretation of the data reported here.

Notes

1. British Department of Employment, *Family Expenditure Survey 1968* (computer file), ESRC Data Archive, Colchester, 1976; and *Family Expenditure Survey 1988* (computer file), ESRC Data Archive, Colchester, 1990.
2. The evidence for this comes from interpretations of Fisher's linear and standardized canonical discriminant functions, which are both difficult to read and take up more space than we are allowed in presentation here. Details can be obtained from the authors.
3. Both showed a very similar capacity to distinguish the self-employed and routine white-

collar workers. The distinction between upper and lower service class proved neither better nor worse than a distinction between professional and managerial workers. This implied a weakly defined, but real, boundary between the service and the intermediate classes in the Nuffield scheme.

Chapter 15

Home-ownership and the middle classes

Chris Hamnett

15.1 Introduction

Why should housing be important for class analysis? The answer is straightforward. Although the housing consumption of any individual or household is primarily a product of their purchasing power – and hence of their past and present position in the labour market, inherited wealth and other sources of finance – the size, quality and cost of housing are a key element of household consumption, social inequality and household life-chances.

In addition, the home is one of the most important aspects of people's lives. It is the base for domestic reproduction, and people commonly expend considerable amounts of money, time and effort to get the home they want, and to maintain and improve it. The home is a crucial social and cultural marker and, for some, an important source of social status and cultural distinction (Bourdieu 1984). It is also a key element of personal identity (Saunders & Williams 1986) and a major source of ontological security (Cooper 1976).

Different types of housing can be seen as an example of what Giddens (1973) has termed distributive groupings, that is, "relationships which involve common patterns of consumption of material goods" (Wolch & Dear 1989). They add: "With their concomitant status implications these goods act to reinforce the separations initiated by differential work-specific capabilities" (Wolch & Dear 1989: 5). This is no doubt correct, but does housing in general, and home-ownership in particular, comprise anything more than just a class-related distributive outcome? Does housing have a specific role in class formation or is it best relegated to the role of index of achieved class position, as Payne & Payne (1977) suggest – the Cinderella waiting at home while everyone else is at the capital–labour ball?

There are arguments that suggest a more significant role for home-ownership, notably the Weberian framework of Saunders (1978). Home-ownership provides access to an important form of potential wealth accumulation that is not open to tenants. Homeowners benefit from any rise in house prices and, when the mortgage is paid off, they own the house outright. Privately owned housing therefore has both use value and exchange value and, in Weberian terms, provides a basis for class formation that theoretically is independent of the ownership or control of the means of production or position in the paid labour market. These arguments will be considered below.

The juxtaposition of home-ownership and the middle class raises a number of additional questions concerning housing tenure and class. The first is whether or not home-ownership can any longer be seen as class specific and, if not, to what extent, if at all, the middle classes occupy a specific position within home-ownership. Do the middle classes own larger, more expensive homes in better areas than other social classes? Do they derive a higher "use value"? The second question is whether or not home-ownership has a specific role or function for the middle class that it does not for other classes. Are there some attributes of ownership that are particularly important for the middle class as sources of social status or cultural distinction? Thirdly, do the middle classes derive financial benefits from home-ownership that are either unavailable to other classes or greater than those available to other classes? Finally, what is the role played by home-ownership in middle-class reproduction and what is the extent of mobility into home-ownership from other tenures? Is it exclusive and self-recruiting or is it open to a wide range of people?

This chapter cannot provide definitive answers to these questions, but it is necessary at least to try to address them if the relationship between home-ownership and class is to be addressed at more than just a descriptive level. I look first at the question of whether or not home-ownership is particularly characteristic of the middle classes and at the nature of middle-class housing consumption that may make it distinctive.

15.2 The changing tenure structure of housing in Britain

Viewed from overseas, the British literature regarding housing has been peculiarly dominated by issues of tenure and class for over 30 years. Although cynics might claim that this interest simply reflects the class-ridden nature of British society and the British obsession with class as the key determinant of social stratification, there is a good argument that it reflects the remarkable transformation in the tenure structure of the British housing market and in housing conditions over the past 80 years (Thorns 1981).

Since 1914 Britain has been transformed from a nation of renters into a nation of homeowners or, more accurately, into two nations: a majority of homeowners and a minority of council tenants. In the process, the distribution of housing conditions, life-chances and financial costs and benefits has been profoundly altered. This transformation has been less marked in other English-speaking countries such as the United States, Canada, Australia and New Zealand where the dominance of home-ownership was established far earlier (Harris & Hamnett 1987, Kemeny 1981). It has also been far less marked in some European countries such as Germany where private renting is still very important. As a result there has been a strong emphasis on tenure in British housing literature (see Ball 1985, Barlow & Duncan 1988, for criticisms of this emphasis).

Home-ownership has been seen as a key element of middle-class life in Britain for many years. This has not always been the case, however. Until the turn of the century, the great majority of the middle class and, indeed, the great majority (about 90%) of the population lived in private rented accommodation (Burnett 1978, Kemp 1982, Daunton 1987). The major difference between the classes was not tenure but housing quality and conditions. Then, from the 1920s onwards, as the economics of private renting increasingly turned against landlords, the inter-war building boom was characterized by a massive increase in the number of dwellings built for sale to homeowners, particularly in the South East (Hamnett & Randolph 1986). The suburban semi-detached house was born (Burnett 1978). Although an increasing proportion of the skilled working class was able to buy in the 1930s as incomes rose and interest rates fell to 5%, home-ownership in the inter-war years was primarily a prerogative of the middle and upper classes (Merrett 1982, Swenarton & Taylor 1985).

The change in tenure structure accelerated after the war as a result of a rapid expansion of both home-ownership and council renting. In 1939, almost two-thirds of households still rented privately, compared with 25% in home-ownership and 10% in the council sector. By 1961, 43% of households were owner-occupiers and 24% were council tenants against just 33% in private renting. By 1971, ownership reached 50% of all households, and by 1991 it reached two-thirds.

15.3 Home-ownership and class: the changing relationship

Considerable changes in the social composition of housing tenures took place as a result of the shifts in the tenure structure. As the private rented sector shrank, growing polarization in the housing market (Hamnett 1984a) meant that council housing increasingly became a preserve of the less skilled working class, whereas the skilled working class began to enter home-ownership in larger numbers. As Donnison & Ungerson (1981) argue: "The opening up of owner occupation to more than half the population – many in houses initially built for renting – has enormously diversified the range of people who buy their own homes" (Donnison & Ungerson 1981: 186).

A similar argument has been made by Forrest et al. (1991), who suggest that the expansion of home-ownership to two-thirds of households has meant that it is no longer the preserve of the middle classes. Instead, home-ownership has become a very diversified and fragmented mass tenure including 1.5 million households who bought council homes under 1980 Conservative "Right to buy" legislation.

The expansion of home-ownership down the social spectrum raises the question of how far home-ownership is still a distinctive attribute of the middle classes? Census data on the incidence of housing tenure by socio-economic group show that, in the past 30 years, ownership has percolated down the occupational structure to a significant degree.

Table 15.1 Homeownership by socio-economic group of head of household, 1961–90 (%).

Social group	1961	1971	1981	1990	Increase 1961–90
Professional/ managerial	67.3	75.8	82.7	90.3	23.0
Intermediate/junior non-manual	53.4	59.3	70.5	78.4	25.0
Skilled manual	40.0	47.9	58.4	73.0	33.0
Semi-skilled manual	28.7	35.6	41.6	49.0	20.3
Unskilled manual	21.9	27.0	30.9	38.0	16.1

Source: Census of Population, 1961, 1971, 1981; General Household Survey 1990.

In 1961, professionals and managers had a clear majority of households (67%) in home-ownership. Other non-manual workers had 53% but the proportion fell to 40% of skilled manual workers and 22% of the unskilled. The proportion of owners in each group steadily increased in subsequent decades, and by 1991 no fewer than 90% of the professional and managerial group were homeowners as were 73% of skilled manual workers. By 1991, all the top three groups had over 70% of households in owner-occupation, and the semi-skilled approached 50%. The only group not to achieve significant access to ownership by 1991 was the unskilled (Table 15.1).

Although marked differentials remain, particularly between the top three groups and the bottom two, it is clear that home-ownership has diffused down the social spectrum to a remarkable degree. Britain is now predominantly a nation of home-owners: or at least professionals, managers, intermediate and junior non-manual workers and the skilled manual groups are. Home-ownership is no longer the prerogative of the middle classes as it was in the 1950s and before. The proportion of the skilled manual group in home-ownership has increased by a remarkable 33 percentage points: from 40% to 73%. This group is now numerically very important within the home-ownership sector. Ball (1982) argues that the shift in the social composition of home-ownership has led to the government redirecting housing subsidies from council housing to home-ownership because the key economically active groups are now homeowners.

This finding raises a major question. If home-ownership is no longer a distinctive attribute of the middle classes, in what ways is home-ownership particularly important for the middle classes? One answer to this is that it is not ownership *per se* that is important today, but the nature of what is owned. Although a growing proportion of the population has become owners, the middle classes may still dominate the most desirable positions within home-ownership. Home-ownership as a positional good (Hirsch 1978) may have become more differentiated and selective.

This is easily shown using British Household Panel Study data to examine the relationships between house type and house price and socio-economic group (see Table 15.2). First, there is a clear pattern in current property value by socio-economic group. In general, professionals and managers own more expensive homes than do other groups. This holds true when region and date of purchase are controlled for. The distribution of house type by socio-economic group is also

Table 15.2 Estimated current mean value of property by socio-economic group of household head, 1991 (£).

Social group	Mean value	N
Professional	103,038	131
Managerial	103,519	600
Other non-manual	74,729	554
Skilled manual	66,351	717
Partly skilled manual	57,775	196
Unskilled manual	58,625	40
All groups	79,744	2,238

Source: British Household Panel Survey, 1991.

Table 15.3 House type by socio-economic group, owner-occupiers only (%).

Property type	Professional	Managerial	Other non-manual	Skilled manual	Partly skilled	Unskilled	Total
Detatched/bungalow	45.3	34.9	16.0	15.6	10.3	7.4	21.3
Semi-detached house	28.0	30.3	31.6	39.1	36.1	29.5	33.7
Terraced house	16.1	18.6	29.5	30.1	37.8	41.1	32.6
Flat	10.0	11.8	20.6	13.0	14.9	17.0	16.6

Source: British Household Panel Survey.

revealing. The professional and managerial groups have a far higher proportion of households in detached houses (45% and 35% respectively) than does any other group. Professionals have 3 times the proportion in detached houses as skilled manual workers, 4.5 times that of semi-skilled workers and 6 times that of manual workers. Conversely, representation of professionals and managers in terraced houses or flats is much lower than that of other groups. The incidence of semi-detached houses is fairly evenly distributed (see Table 15.3).

The relationship between socio-economic group and house type is also found in the South East in an exaggerated form. A survey of 976 homeowners in five areas (Oxford, Chiltern, Milton Keynes, Haringey and Hammersmith) found that 45% of professionals and 40% of managers occupied detached houses, compared with 19% of other non-manual workers, 23% of skilled manual workers and just 2% of semi-skilled and unskilled workers (Hamnett & Seavers 1994). The distribution of current market value by socio-economic group also showed major differences: 56% of professionals lived in houses worth £120,000 or more, compared with 43% of managers, 26% of other non-manual workers, 21% of skilled manual workers and 5% of the partly skilled. It seems that it is no longer home-ownership *per se* that distinguishes the middle classes but the character and price of what is owned, where and by whom.

This conclusion reinforces Forrest et al.'s (1991) view that, as home-ownership has expanded, it has become increasingly differentiated and fragmented. Thus, distinctions within home-ownership, particularly between marginal owners who may own poor condition or difficult to sell properties (such as owners of poor-quality flat conversions or some right-to-buy owners), and those with big negative equity, are as important as those between owners and non-owners.

This conclusion should come as no surprise. In their book *Middle class housing in Britain*, Simpson & Lloyd (1977) showed the continuing importance of Edgbaston in Birmingham, the Park in Nottingham, Hampstead in London, the New Town in Edinburgh and others as middle-class residential areas. These areas still remain desirable and expensive. Indeed, for many members of today's expanded middle class they are unaffordable. A more realistic expectation for most is an inter-war semi or a modern four-bedroom "executive" house. The supply of desirable residences is always limited. As the middle class has grown in number, the type of property they can afford is likely to have declined in quality and size, at least at the bottom end of the middle class. This may help explain the gentrification of inner-city terraced housing (Burnett 1978, Butler & Hamnett 1994)

15.4 Home-ownership, culture and consumption

The home is an important element of social display and a focus for the expression of cultural values and identity for most groups. This is particularly important for the middle classes, not least because of housing's role as an indicator of social status and distinction – a role that was frequently illustrated in nineteenth-century English literature on the middle and upper classes (Bourdieu 1984).

There are many studies of the important role of housing as a source of social status and distinction. In his analysis of gentrification in Melbourne, Jager (1986) argues, after Veblen, that whereas the bourgeoisie occupies a strategic position, setting an example of conspicuous consumption, the middle classes have to fight a war on two fronts between the dominant class and the "lower orders", from whom they must continuously demarcate themselves. He argues that an important way of doing this is via housing: "A change in social position is symbolized through a change in housing." Jager argues, after Baudrillard, that socially produced objects can express the same logic as conspicuous leisure or consumption. They designate the social rank and taste of their owner, signifying aesthetic discernment and "the cultural authority of wealth". Jager argues that the Victorian terraced houses of Melbourne fulfil this function for the middle-class gentrifiers. As he puts it: "urban conservation is the production of social differentiation; it is one mechanism by which social differences are turned into social distinctions" (Jager 1986: 79).

Thrift & Leyshon (1992) have also argued, in a different context, that the major boom in the "country house" market in southern England in the mid to late 1980s stemmed from the rapid increases in income and wealth, particularly among those working in the City and financial services, and from the desire of those who had made money in the City or via Thatcherite entrepreneurialism to buy into the traditional "country gentry" lifestyle. And, outside the country house market, people who are successful in business frequently buy a house that symbolically represents their success through its size and distinctive attributes. The carriage drive and porticoed entrance bear eloquent witness to the desire of "track" to achieve social status. This is not a new phenomenon. Rubenstein (1981) and Wiener (1981) showed that the new wealth elite of Victorian Britain behaved in a similar way. At the other end of the scale, the growing concentration of the less skilled, the low paid, the unemployed and the inactive in council housing (Hamnett 1984a) symbolizes and reflects their lowly economic position. To this extent, housing and residential location are not just an index of class position (Payne & Payne 1977). They can be argued to be an important element in class formation. The housing market works to concentrate particular socio-economic and income groups in particular areas. And, as Robson (1969) has shown in the context of education, the concentration of particular groups in particular areas is associated with different attitudes to education and also in variations in educational attainment. In this respect, housing and residential location may play a crucial part in the maintenance of class differentials in education and job market opportunities (Hamnett & Randolph 1986).

15.5 Home-ownership, accumulation and class formation

It has been argued that the home is a source of use value and a focus for social status, cultural distinction and personal identity. But housing is not just a consumption good. It also has a financial exchange value, and offers both a form of investment and a hedge against inflation. In Weberian terms, ownership of property constitutes an important basis for class formation, and Weber drew the distinction between property classes, whose members share common class situations by virtue of their command over forms of property that could realize income in the market, and acquisition classes, identified in terms of the degree of marketable skills by different individuals.

Rex & Moore (1967) attempted to apply Weberian analysis in their study of the housing market in an inner area of Birmingham. They argued that the competition over scarce and widely desired types of housing could be analyzed in terms of a struggle between different housing or property classes, each commanding a different degree of power in the housing market. Their argument was strongly criticized by Haddon (1970) on the grounds that it confused classes "based on potential power in the system of housing allocation with the empirical identification of housing classes based on current tenurial status" and it confused housing status groups, based on consumption, with housing classes. Haddon concluded that housing cannot provide a basis for class formation because it is an element of consumption.

The concept of housing classes was resuscitated by Saunders (1978), who developed the view that home-ownership is not just an item of consumption, but also provides access to a source of real accumulation. He argued that home-ownership plays an independent part in class structuration although it does not constitute ownership of capital *per se*. As he put it: "If it can be demonstrated that house ownership provides access to real accumulation, then it may be seen as a basis for a distinct class formation in Weber's terms" (Saunders 1978).

Saunders emphasized that this characteristic of domestic property ownership is not open to tenants, who simply pay rent for the use of their property and cannot gain from any increase in its value. Homeowners, by contrast, pay off their mortgage and benefit from any increase in the value of their property. He then argued that house prices in Britain had increased faster than the general rate of inflation since the war and that over the ten years to 1978 they had risen faster than returns on other forms of investment, that mortgage interest rates had been negative and below the rate of inflation for many years, and that tax relief assisted the process of accumulation.

Saunders (1984) has subsequently retracted his claim that domestic property can be an element of class formation, on the grounds that class is based on ownership and control of the means of production and labour market position and that it is difficult to see where housing classes can fit with classes based on labour market position. Instead, he contended that housing tenure and capital gains play a major role in social stratification in general, arguing that class is but one element of stratification. As he put it: "Housing tenure . . . is neither the basis of class formation (as in the neo-Weberian tradition), nor the expression of them (as in the neo-Marxist tradition), but is the single most pertinent factor in the determination of consumption sector cleavages" (Saunders 1984: 207).

Saunders' change of heart does not detract from his claim that home-ownership provides a basis for accumulation and therefore a key axis for social stratification. His thesis has been the subject of considerable debate (Pratt 1982, Ball 1982, Harloe 1984, Hamnett 1989) which will not be repeated here. Suffice to say that the main criticisms of his thesis are twofold. The first was that he failed to assess the degree to which the distribution of housing gains and losses is, in fact, related to labour market position and occupational class. Although Saunders accepted that position in the housing market is, to some extent, related to class and income, he argued that, in principle, gains from the housing market were independent of class.

The second criticism was that the accumulative potential of home-ownership is empirically contingent, and that the conditions that prevailed during the 1970s and mid-1980s were abruptly terminated in 1989 when the home-ownership market in Britain entered a deep slump, from which it has not yet recovered. Average house prices in Britain fell by 20% in nominal terms between 1989 and 1994 and in the South East of England they fell by over 30%. As a result, home-ownership was a source of considerable losses for many owners in the early 1990s. These criticisms are assessed below. First, however, I examine the importance of housing within personal wealth and the distribution of housing wealth and capital gains by socio-economic group.

15.6 Housing and personal wealth in Britain

Until the 1920s, most house property was owned by private landlords, most of whom owned only one or two properties. As such, landlords formed part of a property-owning petite bourgeoisie. The growth of home-ownership in the twentieth century, and particularly since 1945, has transformed the structure of domestic property ownership in Britain. When this was linked to a sharp rise in average house prices from 1970 to 1989, the result was a significant widening of wealth ownership and a reduction of wealth inequality (Atkinson et al. 1989). In 1969, the national average house price was £5,000. In 1989, it was £60,000 – an increase of 1,100% in cash terms and about 2.5 times in real terms. Thus the share of housing in net personal wealth has risen rapidly from about 19% in 1960 to 33% in 1975 and to 50% in 1989. The proportion fell back to 47% in 1991 as a result of the housing market slump, but housing still remains by far the largest single asset in net personal wealth. It is not too strong a claim to suggest that home-ownership has led to the creation of a large new property-owning middle class in Britain (Hamnett 1991b). Not only is housing the most evenly distributed of all assets, but in the middle wealth bands (£25,000–100,000) it accounts for over 60% of all assets, rising in some groups to 70%.

The distribution of housing wealth by socio-economic group

It is impossible using official statistics to determine the distribution of housing wealth or the size of capital gains by social classes because no breakdowns are given. Such calculations have been made by Hamnett & Seavers (1995) using data from the first wave of the British Household Panel Study (BHPS) survey of 5,000 households.

The measurement of housing equity (defined as the current estimated sale price of housing less outstanding mortgage debt) using the BHPS data was not easy (see Hamnett & Seavers 1995 for details), but our results reveal a clear pattern by socio-economic group (SEG) of household heads, which we defined as the principal income-earner. The mean equity for outright owners was £90,600, compared with £48,600 for mortgaged owners, but Table 15.4 shows that mean equity fell steadily by SEG from £63,000 for mortgaged professionals and managers to £34,700 for the partly skilled. A similar pattern exists for outright owners. There were also marked differences in mean equity by region and age of household head, but the variations by socio-economic group remained important when these variables were

Table 15.4 Mean owners equity by socio-economic group of household head, 1991 (£).

Social group	Outright owned	Mortgaged	All owners
Professional	122,200	63,400	71,250
Managerial	134,800	63,900	72,500
Other non-manual	86,500	43,300	50,800
Skilled manual	80,200	39,800	47,400
Partly skilled manual	64,200	34,700	42,400
Unskilled manual	63,900	40,100	46,700
All groups	90,600	48,600	55,850
N	363	1,733	2,096

Source: British Household Panel Survey, First Wave, 1991.

controlled for. We can conclude that the middle classes generally have the highest housing equity and that housing wealth is related to occupational class.

Home-ownership and the distribution of capital gains

We have shown that housing wealth is related to socio-economic group, but what of the distribution of gains and losses from home-ownership? Thorns (1981) suggested that, in absolute terms, the middle classes generally do better than the working classes because they own more expensive houses, which, even if they increase in value at the same rate as working-class housing, provide greater absolute gains. This argument was supported by Forrest et al. (1991). Saunders (1990) has argued, however, that there are only small class differences in relative rates of gain and that, when gains are measured on the basis of the deposit invested, working-class owners have often done as well or better than middle-class owners.

Saunders' findings have been criticized, not least because of his emphasis on relative rates of gain and his belief that the deposit is the correct basis for calculating the gains because this reflects the investment put in by the owner in the first place. However, as many "right-to-buy" owners put down only a small deposit, Saunders' results show that they made largest relative gains. In the limiting case, where the deposit is zero, the percentage gain is infinite. The debate over gains and losses is riddled with measurement problems. Should gains be measured in nominal (cash) terms or in real (inflation-adjusted) terms? Should capital gain be taken as the difference between the purchase price and the current market value, or should any outstanding mortgage debt (and deposit) be subtracted first (see Dupuis 1989).

Hamnett & Seavers (1994) have distinguished a number of gain measures. The first, which we term illusionary gain, is the difference between the current property value and the price paid. Crude gain is the current value minus the original cost of the current property minus outstanding mortgage debt. Gross gain is crude gain minus the original deposit paid. It will be apparent that the illusionary gain is the most favourable measure. The other two measures, which take into account outstanding mortgage and deposit respectively, give smaller gains. These measures can be calculated on either the current property only or the first property owned and on either a nominal or a real (inflation-adjusted) basis.

Survey findings on the distribution of gains and losses

Our empirical work uses two sources of data. The first is a stratified survey of 976 home owners in five locations in the South East of England (Haringey and Hammersmith in London, and Oxford, Chiltern and Milton Keynes) undertaken by MORI in late 1992 and early 1993. The second source is the BHPS national survey data referred to earlier. The data that follow relate primarily to illusionary gain.

Looking first at nominal illusionary gain, the mean gain on current property in our South East sample was £55,000. However, this figure conceals considerable variations, and 19% of owners had made losses even on this measure. When the price paid for the first home (a longer time period) is taken as the base, the proportion of losers falls to 8.5%. When we take nominal crude gain, that is the estimated current market value of the property minus the price paid and any outstanding mortgage debt, the proportion of losers based on the current home rises to 43% and on the first home to 28%. If the figures are recalculated on the basis of real rather than nominal gain they show even larger numbers of losers. It is clear that, *contra* Saunders, home-ownership in the South East of England is not a guaranteed source of accumulation. On the contrary, it has led to substantial losses for some owners. The proportion of losers in the BHPS sample is much smaller because the survey is national and not confined to the South East, where house prices fell most.

It is clear that Saunders' general thesis is reliant on a set of particular empirical circumstances, which ceased to hold in the early 1990s when the home-ownership market entered a severe slump. For many homeowners, the reality in this period has been one of losses, negative equity or repossession. Saunders did not anticipate this possibility but, rather than undermining his thesis, it can be argued that the housing slump generalizes it, and that home-ownership can be a source of real accumulation or of real losses, both of which have important potential implications for class formation and social stratification.

What of the distribution of gains and losses by class? Looking first at mean nominal illusionary gain on current and first property by socio-economic group, Table 15.5 shows clear differences. In the South East, the mean professional gain on current property was £68,900 and the mean managerial gain was £58,300, against £47,600 for other non-manual, £46,500 for skilled manual. The ratio between the mean professional and the mean skilled gain was 1.48:1. Where calculations were based on the first home, the range was from £120,000 for professionals to £50,600 for partly skilled household heads – a ratio of 2.4:1. The BHPS data show similar results. The range was from £57,600 for mean professional illusionary gains on current home to £34,000 for skilled household heads – a ratio of 1.7:1.

These differences are substantial, but the differences based on the period when owners first entered the market are far more marked. Because of the nature of house price inflation, the accumulative potential of home-ownership is a highly time-dependent phenomenon. In general, the longer someone has owned, the greater the potential gains. Evidence from the South East survey shows that, with regard to

Table 15.5 Mean illusionary cash gain, on current property and first property, by socio-economic group, 1991–93 (£).

| Social group | South East Owners' Survey | | | BHPS Survey | |
	Current home	First home	N	Current home	N
Professional	68,876	119,828	129	57,609	128
Managerial	58,335	107,788	242	52,415	579
Other non-manual	47,585	63,462	222	38,306	532
Skilled manual	46,413	50,616	74	34,028	190
Unskilled manual	62,631	60,056	10	37,116	39
Average Gain	54,992	84,482	825	42,031	2,195

Source: South East Owners' Survey and British Household Panel Survey (b).

Table 15.6 Mean illusionary gain, current and first property, by year of first purchase, South East survey, 1992 (£).

Date of first purchase	Current home	First home	N
Pre-1959	105,230	124,934	113
1960–68	97,383	136,741	116
1969–73	65,249	114,317	184
1974–6	64,422	115,294	68
1977–9	68,530	99,892	65
1980–84	35,806	69,828	151
1985–8	9,613	26,624	136
1989–92	4,953	4,651	83
Mean gain	54,992	84,482	834

Source: South East Owners' Survey.

gains on the current home, the range of nominal illusionary cash gains (Table 15.6) was from £105,200 for those who bought pre-1959 to £4,900 for those who bought between 1989 and 1992. When gains are calculated on the basis of the first home owned, the range is from £137,000 to £4,600. In general, calculations based on first home show that owners had locked in larger gains before 1989. This pattern is not confined to the South East, since BHPS data show a similar picture, whereby more recent buyers have made far smaller gains than older purchasers have.

In the home-ownership market, timing is important. Nowhere is this more true than in the case of the 1990s slump. Those who bought at or near the peak of the boom in the late 1980s generally gained far less, or even lost money, compared with those who bought earlier.

The massive variation in gains by year of purchase raises an important question: is class less important than date of purchase? In fact, the "partly skilled" manual worker owners who bought before 1959 had mean nominal illusionary gains of £75,000, and those who bought in 1974–6 had mean gains of £59,000, whereas professionals buying in 1985–8 had gains of £44,800 and professionals who bought in 1989–92 had losses of £3,000. But these figures are not surprising. Social class is an important factor in influencing the distribution of gains and losses within cohorts, but it cannot affect the state of the housing market and, when prices are falling, social class is no guarantor of protection. Cohorts who entered the market earlier, when house prices were rising rapidly, should generally do better than those who entered later. More importantly, the effects of class manifest themselves strongly when date of purchase is held constant. The middle classes made larger gains than other groups in all periods with the exception of 1989–91, when the picture is one of general losses and small gains for managers.

The implications of these finding are extremely important. They confirm that, in absolute terms, the professional and managerial socio-economic groups do consistently better than working-class groups within any given buyer cohort. This may be a result of the fact that they generally buy more expensive property or types of property that rise more rapidly in price, but the outcome is clear cut. But what of the

Table 15.7 Nominal illusionary gain, by socio-economic group of head of household, 1991.

Social group	% gain	N
Professional	356	128
Managerial	429	579
Other non-manual	397	532
Skilled manual	446	688
Partly skilled manual	530	190
Unskilled manual	474	39
Mean % gain	433	2156

Source: British Household Panel Survey, 1991.

distribution of relative gains and losses? Table 15.7 shows that the mean nominal percentage illusionary gain for the BHPS sample was 433%, but there was no clear pattern by socio-economic group. The partly skilled had the largest gains (530%); professionals the smallest (356%). The explanation for this lies in the fact that professionals and managers moved house more frequently and were more likely to have been caught by the sharp fall in prices since 1989.

We can conclude that, although the distribution of relative gains is not class related, the distribution of absolute gains is very strongly class related. This suggests that the differential resources that homeowners put into purchase are reflected in terms of absolute gains. To this extent, gains from home-ownership are not independent of class, but reflect it quite closely.

15.7 Home-ownership, inheritance and class reproduction

The significance of home-ownership in class reproduction is twofold. First, because of its potential as a store or source of wealth, it is possible to transmit this wealth to children or other beneficiaries in the form of housing inheritance. Secondly, it can be argued that, if the parents own, this may help engender a "culture of ownership". This is discussed in the next section. The focus here is on housing inheritance. There can be no doubt that housing inheritance offers some beneficiaries very substantial wealth advantages, which in principle should assist the process of class reproduction. The key questions, however, concern the distribution and value of housing inheritances: are they substantial, and to whom are they likely to accrue?

There are two major forms of thought on the implications of housing inheritance, which can be crudely termed "mass inheritance" and "selective class based". Saunders (1986) is a key advocate of the mass inheritance thesis, arguing that the rapid expansion of home-ownership since the war will lead to a great widening and diffusion of housing wealth.

> With 60% of households now in the owner occupied sector in Britain . . .
> not only is a majority of the population now in a position to accumulate

such capital gains as may accrue through the housing market, but for the first time in human history, we are approaching the point where millions of working people stand at some time in their lives to inherit capital sums far in excess of anything they could hope to save through earnings from employment. (Saunders 1986: 324)

His views were shared by Nigel Lawson, then Chancellor of the Exchequer, who stated in a speech in 1988: "We are about to become a nation of inheritors. Inheritance, which used to be the preserve of the few, will become a fact of life for the many. People will be inheriting houses, and stocks and shares."

On the other hand, there are those who argue that housing inheritance will generally tend to benefit the better off and the middle class as a result of the class basis of home-ownership and the distribution of property type and value. Writing in the *Observer*, Neal Ascherson suggested in the context of London that "the older occupiers of 'fairy money' houses and flats are beginning to die. The heirs do not need the property left to them, and will sell it. What this means is that in the next decade or so the upward mobile middle and professional classes of London will acquire staggering reserves of liquid cash."

This class-based interpretation is also argued by Watt (1993), who claims that, because the middle classes own the most expensive property, their beneficiaries are likely to get more than the children of working-class owners (who are also more likely to have to share the proceeds with more beneficiaries). I too have argued (Hamnett 1991b) that the incidence of inheritance is also strongly class based, as the chance of inheriting house property is currently very dependent on the tenure and class characteristics of the generation of dying homeowners, who were much more likely to be middle class than is the case with owners today.

Given the divergence of views, what does the empirical evidence reveal? Table 15.8 shows the distribution and incidence of housing inheritance by social grade on the basis of a survey conducted by NOP in 1989. Two things stand out from the table. First, the C1s and C2s (the other non-manual group and the skilled manual group, respectively) together receive half of all housing inheritances. When the manager Bs are added, the three groups account for three-quarters of all inheritances. But this is not surprising because the C1s and C2s are the largest groups. When we look at the incidence of housing inheritance, the picture is very different. Some 25% of A

Table 15.8 Distribution of housing inheritance, by social ranking.

Social Class		% inheriting	% in sample	N
A	Professional/managerial	26	6	323
B	Intermediate/junior non-manual	24	26	1,415
C1	Other non-manual	15	27	2,306
C2	Skilled manual	10	24	3,134
D	Semi-skilled manual	7	11	2,005
E	Unskilled manual	5	6	1,461
	Total	12	100	10,664

Source: NOP survey for Hamnett et al. 1991: 101.

and B headed households have inherited house property, compared with 15% of C1s, 10% of C2s, 7% of Ds and just 5% of Es. The chance of inheriting is five times as great for the As and Bs as it is for the Es. This suggests that the incidence of inheritance was strongly class based up to the late 1980s.

Data on the value of inheritances received show that the higher social classes receive more on average than others.

Although the distribution of housing inheritance is likely to widen over the course of the next 20–30 years as the current generation of homeowners begins to die off, the children of tenants are likely to have a far lower chance of inheriting house property than are the children of owners. The advantages of home-ownership based on class (and tenure) are likely to be perpetuated for some time to come, thereby aiding the processes of class reproduction, at least where the transmission of financial advantage is concerned.

15.8 Housing careers and social mobility

Home-ownership appears to confer distinct advantages on the middle classes, at least in some periods. The question must be asked, however, whether or not these advantages are permanently socially fixed. To what extent is it possible for members of other tenures to become homeowners, and to what extent can homeowners move up within the tenure to larger, or more expensive, houses that offer greater use values and potential capital gains? On the first of these questions, there is strong longitudinal evidence (McDowell 1982, Jenkins & Maynard 1983) that the children of homeowners are more likely to become owners than the children of non-owners. However as Savage et al. (1992a) have shown on the basis of their work on Guildford, Surrey, this is not a deterministic relationship and many children of council tenants become homeowners. However, the probability of becoming an owner was strongly class specific. Thus social class strongly influences the probability of housing tenure mobility.

Forrest et al.'s (1991) work on housing careers suggests that there are marked differences in career structure between the upper-middle-class spiralists who move frequently from one area to another for employment reasons (making housing investments as they go) and, at the other extreme, working-class households that tend to remain in one house for much longer periods of time. Their sample was polarized between the two groups so it is not surprising they found a marked difference, but are there sharp structured differences in mobility across classes, with the middle classes tending to move more frequently? The South East survey (Hamnett & Seavers 1994) found that the proportion of owners who had owned only one home varied from just 27% of professionals and 33% of managers to 50% of skilled manual workers, 76% of the partly skilled and 84% of the unskilled. Conversely, the proportion of owners who had owned four or more homes ranged from 19% of professionals to none of the unskilled.

Even if it can be shown that the middle classes tend to move more frequently, what does this say, if anything, about class formation? Is this simply another reflection of differences in class position that enable the middle classes to move more frequently to improve their housing as their incomes rise, or is the frequency of moves associated with the possibility of greater long-term capital gains as households move up-market to more expensive properties? The South East owners' survey suggests that those who have moved more frequently tend to move up-market into larger and more expensive houses, which suggests that mobility is part and parcel of the process of acquiring larger, and generally more expensive, houses with greater potential for capital accumulation and the possible transmission of financial benefits to beneficiaries.

15.9 Conclusions

It has been argued here that, although a higher proportion of the middle class are homeowners than of other classes, the diffusion of home-ownership down the social hierarchy has meant that home-ownership is no longer class specific. It is now quite widely diffused across most social classes bar the unskilled working class. However, the middle classes still have a dominant position in the ownership of more expensive, larger properties, from which they derive a greater use value and a higher degree of social status and cultural distinction. To this extent, home-ownership may play an important role in the cultural basis of class formation. It provides the focus for a wide range of domestic cultural activities.

Financially, home-ownership offers the possibility of both real gains and real losses. Although home-ownership is not a guaranteed source of accumulation, members of the middle classes generally make larger absolute gains than members of other classes, controlling for the time the property was bought. The distribution of relative gains appears not to be class related, however. Home-ownership can function as a vehicle for class reproduction both culturally and via housing inheritance. It was shown that, although housing inheritances are numerically concentrated in the middle of the socio-economic spectrum, the incidence of housing inheritance is greater for professional and managerial households and the value of the inheritance is also higher. Finally, it was argued that the children of middle-class parents are more likely to become homeowners than are the children of tenants, and that the middle classes are also likely to move more frequently, generally to larger and more expensive houses. Home-ownership is important for the middle classes and not just as an index of class position. It appears to play a not inconsiderable role in the process of class formation and reproduction. It does not and could not supplant or replace labour market position or ownership and control of the means of production, but it does play an important, and generally reinforcing, role.

Part Six
Politics and the middle classes

The character of middle class political alignments in advanced capitalist societies has been the subject of lay interest and scholarly debate for many years (e.g. Abercrombie & Urry 1983, Goldthorpe 1982, Savage et al. 1992). The prime issue is whether the middle classes are to be conceived as a radical force for social change or whether, by contrast, they are conservative props of the existing social order. This is no trivial matter, for the view that is adopted on this matter has far reaching consequences for planning viable political strategies as the middle classes become a larger part of the electorate. If the middle classes are an essentially conservative force then it becomes rather difficult to see how radical change can come about. If, however, a contrary view is taken, then it is possible to claim either that a traditional form of left wing socialist politics remains viable even if more dependent on middle-class rather than working-class support (Mallet 1975), or alternatively, that new forms of radical political activism, such as those organized through "new social movements" can be anticipated.

Hitherto, research trying to address such issues tends to fall into one of two types. On the one hand qualitative research using case study methods has examined the sociology of specific political movements and campaigns, examining issues such as the social constituencies that are represented in various political movements, the mobilization process itself, and the sorts of issues and programs raised (e.g. Scott 1990, Eder 1993). On the other hand, survey research has been used to explore aggregate patterns of voting behaviour and political attitudes. These two methods tend to emphasize rather different characteristics of middle-class politics. The former has tended to show that radical political activity is frequently carried out by middle-class people, and that this middle-class constituency appears to be a key base for radicalism. This is true of activists in "new social movements" such as CND (Parkin 1968, and see Bagguley's discussion in Chapter 18), but it has also been documented that members of the Labour Party increasingly tend to be drawn from middle-class ranks (Seyd and Whitley 1992). On the other hand, survey analysis tends to show that *in general*, middle-class people are more conservative than the working classes, and therefore that middle-class radicals should not be seen as representative of their class.

This suggests an intriguing pattern. Although the "typical" middle-class individual tends to be conservative, there appear to be a substantial minority who do not only participate in, but increasingly seem to monopolize, various forms of radical politics. This suggests that the most interesting questions are now not about the politics of the middle classes as a whole, but concern the reasons for these variations (e.g. Heath et al. 1991, Savage 1991, Bagguley 1992). Attention has therefore shifted somewhat towards exploring the sorts of processes that explain systematic sources of division within the middle classes. Are such divisions historical residues that may be eroded as a result of current economic and social changes, with the result that a more homogeneous middle-class politics might develop? Or, by contrast, might such divisions become more accentuated? To put this question another way, are such divisions caused by structural rifts within the middle classes that tend to systematically fragment them, or are they related to more contingent factors such as the specific personal characteristics of different middle-class people?

The two chapters in this part address this issue using survey research (Ch. 17) and a consideration of case study research (Ch. 18). Bagguley examines the nature of new social movements in order to clarify whether they can be rooted in middle-class lifestyles and work, and Heath & Savage use survey data to explore variations in the political identification of different middle-class occupational groups. Despite being grounded in different research methods and bodies of literature there are interesing similarities of argument concerning the way in which middle-class occupations recruit from people with rather different political views

Chapter 16

Political alignments within the middle classes, 1972–89

Anthony Heath and Mike Savage

16.1 Introduction

The examination of the influence of class on political identification and voting behaviour has reached a considerable level of sophistication in recent years (see Heath et al. 1985, 1991, Marshall et al. 1988). However, it is clear that classes are composed of different sorts of people, in a variety of occupations, and it is rare to examine intra-class political divisions systematically. This paper reports a secondary analysis of a pooled dataset of British Social Attitudes Surveys (BSAS) conducted between 1983 and 1990, which allows the nature and extent of political divisions within the "service class" to be thoroughly examined. We are able to carry this out because, when combined into one dataset, the total sample size becomes large enough to distinguish many more groups or fractions within the middle classes than is feasible using the various General Election Surveys that are currently the main tool used for the analysis of political attitudes and alignments (Heath et al. 1985, 1991, 1994). In fact the pooled dataset that we analyze has a total of 3,884 middle-class respondents, all of whom are members of the "service class" as defined by the Goldthorpe class schema, a sample size that compares well with the total sample size of General Election Surveys.

The first step we take is to clarify some of the theoretical issues that are pertinent to the issues we have specified. Here we show that there are two main views on the nature of middle-class political differentiation, one that emphasizes middle-class differentiation as the result of structural factors, and another that explains it as the contingent product of the different personal characteristics of people in various middle-class occupations. Having clarified the nature of the theoretical disagreements, we describe the data used and our methods of analysis in section 16.3. In section 16.4 we explore the patterns of party identification for 39 middle-class groups. In section 16.5 we explore the reasons for such differences by the application of multivariate analysis, and in section 16.6 we briefly consider whether our findings suggest important differences in middle-class politics between the 1970s and 1980s by comparing our results with those derived from the 1972 Nuffield Mobility Study.

16.2 Theoretical issues

As we have seen in earlier chapters of this book, John Goldthorpe (1982) is particularly responsible for the argument that the "service class" has a unitary social structural location. Although he is well aware of significant differences between administrative, managerial and professional workers in advanced capitalist societies, he claims that they all enjoy the benefits of a "service relationship" with their employer rather than the "labour contract" on which other workers are reliant. Goldthorpe argues that "service-class" employees depend upon either expert knowledge or delegated authority. Since their employers are not in a position to monitor these employees directly, they have to trust that they are carrying out their duties. "Employees render service to their employing organization in return for compensation which takes the form not only of reward for work done, through a salary and various perquisites, but also comprises important prospective elements – for example salary increments on an established scale, assurances of security both in employment and, through pensions rights, after retirement, and above all well defined career opportunities" (Erikson & Goldthorpe 1992b: 42).

The service class is therefore a privileged class whose members are given personal stakes in the system by the construction of prospective rewards. It is therefore quite understandable that Goldthorpe sees it as a conservative class, whose interests lie in upholding the existing social and political order. The "service class . . . as it consolidates, will constitute an essentially conservative element within modern societies" (Goldthorpe 1982: 180).

Although Goldthorpe's view is that the common structural position of the service class inclines it towards conservatism, he is well aware that substantial numbers of the service class are not conservative. His explanation of this is couched in terms of the characteristics of the people who happen to be members of the service class rather than in terms of structural features of their class position. His most important argument here concerns the fact that a large proportion of the service class has been recruited from other social classes, with the result that the service class has not yet become "demographically formed". He argues that the rapid expansion of professional and managerial work since the 1950s has meant that many of the service class's members have actually been recruited from other class backgrounds, with the result that the political views of its upwardly mobile members may well be linked to their class of origin and are hence less likely to be conservative. Heath et al.'s (1991) analysis of the 1987 British Election Study confirmed that service-class members from working-class backgrounds were considerably more likely to vote Labour than were the rest of the service class, while De Graaf et al. (1995) have provided an empirical assessment of the political consequences of the service class's lack of demographic formation. Unfortunately we are not able to examine this specific argument in this paper because the BSAS does not include information on parents' occupation. But the general point is still important for us to bear in mind because it has wider ramifications. For instance, Goldthorpe's focus on middle-class political differentiation as the product of the personal characteristics of service-class members rather than of any structural feature can be linked to Heath et al.'s distinction between "old" and "new" sources of political differentiation. The "old" sources of differentiation that they point to (religion, social origins, education) are primarily concerned with contingent factors. Thus religious affiliation plays an important part in affecting middle-class attitudes, with Anglicans being substantially more likely to be Conservative voters than are Catholics and non-conformists. Heath et al. also draw on Inglehart's (1971) arguments concerning the characteristics of "post-materialist values". Inglehart argues that exposure to higher education allows the development of a "critical culture", which might make graduates and other highly qualified individuals more likely to embrace post-materialist values and to support forms of radical politics, for instance those associated with new social movements. Once again, the important point is that the focus here is on the characteristics of the people (in this case, their experience of higher education) that predispose them towards radical politics rather than any feature of their class position.

By contrast, another way of explaining middle-class political differentiation (the "new" sources of differentiation, as phrased by Heath et al.) is to argue that there are structural forces within the "service class" that tend to fragment the political alignments of the middle classes. The concomitant of this point is to suggest that the concept of the service class itself may be of dubious value, at least as a tool for investigating middle-class politics, because it mis-specifies the important causal processes at work in its claim that the service relationship, with its associated prospective rewards, tends to be enmeshed in conservatizing social relationships.

A number of possible structural sources of differentiation have been suggested as significant in fracturing middle-class politics. One that has been particularly widely discussed emphasizes the significance of the distinction between the middle classes in public and private sectors. For Dunleavy (1979) the middle classes employed by the public sector are involved in structural relationships that are likely to predispose them to a state-oriented politics, whereas those employed in the private sector will tend to incline towards market-oriented economic forces (see also Perkin 1989). It is likely that there will be important differences in the work conditions of the service class employed in the two types of situation, with those in the public sector more likely to work in formal bureaucratic settings. However, existing research suggests that sector is only weakly correlated with voting patterns, once occupational group is taken into account (Heath et al. 1991, though see the qualification concerning the differences between the politics of the middle classes in nationalized industries and state welfare jobs in Savage 1991). It might also be pointed out that it is by no means clear that such distinctions override a broader concern that both groups might have to defend the status quo.

A rather more radical view than this can be derived from Bourdieu's (1984) analysis of the distinction between cultural and economic capital. Bourdieu argues that there are two principal axes by which middle-class privileges are constructed and maintained. One of these concerns the accumulation of wealth and property in a way that is analogous, though not identical, to Goldthorpe's arguments concerning the importance of the service class's prospective rewards. But Bourdieu also argues that privilege is dependent upon cultural capital, the construction of forms of cultural distinction that privileged middle-class groups can embrace and pass on to their children by giving them the right "dispositions" to perform well in the educational system. The importance of Bourdieu's idea is that it challenges the notion of a unitary process inclining the service class to conservatism. Thus the attempt by the "cultured" middle class to defend its cultural distinction may put it at odds with the economically privileged middle class whose interests may lie in undermining cultural privilege. In short, because the middle classes are formed round different axes, the potential for structural conflict between middle-class fractions grows more intense than is envisaged by those referring to the service-class concept. Bourdieu's ideas also seem interesting in the light of Heath et al.'s (1991) demonstration that it is the "creative and welfare professionals" who appear to be politically distinctive within the middle classes because of their relatively low degree of support for the Conservative Party. There is *prima facie* evidence that those high in cultural capital tend to be more "left wing" than those with greater amounts of economic capital.

In fact Bourdieu draws back from the implications of his argument by suggesting that both the culturally and the economically privileged middle classes have a common stake in the status quo. He also emphasizes the fluidity of movement between cultural and economic distinction. In the light of this, perhaps the strongest argument in favour of there being structural divisions within the middle classes is that developed by neo-Marxists who point to the different types of employment relationships in which middle-class people are enmeshed. One influential account along these lines is by American Marxist Erik Wright (1985), who has argued for the existence of three independent axes of inequality – property assets, organization assets and skill assets. For Wright, each of these assets is an independent axis of exploitation that does not depend on any other. The result is, for instance, that those who are advantaged through their possession of organization assets need not defend the rights of property at all. As a result the structural relations in which different groups within the middle classes are enmeshed are much more complex than envisaged by Goldthorpe, and it is quite possible that some groups may incline towards radical, anti-capitalist politics.

Wright's arguments are rather formalistic and his concept of "skill asset", in particular, is rather weak. Nonetheless it is possible to develop his arguments in a more viable way. Thus an important distinction may lie between managerial workers exercising delegated authority and professional workers deploying expert knowledge (see Savage et al. 1992). It can be argued – *contra* Goldthorpe – that these groups have rather different relationships to their employers. Because the expertise of managers is specific to the particular organizational context in which they work, they are more likely to be dependent upon an individual firm for position and advancement. Professional workers, however, tend to be able to use their expert knowledge in a greater variety of settings and hence are less reliant on any one employer (Savage et al. 1992). The important implication is that professional workers are less likely to rely on their employers and are more able to develop independent, possibly radical, politics than are managers.

The crucial issue that we have emphasized from the foregoing discussion is whether the causes of middle-class political differentiation are to be found in the personal characteristics of the incumbents of particular sections of the middle classes, or whether there are structural processes that tend to lead to different sorts of political alignments. This is a point of some significance for conceptualizing the nature of middle-class politics, because if the former account is true then middle-class radicalism should be seen as a form of personal deviance from the general character of middle-class politics, whereas if the latter is true then middle-class radicalism can be said to have deeper structural roots.

Of course, the distinctions we have drawn here can be seen as rather crude in some respects. It is not always that easy in practice to distinguish between characteristics of "people" and "places".Thus, although Heath et al. (1991) have shown that highly educated people tend towards left-wing politics, it is unclear whether this is due to their educational background or to do with the sorts of occupations in which they work. Furthermore, there is a particular problem, first noticed by Parkin (1968), concerning the way that selective recruitment to different middle-class occupations means that even occupational position can be seen as a personal, rather than a structural, characteristic. Is it the case that left-wing people choose to go into social work (for instance), or that being a social worker makes you left wing?

There is not much we can do about this particular problem, because only a longitudinal study could explore these interconnections (though see Bagguley in Ch. 17 in this volume). The general point for us to bear in mind is that it is necessary to avoid the temptation to see particular variables as indications of either "individual" or "structural" factors. Rather it is necessary to be sensitive to all the possible interpretations of the way that certain variables may affect the patterns we describe. For this reason much of our exercise is descriptive, attempting to explore the possible interconnections that can be drawn between variables, rather than to find a definitive answer.

16.3 Data and methods

The data we use are drawn from the various British Social Attitudes Surveys carried out in Great Britain (excluding Northern Ireland) every year (except 1988) between 1983 and 1990. We stop in 1990 because the standard occupational classification changed in this year with the result that the categories cannot be readily compared across these years. The aggregated dataset provides a total sample size of 3,884 people who fall within classes I and II of John Goldthorpe's class schema (i.e. the service class). We began by breaking down this sample into smaller component groups so that political differentiation could be examined.

Practically we were constrained by the need to use the occupational categories used in the 1980 Classification of Occupations (OPCS 1980). This classification is very detailed, with 113 different occupational groups containing service-class respondents, and the survey also contains full information on the employment status of respondents (employee, manager, self-employed, etc.), which when used in connection with the occupational codes can provide a very refined level of analysis. However, in order to obtain large enough numbers for statistical analysis, we arranged the different occupational groupings into larger clusters. Our aim was to ensure that the resulting categories would enable us to test the sorts of issues discussed above by differentiating occupations in theoretically relevant ways. Although we sought to avoid using categories with small numbers of respondents and tried to ensure that each group had at least 50 respondents, we did not amalgamate them with others unless good theoretical reasons could be found for doing so. Thus, although there were only four trade union officers in the sample, we kept them separate from other categories because there were no sound theoretical reasons for merging them with any other group. The resulting series of 39 groupings allows a much more refined analysis of the politics of different service-class groups to be drawn up than is possible using the much smaller election surveys, where it is feasible to distinguish only a handful of occupational groups.

Our dependent variable is party identification. We chose this because it is less volatile than actual vote, which might be influenced by specific electoral factors (tactical voting, personalities, particular election campaigns). As we are interested here not in the outcome of particular elections but in people's more general and enduring political alignments, this seemed the appropriate choice.

There is clear evidence that the service class as a whole leans towards the Conservatives, although not to an overwhelming degree. Altogether 47.7% identified with the Conservatives, 20.9% with the Labour Party, and 14.8% with the Liberal, Liberal Democrat or Social Democratic parties (henceforth termed the Centre parties). The rest either had no identification or identified with other parties. The proportion of our sample having no identification, 15.0%, is in line with the proportion of the total electorate expressing no identification (14%) as indicated by the British Election Surveys of 1983 and 1987 (Heath et al. 1991: 12). The proportion of our sample who identified with the Conservative Party is somewhat lower than the proportion of service-class members actually voting Conservative as revealed by the British Election Surveys (which was 54% in 1983 and 1987; see Heath et al. 1985, 1991), but it needs to be remembered that levels of Conservative support tended to be higher in these election years than in intervening years.

16.4 Middle-class political differentiation

In Table 16.1 we show the party identification of the 39 different groups that we have distinguished and the table reveals that the service-class occupational groups do indeed vary in quite striking ways in their degrees of party allegiance. Some groups are considerably less likely to support the Conservatives than is the service class as a whole, whereas others show a remarkable degree of unanimity in their endorsement of the Conservative Party. At one extreme lies a series of occupational groups that appear relatively left-wing in their party identification. Five groups are

Table 16.1 Party identification by middle-class group (%).

	Con.	Lab.	Lib.	Other	None	N
1 Judges and legal professionals	57.1	19.0	16.7	2.4	4.8	42
2 Accountants and financial professionals	60.9	10.9	16.7	0.6	10.9	174
3 Personnel and industrial relations managers	43.7	23.0	17.2	1.1	14.9	87
4 Systems analysts and computer programmers	39.4	19.7	22.5		18.3	71
5 Scientists	31.4	22.9	21.4	4.3	20.0	70
6 Marketing managers and sales representatives	61.0	16.9	11.3	0.5	10.3	195
7 Local government officers and professionals	37.7	21.7	17.4	2.9	20.3	69
8 Senior civil servants	53.3	20.0	26.7			15
9 Higher education lecturers	27.3	39.4	23.2	2.0	8.1	99
10 Teachers	39.0	24.8	22.9	2.8	10.5	459
11 Social workers	30.5	41.8	14.9	0.7	12.1	141
12 Clergy	26.7	26.7	26.7		20.0	15
13 Doctors and dentists	44.7	19.1	19.1	2.1	14.9	47
14 Nurses	40.0	21.0	18.0		21.0	100
15 Health professionals n.e.c.	47.9	18.3	19.0	1.4	13.4	142
16 Authors, writers, journalists	32.4	32.4	17.6	5.9	11.8	34
17 Artists, designers, photographers	37.5	28.1	18.8	1.6	14.1	64
18 Actors, musicians	23.5	44.1	14.7	2.9	14.7	34
19 Civil engineers	50.0	16.7	11.1	2.8	19.4	36
20 Mechanical engineers	45.0	15.0	17.5		22.5	40
21 Electrical and electronic engineers	46.9	16.3	24.5	2.0	10.2	49
22 Engineers n.e.c.	45.2	24.7	12.3	2.7	15.1	73
23 Laboratory technicians	40.0	14.1	18.8	3.5	23.5	85
24 Architects	43.5	17.4	17.4		21.7	23
25 Surveyors, property and estate managers/agents	58.0	17.3	8.6	2.5	13.6	81
26 Air pilots	68.4			5.3	26.3	1
27 Professionals in management roles	59.5	7.1	21.4		11.9	42
28 Production managers	56.8	15.8	13.7		13.7	146
29 Building and mining managers	49.0	23.5	9.8		17.6	51
30 Transport and distribution managers	46.6	31.5	6.8	1.4	13.7	73
31 Office managers	61.3	11.8	11.3	1.4	14.2	212
32 Wholesale and retail managers	51.4	20.4	4.9	2.0	21.2	245
33 Service and leisure managers	41.2	20.6	11.8	1.5	25.0	68
34 Security forces etc	78.6	2.9	4.3		14.3	70
35 Junior civil servants	28.9	36.8	23.7	2.6	7.9	38
36 Clerk supervisors	50.7	20.2	9.2	0.8	19.1	357
37 Trade union officials		75.0	25.0			4
38 Draughtspersons	45.5	22.7	7.6		24.2	66
39 Bourgeoisie	78.4	3.9	7.8		9.8	51
Total	47.7	20.9	14.8	1.5	15.0	3,687

more likely to identify with Labour than with the Conservatives, while another two are equally as likely to support Labour. In descending order of identification with the Labour Party, these groups are trade union officers (where there is a very small sample size); actors and musicians; social workers; lecturers in higher education; junior civil servants; authors, writers and journalists; and the clergy. Most of these groups fall into the category of "welfare and creative professionals" whom Heath et al. (1991) have already pointed out as being distinctive in their left-wing support. However, their sectoral position is much more diverse. Higher education lecturers and social workers are largely employed in the public sector, whereas actors, musicians, journalists and the like tend to work in the private sector. These groups seem remarkably distinct from other service-class groups in their relatively high levels of identification (between 32% and 45%, except for the clergy) with the Labour Party. However (leaving aside the special case of trade union officials), it needs to be pointed out that the highest degree of identification with the Labour Party, 44% by actors, is still only a substantial minority of that group. Goldthorpe seems correct to insist on the generally conservative leanings of the service class.

By contrast, there are some service-class groups that are extremely, almost unanimously, Conservative: 79% of the security forces (which includes the police and the military), 78% of the bourgeoisie (employers with over 25 employees) and 68% of airline pilots identify with the Conservatives. If one excludes those who identify with no party or a minor party, the impression of Conservative strength is enhanced; indeed there were no air pilots who identified with Labour or the Centre parties at all. Using this measure of three-party identification, we can detect a number of groups where a very hefty two-thirds or so identify with the Conservatives rather than with Labour or the Centre: office managers; sales representatives; accountants and professionals in management. Although these are predominantly employed in the private sector, it is once again interesting to point out that one of the most Conservative groups of all, the security forces, is located firmly in the public sector. Indeed, looking at the distribution of other groups in Table 16.1 shows several cases where predominantly private sector groups are similar to predominantly public sector ones (for instance senior civil servants and electrical engineers; nurses and service and leisure managers).

Considering the spread of groups as a whole there does appear to be a broad axis of differentiation between those occupational groupings relying on managerial authority, who tend to lie on the more conservative wing of the service class, and those more likely to rely on cultural expertise, who appear more drawn to left-wing politics. Thus there is no managerial group where less than half of its members with a political identification support the Conservative Party. By contrast, most groups in creative, teaching and research-based occupations or in caring jobs tend more towards left-wing politics (although they have substantial numbers of right-wing supporters). The established professions appear towards the centre of the distribution. This general contrast between business and humanities, with the professionals lying between the two poles, is actually quite familiar from Bourdieu's analysis of middle-class cultural taste (e.g. Bourdieu 1984: 128–9).

16.5 Modelling party identification

Table 16.1 therefore shows considerable variation between occupational groups – variation that casual inspection suggests may be more related to employment status (employer, manager, employee) than to sectoral location (public, private). The next stage in our analysis, therefore, was to check these first impressions with more formal modelling of the data. Since we have a trichotomous dependent variable (Labour, Conservative or Centre identification), a multinomial logit is the appropriate technique. However, a multinomial logit generates a large number of parameters and is not altogether easy to interpret. So here we settle for a simpler logistic regression model in which the dichotomous dependent variable distinguishes Conservative and non-Conservative identifiers.

Table 16.2 presents the results of a series of logistic models. The basic model, on the right of Table 16.2, measures the extent to which the occupational groups deviate from the service-class average (represented by the health professionals n.e.c.). If the figure is positive, it means that the group deviates towards the Conservatives; if it is negative the group deviates away from them. The higher the number (whether positive or negative), the stronger the deviation and the more unusual or specific is the political identification of that group *vis-à-vis* the service class as a whole.

At the bottom of Table 16.2 there is an indication of the goodness of fit, using the chi square statistic. (Strictly speaking, this statistic shows the improvement of the model in question over a model that contains no explanatory variables.) The higher this figure is, the more the model in question accounts for the patterns found in the data. However, it is very important to note that this statistic shows how well the model accounts for individual not group patterns of party identification. A variable such as education might explain individuals' patterns of party support but if, to take an extreme possibility, all the occupational groups had the same mix of qualified and unqualified individuals, education would nonetheless fail to explain the group differences. To check whether a particular model has succeeded in explaining the group differences, therefore, we have to look at the changes in the sizes of the group parameter estimates. The more these move towards zero, the more successful the model has been in explaining the group differences.

The other important set of figures to watch is levels of significance. Since significance levels estimate the probability that the results could be due to chance, low levels of significance do not necessarily indicate that the parameters are incorrect; it would be wrong to assume that deviations from the mean exist only where there are high levels of significance. A good example of this point is the estimate for trade union officials. This is very strongly negative, indicating that trade union officers tend to be relatively left-wing. However, this figure has a low level of significance because there are only four cases in the sample. We would be foolish to assume that the low level of significance means that trade union officers are not left wing.

Look first at the basic model in the right-hand column. The parameter estimates indicate the extent to which each occupational group deviates from the service-class norm. Formally speaking, the estimates are fitted log-odds ratios. Consider for example the security forces. Their odds of supporting the Conservatives are $92 : 8 = 11.5 : 1$ (since 92% identify with the Conservatives and 8% with the other two main parties). The overall odds for the service class as a whole are $57 : 43 = 1.3 : 1$, and thus the odds ratio for the security forces as a whole is $11.5 : 1.3 = 8.8 : 1$. The log

Table 16.2 Parameter estimates for occupational groups, using different models.

Group	Employment status	Sector	Education	Basic model
		Model		
Judges	0.15	−0.35	0.22	0.22
Accountants	0.43	0.06	0.39	0.54[a]
Personnel managers	−0.32	−0.71[a]	−0.29	−0.17
Systems analysts	−0.20	−0.85[a]	−0.51	−0.32
Scientists	−0.47	−0.87[a]	−0.58	−0.59
Marketing managers	0.15	−0.06	0.36	0.52[a]
Local government officers	−0.30	−0.15	−0.38	−0.29
Senior civil servants	−0.47	0.17	−0.38	−0.16
Higher education lecturers	−1.00[b]	−0.81[b]	−1.00[b]	−1.09[b]
Teachers	−0.36	−0.33	−0.30	−0.45[a]
Social workers	−0.92[b]	−0.77[b]	−0.98[b]	−0.87[b]
Clergy	−1.06	−0.82	−0.83	−0.94
Doctors/Dentists	−0.37	−0.43	0.12	−0.10
Nurses	−0.58	0.01	−0.46	−0.22
Mechanical engineers	0.24	−0.32	0.05	0.08
Authors, journalists	−0.92[a]	−1.47[b]	−0.68	−0.68
Artists, designers	−0.79[a]	−1.16[b]	−0.58	−0.47
Actors, musicians	−1.54[b]	−1.90[b]	−1.25[b]	−1.17[b]
Civil engineers	0.38	0.03	0.36	0.34
Electrical engineers	0.04	−0.60	−0.16	−1.10
Other engineers	0.11	−0.56	0.12	−0.05
Laboratory technicians	−0.02	−0.05	−0.35	−0.06
Architects	−0.15	−0.32	−0.04	−0.03
Surveyors, etc.	0.54	0.05	0.42	0.56
Air pilots	4.79	4.55	4.74	4.95
Professionals in managment roles	0.24	0.15	0.35	0.48
Production managers	0.06	−0.17	0.31	0.41
Building, mining managers	0.21	−0.41	0.04	0.14
Transport managers	−0.41	−0.76[a]	−0.18	−0.06
Office managers	0.38	0.15	0.54[a]	0.73[b]
Wholesale, retail managers	0.11	−0.02	0.27	0.46[a]
Service, leisure managers	−0.36	−0.57	−0.19	−0.01
Security forces	2.13[b]	2.42[b]	1.92[b]	2.15[b]
Junior civil servants	−1.34[a]	−0.62	−1.16[b]	−0.99[a]
Clerk supervisors	−0.06	−0.20	0.08	0.30
Trade union officers	−5.28	−5.18	−5.25	−5.44
Draughtspersons	0.20	−0.36	−0.01	0.16
Bourgeoisie	1.03[a]	1.56[b]	1.55[b]	1.65 [b]
Goodness of fit (chi squared)	275.5[b]	287.5[b]	305.5[b]	249.3[b]

Note: Health professionals n.e.c. are excluded from the table. As they have been used as the reference category, their distribution closely matches that of the sample as a whole. a. Significant at .05 level; b. significant at .01 level

of this is 2.15. Inspection of Table 16.2 shows that this is a very high figure relative to those of other groups, which is exactly what we would expect given that we already know they are a very right-wing group. The basic model in Table 16.2 shows that in 10 out of 38 cases the deviations are statistically significant. There are five left-leaning groups whose deviation reaches standard levels of significance. In descending order these are actors and musicians, higher education lecturers, junior civil servants, social workers, and teachers. There are a further six that show statistically significant deviations towards the Conservatives: the security forces, the bourgeoisie, office managers, marketing managers, accountants and wholesale and retail managers. However, we must remember that the levels of significance depend both on the size of the parameter estimates and on the numbers in each group. With an even larger sample, even more groups would be significantly different from the service-class average, and vice versa.

Let us now consider how the parameter estimates change once various models are applied. The first column considers how employment status affects the patterns, thus allowing us to examine Wright's arguments concerning the distinction between employed, self-employed and managerial workers. The chi squared figure at the bottom of Table 16.2 indicates that the inclusion of employment status does improve the model somewhat, but this improvement is by no means dramatic. This improvement indicates that, in general, individual managers are more pro-Conservative than are the rank-and-file employees. In fact, in the service class as a whole, 63% of managers support the Conservatives compared with 48% of rank-and-file employees, while 68% of the self-employed favour the Conservatives.

Employment status does, then, have some power in explaining individual differences. Can it also explain the group differences? If we inspect the parameter estimates for the managerial groups, we find that most of the estimates are indeed reduced in size compared with the baseline model, suggesting that it is their position of managerial authority that accounts for the conservatism of these groups. The exceptions are transport managers and service managers, who now appear somewhat more left wing than would be expected for a managerial group (although not to a degree that is statistically significant).

The employment status theory is, however, weakened by the fact that the parameter estimates remain high for many of the left-leaning occupations. In other words, employment status has failed to account for the political preferences of these particular groups. Indeed for social workers, junior civil servants, authors and journalists, artists and designers, and actors and musicians the parameter estimates become even more negative compared with the baseline model, and are now in all five cases statistically significant. That is to say, these groups are significantly more left wing than would be expected given the general relation that holds between employment status and party identification in the service class as a whole.

One way of considering the overall effectiveness of employment status in explaining the group differences is to see whether the inclusion of employment status in the model tends to move the parameter estimates for the occupational groups closer to zero. If employment status could explain the occupational differences, one would expect the parameter estimates in general to be closer to zero than in the original model. But in fact there is no general tendency in this direction: in 19 cases the estimates move towards zero while in 19 they move further away from zero. In short, there is limited evidence that employment status can provide a general explanation for service-class differentiation.

The second column of Table 16.2 gives the parameter estimates when sector is included in the model (and employment status is removed). The chi square figure increases somewhat, suggesting that sector is slightly more powerful than employment status in explaining individual differences. Indeed, within the service class as a whole, 66% of the people in the private sector favoured the Conservatives compared with 44% in the public sector (nationalized industries falling in between with 53%) – slightly larger differences than those between managers and employees.

Moreover Table 16.2 shows that the parameter estimates for many of the left-leaning public sector professions such as the higher education lecturers are reduced once sector is taken into account. This suggests that some of the left-wingness of these groups is indeed due to their location in the public sector. However, many of the reductions are small and a number of the left-wing public sector professions continue to be strikingly left wing, even taking their sectoral location into account. Furthermore, some new anomalies emerge when we include sector in the model. Thus personnel managers, systems analysts and scientists all prove to have statistically significant negative parameters once sector is included. This indicates that these groups are significantly more left wing than are other occupations with a similar sectoral location.

As with employment status we can check whether the inclusion of sector in the model tends to give group parameter estimates that are in general closer to zero. There is a modest general tendency in this direction: in 21 cases estimates move towards zero, but in 17 they move further away from zero. This is slightly better than the comparable results for employment status, but is scarcely an impressive demonstration of explanatory power.

If we turn to the third column of Table 16.2, we can begin to consider the effects of education (measured in terms of the age at leaving full-time education). In general, 55% of respondents who left school at 15 or less identify with the Conservatives rather than with Labour or the Centre compared with 62% of those who left school at 16, 68% of those who left school at 17, 59% of those who left at 18, and a strikingly low 43% of those who left after the age of 18. This indicates a curvilinear relationship between the age at which respondents leave full-time education and party identification. Those who leave at 15 or younger tend to be less Conservative in orientation than the service class as a whole, probably because they are more likely to come from a working-class background and hence are more likely to adopt left-wing politics. Those who left full-time education between 16 and 18 are more likely to be Conservative in orientation. However, those leaving education after the age of 19, presumably graduates in many cases, tend to be markedly more left wing.

The chi squared figure for this model suggests that the addition of education to the model provides a more powerful prediction of individual party identification than does employment status or sector. This much is not surprising, given our discussion in the introduction. What is especially important for us to consider is how education affects the estimates found for specific occupational groups.

Here we find that the parameter estimate for a relatively left-wing profession such as the higher education lecturers is reduced by very little (compared with the basic model) while in the case of social workers and junior civil servants the parameters actually increase. This may initially be surprising, since one might expect that the radicalism of these groups is due to their educational background rather than to the nature of their job. We must remember, however, that the service class as a whole is generally well educated and that even higher education lecturers do not reach the educational levels of, for example, doctors. Moreover some of these radical groups such as social workers actually have lower-than-average educational levels.

In general Table 16.2 shows that there is a slight tendency for the occupational parameters to move closer to zero once education is included in the model: this occurs for 23 groups. So in fact education does perform slightly better, in explaining both the individual and the group differences, than does sector or employment status. The fact that educational level appears to be the best predictor of party identification suggests that it is the individual characteristics of particular members of the service class that are of greatest importance in shaping patterns of political differentiation. This is especially true because the variable we used (age at leaving education) is not a good proxy for the educational qualifications demanded by specific occupations.

Another way of looking at the role of occupation *per se* is to see whether or not some occupations tend to have similar parameters under all four models. This might indicate that it is the specific character of the occupational group that explains the variation rather than the general characteristics of sectoral location or employment status. Table 16.2 shows that a small number of occupational groups do appear utterly distinctive in their politics, deviating from the service-class mean under all three models. The most striking are the security forces and the bourgeoisie (who lean to the right), and the higher education lecturers, social workers, and actors and musicians (who lean to the left). These are the only groups for whom the parameter estimates have high levels of significance in all four models. None of the general theories that we have considered in this chapter seems to be able to account for the partisanship of these groups, and since these are the most striking groups we are therefore inclined to the view that these general theories of political differentiation are of relatively modest value.

An important point to make, moreover, is that there are many other occupational groups that lack distinct political leanings. The conclusion from Table 16.2 is that the majority of service-class occupations do not have particularly distinctive political leanings but share the general pro-Conservative tendencies of the service class.

16.6 Change over time

The analysis so far has allowed us to peer inside the service class in the 1980s in order to explore the nature of occupational divisions within it. However, in order to carry out this analysis we have had to adopt a purely cross-sectional approach and have not been able to examine change over time. In this final section we put our earlier analysis into a historical context by comparing these findings with those from an earlier survey, the Nuffield Mobility Survey, carried out in 1972. Although this survey was carried out just over a decade earlier than the British Social Attitudes Surveys that we have used, it allows us to consider whether the politics of the service class has changed in any significant ways following the Conservative hegemony that began with Margaret Thatcher's election victory in 1979 and that marked a significant shift in the political climate (see Jessop 1990). There are indeed a number of largely unproven notions that claim that alignments within the middle classes have changed recently. Perkin (1989) has emphasized the growing division between public and private wings of the salariat brought about by the Thatcher government's attempts to rein back the public sector. Jessop (1984) have echoed these arguments by claiming that Thatcherism distinguished a private sector productive class against a public sector middle class. Savage et al. (1992) have argued that Thatcherism's policies towards the state led the professional middle classes towards the left whereas the managerial middle classes have moved, less spectacularly, towards the Conservative Party.

Hitherto it has been difficult to prove or disprove such claims owing to the lack of appropriate historical data. Although the British Election Surveys go back to 1964, we have already seen that the sample size is too small to allow the detailed occupational analyses that we have carried out here. The Nuffield Mobility Survey (NMS), however, carried out in 1972, asked questions on occupational position as well as party identification and has sufficient respondents (over 10,000, 2,480 of whom fall into the service class) to allow an occupational breakdown. And, although the Nuffield survey is only slightly more than a decade before the BSA surveys, this is far enough apart to allow possible trends and shifts to be identified.

Having said this, it is no easy matter to compare the Nuffield survey with the pooled BSAS dataset. One problem is that the Nuffield survey covered only men living in England and Wales, aged 20–64, whereas the BSAS include women, older and younger age groups, and Scots. In order to allow comparison, our analysis of the BSAS dataset has been rerun so that it includes only equivalent respondents to the Nuffield study, that is, men aged 20–64 living in England and Wales. On the whole, these alterations do not change the patterns we revealed above, although they do of course sharply reduce the sample size. This will make it more difficult to detect statistically significant changes over time.

A more serious problem is that the Nuffield survey is coded to the 1970 Occupational Classification (OPCS 1970), whereas the BSA surveys were coded to the 1980 Occupational Classification. No exact comparison is possible because individuals who would be classified to a specific group in 1970 might have been reallocated to two or more 1980 groups, and vice versa. The biggest problem arises since the 1970 scheme specified a number of amorphous categories that were coded to more precise occupational groups in 1980. In particular, individuals who were placed in the 1970 occupational groups 220 (technical and related workers n.e.c.), 217 (professional workers n.e.c.), and 180 (managers n.e.c.) were dispersed to a variety of specific occupational groups in the 1980 classification.

These problems mean that we cannot carry out a comprehensive comparison between the NMS and the BSAS. It is sensible to compare the results only in those cases where it is possible to match up the 1980 categories to the 1970 ones. We can in fact judge whether specific groups could be matched up because the 1983 British General Election Survey was coded to both the 1970 and the 1980 schemes, making it possible to examine the proportion of individuals who would be classified to the same occupational group under the two classification schemes. For 11 of the groups we have specified above there was a perfect or close to perfect matching: 95% or more were classified to the same group under both schemes. In a further 12 cases there was a reasonable tie up, with 75–94% being classified to the same group. This leaves 16 groups where the comparison is clearly questionable. In the analysis that follows we examine only those groups where meaningful comparisons can be made.

In general terms the service class as a whole appears to have switched relatively little in its allegiance since 1972. In 1972, 46.8% identified with the Conservative Party and 19.6% with Labour. By the 1980s these figures had changed to 49.6% and 21.7%, so that both major parties gained slightly. The reason for this is that the proportion of non-identifiers fell slightly (from 18.6% to 14.3%) as did those identifying with a minor party (2% to 0.9%). If we examine only those respondents who identified with one of the major parties, a slight swing from the Conservatives to the Centre parties becomes evident. The Labour share of identification held stable, scarcely changing from 25.7% to 25.5%, while the Conservative share fell from 61.4% to 58.4%, and the Centre increased slightly, from 12.9% to 16.1%.

Although a marginal shift is detectable, in general there appears to be a considerable stability of political identification at the aggregate level. What we need to examine, however, is whether this aggregate stability is repeated at the level of individual occupational groups, or whether it actually hides a growing polarization in the allegiances of groups within the service class. If there were signs of growing polarization or fragmentation over time, this might begin to call into question some of John Goldthorpe's expectations about the future of the service class.

Table 16.3 compares the levels of identification found in the NMS and the BSAS for two sets of occupational groups: those that are comparable in the 95% level at the top part of the table, and those comparable in the 75–94% level at the bottom part of the table. We should emphasize that many of the groups that have been specified are small and we cannot be confident that the patterns revealed are statistically reliable; the results should be treated as suggestive only. However, it is striking that considerable shifts in alignment are evident among many of the groups. In most cases shifts are over 10 percentage points. Six groups swing markedly away from the Conservatives: doctors and dentists; actors and musicians; artists; social workers; scientists; and authors, writers and journalists. More modest left-wing shifts can be detected amongst teachers and the clergy. On the other hand, air pilots, bourgeoisie, other health professionals, other engineers, service managers, draughtspersons and clerk supervisors shift markedly to the right.

Although we cannot be confident about the reliability of the figures here, the evi-

Table 16.3 Conservative share of party identification in selected middle-class groups, 1972 and 1980s.

Occupational group	1972 Tory identifiers		1980s Tory identifiers		Shift
	%	No.	%	No.	
95 % compatibles					
Judges	64.7	17	57.1	15	−7.6
Teachers	49.2	199	40.0	95	−9.2
Clergy	55.6	18	40.0	10	−15.6
Doctors, dentists	81.5	27	50.0	21	−31.5
Nurses	40.0	17	50.0	2	+10.0
Authors, journalists	56.3	16	37.5	18	−19.2
Actors,	54.5	11	25.0	16	−29.5
Air pilots	44.9	46	100.0	10	+55.6
Service managers	56.5	46	68.8	16	+12.3
Draughtspersons	45.3	64	59.0	39	+13.7
Bourgeoisie	75.0	26	92.0	42	+17.0
75% compatibles					
Scientists	58.6	29	38.9	36	−19.7
Social workers	37.5	16	11.5	26	−26.0
Other health professionals	50.0	16	66.7	21	+16.7
Artists	65.0	20	36.0	25	−29.0
Mechanical engineers	58.6	29	57.8	45	−0.8
Electrical engineers	53.2	47	54.5	33	+1.3
Other engineers	42.9	35	58.0	50	+15.0
Surveyors	71.4	35	61.5	52	−9.9
Building managers	61.0	41	54.8	31	−6.2
Service managers	73.1	52	68.8	16	−4.3
Clerk supervisors	56.0	100	67.3	55	+11.3
Total, all groups	61.4	1,879	58.4	1,464	−3.0

dence does appear to suggest that there was considerable internal movement within the service class between the 1970s and the 1980s, and some of these shifts are quite striking. Most notably doctors and dentists, overwhelmingly Conservative in 1972, became more divided in their loyalty by the 1980s, a possible response to NHS policy, while social workers also show a marked move to the left. It might also be suggested that changing government arts policies might have affected the political orientations of actors and authors. On the other hand, air pilots, who in 1972 had been one of the most pro-Labour groups, swung to the Conservatives to an almost astonishing degree, although we should note the very small numbers involved in the BSAS dataset. Another major shift to the right was made by the bourgeoisie, one of the groups that has been particularly favoured by Conservative policy.

This suggests that contingent political factors may have been at work – ones that may well be reversed when there is a change of government. There is little sign that longer-term or more general processes are at work: for example, whereas doctors, dentists and social workers are primarily located within the public sector, the creative professions are not. The analysis presented above is exploratory only. As we have emphasized, our comparisons have faced problems both of occupational aggregation and of adequate sample size. All we would argue at this stage is that there is *prima facie* evidence that some realignments may have taken place within the service class between the 1970s and the 1980s. These realignments did not materially change the aggregate identification of the service class, because shifts took place in both directions and tended to cancel each other out. Although there are examples of left-wing groups such as social workers becoming even more left wing over time, and right-wing groups such as the bourgeoisie becoming even more right wing, there are contradictory processes too, such as the scientists who move from right to left and the engineers who move from left to right. Since they cancel out, we must therefore reject the claims that the service class has in general become more fragmented or polarized over time.

16.7 Conclusions

Let us now return to the broad themes of the paper to summarize what our analysis suggests about the nature of service-class political identification. Focusing simply on the BSAS dataset, we have shown that there is a considerable degree of political differentiation within the service class, although only a relatively small minority of the class are notably left wing. Aside from the trade union officials, the most left wing of all the occupational groups within the service class were the actors and musicians, of whom 52% favoured Labour; only three other occupational groups within the service class had 40% or more favouring Labour. We can put these figures into perspective by noting that, in the electorate as a whole, 40% favoured Labour, whereas the working-class average was just under 60% in favour of Labour. In other words, not one of the main occupational groups in the service class was as pro-Labour as the working-class average.

Turning now to the issue of why service-class occupations differ in their political outlooks, a number of possible points suggest themselves. The idea that there are distinct structural forces inclining specific service-class groups to the right or left has only limited explanatory power. Partly this is because the most powerful model for explaining occupational differentiation is that of educational level, which we take to be an individual characteristic, rather than the structural characteristics of employment status or sector. Partly, the apparent fluctuation in the political orientations of occupational groups between the 1970s and 1980s suggests that the political views of the incumbents of particular occupations may actually be rather fluid and responsive to political events, rather than fixed in a predetermined, structural, sense. Admittedly the hypothesized occupational shifts need to be tested more rigorously than we have been able to do here, but there is an interesting suggestion that minor change at the level of the class as a whole may coincide with considerable fluctuation at the level of the specific occupational groups that comprise the class.

Finally, let us turn to the question of self-recruitment and occupation. One possible reason for service-class political differentiation, as we stated in the introduction, is that left-wing people seek occupational shelter, as it were, in left-wing jobs associated with public sector employment, the caring professions or, to use Gouldner's phrase, the "culture of critical discourse", whereas right-wing people deliberately seek out occupations involved with security or money making. The distinctive political character of occupations such as social work and the security forces, and our inability to explain this distinctiveness by structural forces, are consistent with this idea, although we would need longitudinal attitude data to provide a firm test of this hypothesis. But if this idea is correct, it suggests that much middle-class radicalism of the kind described by Parkin and others and reviewed at the beginning of this chapter may occur despite the structural position of the service class rather than because of it. Incumbents of service-class positions may behave in radical ways for reasons that have nothing to do with their current class positions: not everything that happens in the service-class happens because of the service class.

Chapter 17

Middle-class radicalism revisited

Paul Bagguley

17.1 The perils of prophecy

Today it seems remarkable that only 40 years ago the American social scientist C. Wright Mills could claim that "there is no probability of the new middle classes forming or inaugurating or leading any political movement" (Mills 1951). Rather, it is now widely believed that the middle classes are the basis of the only significant class conflicts remaining, a view that finds recent expression in Berger's observation that, "Contemporary Western societies are characterised by a protracted conflict between two classes, the old middle class (occupied in the production and distribution of material goods and services) and a new middle class (occupied in the production and distribution of symbolic knowledge)" (Berger 1987).

Contrary to Mills' prophecy, by the end of the 1960s it was widely accepted that younger members of the new middle class were the basis of the US "New Left". It has become widely held that the new middle class, especially the state-employed professionals, provides the demographic base for, if not the leadership of, what have become known as "new social movements" (Cotgrove 1982, Byrd 1985, Eckersley 1989, Kriesi 1989, Mattausch 1989, Kitschelt & Hellemans 1990, Rudig et al. 1991, Eder 1993). Social movements such as environmentalism, contemporary feminism and the peace movement are all believed to be causally related to the growth of the new middle class. Such movements have been designated as distinctly "new" on the basis not just that they share the characteristic of being based in the new middle class, but that they also aim to transform values and lifestyles through direct action organized via networks and similar informal patterns of interaction (Scott 1990: 19).

It is my aim in this paper to show that the standard causal implication about the new middle class (NMC) and the new social movements (NSMs) is based on dubious theoretical constructs, methodological inadequacies, and a selective reading of some of the key empirical studies in this area. Principally, these confusions result from a failure to consider the interactions between individual biographies, political protest and job choice at the levels of both methodology and theory. Once these issues are examined in these terms, the apparent correlation between employment in certain fractions of the new middle class and participation in new social movements can be seen to be an emergent property of individual job choice shaped by political values, and operating in the context of education and labour market constraints.

17.2 The partial Parkin

The title of this paper makes a quite deliberate reference to Parkin's influential study of Britain's Campaign for Nuclear Disarmament (CND) during the 1960s – *Middle class radicalism* (Parkin 1968). I want to argue that most subsequent accounts of Parkin's explanation of middle-class radicalism have provided a partial version of his analysis. They have paid undue attention to his discussions of political alienation, and, especially, expressive politics motivated by moral concerns, while ignoring his analysis of the influence of political commitments on job choice (Byrd 1985: 67, Eckersley 1989: 222, Kitschelt & Hellemans 1990: 103).[1] I believe it is this latter aspect of Parkin's analysis that provides a better account of the relationship between state-employed professionals and NSMs, despite the overwhelming impression in the literature.

Parkin's account proceeds by initially making a distinction between working-class politics and middle-class politics that has become something of a leitmotif of virtually all subsequent accounts of new social movements and middle-class radicalism. He begins with the observation that working-class politics is principally concerned with economic and material issues, whereas middle-class radicalism is largely moral in content. Working-class radicalism is sectional and class specific; it seeks economic and material gains for the working class at the cost of the upper and middle classes. In contrast, middle-class radicalism has no sectional benefits for the middle class because the benefits are public, or are specific to other groups. The benefits of middle-class radicalism are emotional and expressive (Parkin 1968: 2). Parkin therefore provides the basis for the now familiar dichotomies that are frequently used to distinguish old from new social movements (Scott 1990). This is not surprising – much of this contemporary debate about the characteristics of new social movements can also be seen in the mass movements' literature, largely concerned with the 1930s, that Parkin considers (Parkin 1968: 10). His account identifies three characteristics of mass politics: no formal membership, lack of bureaucratic structures of authority, and mobilization of support for specific public protest events. These are all familiar themes of contemporary writing on new social movements that reinforce the case of those who argue that there is not much that is new in them after all.

Parkin was critical of the idea that political alienation was a possible cause of middle-class radicalism. The only evidence he found of political alienation among the middle-class supporters of CND was in terms of alienation from dominant social institutions and values, especially the monarchy, capitalism and private property, and the Church. One might object that these represent left-wing socialist values in the British context, and hence might be more indicative of sympathy for radical working-class politics than for expressive middle-class politics. Nevertheless, he goes on to argue that prior value orientations created a predilection to become involved in CND, and that these orientations were grounded in family socialization (Parkin 1968: 145–61). However, his survey was of those who were already involved, so the question of causality in this context remains somewhat speculative. His argument is further muddied by his later discussion of the impact of CND on the politics of those who became involved. There he makes clear from his evidence that CND was for many people a major route in to wider radical politics. Involvement in CND in effect transformed many participants' political attitudes, principles and practices.

Parkin's analysis of the moralist and principled concerns of middle-class radicals operates on several levels. For the middle class in general he argues that the economic security of their class position enables them to become concerned with expressive politics, unlike the working class. This is a theme that Inglehart has pursued in much more detail (Inglehart 1977, 1990). Parkin notes that all movements need intellectuals for their communication skills. CND was in effect a creation of a group of nationally known intellectuals. Parkin considers a wide range of putative explanations of intellectuals' radicalism, including their loss of social status, their lack of knowledge of practical politics, and their critical skills, that might propel them towards radical politics. However, he points out one peculiarity of British intellectuals – *their location as solid conservative middle-class individuals*. Hence the difficulty of generalizing about conditions in Britain from comments about intellectuals in Europe and elsewhere. However, he does identify a distinct stratum of intellectuals, often playwrights and actors, who became centrally involved in CND. What characterizes these groups, according to Parkin, is their economically marginal and precarious positions. Added to this was the role of many of these individuals in cultural innovation in Britain at the time; they included people such as John Osborne, Arnold Wesker, Doris Lessing and Vanessa Redgrave, and many of them had not been to university or even grammar school. They were, therefore, not part of an "establishment intelligentsia". In addition, many CND intellectuals were upwardly mobile from the working class. In contrast to this distinct group, Parkin argues that employed intellectuals are constrained to "behave themselves", as they might be threatened in their secure employment if they engage in deviant political activity. Intellectuals with bureaucratic careers are not as free to engage in protest as are those who are freelance. This interpretation is largely against the grain of much subsequent analysis and commentary, which suggest that it is precisely because certain sections of the middle class are in secure employment that they protest about "post-materialist" issues (Eckersley 1989). Furthermore, this argument seems to contradict what Parkin has to say about intellectuals in higher education and his main conclusions about job choice. Finally, in relation to intellectuals he argues that higher education encourages critical thinking, especially in the humanities and the social sciences. Although there were relatively few scientists involved in CND (Parkin

1968: 105), the organization did appear to be exceptionally attractive to sociology students and sociology lecturers in higher education!

It seems indisputable that the ranks of CND, and one might add of most other putative new social movements such as contemporary feminism and environmentalism, are drawn from the educated middle class. Parkin argues that this is not just an effect of the liberalizing consequences of higher education, but also due to the fact that these categories do not depend on the private ownership of capital for their income. Consequently they are not predisposed to pro-capitalist values and politics. Generally, they come from the welfare and creative occupations. At this juncture Parkin draws upon Parsons' distinction between the acquisitive values of commercial businessmen and the detached service ethic of the professions. He considers the possibility that such professional values predispose them to become involved in radical politics, as well as Lenski's view that status inconsistency, in this case high education alongside low economic status, is a cause of middle-class radicalism. However, he rejects both approaches in favour of the following:

> An alternative and more satisfactory hypothesis may be suggested; namely, that middle-class radicals are necessarily highly selective in their choice of occupation, and that the welfare professions provide the kind of milieux most amenable to their political orientations. That is, the connection between these particular occupations and political radicalism is to be explained not in terms of the strains created by status inconsistency, nor as a result of individuals adopting the humanistic values generated within the professions, but rather as a result of the tendency for individuals who are *already* radical to enter these fields of employment rather than others. (Parkin 1968: 168)

Not only do people choose jobs that are generally in line with their values, but they also avoid employment where being a radical could be a career disadvantage. Indeed, Parkin cites evidence where CND activists had been discriminated against in the job market. Those who do enter capitalist organizations may change their views, or get other more amenable jobs. There is a kind of selection process involving interaction between individuals and jobs positions. Consequently radicalism can be carried into certain sections of employment more readily than it may be generated by the structural characteristics of these job positions. The standard accepted interpretation of Parkin is quite alien to his main conclusion. Many authors seem to have concentrated too much on the discussion of expressive politics and political alienation from dominant values. Perhaps they would do better to read the conclusion of the book, which is that "the welfare and creative professions provide acceptable sanctuaries to those who wish to avoid direct involvement in capitalist enterprises by affording outlets for the exercise of their talents that entail no compromise of political ideals" (Parkin 1968: 192).

To put my own gloss on this account, I believe that this is still class analysis. However, we should be clear about the "classed" nature of the explanation being offered.

It is about a process of class formation that is simultaneously political, cultural and economic, and one that operates through the accumulation of individual decisions in relation to social institutions. Class formation, in this specific instance of the creative and welfare professionals of the new middle class, appears as the emergent property of individual decisions about jobs based on the agents' value orientations enabled or constrained by their educational qualifications, and on the structure of labour market positions that they perceive to be available to them. Broadly speaking it is a process of structuration more generally considered by Giddens (1984).

17.3 The critique of Parkin

Mattausch makes a number of criticisms of Parkin. He claims that Parkin does not consider the effect of employment on respondents' views and attitudes; that Parkin does not consider the development of radicalism; and that Parkin ignores the motives and accounts of agents (Mattausch 1989: 8). Furthermore, he claims that Parkin's job choice model assumes uniform reasons for choosing jobs (Mattausch 1989: 15), and that Parkin overlooks the fact that welfare state employees form the core social base of CND.

Let me take each of these points in turn. Parkin does consider at some length the impact of employment on political attitudes (in a section entitled "occupation and political values"!), and this is the section of his book where he concludes on the basis of his empirical evidence that such a causal inference is too crude, and he develops his job choice model as an alternative (Parkin 1968: 181–92). Parkin considers the development of radicalism in terms of familial socialization (ibid.: 145–61), education (ibid.: 171–2) as well as the radicalizing impact of being part of CND, especially for young people (ibid.: 163–5). Regarding the motives and accounts of the members of CND, Parkin refers to the importance of principles and moral questions to their motivation to join (ibid.: 36), as well as job choice (ibid.: 186–7). He also discusses a range of factors influencing radicals to choose professional employment, not just avoiding capitalism, but also a general desire to work with people (ibid.: 187). Finally, a significant section of Parkin's book (ibid.: 181–92) discusses why CND should have a social base biased towards those professionals employed in non-commercial organizations, principally the welfare state. In short, much of Mattausch's critique is based on a mis-reading of Parkin and the creation of a straw man. As an alternative, Mattausch develops the account that Parkin rejected: "welfare state employed CND members participate in common forms of life which engenders particular social and political orientations and a duty and proficiency to express them" (Mattausch 1989: 54).

There are a number of problems with this account from a "Wittgensteinian ethnomethodologist" (Mattausch 1989: 16–19). Clearly, most welfare state professionals do not become involved in CND or anything like it, because if they did such groups would have millions of members. He does not consider how to explain this lack of protest, which is surely required by the strong kind of causal claim in the above quote. Furthermore, it operates with an unacknowledged and undeveloped Parsonian trait model of the professions. As such it takes the professions' accounts of their moral high standing at their own face value. However, even his own empirical evidence is not unambiguous on this central theoretical issue. The central implication is that the experience of professional work and training provides the impetus for radicalism. Among his sample of teachers, only one of them mentions the experience of teaching as radicalizing. Others mentioned their experience of higher education as most important. More generally, in his empirical chapters Mattausch emphasizes the uniqueness of individual biographies in the sources of radicalism. More often than not these individuals see their choice of job in the first place as the expression of political or more general moral concerns. Yet in the end Mattausch imposes his own structural explanation onto these accounts, which is apparently what he thought was wrong with Parkin.

We can see, then, that these critical points against Parkin are somewhat inadequate. However, there is a much wider literature concerning the radicalism of the new middle class, and it is to a consideration of this literature that I shall now turn.

17.4 Broader class-theoretical explanations of NSMs

In this broader literature about the new middle class (NMC) and new social movements (NSMs) there is frequently a problem of over-generalization from particular empirical studies of particular movements or broad measures of individual political attitudes to all NSMs or politics in general. Many of the studies of NMC radicalism are concerned only with environmentalist attitudes or the membership of particular organizations such as CND or the Greens, to the neglect of contemporary feminism (Bagguley 1992). The claim that the NSMs grew as a result of the growth of the NMC is fraught with difficulties. Were they contemporaneous in time, or did the NMC grow first followed by the emergence of NSMs? Such technical niceties are important considerations for the empirical validity of the theoretical claims made in this literature. In one sense I want to argue that they grew together as part of a contemporaneous process of political, cultural and economic class formation of a particular fraction of the service class – welfare and creative professionals. In this process there is a certain historical contingency in the fortuitous creation of a particular political generation and the creation of a substantial number of class places where such radicals could "hide from capitalism" and continue to pursue the delights of protest into middle age.

The correlation with employment in public sector professions is frequently noted, but sometimes not discussed in any detail. Byrne's study of CND from the mid-1980s confirms the social base as in Parkin's (1968) account, but remains essentially descriptive and avoids the thornier theoretical issues. The appendices to Mattausch (1989) summarize the results of a range of studies of CND members highlighting the social base in the welfare state professions. Similarly a recent study of the British Green Party concluded that the typical member is "41 years old, lives in the South of England in a small town or rural area, is not religious, has a university degree in an arts or social science subject . . . is an owner-occupier, and works as a 'professional' in the public sector, most likely in education . . . they are not drop-outs completely alienated from society" (Rudig et al. 1991: 30).

The sociological consensus seems to be that professionals employed in the state sector, provide the social base of contemporary peace, environmentalist and feminist movements in virtue of their class position. It is usually claimed that in some sense the characteristics of the class location of these strata propel or enable them to be the basis of new social movements. Most theorists share the view that by grasping class position we can immediately prophesy about political action. Eckersley, Byrd and Kitschelt & Hellemans are typical representatives of this mode of reasoning:

> Their relative independence from the vagaries of the market sector explains why the new class (especially public sector employees) are more inclined than the working class to be critical of the system and actively involved in seeking reform. (Eckersley 1989: 222)

> Parkin elaborated the concept of "expressive politics" to fit middle-class membership of CND into a wider set of radical middle class values which emphasised the promotion of principles . . . and the benefits and satisfaction gained from that promotion rather than the achievement of specific materialist goals . . . Parkin found CND membership dominated by an educated middle class employed in welfare, teaching and social work rather than commerce and industry. (Byrd 1985: 67)

> The theory maintains that in advanced capitalist democracies the educated new middle class of white-collar employees and professionals in the social service sector develops a new style of politics, detached from traditional class, religious, or territorial cleavages and more concerned with intangible social, cultural, and military policy issues. These groups engage in protest politics demanding a more participatory and egalitarian society. (Kitschelt & Hellemans 1990: 103)

More widely, class-theoretical explanations of NSMs are partly embedded in debates about the political and cultural consequences of post-industrialism. This is most evident in the work of Bell (1974) and Touraine (1974). Bell identifies a range of political issues that he believes are emerging as a result of post-industrialism, and that are displacing class conflict between workers and employers. These emergent political questions include: conflicts around the organization of science, the organization and financing of non-market welfare provision, resistance to bureaucratic forms of organization, environmental issues and the emergence of an adversary culture. In addition he discusses the proliferation of citizenship rights claims in the form of positive discrimination for blacks and women, and the transformation of cultural issues into political conflicts. His view of these developments is generally rather conservative in tone: "cultural issues are transformed into political issues as women press for the repeal of the anti-abortion laws, young people for the legalisation of marijuana, and sexual deviants for the end of discrimination" (Bell 1974: 482).

Fundamentally he sees the issue in terms of how to manage an increasingly politically mobilized society with a proliferation of conflicts. In terms of the NMC he sees the question principally in terms of an internal, largely cultural conflict within this class. This is a theme reiterated by many writers since, such as Berger (1987), but Bell sees it purely as a split between intellectuals rather than within the middle class as a whole:

> In the social structure of the knowledge society, there is, for example, the deep and growing split between the technical intelligentsia who are committed to functional rationality and technocratic modes of operation, and the literary intellectuals, who have become increasingly apocalyptic, hedonistic, and nihilistic. (Bell 1974: 214)

These themes are recurrent among "left" accounts of the politics of the "new class", such as in the self-styled "Hegelian sociology" of Gouldner, who saw the political radicalism of the new middle class as indicative of its Hegelian "mission" as a flawed "universal class" (Gouldner 1979). However, other accounts have been more structural in nature. Cotgrove & Duff (1980, 1981) explain public sector middle-class support for environmental values in three ways. First, their class location is peripheral to the core institutions of capitalist society. Environmental protest reflects their alienation from and powerlessness relative to the key centres of decision-making. Secondly, environmentalism constitutes a challenge to the logic of the market and the dominant class of capitalism. Thirdly, because they are located in the non-market sector, enviromentalists' interests lie in opposing the dominant ideology of industrial capitalism.

Cotgrove's later development of these issues is somewhat contradictory. On the one hand he argues, on the basis of a study of job preferences among University of Bath students in the 1970s, that political values shape occupational choice:

> Environmentalists will try to choose occupations congruent with their public post-material values and social ideals . . . they tend to choose occupations which do not involve direct commitment to the goals and values of industrialism, and which are congruent with their generally anti-industrial sentiments. (Cotgrove 1982: 45)

Nevertheless, he makes the valuable point that "choice" of occupation here is only really an option for those with higher education. Hence the widely noted correlation among the public at large between environmental values and occupational groupings. On the other hand, Cotgrove argues for a class-interest explanation of environmentalism. In this account the crucial aspect is the role of certain middle-class groupings employed in the non-market sector of the economy:

> . . . environmentalism is an expression of the interests of those whose class position in the "non-productive" sector locates them at the periphery of the institutions and processes of industrial capitalist societies. Hence their concern to win greater participation and influence and thus to strengthen the political role of their members. It is a protest against alienation from the processes of decision-making, and the de-politicisation of issues through the usurpation of policy decisions by experts, operating within the dominant economic values. (Cotgrove 1982: 95)

However, nowhere does Cotgrove make clear the relationship between this explanation of middle-class radicalism and the job choice model. A further problem is that this type of class interest explanation tends to devalue the distinctive characteristics of the issues raised by environmentalism. It would seem to imply that the distinctive issues of environmentalism matter rather less than the class interests. One might speculate that if the issue was not environmentalism then it could be some other political question. The class interests identified by Cotgrove are not really class interests at all in the conventional sense, but are issues of political representation regarding the influence of decisions about environmental risks. There would seem to be nothing distinctively middle-class about this question, since in the case of environmentalism does it not equally affect the interests of the working class?

Rather like Cotgrove & Duff, Day & Robins (1987) develop an argument concerning the contradiction between the repressive and reproductive arms of the state. This leads to those employed in the reproductive arm – the welfare and educational sectors – becoming involved in CND. This leaves open a number of issues. First, why are only the more highly educated in those sectors active in CND? Secondly, what about CND in the 1960s when education and welfare were still expanding? Finally, they also fail to examine the issue of job choice raised by Parkin.

Sociology in the USA has focused largely on the issue of the "new class" and its related political attitudes. Berger's (1987) summary and analysis of this is especially elegant, and some themes apparent in the British debate recur. He sees the new class as the producers and disseminators of symbolic knowledge, including not just professional intellectuals but also various counsellors and advisers. This class he sees as basically left wing and anti-capitalist in orientation owing to two sets of material interests. First, they have an interest in the use of educational credentials in the labour market. Therefore, they tend to be opposed to success in purely market capitalistic terms such as the classical entrepreneur of free-market capitalism. Secondly, they are largely dependent on state sector employment, hence they have a material interest in the expansion of state employment, especially the welfare state, and in increased taxation on the productive capitalist sector of the economy. However, Berger notes this is perhaps less the case in the USA than elsewhere. The USA has a smaller welfare state, and more of the new class depend on the capitalist market for their income. Consequently, this may explain a major difference in their political proclivities between the USA and Europe. Nevertheless, Berger does conclude, in a fashion that neatly summarizes the view of many US analysts, that the class conflict of contemporary capitalism is characterized as one between the old middle class and the new middle class (Berger 1987: 66–70).

Brint's (1984) analysis of these issues is especially valuable because he assesses the utility of four different concepts of the "new class" – those of the Ehrenreichs, Ladd, Gouldner and Kristol. For those familiar with the work of these authors, one striking feature of the US debate is the way in which these phenomena have been discussed in similar ways by authors sympathetic to both the political left and the political right. Brint's approach is to see which of the four versions of the new class hold liberal attitudes. Only Kristol's new class shows any disproportionate tendency to hold such views. However, Kristol's definition is restricted to the occupational grouping of professionals in education and cultural industries. This new class concept is very restricted, at best being only a fraction of the new middle class. Furthermore, only the younger individuals in this segment are the exception to new class conservatism. As Brint summarizes:

> . . . the theorists were simply incorrect in many of their fundamental assertions. They exaggerated the levels of dissent and even the levels of liberalism found in the new class . . . the theorists mistook the confluence of several distinct demographic and temporal forces for the rise of an oppositional new class. This oppositional new class . . . is . . . a fictional entity made possible by the conjunction of the following forces: the liberalizing effects of a much expanded higher education system, the traditional liberalism of a now larger category of social and cultural specialists, and the coming of age of a notably liberal cohort. (Brint 1984: 60)

Brint's work has been widely and positively cited in the subsequent literature on new social movements and the new middle class as well as more conventional analyses of political attitudes. However, there are a number of weaknesses in his approach that should urge us to be cautious. First, his account is of attitudes, and attitudes are not political actions, even less do they constitute a social movement. They may be causally related to both in complex ways. Hence it would be risky simply to use Brint's account directly in debates about NSMs and the NMC, as some authors seem inclined to attempt. More importantly, his category of liberal attitudes does not really reflect ideologies or attitudes associated with NSMs. This is partly due to the national specificity of certain political ideologies and attitudes. In the European context, what Brint regards as liberal attitudes correspond to individual freedom, pro-working class, pro-welfare state, and anti-racist attitudes. There is nothing in Brint's list of liberal attitudes about the paradigmatic NSMs such as feminism, pacifism or environmentalism.

Brint produces a "cumulative trend" theory of liberalism and the new class, where a particular combination of factors at a specific historical conjuncture accounts for the liberal attitudes. However, we are left with little understanding of why liberalism is concentrated among social and cultural professionals. Brint's only suggestion is education, but even this he leaves ambiguous. Again the issue of job choice is neglected, ignoring agency–structure interactions and leaving the analysis vague and muddled. Perhaps it is not surprising, then, that others have challenged Brint's account.

McAdams (1987) sees the new class as an elite that has achieved economic advantage in the arena of politics rather than the market. He does not see any real conflict between market capitalism and specialized knowledge, as long as there is a lucrative market for that knowledge. For the new class this market emerges with the growth of government. He found that conservatism is concentrated among those with modest education and high incomes, whereas those with better education and modest incomes have more liberal attitudes. McAdams is one of those who sees this as explaining the emergence of NSMs. However, he does see these new class attitudes as linked to its economic interests in the expansion of state employment and education. Thus McAdams sees liberal attitudes as linked to class conflict.

The concern to explain NSMs in a class-theoretical manner is principally an Anglo-American one. However, the notion has also been taken up by mainstream European theorists of social movements. Melucci, for instance, accounts for the NMC participation in NSMs in the following manner:

> Their capacity for constructing a collective identity is rooted in the set of resources (such as educational achievement, professional skills and social activities) available to them. (Melucci 1989: 53)

Broadly I would concur with this claim, but with some critical reservations. First, Melucci tends to see these resources as traits of individuals, rather than as social resources; that is, as the characteristics of social categories, which are then realized through the actions, biographies and so on of individuals. Secondly, the claim as Melucci puts it in this instance has an oddly conservative, even reactionary, ring to it, because it implies that the working class does not have the capacity to construct a collective identity. I think this flows from Melucci concentrating too much on the collective identity aspects of NSMs and ignoring other capacities for collective identity formation and other social factors that influence social movement participation. Finally, the evident economic, social and political heterogeneity of the new middle class (Savage et al. 1992, Savage & Heath in Ch. 16 in this volume) makes the construction of a collective identity rather unlikely. Add to this the openness of the new middle class in terms of social mobility (Goldthorpe 1990) and a plurality of identities is a more probable outcome.

Rootes (1995) has argued that the NMC is too heterogeneous, so that the "new class" theories of middle-class radicalism are at best restricted to those in the welfare and creative occupations. He concludes by arguing that higher education is the source of radical values that engender sympathy towards NSMs. In a similar fashion

Eckersley (1989) points out that the heterogeneity of the NMC makes identification of its class interests in order explain NSMs difficult. He regards the tendency of the "new class" to be active in environmentalism to be due to two factors. First, higher education develops the culture of critical discourse as Gouldner termed it. Secondly, sections of the NMC are relatively autonomous from capitalist production and are therefore politically alienated from the system. Although the latter argument is open to serious question, I believe Eckersley's account of the importance of education develops the more fruitful line of analysis, as higher education "not only increases an individual's ability to acquire information but also helps to cultivate the ability to think critically, question everyday assumptions, form an independent judgement and be less influenced by the judgement of others" (Eckersley 1989: 221).

What becomes clear from much of this literature (which reinforces some of Parkin's original findings) is that only a particular section of the new middle class has a propensity towards radicalism in general and support for new social movements in particular – those in the welfare and creative occupations, whose numbers increased from some 621,000 in 1961 to 1,257,000 by 1991 (figures from the Census). This section of the middle class basically corresponds to Kristol's "new class". It has seen a threefold increase in its size since 1951, mostly between 1951 and 1981, from about half a million to one and a quarter million in 1991. In the 1960s and 1970s this group grew by half a million, so during this period there were plenty of job opportunities for those British activists of the "60s protest generation". Since the early 1980s there has been low growth in the numerically significant state sector, e.g. teachers and social workers. This raises some interesting issues regarding the future possibilities of intergenerational mobility into this section of the middle class. However, it is clear that that the period from the early 1950s to the late 1970s was one of rapid growth for this section of the middle class, and this now seems to have come to an end.

Family socialization appears to play a part in the political behaviour of the middle class. Savage et al. for instance found that the "inter-generationally stable professional middle class", i.e. those professionals whose fathers were in professional occupations, were the most "anti-Conservative" in their voting behaviour in the 1987 general election (Savage et al. 1992: 198). Butler (Ch. 11 in this volume) shows that middle-class gentrifiers often come from professional middle-class backgrounds as well as working in such occupations themselves, and have distinctly left-leaning politics as expressed in their support for the Labour Party. Ley (1994a) obtained similar results in a study of gentrification and politics in Canadian cities, where welfare and creative professionals living in gentrified areas supported left and radical parties. Parkin (1968: 145–61) found that young CND supporters typically came from middle-class backgrounds where the parents were supportive of CND, but not usually activists, and frequently were Labour party supporters. In a very different context, Fendrich (1993: 52) found that black civil rights activists came from backgrounds that were supportive of their political tendencies, although normally they came from working-class origins.

Heath and Savage (Ch. 16 in this volume) show that social workers, higher education teachers, actors and musicians, authors, writers and journalists, and junior civil servants appear to be strong identifiers with the Labour Party compared with the rest of the service class. In considering the support of the "public sector salariat" for the Labour Party between 1964 and 1987, Heath et al. found that it split evenly between the parties, concluding that:

> This finding must cast serious doubt on the theories of public-sector or specialist interests. After all, if there were distinctive public-sector interests, we would expect these to affect the behaviour of public-sector administrators and managers as well as public-sector welfare workers. (Heath et al. 1991: 95)

Nevertheless, the more narrowly defined welfare and creative occupations, which correspond to Kristol's "new class", do seem to be distinctive in terms of their support for parties other than the Conservatives. Furthermore this seems to be a recent development. Heath et al. (1991: 93–6) show that levels of support for the Conservative Party among those in welfare and creative occupations fell from 50% in 1964 to 32% in 1987. However, like Heath et al. I am somewhat reluctant to see this as a permanent feature or an aspect of structural change. As Savage et al. imply, much of this could be a response to the Conservative government policies during the 1980s.

Finally in this context I should add the reservation to all of this discussion that voting for or supporting the Labour Party, although a distinctive feature of this welfare and creative fraction of the new middle class, is not directly equivalent to support for NSMs. Indeed, many commentators would see NSMs and the Labour Party as somewhat opposed or competing political movements (e.g. Offe 1985).

Generally, this literature is based on the simplistic structural model of class analysis castigated by Pahl (1989), where structural class location determines social consciousness, which leads to political action. This literature frequently fails to take up the issues raised by Parkin with respect to political protest and job choice. This is a theme that I have been highlighting in terms of subsequent debates about class formation – that social movements can have a formative impact on the particular character of classes or sections of classes. However, there were weaknesses in Parkin's analysis. He was, for instance, somewhat contradictory concerning the factors behind intellectuals' participation in CND, and there remains uncertainty around the relationship between CND and people's political values. Did social movement participation have an impact on those values or not? A further objection might be raised regarding the more general validity of his case study. How general is it? Is it simply an exceptional instance? Fortunately we have alternatives with which to assess this issue. In another country, the United States, at the same time (the early 1960s) many young, well-educated people were also becoming involved in protest politics. However, the issues were different: they concerned the civil rights of black Americans.

17.5 The influence of social movement participation on job choice: the case of "Freedom Summer"

In this section I shall consider some North American studies of the longer-term consequences of social movement participation during the 1960s. These not only introduce a comparative dimension to my argument relative to Britain, but also involve a very different social movement – civil rights – and, in the case of Fendrich, examine the racial dimensions of social movement participation and class formation.

Doug McAdam's study *Freedom summer* (1988) is especially interesting. Both survey-based and case-study approaches to political mobilization share a common drawback. They both approach the relationship between class and politics *statically*, and ignore the *dynamic interaction between class and politics*. Thus, despite the attempts of both Mattausch and Parkin to develop dynamic accounts, their methodologies are "snap-shots" rather than longitudinal. McAdam, however, was principally concerned with the impact of social movement participation on personal identity, and the way that the lives of radical Freedom Summer (FS) volunteers (who spent several months in the early 1960s working in black southern communities, often under considerable threat from local whites) developed in subsequent years. These FS radicals were not alienated from mainstream US society. They were in many respects all-American, middle-class, educated youngsters, optimistic about their personal future as well as that of the USA. They were idealistic and often involved in some kind of social movement or community activity, quite often by no means left wing or radical.

McAdam shows that many FS volunteers subsequently entered the liberal professions in greater proportions than their age-group peers in the US population at large. In particular, the FS volunteers show an aversion to entering the corporate professions such as accountancy and business executive and managerial jobs. His qualitative interviews showed that FS participants eschew monetary reward in favour of the political or moral value of employment. From his quantitative material he demonstrates that almost half of the FS volunteers strongly agreed that social movement participation had affected their choices about employment. More generally, the FS volunteers felt socially isolated from the mainstream of US society, especially during the Reaganite 1980s.

We can "read" several of the classic interpretations of middle-class radicalism in a rather different light as a result of this account. Parkin's thesis of middle-class alienation from the core values of British society leading to participation in CND might easily be seen in the reverse manner – that participation in social movements leads to social isolation and alienation from dominant values. From McAdam's interpretation it might be suggested that political alienation does not cause protest, but that protest leads to political alienation! Similar arguments could be applied to the claim that NSMs reflect the structurally determined interests of the NMC that is dominant in the literature discussed above. It is not their interests that determine their protest, but their protest that leads them to seek jobs with interests contrary to those of the dominant social order.

More widely, McAdam identifies a "fan effect" of Freedom Summer. Activists securing jobs within a particular segment of occupations may have a further radicalizing effect on their immediate occupational peers, who may in any case already be susceptible to radical politics. Another aspect of this lies in recruitment networks. A now burgeoning literature in the social movement (SM) field demonstrates the importance of these networks in the process of SM mobilization. Where better than the workplace for the embedding of a recruitment network?

Using a similar longitudinal methodology to that of McAdam, Fendrich (1993) followed up cohorts of both black and white civil rights activists into the 1980s in comparison with those from the same cohort who were not politically active. He found that only 20% of white activists participated in protest events, whereas over 70% of black students did so. The white activists came from middle-class backgrounds and had very little support from their families for their politics; the black activists overwhelmingly came from what Fendrich terms "striving working-class" backgrounds and generally had the support of their communities for their politics. These black activists experienced considerable upward social mobility. Their fathers worked in "relatively low status, low paying jobs as roofers, tailors, parking attendants, truck drivers, laundry workers, janitors, hospital attendants and soda fountain workers" whereas the black activists became "teachers, social workers, managers . . . public administrators" (Fendrich 1993: 52). However, the white activists did not experience such significant upward social mobility.

Similarly Fendrich identifies issues of job choice in relation to political ideals. One of the black activists rose to the level of Colonel in an Army intelligence unit in Vietnam. Disgruntled with army racism, he eventually found a university administration post that was more congruent with his own values (Fendrich 1993: 61). Generally, black civil rights activists aimed for careers consistent with their personal political values and commitments:

> The activists' choice of careers reflected their distinctive values and commitments to fostering the public good. They were much less committed to making money and having a secure high-status job. They also were strongly committed to being agents of social change. In their jobs they wanted to redistribute wealth, reduce social inequalities, and improve democratic institutions and procedures. The long-range consequences of the 1960s students' protest movement were not limited to adult politics and behaviour. Activism significantly affected the type of values associated with careers as well as the particular careers chosen. (Fendrich 1993: 100)

Following Mannheim, Fendrich makes the significant point that within the 1960s generation there were distinctive political units. Overall the activists were a minority of this generation, and partly in response to the successes of the activists in terms of civil rights legislation, etc. other members of that generation have formed the political activists base of the emergence of Reaganism in the 1980s. The new generation of Democrat and Republican political leaders of the early 1990s to some extent reflects these separate generational units. So the popular image of the 1960s radical becoming a conservative during the 1980s and 1990s is shown to be a media myth.

These studies, like Parkin, provide job choice models of the development of middle-class radicalism in a complex process of interaction between structural class places, political processes and individual biographies. I want to suggest that they have identified a recursive relationship between protest and occupational class that operates through individual biographies. There are a number of mechanisms that may link individual biography to the wider "structural" processes:

- a) sensitivity to political issues generated through family socialization and higher education;
- b) identity transformation through participation in NSMs leading to politicized job selection;
- c) subsequent recruitment networks;
- d) the impact of a and b on occupational peers;
- e) the impact of a and b within middle-class residential zones.

These mechanisms will tend to be localized in their empirical effects (Bagguley 1992). The real NMC politics of class takes place principally in trade unions and professional organizations, in the sense that they deal with transparently narrow class issues such as wages and conditions. These tend to be national and workplace based in their spheres of action. Very often NSM activity has a local sphere of action.

17.6 Concluding remarks

In the early 1980s the two principal contributions to the debate on the service class – Goldthorpe (1982) and Abercrombie & Urry (1983) – made diametrically opposed claims about the political tendencies of the service class. Abercrombie & Urry (1983: 138–47) emphasized the role of the service class in leading the labour movement and in generating new social movements. Although they mentioned the emergence of right-wing politics among the service class (e.g. 1983: 142), the conservatism of the service class was not systematically considered. In contrast, Goldthorpe argued that in terms of structural, but "empirically determinable", interests in relation to other classes the service class is fundamentally conservative (1982: 179–85). Subsequent analyses of the service class, which emphasize its diverse nature and fragmented patterns of class formation, have pointed to the significance of divisions within or among the middle classes (Savage et al. 1992). Indeed, the divisions that they identify between the public and private sector professional and managerial middle classes' voting patterns may in part be intelligible in terms of a job choice model. Young Tories choose to become managers, whereas young socialists and liberals choose to become teachers. In the end Goldthorpe may prove to be correct. In terms of structural interest and political action, the service class or new middle class is broadly conservative, but we should add the rider that some within it will choose jobs in line with their strongly held radical political beliefs, jobs that are sheltered from the immorality of directly serving private corporate capitalism.

This chapter has been inspired by the evident weaknesses of many currently accepted sociological analyses of the relationship between the new middle class and the new social movements. I do not wish to deny the ontological reality of class and class processes that has recently been trenchantly and soundly reasserted (Goldthorpe & Marshall 1992, Lee 1994). However, I have been at pains to argue that the relationship between class and social movement activism in the case of the middle classes is best seen as an emergent property of politicized job choice, enabled by educational qualifications, and structured by the wider labour market opportunities for educated labour. This way of thinking of class formation and social movements links social structural changes and social conflicts at the macro level with individual level decisions, and can be examined empirically only using biographical or longitudinal methodologies.

Note

1. Exceptions to this include Kriesi (1989) and Cotgrove & Duff (1981: 102–3).

Part Seven

Conclusions

Chapter 18

The service class revisited

John H. Goldthorpe

18.1 Introduction

In this paper my aim is to respond to a variety of arguments concerning "the service class" that have been advanced since the time I took over the concept from Renner (1953), via Dahrendorf (1959, 1964), for use in analyses of class structure and mobility (Goldthorpe 1982, Goldthorpe et al. 1987). Most of these arguments were developed with reference, critical or otherwise, to my work, and most are at least rehearsed in contributions to this collection, even if in some instances their fullest presentation is to be found elsewhere.

In pursuing my aim, the difficulty of which I am chiefly aware is that arising from the situation alluded to by Savage (p.16 above); namely, that recent debates on class and class analysis have largely failed to produce real dialogue, because those involved have had "such different conceptions of what social science is all about". This is a judgement I can only endorse (although with the aside that, in some instances, it is hard not to conclude that the idea of social science has been abandoned altogether). In these circumstances the danger is that any discussion of substantive issues becomes interlarded with the treatment not just of methodological, but of yet more basic philosophical disagreements, the resolution of which can scarcely be hoped for. I shall, however, seek to focus attention so far as possible on what to me, at least, is of ultimate interest: that is, arguments that have evident sociological content and that, by the same token, are open to critical evaluation on the basis of appropriate exercises in data collection and analysis.

What follows will be divided into five sections. The first four will deal in turn with issues relating to the concept of the service class and its application in sociological research, the historical development of the service class, the nature and extent of its internal differentiation, and the political orientations and action of its members. In the concluding section I will then seek to argue that, despite the questions now being raised about the future stability of the service class, the central problem that arises from current research is that of accounting for various notable features of its social reproduction.

18.2 The concept of the service class

The service class is a class of employees. This much at least is common to the concept as developed by Renner, Dahrendorf and myself. In my own formulation (1982: 162), it is the class of professional, administrative and managerial employees. I am therefore entirely happy with the synonym of "salariat", introduced by Heath et al. (1985), which has indeed the advantage of avoiding confusion between the service class and "service workers". On the other hand, though, I am disturbed that authors such as Herz (1990) and Savage et al. (1992: 8–9), and likewise several contributors to the present volume, should suppose that the service class, in my understanding of it, comprises employers and proprietors as well as employees. This misapprehension, I take it, arises from a failure to distinguish between the concept of the service class itself and the way in which the concept has been applied in research, in particular via the class schema that I have developed with colleagues over the past 20 years or so. As is at various points explained (e.g. Erikson & Goldthorpe 1992b: 37–41), difficulties are regularly encountered in dealing with individuals described, or describing themselves, as "employers" or "proprietors" – or again as "independent" or "self-employed" professionals. It is often unclear just how far such individuals are actually differentiated from salaried managers or professionals in sociologically significant ways rather than merely formally, in consequence of legal arrangements set up for reasons chiefly of financial or fiscal convenience. This being the case, some slippage between concept and practice – as indeed is likely to occur in any kind of empirical research – cannot be avoided. In applying the class schema, the procedure that has so far been adopted is for all "large" employers and proprietors – i.e. those not obviously better assigned to the petite bourgeoisie – and all professionals, regardless of employment status, to be coded to the service class. But, it must be stressed, it has then been quite explicitly recognized (see e.g. Goldthorpe et al. 1987: 41, Erikson & Goldthorpe 1992b: 40–1) that this procedure is *faute de mieux* and means introducing some, though in all probability only a quite small, degree of error. It follows, therefore, that if researchers are confident – as, for example, Heath and Savage (Ch. 16 in this volume) claim to be – that they can identify genuine categories of large employers (or likewise of independent professionals), and ones of sufficient size to permit separate analysis, then these categories should certainly be excluded from the service class.[1]

Given, then, that the service class is a class of employees, the main "boundary problem" that arises is that of demarcating the service class from other employee classes.[2] Further consideration of this particular problem has in fact led me to reformulate the way I would represent the basis of class differentiation in general – although with the aim more of clarifying than of significantly changing my initial approach. In earlier work (e.g. Goldthorpe 1982, Goldthorpe et al. 1987: 40), I referred (following Lockwood 1958) to market and work situation as being the two major components of class position, and sought to implement this view in the development of the class schema. However, I now believe it better simply to say that class positions are differentiated in terms of employment relations. The primary division here is then according to employment status, that is, between employer, self-employed and employee positions; while the secondary division is according to different types of employee relationship (or different forms of the regulation of employment), with the "service relationship" being counterposed to the "labour contract" (cf. Erikson & Goldthorpe 1992b: 37–40 and Fig. 2.1 esp.). This reformulation appears to me desirable chiefly in order to bring out that the view of class that I take – in contrast to that of, say, Marxists of the "labour process" school inspired by Braverman (1974) and also, it seems, of most feminists – is not a "work-centred" one (cf. Wright 1989a); that is to say, it is employment relations that determine class positions, not the nature of work tasks and work roles *per se*, nor yet the degree of autonomy, authority, etc. that is conferred on the individuals performing them.

Thus, in seeking to draw the boundaries of the service class, the crucial question is whether or not a service relationship could be said to prevail. That is, a relationship in which, as Erikson and I have put it (1992b: 41–2): "Employees render service to their employing organization in return for 'compensation', which takes the form not only of reward for work done, through a salary and various perquisites, but also comprises important prospective elements – for example, salary increments on an established scale, assurances of security both in employment and, through pension rights, after retirement, and, above all, well-defined career opportunities." There are, to be sure, good reasons for expecting that those positions that are defined by a service relationship will tend to be ones that do involve their incumbents in the exercise of some degree of professional autonomy and/or of managerial or administrative authority (cf. Goldthorpe 1982: 168–9). But where any discrepancy in this respect occurs, it is the nature of the employment relationship, and not of work tasks and work roles, that is relevant. Thus, for instance, in the case of positions supposedly carrying managerial titles for purely "cosmetic" reasons (cf. Crompton 1980), what matters is whether or not a service relationship exists (Goldthorpe 1980b). If it does, then such positions are service class positions – and even if those fortunate enough to hold them are required to do no more than sort paper clips.

Two other advantages may also follow more incidentally from the reformulation in question, both of which, however, have particular importance for discussion of the service class. First, it will, I hope, become more difficult for commentators to misunderstand the sense in which the class schema, referred to above, is an "occupationally-based" one. It ought now to be clear, if it was not before, that although, ideally, class positions would be determined on the basis of information directly about employment relations, in research practice occupation – and employment status – serve as proxies in this respect. In other words, the class schema is "occupationally based" only insofar as it is supposed that groupings of occupations, with the same employment status, will be characterized by similar employment relationships. It follows, of course, that this supposition is crucial to the validity of the schema. That is to say, what is at issue is not just how well the schema performs in the analysis of dependent variables ("construct validity") but, further, how well it captures what, conceptually, it is intended to capture ("criterion validity"). In fact, Evans (1992, 1994) has shown that, in this latter regard, the schema is rather successful. The major divisions made, on the basis of occupation and employment status, do turn out to be aligned with differences of the kind that would be expected in employment relationships. Thus, when Crompton (1993: 115) argues that the schema – and particularly in the case of the service class – "involves the aggregation of non-comparable jobs and occupations", one can only say that this is to miss the point. It is the very purpose of the schema to "aggregate" occupations that in many of their attributes, including the work tasks and work roles they involve, will be heterogeneous, provided only that – as seems in fact largely the case – they are alike in their associated employment relationships or, that is, in what is taken to be the key differentia of class positions. And, it may be added, Crompton is again mistaken in asserting (1993: 59) that the class schema is "not particularly suitable as far as women's employment is concerned". To the contrary, its construct validity differs rather little whether tested by data for women or for men (Evans, 1994).

Secondly, to underline that the concept of class I seek to develop is not a "work-centred" one should also help clarify the grounds for my further conceptual prefer-ence for giving the conjugal family priority over the individual as the unit of class composition (Goldthorpe 1983, Erikson & Goldthorpe 1992a). If a "work-centred" view is taken, the implication must then be that the experience of class occurs pri-marily within the workplace itself; it is, for example, the experience of autonomy or control in work or of authority or subordination. And, in this case, the idea of one individual's class position being "derived from" or "mediated through" the employ-ment of another is obviously problematic. But if the emphasis is placed, rather, on employment relations, the experience of class that is implied is of a different kind: it relates not primarily to the nature of work performed but rather to the nature of the rewards obtained from this work, both currently and in life-course perspective. In other words, the experience of class, extending outside the workplace, will also include, for example, that "of affluence or hardship, of economic security or insecu-rity, of prospects of continuing material advance or of unyielding material con-straints". And these are, then, "experiences that the members of a conjugal family will tend for the most part to share in common" (Erikson & Goldthorpe 1992b: 236). That this point is one of recurring relevance for debates on the service class will become apparent as the paper proceeds.

18.3 The historical development of the service class

There is general agreement that the service class, wherever its exact boundaries may be taken to lie, has been in more or less continuous expansion in all advanced socie-ties since at least the end of the nineteenth century, and especially in the period since the Second World War. However, as regards the way in which this development should be understood, and related to other aspects of the sociology of the service class, dissension prevails. The main criticism that has been levelled against my own position (see e.g. Crompton 1989, 1993: Ch. 5, Savage et al. 1992: Appendix 1, cf. Witz, Ch. 3 in this volume) is that, having noted the expansion of the service class, I then simply take this as given and proceed directly to analyses of social mobility and of other processes relevant to the formation of the service class at the "demographic" and "socio-cultural" levels. That is, I neglect, and indeed seek to place outside the scope of class analysis, the entire question of how the actual structure of service class positions has itself been created. Thus, it is held, I fail to see how particular features of what Witz would call the "socio-structural" formation of the service class – in particular, the extent to which this has from the start been "gendered" – carry major implications for those issues on which my own attention is focused.

To respond at all adequately, I must make several different points. To begin with, it is correct to say that, for reasons I have already indicated (1990) but to which I return below, I take class structures, as they exist, as providing the context for the study of class mobility and of other issues falling within the research programme of class analysis, rather than being themselves among the explananda of this programme. However, it is certainly not the case that I then disregard the way in which features of class structural development are likely to be consequential for the treatment of these issues. To the contrary, much of my work on class mobility, both in Britain and in comparative perspective, has been concerned precisely with such "structural" effects (Goldthorpe 1980a: Chs 2 and 3 esp., Erikson & Goldthorpe 1992b: Ch. 6 esp.).

Moreover, as regards specifically the effect on mobility of the gendered construction of service class positions, I may claim to have pointed out (Goldthorpe & Llewellyn 1977) a good deal in advance of my critics how, in Britain, the progressive redeployment of the female labour force from manual into routine non-manual employment, rather than into professional, administrative or managerial occupations, increased the opportunities of men of all social origins to gain access to the service class. Subsequently, though (Goldthorpe 1980a: 299, n.23, and cf. McRae 1990: Table 8.1), I have also attempted something of which my critics have notably fought shy: that is, to provide an estimate of the quantitative importance of this effect. The results suggest that, although not negligible, it is not all that large. If (as of 1983) existing service class positions had been "ungendered" – that is, shared equally between men and women in employment – then, all else being unchanged, men's chances of being found in higher-level service class positions would have fallen from an actual 16% to 11%, while as regards lower-level service class positions their chances would have remained exactly the same, at 18%. All such counterfactual analyses do, of course, have their uncertainties, but they serve at least to give a sense of orders of magnitude. And, in this case, the indication clearly is that the gendering of different kinds of employment is very far from having the pre-eminence that standard feminist rhetoric would imply (see, e.g., Witz, pp. 47–54 above) among the range of other factors – differing trajectories of industrial development, national political economies, configurations of international trade, etc. – through which class structures, and in turn mobility rates and patterns within them, are shaped and reshaped.

Further in this connection, I might add that, even though certain sectors of professional, administrative and managerial employment have been constructed as

317

largely male preserves, it does not then follow that it makes sense to regard the service class as itself "gendered" (Gregson and Lowe, p. 149 above, cf. Crompton 1986). Such a view derives logically, but at the same time rather nonsensically, from the insistence on the individual rather than the conjugal family as the unit of class composition. It means in effect leaving entirely out of account the way in which women have also benefited from the expansion of service class – that is, if only through marriage to those men who took up the growing career opportunities that were created. For even where such women have been confined to employment at a lower level than that for which their abilities or education would have qualified them, or indeed to housework, it would still seem merely perverse not to recognize them as holding more advantaged class positions than women – or men – with similarly poor employment chances but also unable to enjoy the level of living, security and prospects of material advancement of a service class wife.[3]

Finally, then, I revert to the question of why, if I do accept the far-reaching implications of the way in which class structures themselves develop, I do not see the explanation of this development as being itself central to class analysis. The answer is that, as I have previously argued (1990: 417, cf. also Erikson & Goldthorpe 1992b: 213–16), the factors involved are in fact so diverse, and often so specific from one national case to another, that there seems to me no serious possibility of sociological theory being deployed in order to provide such an explanation. Sociologists will rather have to be content with taking primarily historical accounts of the development of class structures, capable of doing full justice to the particularities of each case, as the starting point – the context – of their treatment of problems on which they may hope that the research methods and analytical techniques of their own discipline will give them a greater purchase.

Such a position is obviously not congenial to those who have in this regard invested heavily in programmatic statements of a more ambitious kind than I would believe viable. However, it is clearly *their* task now to turn programmes into performance. For my own part, I would only note that, so far at least, both they and others who have sought to give accounts of the "socio-structural" formation of the service class in particular have very effectively made my case for me. That is to say, these accounts have in fact been of a historical, not a theoretical, character. Consider, for example, the treatment by Lash & Urry (1987: Ch. 6) of the emergence of the service class in the USA and several European countries, or by Savage et al. (1992: Ch. 3) of the British case, or again work from a feminist standpoint such as that of Crompton & Sanderson (1990) or Witz (1992). What we have here are essentially historical sketches, built up from secondary sources, with decidedly ideographic emphases. Little is to be found in the way of the attempted description, let alone explanation, of general tendencies or of systematic variation of a temporal or cross-national kind. I do not say this disparagingly, because I do not believe that attempts in these directions would prove rewarding. But what I would maintain is that theory is something very different from such "potted" history (and it is far more difficult to produce), and that there is no excuse at all for confusing the one with the other.[4]

18.4 The internal differentiation of the service class

In initially taking up the concept of the service class, I noted (1982: 169–70) that one of the most frequent objections to it was that it brought together two broad occupational groupings – professional employees, on the one hand, and administrators and managers, on the other – whose members had typically different positions and roles within production units. Although not seeking to deny the fact of this division within the service class, I suggested – and for reasons that the first section of the present paper have perhaps made more apparent – that it might be seen as simply one of situs, of a kind readily identifiable within other classes.[5] Subsequently, though, several authors have wished to accord it a larger significance. For example, Savage et al. (1992) have set against the idea of the formation of a relatively homogeneous service class the alternative possibility of contemporary "middle classes" forming in a more fragmented way around three different kinds of "asset": that is, property, cultural and organizational assets. Insofar as property assets are associated with an entrepreneurial middle class, there is, at least at an empirical level, no major divergence from my own approach (see p. 314 above). However, the suggestion that the potentialities for class formation among professional employees are to be linked to their command chiefly over cultural assets, but among managerial (or administrative) employees to their command over organizational assets, is clearly at odds with my emphasis on the basic commonality in their employment relationships. Esping Andersen (1993: 13) has likewise argued, and indeed more unequivocally, for differentiating the class positions of "scientists–professionals" and "managers– administrators". Although members of both groupings exercise autonomy and control, they do so, he maintains, increasingly on the basis of different kinds of human capital and of productive (or non-productive) activities. Both of these positions have groundings that I do not find persuasive: that of Savage et al. in Wright's attempt (1989b) to derive class positions from a theory of exploitation that involves counterfactuals of a quite arbitrary and implausible kind (cf. Van den Berg 1993, Mills 1994); and that of Esping Andersen in the Fordist/post-Fordist contrast, which sets up a crude qualitative dualism in place of the serious (i.e. quantitative) analysis of actual trends in industrial organization. None the less, it is still possible for the differences that arise to be pursued at an empirical level, and especially so since there is in fact agreement that a key indicator of the extent and nature of differentiation within the service class is provided by the patterns of social mobility associated with its component elements.

So far as intergenerational mobility is concerned, Savage et al. recognize (1992: 146–9) that for professionals and managers these patterns are rather similar – pointing to a "fusion" of cultural and organizational assets that give the children of the service class a generalized advantage in their mobility chances over the children of all other classes. However, as regards intragenerational, or work-life, mobility, Savage et al. (1992: 139–46) seek to show that a notable degree of differentiation occurs. They replicate my own finding (1982: 178–9) that professionals quite frequently move into managerial positions in the course of their careers but claim that, even so, they still display far greater career stability than do managers and thus "can be said to be much more cohesively formed" as a collectivity. This latter argument is essentially reiterated by Fielding (Ch. 10 in this volume).

Savage et al., and likewise Fielding, draw on data from the OPCS Longitudinal Study – the former for the period 1971 to 1981, the latter for 1981 to 1991 – and their analyses are based on the official socio-economic groupings (SEGs). However, a problem then arises not only with SEG 1.1, "Large Employers", but further, and more seriously, with SEG 5.1, "Ancillary Workers", which comprises both professionals and managers as well as other groupings, of technicians etc., that under the class schema earlier discussed would be treated as falling outside the service class altogether. On this account, I believe, the claims made by these authors are exaggerated and, in the case at least of Savage et al., this can be demonstrated. A simple re-analysis of the reported results for 1971–81 in which both SEG 1.1 and SEG 5.1 are discounted and, further, the two professional SEGs (3 and 4) and the two managerial SEGs (1.2 and 2.2) are combined provides a rather different picture from the original. Contrasts in career stability, as measured by the proportion of professionals still being professionals and managers still being managers at the end of the ten-year period covered, are not now all that striking: 49% as against 43%, respectively, for men and 26% as against 22% for women. Fielding's results for 1981–91 are not, unfortunately, presented in a form that makes a comparable treatment possible.[6]

Furthermore, important new light is thrown on the issues in question by Mills (Ch. 6 in this volume), who has constructed a dataset with far greater potential for the analysis of change than any hitherto utilized, at least in the British case. Two of Mills' findings, for men at least, are of particular relevance: first, that, although professional and managerial careers still unfold at a rather different tempo, they are tending overall to become more rather than less similar; and, secondly, that work-life mobility between professional and managerial positions is growing increasingly frequent, with, by the mid-1980s, the entry of professionals into management being no more common than the reverse transition.

This latter result may appear rather surprising but it is, one may observe, confirmed by Fielding's results (Table 10.1b, p. 171 above) – subject to the qualifications noted. Mills believes that one sees here the outcome of the proportionate growth of lower-level professions, which more readily allow for mid-career entry on the part of those previously employed as managers. But it might additionally be suggested that, quite contrary to Esping Andersen's view, in some kinds of modern production unit the division between professional and managerial functions is becoming increasingly blurred – with consequent difficulties for maintaining the validity of the classificatory distinction at the level of individual employees.[7]

Overall, then, research findings on mobility, rather than showing a widening division between the professional and managerial components of the service class, would seem to point to a growing homogeneity. There is, moreover, one other result reported by Savage et al. (1992: 155 and Table 7.9) on a rather different topic that I would see as reinforcing this conclusion: namely, that "there is considerable inter-marriage between professionals and managers". Savage and his associates take this finding as indicating that "different assets may be combined within one household" – but also that there are "important tendencies towards middle-class endogamy". This seems scarcely consistent. If the individual, rather than the family, is to be viewed as the unit of class composition, and if there are divergent processes of class formation in train based on cultural as distinct from organizational assets, then what should be recognized here is of course evidence of class exogamy. In contrast, from the standpoint I would adopt, a quite straightforward interpretation presents itself: that the professional/manager distinction within the service class, whether taken as referring to "family of procreation" or, I would be ready to add, to "family of origin", is just not a significant barrier to marriage.

I would therefore maintain that, in the light of current research, prevailing mobility and marriage patterns must be regarded as alike contributing to, rather than working against, the process of service class formation. However, there is one other respect in which I would regard my earlier speculations on this matter as remaining still very much open to debate. I suggested (1980a: 178) that so far as differentiation in lifestyles was concerned, not only were situs effects likely to be slight but, further, that, as recruitment to all sections of the service class became increasingly channelled through higher education, a greater overall similarity was in fact to be expected. In obvious opposition to this view are now arguments, advanced or reviewed in several contributions to this collection (see esp. those of Butler, Ch. 2, Urry, Ch, 12, and Cloke, Phillips and Thrift, Ch. 13), that claim a growing diversity of tastes, preferences and cultural values within the service class, which, backed by rising discretionary income, find expression in a "post-modern" proliferation of lifestyles.

The issue is one of undoubted interest; but the main point that I would wish to make here is that, in marked contrast with the situation regarding mobility and marriage patterns, the evidence so far available is seriously inadequate. Far too little attention has in fact been given to questions of data collection and analysis, and too much to what Warde and Tomlinson (p. 241 above) refer to as "the prevailing wisdom among new cultural intermediaries" – that is, advertisers and market researchers and, I would like to add, fashionable purveyors of "cultural theory". Thus, for example, when Butler argues (p. 204 above), from a study of the subcultures of "gentrifiers" in Hackney, that "middle-class life has become much more individualistic" or Cloke, Phillips and Thrift (p. 238 above), from research in three southwestern rural areas, that "the middle class is now discursively constructed to a much greater degree than previously", it must be recognized that the empirical grounding of such arguments – even supposing that we know what they mean – is remarkably weak. What is claimed relates to long-term processes of societal change: the evidence adduced is from one-off case studies of limited, and possibly quite unrepresentative, milieux. And, indeed, by just what processes of inference conclusions of the kind illustrated are actually arrived at is far from clear.

From this standpoint, I would then see the chief importance of Warde and Tomlinson's own contribution as being methodological. They make a valiant effort, on the one hand, to provide the kind of data on aspects of lifestyle that are actually required: that is, data extensive in both time and space; and, on the other hand, to subject such data to a form of analysis that is adequate to sustaining arguments about increasing variation, whether between or within classes. Commendably, given the difficulty of their undertaking, they present their substantive conclusions on the particular topic of tastes in food in a cautious and qualified way. But it is, I believe, still significant – and at all events salutary – that, overall, they are led to put almost as much emphasis on long-term continuity as on change. The development of contemporary lifestyles and the issue of their degree of autonomy from class or other social structural locations can surely be identified as an area where further research, and especially in regard to the service class, is needed and could prove highly rewarding. But it seems to me vital that such research should be rescued from both the theory and the methods of exponents of "the cultural turn" in sociology, and provided with a more coherent intellectual basis.[8]

18.5 The politics of the service class

Perhaps the most disputed passage in my original essay has proved to be that in which I maintained (1980a: 180–3), in opposition to various "new class" theorists (see e.g. Mallet 1975, Bruce Biggs 1979, Gouldner 1979) that, as the service class consolidates, it will become "an essentially conservative element within modern societies". In particular, I argued that members of the service class, occupying, as they do, the more rewarding and generally desirable positions within the social division of labour, are unlikely to be attracted to movements or parties that uphold egalitarian values or policies, but will rather seek to preserve the status quo within which their positions of relative power and advantage are established. The most sharply divergent view that has emerged is that of Lash & Urry (1987, cf. also Abercrombie & Urry 1983). For them, the service class, itself a product of the "organized" phase of modern capitalism, is now "an important and driving factor in capitalism's disorganization process". In modern societies the service class has "realized considerable powers" and is now transforming these societies "from within". This transformation comes about as the result of the service class acting in its own complex interests (rather than as a "universal class" in the sense of the "new class" theorists), and it is, it should be said, on the innovative and disruptive, as much as the specifically radical, character of this action that Lash & Urry place their main emphasis. Thus, as regards politics, two cross-nationally common features that they identify are the rise of "new social movements" and the weakening of old patterns of affiliation between class and party (1987: 209–31, 330–13 esp.).

So far as "new social movements" are concerned – for example, the environmentalist or feminist movements – I have no difficulty with Lash & Urry's claim that service-class members play a dominant part in their leadership and organization, although I see no reason to change my view (1982: 183) that within the service class as a whole such participation is, and is likely to remain, minoritarian, intermittent and localized. But it is quite another matter when Lash & Urry in turn contend

(1987: 195) that the rise of such movements, which are "not directly structured by the relations of production", has led to "the redrawing of the boundaries of social division, political conflict, and cultural experience". This I can only regard as a wild exaggeration that goes far beyond any research findings that could conceivably be cited in its support. Furthermore, in the case of the supposed transformation of electoral politics, to which Lash & Urry give major attention, it can be said that their argument is simply mistaken. There is, they believe, evidence for the recent past of a declining propensity of members of the working class to support parties of the left, which has, however, been in part at least offset by greater service class voting for such parties – and especially to the extent that they have managed to shed their "proletarian" character. In other words, in most Western democracies a significant "class dealignment" in voting has occurred. Here, though, Lash & Urry rely on seriously flawed analyses, and in particular on results from the now discredited "Alford Index", which, in the British case at all events, had already been called into question before their own work appeared (Heath et al. 1985). Subsequently, a series of studies have shown that in Britain (Heath et al. 1991, 1994, Evans et al. 1991, Goldthorpe 1995), the USA (Hout et al. 1994) and several continental European nations (Weakliem 1991) no consistent long-term tendency exists for the net association between class and vote to weaken. Left parties have often been disadvantaged at the polls on account simply of the declining size of the working-class electorate and also, in some instances, have lost the confidence of voters "across the board"; but underlying class–party linkages have tended to display a marked temporal stability. Moreover, also damaging to Lash & Urry's position is the associated finding that the "new agendas" that they see as being promoted by the service class have typically failed to displace the "old agendas" – of jobs, pay, taxes, etc. – from the centre of electoral politics (see esp. Weakliem 1991, Evans 1993).

A more limited, but more plausible, alternative to my view of the service class as "essentially conservative" is advanced by Savage et al. (1992: Ch. 9 esp., cf. also Savage 1991a). These authors, to be sure, sometimes write as if they too believe in the thesis of class dealignment, at least as applied to Britain: for example, when they claim (1992: 204) that "Thatcherism has had the effect of reconstituting Tory support on lines which rely less on the middle classes: a development of major historical importance". However, what I take to be their serious argument – and one more consistent with their general position – is that a distinction must be recognized between the politics of managerial and of professional employees. The former, reliant chiefly on organizational assets, tend, like employers, to be politically conservative; but the latter, through their command over cultural assets, have greater independence of employers or employing organizations and are thus more free to develop their own political orientations, which are more often of a radical or at least non-conservative kind. I would regard the attempts initially made by Savage and his associates actually to demonstrate such systematic differences in the voting patterns of professionals and managers as having some questionable features.[9] Fortunately, though, the contribution by Heath and Savage to the present volume (Ch. 16) can be taken as superseding these earlier analyses, both technically and in its specification of the key issue involved: that is, to the extent that differences in partisanship between professionals and managers do exist, how far do these reflect a structural division within the service class and how far simply personal characteristics, associated, perhaps, with processes of occupational self-selection – of the kind discussed in Chapter 17 above by Bagguley.

The results that are reported by Heath and Savage would seem largely to favour the latter of these two possibilities. Professionals are, overall, somewhat more left oriented than managers, although with many occupational groupings representing exceptions to this generalization. But the important finding is that, especially when education is controlled, patterns of party identification within the service class appear fairly homogeneous and, in aggregate at least, quite stably so.[10] It can, moreover, be calculated from the data of Table 16.1 of Heath and Savage's paper that, among occupational groupings that together account for some two-thirds of all service-class members, identification with the Conservative Party is at least twice as likely as identification with the Labour Party. On this evidence, I would then believe that my characterization of the service class as a politically conservative force still stands – for British society at least; and I would continue to place major explanatory emphasis on employment relationships and associated returns from employment that are of a relatively privileged kind.[11] The possibility cannot of course be ruled out that, in some future instances, service class support for parties usually counted as being on the left will increase – and even, perhaps, as support for such parties from other classes is falling, thus creating class dealignment (or at least realignment) in voting patterns. Political pundits have of late been speculating that something of this kind might happen in Britain once the Labour Party has completed its "modernization" programme. However, in any such eventuality, it would be important to ask not only how far class dealignment had occurred, but further how far it was the accompaniment of *party* dealignment; that is, how far the new enthusiasm of the service class for Labour followed an attempt by the party specifically to increase its appeal among this growing component of the electorate by moving rightwards – especially, say, in regard to redistributional issues and its relations with organized labour. It might, in other words, be that, when at last the nature of the "new model" Labour Party stands fully revealed, the conservative influence of the service class on British politics could want no better testimony.

18.6 The service class: disruption or reproduction?

In much of the most recent discussion of the service class – and several contributions to this collection illustrate the point – the issue is raised of the threats that now apparently exist to the very basis of this class, at least as I would wish to view it: that is, the service relationship. It is not just that tendencies for the "downsizing" and "delayering" of business and administrative organizations appear likely to reduce the number of positions to which such a relationship might attach; it is further suggested that employers are increasingly inclined to buy in the specialist services that they require from freelance operators and, moreover, to place their own professional and managerial staff on short-term or "payment by results" contracts that would seem clearly to contradict the defining assumptions of the service relationship.

In this regard, I would adhere to the position, outlined though not entirely accepted by Halford and Savage (Ch. 7 in this volume), that holds that the bureaucratic career will prove more resistant, or adaptive, to change than is often supposed and that reports of its "imminent demise" need not be taken all that seriously. I would not find it surprising if the number of professionals who were self-employed (if only technically) were to grow; nor if what the service relationship came in some cases to imply was less continuity of employment than continuity of employability – with a consequent increase in inter-organizational mobility among both professional and managerial employees. But, I would urge, it is important here not to be misled into constructing long-term trends out of the expedients of recession or the passing fads of management consultants. Although changes over time may surely be expected in the particular groups of employees to whom the service relationship is extended, its logic in the case of those who actually do exercise special expertise or delegated authority is a powerful one, and will not readily be superseded.[12]

Furthermore, it would in any event be unfortunate if speculation on possible threats to the stability of the service class in the future were to distract attention from the rather remarkable degree of stability that has in fact characterized this class during the recent past. Indeed, what I would wish to argue in concluding this paper is that, for sociologists interested in the service class, it is the very effectiveness of its processes of reproduction that must, so far at least, be recognized as the obvious and central explanandum. As already noted, the service class has grown throughout the twentieth century, at an accelerated rate in the decades since the Second World War, and with significant changes in its occupational composition. Over more or less the same period, educational provision has been enormously increased, at the secondary and then at the tertiary level; and most national governments have become committed, in principle at least, to increasing equality of educational opportunity, and most employing organizations to recruiting and promoting personnel according to attested ability rather than social provenance. Nevertheless, what is now apparent from a substantial body of research (cf. Erikson & Goldthorpe 1992b) is that the capacity of the service class as a collectivity to maintain its advantages from generation to generation, as against the members of other classes, has been remarkably little altered.

Thus, as just one possible indication of the extent of the inequalities that have persisted, one might take the finding that in Britain the odds of children of service-class origins being themselves found in service-class positions rather than in non-skilled wage labour are around 15 times greater than these same odds for children of non-skilled working-class origins, and appear to have remained so from at least the early decades of the century. Nor is Britain in this respect at all exceptional. Disparities in chances of access to service-class employment of much the same order of magnitude have been shown to operate across a wide range of other advanced societies, regardless for the most part of differences in national institutions, cultural traditions or political regimes. Moreover, the failure of educational expansion to bring about any substantially greater equality of opportunity can, in an immediate sense, be easily enough explained. Although educational qualifications have become of particular importance in obtaining service-class positions, the relative rates of success of children of differing class backgrounds in making key "transitions" within educational systems have themselves proved extremely difficult to modify (see Shavit & Blossfeld 1993). In other words, although educational levels have substantially risen overall, the clear competitive "edge" enjoyed by the service class would seem in this respect also to have been largely preserved.

Here, then – and in contrast with the question of the "socio-structural" formation of service classes – an entirely legitimate challenge to sociological theory must be recognized. Since the regularities that express the vitality of service class reproduction are ones established on a wide cross-national basis, historically grounded accounts, attentive to the specificities of particular places or periods, cannot be of primary relevance. What is required is some explanation of how these regularities are actually generated, at the "micro" level, by processes of social action and interaction that can themselves be shown to occur in a similarly generalized way.

The development of theory adequate to this purpose must be reckoned a major undertaking, which I shall not in the present context try further to advance. However, one point at least (see Erikson & Goldthorpe 1992b: Ch. 8) seems apparent enough. That is, a major concern of such theory will need to be with the strategies pursued by service class families in seeking to ensure that, in changing circumstances, the various resources that they command – economic, cultural, social – are used to the best possible advantage to help their children maintain their class position or, at very least, to avoid any threat of downward mobility of a decisive kind. This point I see as requiring emphasis here, not only because it again brings out the importance of treating the family rather than the individual as the unit of class composition, but further because elsewhere in this collection it appears rather neglected and is indeed in some cases obscured as a result of feminist preoccupations with gender conflicts occurring within the family.

Thus, when Witz refers to "the relatively undertheorized status of the family within sociological accounts of class formation", her interest is clearly not in understanding strategies of the kind in question, but rather in advancing the claim that "conventional" class analysis has attributed to the family "a unitary status curiously lacking in real social content" (pp. 41, 45 above). And a yet more striking illustration of the blinkers that a feminist perspective may impose is to be found in the contribution by Gregson and Lowe (Ch. 9). Although these authors are directly concerned with family strategies, these are ones simply of "domestic servicing", and the larger significance that they give to the growing and varied use of cleaners and nannies by professional and managerial families relates, on the one hand, to the "gender politics" of domestic labour, and, on the other, to the loss of any commonality in the organization of such labour which they see as in fact "forestalling" class formation. What Gregson and Lowe entirely overlook is that decisions made by service class couples to employ domestic labour of one kind or another may form part of strategies, whose aims extend beyond coping with problems of household chores and routine childcare and centre on the optimal use of family resources in promoting children's chances of educational, and subsequent career, success; for example, by obtaining the best possible trade-off between family income (present and future) and the amount of "quality time" that parents can devote to their children. Assumptions about gender roles may well be involved that Gregson and Lowe would not regard as "progressive". But the ultimate purpose and effectiveness of the resulting arrangements – their "real social content" – could go some way to explaining what for these authors is their "most depressing" finding: that is, that their definition of the situation prevailing in the families they studied, couched in terms of "gender politics", was one that many of the women they interviewed failed to share.[13]

As regards class formation, then, just the opposite of the view taken by Gregson and Lowe could be maintained: that the increasing ability of service class families, and especially "dual-career" families, to pay for domestic labour, as in effect an element in a strategy of social reproduction, represents one further aspect of the way in which the growth of women's employment has itself made for a hardening of class inequalities in life-chances. Insofar as feminists acknowledge this effect, it is notable that they regard it as being "paradoxical" (e.g. Crompton & Sanderson 1990: 166, Witz, p. 46 above). But from the standpoint here adopted, in which the conjugal family represents the unit of class composition – and of economic decision-making – it is difficult to see what else might be expected.

In sum, although sociologists should of course remain alert to the possibility of changes in the organization of economic or family life that might weaken the basis of the service class, as also to any tendencies towards its greater internal differentiation, this should still not prevent them from recognizing, and responding to, the very ample evidence to suggest that, thus far, these are not developments of major consequence – that is, primarily the evidence of research on class differentials in educational attainment and on class mobility rates and patterns as viewed in both work-life and intergenerational perspective, with which the findings also reviewed on the prevailingly conservative, or at all events far from radical, character of service class politics would seem congruent enough. In other words, the evident sociological task, for the present at least, is that of providing theoretically directed, but empirically testable, accounts of the processes through which it has been possible for service class growth and the consolidation of service class advantage to go ahead together, and which would appear to operate in essentially similar ways, regardless of institutional and cultural variation, across the societies of the modern world.

Acknowledgement

I am indebted to Jeff Manza, Mike Savage and Alan Warde for helpful comments on an earlier version of this paper. The usual disclaimers apply.

Notes

1. If such circumstances were recurrent, it might be appropriate to make explicit provision for "large" employers within the class schema; for example, by distinguishing for this purpose a Class Ia. However, it should not be supposed that this would then provide an adequate representation of the "capitalist class". For the employers in question would of course be "large" only in the context of enterprises that remained unincorporated – i.e. mostly ones of a quite modest kind. For an illuminating treatment of this issue, see Marshall et al. (1988: 54–9).

2. There is of course the other "boundary problem" – that of who it is that the service class serves. On this, I have myself nothing to add to what I said in my earlier paper (1982). For further discussion, see Abercrombie & Urry (1983: 122–5).

3. Feminist sociologists, insofar as they have addressed this issue, have sought to minimize its significance by claiming that wives typically enjoy a lower level of intrafamilial economic welfare than do their husbands. However, so far as I can discover, the research supposedly supporting such claims turns out either to relate to other matters – e.g. different systems of household financial management – or to be based on small samples of very questionable representativeness.

4. As an illustration of what I would understand as a theoretical account of structural change, I might cite the classic analysis of Clark (1940: Ch. 5) of the progressive shift of labour, in the course of economic growth, from the primary to the secondary sector of the economy and in turn from the secondary to the tertiary sector. Clark seeks first of all to establish that this empirical regularity actually exists, and then proposes two mechanisms or processes through which it is in all cases generated: briefly, those of relative changes in demand for the products of different sectors and differential increases in productivity across sectors. From this point of view, what is then required of a theory is that it should offer some explanation of how an observed regularity is created and sustained – which explanation is in turn open to empirical test. Unfortunately, in much contemporary sociology the very idea of theory has become seriously degraded – one symptom of which is the widespread use of "theorize" as a transitive verb.

5. I used the concept of situs in the sense of Morris & Murphy (1959) to refer to "the functional context" of an occupation or group of occupations, which may exert an influence on the lifestyles and patterns of action of their incumbents, independently of that of the class, or status, positions that they simultaneously hold.

6. Fielding (Table 10.1, p. 171 above) does actually combine SEGs 1.2 and 2.2 as managers and SEGs 3 and 4 as professionals but then adds to the latter not only SEG 5.1 but also SEG 1.1 – that of "Large Employers". This seems entirely inappropriate.

7. Such a development appears most likely where the production process, whether of goods or of services, has a relatively advanced technological basis, knowledge of which is necessary to the performance of managerial functions. If the professional/managerial distinction is thus breaking down, then the implications for the "asset" theory of differentiation within the service class are of course even more damaging than those that follow from evidence of increasing mobility between professional and managerial positions.

8. The crucial issue here is that of the relationship between theory and evidence (cf. Lieberson 1992, and esp. the references to Bourdieu), which relates to much more than the problem referred to in the text of generalizing from case studies. It is a basic problem of cultural theory that, for the most part, it falls under the rubric of "not clear enough to

be wrong". I learn from Cloke, Phillips and Thrift (p. 224 above) that, on the authority of Bourdieu & Wacquant (1992), "the vague and indefinite" may indeed be of "positive value" where questions of culture are concerned. That such an argument should be taken seriously certainly explains a good deal. None the less, it still does not help me, in reading recent works of apparent relevance to this paper such as, say, Lamont (1991) or Eder (1993), to work out just what is being claimed and on just what grounds.

9. That is, ones again arising from their treatment of SEGs (see pp. 320 above) and, in particular, their inclusion of SEG 5.1, "Ancillary Workers", in the professional component of the service class.

10. The strongest evidence of which I am aware of diverging political orientations as between professionals and managers is that showing a greater propensity on the part of the former to vote Democrat rather than Republican in US Presidential elections since 1972 (Hout et al. 1994, Brooks & Manza 1994), which appears related to their greater "social liberalism" on issues such as civil rights, abortion and gender equality. Education is not, however, included in the analyses in question. Insofar as interest centres on the political differentiation of the service class, I would suggest that at least as profitable an axis to consider as that of professionals versus managers would be that of higher versus lower echelons (as, for example, represented by Classes I and II in the schema earlier referred to). For a suggestive, though technically questionable, exercise relating to the German service class, see Herz (1990).

11. Note also that, as Heath and Savage acknowledge, their analysis takes no account of the effects on party identification of class mobility. There is, however, good evidence that such effects occur (see e.g. De Graaf et al. 1995); and it is then at all events a plausible hypothesis that if, as seems likely, an expanded service class becomes to a greater degree self-recruiting, rather than reliant on "recruitment from below", the conservatism of its membership will *ceteris paribus* increase. Some evidence of such a shift as between 1972 and the 1980s is reported by Heath and Savage, although, as the analysis stands, this could simply reflect a right-wing movement among the electorate as a whole.

12. It is here again important not to highlight present developments against a largely fictitious "past". As Fielding observes (p. 175 above), the results on middle-class mobility (occupational and geographic) that he reports for the 1980s clearly recall contrasts drawn in studies of the 1950s and 1960s between "locals" and "cosmopolitans" or "burgesses" and "spiralists".

13. It may be noted that a concern with family strategies aimed at maximizing children's chances of educational success – including the possible use of private education – is apparent (p. 203 above) even among Butler's *Guardian*-reading, Labour-voting, discursively reflexive gentrifiers. Although I would then entirely agree with Gregson and Lowe that their findings provide an important counter to arguments that stress the radical nature of middle-class politics, their preoccupation with gender issues means that they miss an opportunity of showing how their point applies far more widely.

Chapter 19

Reflections on gender and geography

Doreen Massey

19.1 Class and other axes of division

One strand of change within class analysis over the years, and one that is widely if not universally reckoned to have represented "progress", has been the increasing attention paid to the intersection of class with, or its incorporation of, other axes of social differentiation and inequality. A number of papers in this collection pay central attention to this issue (Witz, Crompton, Gregson and Lowe and Phillips and Sarre) and many of the others engage with the question in some way or other.

It also seems clear, from reading these papers, that the debate over what one might call the "depth" of the relationship between class and other axes, has shifted. On the whole, it seems, the claims now being made are for a deeper level of interaction. At a number of points it is argued, for instance, that not only are social classes in their social outcomes empirically gendered or racialized but so too are the processes of class formation themselves. Thus Anne Witz, focusing on gender, provides a detailed explication of this in her examination of occupational structures, arguing that "gender matters in a *further*, more embedded, sense that has much more to do with the processes and mechanisms . . . underlying the historical specificities of forms of the social division of labour, of which occupational structure is one aspect" (p. 43 above). In other words, the construction of occupational positions must be taken to be part of class theory, and not assumed to be pre-given to it, and moreover that process of construction is itself gendered. For these reasons, she argues, "we need a new concept of class formation in order to describe the processes and mechanisms whereby occupational structures of 'places' emerge and gendered 'persons' come to be associated with them over time and, indeed, how these two processes are not necessarily sequential" (p. 43). Now, there are a number of ways in which such processes and mechanisms may operate, and both Witz and other authors in the collection engage with a range of them. There is, for instance, the way in which the bureaucratic career has been constructed as a male career. There is the dependence of career jobs on the existence of routine and non-career jobs, the former held more by men, the latter more by women. There is the legitimation of certain jobs as being of high status simply because of the maleness of those who hold them. There are gendered processes of exclusion, demarcation and segregation enacting social closure around, for instance, positions based upon the possession of specialist knowledge.

I want here to take this argument a little further. Most of the mechanisms referred to above are examples of the joint operation of class and gender in the production of gender-exclusive, or dominated, occupational positions. It may be, however, that the intermeshing of class and gender operates at an even deeper level, and that the process is one not only of class (or occupational structure) formation, but also of gender formation.

The co-constitution of class and gender

Take, as an example, the relatively recently established, and growing, occupation of research-scientist in high-technology industry. It is an occupation that has emerged as a separate element in the social division of labour with the increasing separation of knowledge-based jobs (such as research engineering) from the process of direct physical production (see Massey et al. 1992). The jobs that now fall into this occupational grouping involve intellectual research, quite high levels of abstract thought, and the concentrated application of scientific logic. They are reasonably paid and, more important than that, are surrounded by a high level of hype, both journalistic and academic. They are jobs with a high degree of cachet, and are seen as being "on the frontiers"; their holders are sought after and applauded, in different ways, by politicians on both left and right of the political spectrum. Approximately 95% of the holders of these jobs in the UK today are men.[1]

How are these facts to be interpreted? Certainly there are issues here of social closure around these jobs based on specialist knowledge. Much has, for instance, been written about the culture of high-technology workplaces and the difficulties that it frequently presents to women. The time–space organization of the jobs is also highly demanding, and thus restricts the range of people who would be prepared to take them up. The hours are frequently very long and – equally important – unpredictable. Work continues into the night, over weekends, into Bank Holidays. And although in some ways these knowledge-based jobs might be done anywhere (so long as you have a computer on hand), in fact considerable geographical demands are placed on these employees. They may have to be "on call" to go out and fix problems, they may have to fly off to California at a moment's notice, their very progress in their careers may require a period of worldwide geographical mobility. These are jobs that demand a particular form of what is now usually referred to as flexibility – in this case time–space flexibility. They are also, and for that reason, jobs that prefer that you don't have too many commitments outside work, and certainly not commitments – such as those of caring for others – which themselves require a degree of time–space flexibility. In our interviews we found no-one to disagree with the statement that "a single parent could not do this job". In these and a multitude of other ways, then, already-gendered persons have highly differential abilities (whether through availability or through inclination) to enter this profession.

Certainly, too, it is the case that the way in which these jobs are socially constructed generates a demand for help with personal servicing. In our interviews the younger single men sometimes got by on junk food and night-time visits to the launderette, there was a medium degree of reliance on other family, on cleaners and on childminders, but the bulk of the burden fell, in the 66% of cases where the scientists were cohabiting, on the female partners. It is, then, a classic segment of the service class whose possibility of existence in this form depends on the existence also of "service wives" (Crompton, Ch. 4 in this volume). And this in turn of course made it even more difficult for these (mainly professionally qualified) women to enter fully into their own professional careers.[2] And thus the masculinity of the occupational middle class is further reinforced.

It is also surely the case that the fact that these occupations are peopled by self-confident (and mainly young) men further reinforces the high status in which they are so frequently held. The mythologizing of the lives of young male scientist–entrepreneurs was, particularly in the 1980s, a regular feature of newspaper business pages (see Massey et al. 1992).

In all these ways, then, gender makes these occupations what they are: in terms of who fills these spaces in the social division of labour, in terms of the design of the spaces and of their dependence on other gendered work, and in terms of the status that they are thereby accorded.

It may be, however, that the nature of this patch within the overall social division of labour is even more fundamentally gendered than this. These jobs are the apex of abstract thought within the overall process of production. They are the result of a long process (which even now may be being re-evaluated) of separation, within industry, of conceptualization from execution. These jobs are at the "conceptualization" end of that dualism. They are occupations/roles in society whose status derives from the (perceived-as) elevated abstraction of their work-content. And, as Butler pointed out in Chapter 2 (p. 30), Lash & Urry among others have argued that conceptualization is one of the three distinctive functions performed by the service class. Moreover, they speak of this function as being "for capital".

Certainly, the separation of conceptualization from execution is part of a process of the division of tasks propelled by the requirements of competitive production, by the requirements of capitalist calculation (see, for instance, Braverman 1974). It is a necessary part of the capitalist division of labour. However, the fact that the division of tasks historically took the *form* of the separation of conception from execution can also be read in the light of a longer historical distinction – the philosophical separation of Mind from Body that has been so prominent in Western philosophy since Descartes and that was itself a more precise, and in many ways more extreme, version of an even longer-lasting distinction between Reason and non-Reason. The separation-out of conceptualization as a social function is not particular to capitalism, although of course its forms in this case are distinct. Nor is it only a distinction around which *class* divisions may be articulated. Genevieve Lloyd (1984) among many others has pointed to, and analyzed in detail, the imbrication of the establishment of these dualisms with the establishment of the dichotomous gender system and its particular ascribed characteristics. It was with masculinity that were associated the "Reason" and the "Mind" sides of these dualisms. And it was with the establishment of masculinity as dominant that the very nature of these dualisms (the fact of their mutually-exclusive dichotomous nature, the lines of divide that they describe) was associated. More generally, indeed, it might also be remembered that such dualisms are by their very nature "relational" in the terms discussed by Savage and Butler (in Ch. 20), but that the *form* of this relational connection is precisely what has been argued to be characteristic of, and related to, our societies' dualistic approach to gender definition (Lloyd 1984, Massey 1992).

On the one hand, then, it is perhaps no more than the continuance of a long tradition that men should be the ones to get the high-status jobs at the conceptual end of the current spectrum in the social division of labour. But on the other hand, and in the end much more importantly, the very fact and nature of the divide itself is utterly tied up not with already defined genders, but with the processes of gender-dividing and the ascription of gender characteristics – the formation of gendered identities. David Noble (1992) has written of the gendered history of this set of dualisms and of some of its practical effects in modes of social organization. The subtitle of his book is "The Christian clerical culture of Western science". Maybe the high-tech research laboratory of the late twentieth century has much in common – in status, in symbolism, in the construction of a particular form of masculinity – with the medieval monastery. The long Western (and not only Western) construction of a division of labour that separates Reason from non-Reason, abstract thought from concrete production, conceptualization from execution, has been at the same time a process at the heart of the construction of gender.

Moreover, the process continues today. In the scientific workplace of today this clerical–scientific culture is one that both reflects and helps further to define and reinforce particular aspects of a particular kind of masculinity – that bound up with science, logic and rationality. What is at issue is not individual empirical men – individual men cope with the culture in a variety of ways and with varying degrees of difficulty and ease – but a form of *masculinity*, socially defined.[3]

So, it is being argued here, the terms on which the social division of labour is constructed (the criteria of its lines of divide) are imbued with gender, and the construction of this social division of labour is itself active in the constitution of gender, both the nature of its divisions and the characteristics that they are socially ascribed.

Moreover, the fact of the continued salience of this process of gender-constitution then curls back into another argument that has been addressed in this collection. Nicky Gregson and Michelle Lowe argue in Chapter 9 (and our own research, cited in note 1, would completely support their conclusions) that there is a strong unwillingness on the part of middle-class men "to do more than the bare minimum in the way of domestic labour" (p. 158). They go on to explore "the place of domestic labour in the identities of middle-class men and women" (p. 158), using a performative account of class in an analysis of domestic labour to distinguish between those elements that such people will do (which they see as being compatible with or con-firming of their identities) and those elements that they are happy to delegate to others, given their time-constraints and their financial abilities. The authors urge the need to address "the gender politics of domestic labour" (p. 163). Perhaps, again, the argument can be taken a step further. First, as Gregson and Lowe would concur, there is variation on this issue between masculine and feminine identities. But secondly, and to bring the argument in a sense full-circle, the construction of certain types of middle-class masculinity as not including domestic labour is also, in part, a product of the social division of labour in paid employment. For some of the scientists in our research it was important to their self-conception as scientists to play down their interest in and ability at domestic labour (see Massey, 1995b). Thus, the construction of masculine incompetence about the house, and therefore the construction of a gender politics of domestic labour, happens in part through the joint constitution of gender and occupation within the wider field of the social division of labour.

The relation of the categories

The basic argument here, then, is that the interrelation between class and other axes of social differentiation, such as gender, operates at a very profound level and that what will frequently be involved will in fact be the *joint*, or simultaneous, consti-tution of the dimensions and the character of both class and these other axes. The status of the particular kind of specialist knowledge possessed by the men in these examples reflects and confirms, and constitutes, both their middle-class status and their masculinity.

It is still, none the less, the nature of *class* that is the focus of attention in this vol-ume, and to argue that things are interrelated is by no means to argue that they should be collapsed into each other. Indeed, to retain any notion of interrelation one must previously have established a distinction. The categories race, class, gen-der are not *the same*, as Mills (p. 99) points out. In that sense, I find it difficult to understand the occasional insistence in the papers here on abandoning the *analyti-cal* distinction between class and gender (perhaps I misunderstand what this means) and would query the formulation in the Editors' Introduction to Part II concerning "whether gender and ethnicity should be seen as independent social processes from those of class, or whether there are inter-dependencies between them".

A similar point might be made in relation to Phillips and Sarre's argument in Chapter 5 about the relation between "race" and class. They criticize Savage et al. (1992) for maintaining race and gender as "contingent" to the process of class for-mation. The alternative is, in the terms of realist explanatory categories, that they are "necessary". It seems to me that there is an implicit reading here of "contin-gent" and "necessary" as less and more significant respectively. Certainly in this context quite the opposite is the case. For race and class to be *contingent* causal axes to the process of class formation means that they have an analytically autonomous causal structure. It means, precisely, that they are not subsumed within the logic of

334

class, as would be implied by the term "necessary". To say that, empirically, class and race and gender are often (always? how would we know?) mixed up together is *not* to establish that they are part of the same necessary logic.

However, at this point I change horses as far as the foregoing chapters are concerned. Goldthorpe, Mills, et al. seem to wish to maintain this analytical separation in order that the "relative impact" of each axis can be evaluated (see Crompton, Ch. 4, and Mills, Ch. 6 this volume). This implies a very weak notion of interrelation. What is at issue is not accounting for proportions of variation in outcomes, but recognizing the active mutual engagement of dimensions of social differentiation so that they produce an outcome in which specific forms of gender and class relation are in effect fused. But here there is a problem that some recent formulations of class, notably Goldthorpe's own (1983, Erikson & Goldthorpe 1992b), are couched in such a way as to make it difficult to examine this interface. Goldthorpe's recent formulations emphasize that class is based around employment relations rather than the experience of work itself. An important thread in this argument, however, is that the experience of class on the second view happens primarily within the workplace, whereas on the first view the experience extends to the members of the worker's family. This poses two problems. First, as Gregson and Lowe (Ch. 9) argue, and as the cases put by Witz (Ch. 3) and Crompton (Ch. 4) also demonstrate, the experience of class within the workplace helps construct individuals with particular identities, which they continue to inhabit outside the workplace as well. The construction of one's identity around status and career, for instance, is not something one leaves behind in the office. You take it, for instance, back home to the domestic sphere. Nor are such characteristics exclusively ones of class. In the case of the scientists–professionals in my own recent research, they were also characteristics of (a particular form of) masculinity. And as both my own research and the paper by Gregson and Lowe demonstrate, the construction of such work identities has considerable effects on people outside of the workplace, not least the other members of "the conjugal family".

Secondly, there is a problem for those – such as Goldthorpe – who insist that the family is the unit of class analysis. As the research cited above shows, the effects of work relationships are frequently brought back into the home in ways that are divisive. This is particularly true of non-economic effects. Thus scientific masculinity on occasions discouraged the performance of domestic work, and, as Gregson and Lowe point out, the impact of careerism (and the possession of a career is a central criterion in Goldthorpe's definition of the middle class) can have similar, contradictory impacts. Moreover – and this is the point – these can set up members of a conjugal family with conflicting interests. And, although Erikson & Goldthorpe state that they are aware of possible gender divisions within the family (Erikson & Goldthorpe 1992b: 233), it seems important not just to admit these as a possibility, but to point to clear links between the construction of specific forms of class identity and domestic relationships. There is widespread evidence both that the man's career is pursued as much for himself as for his family (in our group, for his status as a scientist rather than for monetary reward) and that (certainly in many of our cases) the women could have had equally well-remunerated careers – it was just that their priorities were different (they put family and children higher up the list).

19.2 The geographies of class

At a number of points in the course of this book reference has been made to the importance of "place" in any consideration of the nature of class and of the middle class in particular. There is something intuitively appealing about this – the sharpness of the spatial differentiation between social groups in Western society is such that it is easy to think of emblematic class-related places. The more difficult questions are those that try to push beyond this (not unimportant) level of analysis; and access to a number of these questions is provided by the foregoing chapters. There are two particular lines of thought that I wish to pursue here. The first is to argue that what is at issue is somewhat wider than simply "place". Rather, I think, what we may be able to begin to think about is different relations between particular social groups and *geography*. "Geography" in its usual "officially recognized" definitions embraces consideration of a classic triad: space, place and nature. In Chapter 12, John Urry begins to make some inroads into the third of these terms – in his consideration of the changing character of tourism, of environmentalism and of outdoor activities, for instance – and I will not pursue this one any further here. What *will* be argued, however, is that, as well as distinctive relations to *place*, different social groups may also have particular identifiable and characterizable relations to space – what I shall term here *social spatialities*. The second aim is to explore the nature of the relationships that may exist between these aspects of geography and distinct social groups and – even more difficult to pin down – the nature of the connection (if any) to class. The two themes are intertwined in what follows.

Space

Tony Fielding's chapter (Ch. 10) provides a good way into this issue in his demonstration of the important role of differential spatial mobility in class formation. There are two issues here (though Fielding concentrates mainly on the first). First, interregional spatial mobility is shown to be an important part of the process of gaining access to certain social classes. In particular this is true of his three categories of the middle class: managers, professionals and petits bourgeois. For all these groups, entry seems to be importantly facilitated by spatial mobility. Specifically, it is facilitated by movement to the South East of England from other regions of England and Wales. Some caveats might be noted (the proportions of movers are still only small; and since the largest component consists of those leaving education it may include a percentage returning to their "home" region after a period away at university), but none the less the results are significant and interesting. Secondly, moreover, not only is spatial mobility important in class formation in some cases, but the *differences* in its importance between social groups are also marked. The difference, for instance, in the role of spatial mobility between professionals and blue-collar workers (in England and Wales between 1981 and 1991) is very marked. So spatial stability or mobility could be a differentiator between classes defined in these terms: some classes appear to be formed *in situ* far more than others.

This is mobility in class formation. There is also the question of spatial mobility as a characteristic of the class itself. Here again Fielding provides a pointer. As his results show (Table 10.3, final column) once again there are clear differences between classes defined in this way and levels of interregional migration over that ten-year period. Moreover two points stand out in relation to the middle class. First, two of its three elements, the professionals and the managers, are quite dramatically more mobile than any other social groups. The most notable contrast, again, is between professionals, at over twice the overall average of mobility, and blue-collar workers, at less than half. Clearly, there are sharp distinctions between social groups and spatiality. The second point is a differentiation on these terms *between* the groups that Fielding assigns to the middle class (an assignment to which, I should add, I am sympathetic). For, in stark contrast to the professionals and the managers, the petits bourgeois display a very low rate of interregional mobility, coming in second bottom after blue-collar workers.

Now, of course, this is a very restricted aspect of mobility. Fielding's concern was to examine change between regions in place of residence. But mobility is more than this: in terms of a wider notion of culture and lifestyle, mobility might be thought of rather as (differential) flexibility in relation to the spatial dimensions of life. So far as I know there is little systematic empirical research on this issue. But John Urry, among others, has effectively argued that, in order to understand the social construction and delineation of modern society, we need to go beyond the spheres of work and residence and examine also such activities as tourism, travel and leisure. Work within geography has pointed to what appear to be broadly systematic patterns of differentiation between social groups (including both class and gender) in both degrees and types of spatial mobility. These arguments have often been made within the context of the wider debate about "globalization" and have sought to point out that the geographical flexibility so frequently associated with "the postmodern condition" is in fact very unevenly distributed (see Massey 1994). The relationship of different social groups to the general phenomenon of globalization varies widely. This, moreover, is a question not just of degrees of spatial mobility, but also of their type and quality – the degree of control one has over one's own and others' movement, even the ease and style with which one travels. A simple example from Fielding's paper illustrates the point. In his tables professionals, managers and the unemployed exhibit relatively high degrees of interregional movement. Yet the terms on which this spatial mobility takes place, its social meaning and its character as an experience, indeed the way it becomes part of the process of identity-formation, must be very different between the groups: the spatial mobility of the unemployed building worker coming down from the North represents a very different experience of spatiality from that of the new Oxbridge graduate coming down to London to begin a professional career.

It would be fascinating to map these power geometries of different groups in society, to assess how coherent they are within classes, how differentiated between them, and on what terms these social spatialities intersect. It may well be, although I have no systematic evidence to back up this speculative thought, that "the middle classes" have, or are establishing, distinctive relationships to spatiality.

Place

The relationship of social groups to place is more generally recognized to be significant than is that to spatiality, even though the nature and coherence of the relationship are disputed. The connection of the middle class to the countryside, which is the focus of a number of discussions in this book, raises a range of issues.

To begin with, it underlines that what is at issue here is not just the happenstance congregation of different social groups into distinct geographical locations but the active *making of places*. Moreover, this making of places is itself part and parcel of constructing and confirming the identity of the social group. A social group does not merely make a place after its own (thus pre-given) image; rather the process of construction of the place is integral to the imagination and affirmation of the social identity itself. That this is so is evident from many of the discussions of the relationship between elements of the middle class and the countryside, both in the articles in this collection and elsewhere. (This is emphatically *not* to argue, as none of the papers here would argue, that there is some one single coherent relation between the middle class and the countryside. It is simply to argue that, insofar as there are such relationships, fractured and complicated as they may be, they take this form of constitution rather than merely correlation.)

To the extent, then, that there are constitutive relationships between place and group, they involve not only (re)making the place, for instance the countryside, but also (re)making the group. Both the paper by Cloke, Phillips and Thrift (Ch. 13) and – particularly – that by Phillips and Sarre (Ch. 5) pick up on an element of this that links back to the discussion in the opening section of this chapter. The countryside (and the discussion is mainly, though not exclusively, of the English countryside) is white. If the notion of the middle class in Britain brings with it images of whiteness, then that is reinforced when the middle class is linked to rurality. All the classic images of villages and "quintessential" (it seems obligatory to use that word!) English countryside hark back to an imagined past before immigration and stand in rebuke and rejection of the ethnic chaos of the inner city. Cloke, Phillips and Thrift cite evidence of geographical avoidance of ethnic minorities as part of the reason for some white people's desire to live in the countryside. What is going on here is certainly exclusion (Phillips and Sarre talk of "reluctant admission" to the middle class) from both place and the culture of the social group. And it is also the active *making* of both place and culture in a process of mutual reinforcement. In a programme of work on the (re)making of the South East of England during the 1980s we uncovered just such processes under way.[4] What began to emerge was a picture of the Outer South East of England, at least in its more rural parts, as a region – or a set of localities –

being produced as part of a project to construct a particular kind of (middle-class) white ethnicity. The place, the particular nature of the articulation of the ethnicity, and the identity of the social groups involved were being constructed together and as largely mutually reinforcing. This is a particular kind of English whiteness, and a particular way of being middle class, articulated into and through a particular kind of place. As Phillips and Sarre so aptly put it in this volume, "The whiteness of the British middle classes turns out to be not just an assumption or an oversight, but an implicit goal of British culture" (p. 91). And, to mirror the argument in the first section, this is not just a matter of exclusion and of discrimination (although it is also both of these); it is also a matter of co-constitution, in which the co-constitution of place may also be a significant element.

It was probably without a flicker of surprise that you read, in Tony Fielding's paper, that the process of class formation for managerial and professional strata involves not only interregional migration but migration specifically to the South East of England (and were it possible to draw the boundaries of that region rather more generously I am certain that this observation would be even more emphatic). Yet why should we accept, as though it were apparently "natural", that these social groups should cluster so strongly (although not exclusively) within one corner of the country? Here is a clear correlation between social class (in the most general of terms – I shall return to this) and geography, and one that appears to have been reinforced over recent decades. One way to interpret this geography is as the spatial expression of the (changing) social relations of production (Massey 1995a). Managers may be defined in terms of their control over the relations of economic ownership and possession; and professionals through their autonomy and their possession of specialist knowledge (to remain with the case of scientists and technologists, through their control over conceptualization within the overall process of production). As the social relations involved in both of these dimensions have become more elaborate, as long hierarchies of management have developed (with the concentration of ownership, and so forth) and as conceptualization has become increasingly divorced from execution, so their geographies have changed. It has become less necessary for the upper echelons of these hierarchies to be located alongside the direct process of manual production. Increasingly, in fact, they have pulled away from it. Over the past 100 years the geography of the control over production has become increasingly distinct from the geography of "production itself". And the geography of Research and Development has become more and more removed from the geography of factories. In the process these newly emerging groups have made places that both reflect and actively reinforce their (social) distinctiveness. *They have created a geography of difference.*

The complexities of causality involved in all this are fascinating. At first sight what is going on is that changes in the division of labour (the proliferation of occupational places) along the managerial and conceptual aspects of the social relations of production have enabled a parallel proliferation, and mutual distancing, of spatial locations. (Just note, at this point, that they have only *enabled* these spatial changes; they have not necessitated them.) As the hierarchies of management and conceptualization have been stretched out over space they have responded to other locational demands (other than proximity to production), they have been attracted to other geographical environments, they have established a distance between themselves and manual production and the working class. Yet in fact the changes in the division of labour and the establishment of new occupational categories have not been the simply autonomous "independent variable" from which the definition of new social groups and new social geographies has been a dependent derivation. It has been argued in the first section of this chapter, and in other papers in this book, that the emergence of occupations does not happen as some kind of ineluctable technological necessity. The relation between gender and the splitting of conceptualization and execution was discussed above. And the same point can be made in a more general way here: the pushing forward of the division of labour itself has been both stimulated and influenced in its character by forces pushing towards social differentiation and by the possibilities offered by geographically uneven development (see Massey 1995a). Moreover, once again, the different aspects have in many ways reinforced each other. Most importantly, the possibility of spatial distancing from the manual working class and of establishing a social exclusivity of place has been both a stimulus to the development of the division of labour and a reinforcement of the social differentiation that it enabled. In the UK (and there are differences between cultures here) functional distance from production has gone along with, and in its social effects has been reinforced by, geographical distance. The spatial symbolism of science parks may be seen as emblematic of this process (Massey et al. 1992). Their whole construction as places is designed to this effect. Occupational, social and spatial identities are constructed together.

This, of course, has been to concentrate on the relation of "place" to employment and to residence. There are many other ways, as Urry (Ch. 12) again reminds us, in which the symbolism of place can be a significant component in the struggle to construct and demonstrate a particular social identity. If the working class goes to Benidorm and Bowness, there are middle-class "honeypots" too. There is (apparently) significance attached to the choice of ski resort; there are highly developed relationships, bearing well-established meanings, with particular parts of continental Europe – the Dordogne, or Tuscany; there is a knowing cultural geography of the sources of consumption – olives from the right grove, olive oil from the right region (even if you have gone out on a limb and found a little place no-one else has ever heard of, the *fact* of geography, and of having an awareness of this kind of "cultural geography", is important). But to wander thus is to raise again a central question. There certainly seem to be important connections between the establishment of social identity and place/spatiality, but what is their nature and how, if at all, are they related to class?

The character of the connections

First, then, it is important to remember that the constitution of social groups necessarily occurs "spatially"; that is, in places and through spatial mobility and interaction. It is, moreover, all these elements, rather than just the "in place" aspect of things, which are important. Indeed, it may be the combination of these things, rather than any one of them individually, that produces the greatest degree of distinctiveness between social groups. Thus the commitment to some idea of "village life" by certain middle-class elements is referred to a number of times in these papers. So too is the fact that this space of the village may be shared by other groups that are in no way middle-class. The social difference between these groups is sometimes characterized in terms of the distinct images and symbolisms of the village that each mobilizes. But there is also a clear differentiation between such groups (and also between genders) in terms of the wider spatiality within which this village location and imagery are set and indeed with which it interplays.[5] The "idyllic village in the mind" is in fact most likely to be found precisely in the minds of those who are more spatially mobile, those who travel abroad for holidays, who go frequently to London for business and for culture, who travel frequently and internationally as part of their working lives. The one aspect, indeed, could well be the stimulant to the existence of the other: the rapid and perhaps disorienting spatial flexibility on the one hand generating a desire for stability in place on the other. The (tentative) argument being developed here, then, is that maybe it is possible to think in terms of different social groups being characterized by distinct spatialities, where that term is used in the widest possible way – as degree of and relation to spatial flexibility, as commitment to place, as level of control over both. And, if that is so, then maybe at least some significant elements in the middle class in the UK today (I am thinking particularly of the upper echelons of professional, managerial and new petit bourgeois groups) embody in their own lives, and more than any other group in society, that tension between the global and the local (between spatial mobility on the one hand and a commitment to place on the other) about which so much is currently being written. It is, perhaps, a measure of their cultural hegemony that it is *their* experience that is taken as the sign of the times. And it is, of course, primarily they who write about it.

A second reflection on the nature of these connections between spatiality and the social is simply that geography plays an "active" role in the constitution of the social. Distinctions of spatiality and place reflect, are actively drawn upon by, and mould and reinforce other social distinctions.

Moreover, thirdly, and leading directly on from this, if the constitution of class-related social groups is, or should be interpreted as, relational (and I would argue so) then distinctions of geography most certainly fulfil this criterion. It is not only that different social groups have different social spatialities and relationships to place but that these distinct spatialities are in many ways mutually-constitutive. At the simplest level, the middle class has in general more *spatial power* than working-class groups. Such power may operate in a variety of ways: through market-power, for instance in the housing market, through greater degrees of mobility through access to transport and the availability of opportunities, and through its power over location in the employment relation (see Massey 1995a), and so forth. And in many ways this power works, and is worked, to reinforce already existing differences. The

341

importance of *distancing*, from direct production, from economic decline and der-eliction, *from the working class*; the importance of *exclusion*, from the residential area, from the employment location (the very term "exclusive" being often used in adver-tising); the importance of "seclusion"; the power of *relative* (rather than absolute) mobility in reinforcing social advantage – all of these are social relationships of geography that are established relationally with other social groups. These things are important at a range of spatial scales: within towns and cities, between urban and rural, and between the South East of the country and "the rest". Indeed, it is the combination of the social and spatial power of middle-class groups that is the most intractable problem standing in the way of addressing the gross inequalities of geographically uneven development in the UK today. Whether it be the commit-ment to certain kinds of exclusivities of place or the simple refusal of "high-level" managers and civil servants to move outside of the home counties, the mutually reinforcing social and spatial power of these groups is consistently wielded against attempts to tackle problems of spatial inequality. Between them, the upper echelons of managers and professionals more or less control the geography of employment in the UK (Massey 1995a). Earlier in this chapter it was asked on what terms the so-cial spatialities of different groups might intersect. The answer must be, at least in part, that they intersect relationally: they constitute, and reinforce the characteris-tics of, each other.

Yet how, if at all, is all this related to *class*? Much of the foregoing discussion in this chapter has been cautiously (prudently) in terms of "social groups". And even when, as in Fielding's chapter (Ch. 10), the analysis is in terms of clearly defined classes, what is demonstrated is the empirical fact of notable degrees of variation. At the em-pirical level this leaves open the question whether an even greater degree of inter-group variation in interregional mobility would have been identified between groups defined along different lines. Moreover, when a wider range of characteristics of spatiality is taken on board (other, that is, than interregional residential migration) it becomes clear not only that there is variation between subgroups of the middle class (Fielding demonstrates such variations between professional, managerial and petit bourgeois), but also that there is considerable variation at a more detailed level. The chapters in this collection amply demonstrate, and reflect upon, this point. Urry's paper (Ch. 12) considers it in some detail, and Cloke, Phillips and Thrift (Ch. 13) also identify variations. There are even greater divergences evidenced *between* the papers. Cloke, Phillips and Thrift argue that there is a close relationship between ru-rality and the middle class, whereas Butler's analysis is of gentrification in an ex-tremely *un*-rural area, in the heart of the inner city. It seems to me, therefore, that it is not possible to argue for a single geography of the middle class if this is to be defined in terms of place-outcomes (that is, the actual places chosen, whether for residence or whatever). However, such choices may be interpreted as the operationalization or non-operationalization of spatial powers, and it may be that it is the possession of these spatial powers, rather than the particular way in which they are operational-ized, that middle-class groups have in common. In other words, it may be the wider *spatialities*, in the broad definition outlined above, that the middle class coherently exhibits, rather than any particular specific set of locations.

However, if such a spatiality can be demonstrated to be a common property of the middle class in what way is that relationship established? Fielding's evidence of a clear empirical correlation, for instance, is just that. We have yet to theorize any *necessary* (constitutive) relation between the middle class and particular spatialities. Indeed it seems to me that this is very difficult to do. It may possibly be the case that spatial powers can be derived from an asset-based analysis, for instance from a combination of property and culture assets, but the connections do not seem to be very direct. On the other hand, an approach to class based in the relations of production does offer some pointers. It is evident, for instance, that the spatial flexibility of managerial and professional groups in terms of employment and residential location derives quite directly from long-term shifts in the organization of capitalist production and that the hierarchies of occupations are quite directly reflected in their geographies. The relational definitions of class in these terms, and their relational geographies, are connected and mutually reinforcing.[6] And what this represents is the operationalization of a potential, located in the social division of labour, where the division of labour is itself in part a response to the possibility of such operationalization (see above). In this sense, it would be possible to see the geographical hierarchies of professional and managerial groups as deriving from their socio-spatial causal powers and as feeding back into the process of consolidation of their social distinctiveness. It is also possible to pursue this line of analysis at a finer level of disaggregation and in particular to explore the distinction between managerial and professional groups. Thus, it can be argued that the different places of these two groups within the class schema based on relations of production (drawing on Wright 1976) produce distinct spatial potentials in relation to the geography of employment and residence (Massey 1995a). In direct reflection of their contrasting functions within the overall relations of production, and the distinct locational pressures which relate to them, whereas in the UK managers tend to be more concentrated within conurbations (and especially London), scientific professionals have the greater tendency to be in the more rural parts of the outer South East. This is a difference in geography that is noted in passing in a number of chapters here, especially in the contrasts between London and Berkshire. What I am arguing here is that it can be clearly related to differences in location within the relations of production. Such tentative suggestions, it seems to me, may offer a way forward. What they do not do, of course, is to link up with those aspects of social spatiality that go beyond the sphere of work and home location – the wider social characteristics connected with leisure, tourism and the more elaborated spatialities of social life.

The causal logic of the connection between social class and spatiality may, then, not have been fully established, and may not be there to establish. But what does seem clear is that spatiality in its widest sense is an important differentiator, and moment in the formation, of social identities more generally.

Notes

1. See, for a general analysis, Massey et al. (1992). The research that is reported on below was carried out at the Open University with Nick Henry, under the title of "High-status growth? Aspects of home and work around high-technology sectors", ESRC: R000233004.
2. This reinforces the general point made by Crompton (p.60), but extends it also into certain kinds of professional employment.
3. The relations between these occupations and the dualisms Reason–non-Reason and Transcendence–Immanence are spelled out in Massey (1995b).
4. The research is "The South East Programme", based in the Faculty of Social Sciences at the Open University and funded by the Economic and Social Research Council. "Occasional Papers" are available from the Geography Department.
5. Again this argument draws on the OU's South East research programme.
6. Savage et al. (1992) argue that a critical realist view of class relations leads to the adoption of an asset-based approach to class. I certainly agree that Savage et al.'s asset approach is compatible with a critical realist position. However, I would also contend, and it is implicit in the argument at this point, that other approaches may also be compatible – in particular here the approach based on social relations of production.

Chapter 20

Assets and the middle classes in contemporary Britain

Mike Savage and Tim Butler

20.1 Preamble

This book has considered one general issue – the contemporary relevance of class analysis in social research – in the light of one more specific issue, the general role of the middle classes in understanding various facets of social change in contemporary Britain. Readers will be able to see that, although all contributors to this volume share a commitment to the need for one form or another of class analysis, they show little agreement as to what form this analysis should take. A number of differing conceptual frameworks have been debated in this book, principally Goldthorpe's view of the service class, Marxist approaches to the middle classes, the newer "asset-based" approach, the culturalist approaches of Bourdieu and Eder, along with gender- and race-sensitive approaches to class. However, it is clear that the contributors differ in their assessment of the merits of these various perspectives.

This proliferation of views could of course be taken as a weakness, as an indication of the breakdown of any clear "class paradigm" that helps to shed light on contemporary social relations. We take a rather different view. In our view, the concept of social class retains much of its interest because of its ability to allow bridges to be built between different research traditions, conceptual approaches, methodological perspectives and political orientations so that meaningful dialogue between researchers working within different paradigms can take place (see further Savage 1994). Bauman's (1987) distinction between legislative and interpretative intellectuals is helpful in elaborating what this entails. Legislative thought is concerned with delineating what is "true" and "correct", whereas interpretative thought is more concerned to filter and translate ideas between different communities.

Of the contributions in this book, perhaps Goldthorpe's approach (along with that of his supporters such as Mills) fits most closely into the legislative camp, with its clear commitment to distinguish class from other social phenomena so that its salience can be tested and empirical adjudication. On the other hand, the arguments of Crompton, Witz, Massey, Urry, Cloke et al., as well as several others, are more concerned to emphasize the ambiguities of class, the difficulty of locating it in only one dimension, and the "messiness" of its connections with other social phenomena. For these writers the topic of "class" operates within Bauman's interpretative paradigm, by exploring interconnections between diverse social phenomena.

In the spirit of this interpretive perspective we do not attempt to "sum up" the book in our conclusion. Rather, we offer a "partial" conclusion, which should be read alongside those of Goldthorpe (Ch. 18) and Massey (Ch. 19). Given that one of the themes that several contributors have examined has been the applicability of the "asset-based" approach to the middle classes, and given that one of the editors of this book has defended such a perspective in earlier work (Savage et al. 1992), this seems the place to consider more directly what implications the articles in this book have for its current relevance.

This conclusion has three sections. We begin by returning to some of the broad conceptual issues in class analysis that were raised in Chapters 1 and 2 and taken up by various other papers, in order to consider how the asset-based approach to class avoids existing pitfalls in class analysis. In section 20.3 we examine the changing relationship between class and employment, a point that has surfaced in various papers in this volume and warrants fuller discussion here. Finally, in section 20.4 we consider, in more empirical vein, how the middle classes are changing in the light of the various findings reported in this book, as well as elsewhere.

20.2 The asset-based approach to the middle classes

As David Lockwood mentions in Chapter 1, the "classic" problematic of class has been traditionally couched within a historical teleology. Both Marxist and Weberian approaches to social class anchored their account of class in what might be termed a "meta-narrative" of historical change and development. Thus changes to the class structure and class relationships more generally were locked into macro-based accounts of historical development – such as proletarianization in the case of Marx, bureaucratization and rationalization in the case of Weber, and so on (see also Goldthorpe & Marshall 1992). Lockwood himself discusses how the class formation problematic was originally designed to explore the way in which the working class gained entry to citizenship rights, and (amongst other issues) poses the question as to whether or not this problematic is useful for considering middle-class formation, given that the middle classes have not had to fight hard battles to gain inclusion. He therefore suggests the problems of a class analysis rooted in what he terms "the problematic of the proletariat", where the proletariat has never lived up to its Marxist-inspired mission – and wonders where the subsequent dissolution of the "class-in-itself" and " class-for-itself" paradigm leaves class analysis itself.

Interestingly, Goldthorpe also raises the issue of history in his work (Goldthorpe 1991, 1994, and Ch. 18), but largely in order to argue that the historical dimension to class analysis should not be given prime focus, especially if it carries with it a teleological, historicist baggage (see also Goldthorpe & Marshall 1992). One problem, of course, with the sorts of teleological accounts Goldthorpe criticizes is that they tend to endorse the view that members of classes are bound to be the historical bearers of class interests and goals, with the result that class analysis itself takes on a deterministic character that most contributors in this book would wish to distance themselves from.

In our view it is essential to develop a form of class analysis that avoids historicism of this type. However, it also remains important not to throw out the baby with the bathwater, by disregarding the connections between social change and social class *per se*. Indeed, one of the unifying facets of the various papers in this book is their common concern with examining historical change over the past 30 years or so. The quantitative papers (Mills, Ch. 6; Fielding, Ch. 10; Warde and Tomlinson, Ch. 14; Heath and Savage, Ch. 16) have all compared surveys carried out at different times to ground their analyses of change. Many of the qualitative papers have also centred their analysis on historical change, for instance Urry's account of the countryside (Ch. 12), Carter and Fairbrother's analysis of the Civil Service (Ch. 8), and so forth. The asset-based approach, we contend, is of considerable value in facilitating historical, but not historicist, analyses. This is because it roots class relations in the specific social mechanisms producing and sustaining social inequality, but not in a macro-social structure with teleological dynamics that can then be said to determine the future course of class relations. Various class assets are not themselves constituted at the macro level (although their operation and reproduction may depend upon the existence of appropriate macro-institutional forces such as the nation-state, as suggested by the Regulationist school of Marxism) but can exist at a variety of spatial and social scales. Further, the extent to which class assets are common in any society, the way they may or may not give rise to the social collectivities that can be called social classes and the extent to which they shape other social processes cannot be pre-ordained and need to be ascertained in the course of social research. One great advantage this leads to, we would maintain, is that we can be made aware of issues of agency (both individual and collective), because social actors themselves make (or do not make) assets salient in their everyday life.

A further advantage is suggested here. Currently, opinion is divided between those (notably Goldthorpe, Ch. 18) arguing for the perpetuation, or, at most, consolidation, of long-standing patterns of social inequality, and those who point to the onset of dramatic social and economic change in the past two decades or so that have fundamentally transformed the social relations of capitalist societies such as Britain, a view developed in a variety of forms recently, for instance in accounts of postmodernity (Harvey 1987), or reflexive modernity (Beck 1992). Urry's paper (Ch. 12), and that of Cloke et al. (Ch. 13), are the clearest elaborations of this perspective in this volume (see also Lash & Urry 1994). Readers will see, however, that most of the empirical contributions in this volume offer hybrid accounts that point neither to fundamental change nor to stability. The task appears to be that of exploring change and continuity simultaneously, rather than as alternatives. Here, we would argue that a crucial advantage of the asset approach is that it can offer valuable tools to conceptualize both continuity and change. This is due to the fact that the asset-based approach is interested in exploring the ways in which particular assets allow privileges to be stored and so transmitted to future generations (and here we have many points of agreement with Goldthorpe's own discussion in this volume), but it is also attentive to the way in which assets can be "traded" by social actors, and also to the way in which differing historical circumstances may alter the way in which assets can be drawn upon by social actors, leading to different types of social collectivity. We argue that this conceptual schema makes it possible to find a middle way between a recognition of stability and continuity on the one hand, and of change and dynamism on the other.

There is another issue here that should be considered alongside time and history, and that is the question of space. It is noteworthy that Goldthorpe, who emphasizes continuity, says nothing about space in his conclusion, whereas those who emphasize change do so largely by stressing spatial upheavals current in recent times. Some writers articulate this as the extension of "time–space compression" (Harvey 1987), others as the "emptying out" of objects from places (Lash & Urry 1994). No matter. What is significant is that those who use a theoretical framework that offers no purchase on the significance of space for social relations are more likely to miss one of the possible ways in which contemporary societies are being transformed, a point that may help account for Goldthorpe's position. If the nation of Britain is taken as the unit of analysis, then it may be the case that change appears limited, but this may ignore the extent to which Britain may be becoming a less salient entity, both as a result of globalization and also owing to the character of local and regional restructuring as well as to the changing dynamics of spatial mobility possible with enhanced transportation and communication facilities. Indeed, it is clear from the papers examining the spatial aspects of middle-class formation in contemporary Britain that classness is bound up with relationships to place and space, and increasingly that places are important not simply as communities, as sites of residence of particular classes (the way they have usually been seen in sociology), but as places visited, gazed at, represented and so forth (see Massey's remarks in Ch. 19).

Again, we would maintain that an attractive feature of the assets approach is that it recognizes that classes are not formed "on the head of a pin". Assets differ in the extent to which they are spatially mobile. Property, in the form of stocks and shares is highly mobile; organizational structures are mobile but rather less flexibly; while it might be argued that cultural distinctions are still largely rooted in specific national cultures and education systems and can only with difficulty be moved (see, for instance, Lamont 1991 on the ingrained differences between French and American middle-class cultural values), though even here there are some tendencies towards a more global, cosmopolitan culture. Just as we would insist on the need to recognize continuity with change, so we would emphasize (along with Harvey 1985) that spatial fixity and mobility are interdependent.

It should be clear that we view one of the main attractions of the asset approach as its ability to articulate an analysis of class that is sensitive to issues of temporality and spatiality. But this is a defence of the asset approach that judges it by its implications rather than by its direct theoretical claims. So we now turn to consider the merits of the asset approach head on. In summary, we would see its strength as lying in its relational perspective on class, which allows theoretical approaches to class to avoid becoming merely descriptive summaries of degrees of advantage and disadvantage. Thus to say that people draw upon organizational assets, for instance, does not simply mean that managers are better off than their employees (though in practice they do indeed tend to be), but rather that the advantaged position of such managers is crucially tied to the subordination of others, so that the two are interdependent and necessary to each other. There is an interesting point of contrast here with John Goldthorpe's defence of the service-class concept in this volume (Ch. 18), which also stresses the relational character of class. For Goldthorpe, the difference between the service class and other employees does not rest in the direct relationship between these two groups themselves, but in their respective relationships to their employers (with employees being employed on a labour contract, the salariat on a service contract). This formulation is not one that we subscribe to for reasons elaborated elsewhere (see Savage et al. 1992), but here the main point we wish to make is that Goldthorpe's analysis does not allow any direct relationship between the salariat and employees to be delineated (see also Wright 1985: 84).

Let us now pose an objection to the asset-based approach, that is that it contains a certain imprecision as to how assets are to be theoretically recognized as assets. Why do we select property, cultural and organizational assets as being the crucial ones we use in our analysis of the middle classes? And how do we distinguish an asset from any form of social advantage? The original articulation of the assets approach was loosely couched within rational choice theory, and argued that assets could be defined as the process which allowed "one person's welfare to be obtained at the expense of another" (Wright 1985: 65). This definition begs many questions, notably how do we know when one person's welfare is obtained at the expense of another (see the general discussion in Carling 1990, Wright 1989b, Mills 1994)? In our view the looseness of this definition is not, in fact, a great problem. It is actually unhelpful to try and define *a priori* what specific criteria must be met, because this is to prejudge the issue and to create one "benchmark" form of exploitation against which all others must be measured. In general accordance with the methodology of critical or theoretical realism (e.g. Sayer 1984, Layder 1990), research should be able to show how specific sorts of social inequalities can plausibly be shown to be the product of given causal processes operating under certain conditions, a process that involves both theoretical reasoning about the necessary relations involved in processes of exploitation, and the appropriate empirical research that is able to detect that the proposed effects can indeed be found in situations where the appropriate conditions exist.

This may sound rather vague, but in fact it is the only alternative to theoreticist definitions of class on the one hand, or purely descriptive accounts on the other. A good example of how this reasoning can be used to improve our understanding of assets concerns the delineation of the "skill assets" that Wright (1985) saw as being one asset underlying class formation. However, as various commentators pointed out, and as Wright (1989b) himself came to recognize, it is difficult to determine how someone with a skill in short supply directly exploits those without this skill –

no direct relational process can helpfully be delineated. Savage et al. (1992) suggested that it is more helpful to invoke Bourdieu's conception of cultural capital, which seems better able to explain how those who claimed cultural distinction did so by excluding those other cultures as "low" cultures. In this case there is a distinct mechanism connecting the privileging of one group through the exclusion of another. But of course this formulation is also open to challenge; see, for instance, the critical comments of Cloke et al. in relation to Bourdieu in Chapter 13.

This brings us to another serious issue in class analysis that has been rehearsed in this book – the relationship between class, gender and ethnicity. The asset approach has two main features. First, it agrees that patriarchal and ethnic bases of domination have their own independent axes, which run throughout the social spectrum, and which should be distinguished from class assets. These can exercise a powerful influence on how classes form. Secondly, the various class assets do not operate in gendered or ethnically neutral ways. In particular, organizational assets tend to be more difficult for women and ethnic minorities to draw upon than cultural assets. Both Crompton (Ch. 14), and Phillips and Sarre (Ch. 5) bring interesting evidence to bear on these arguments, which in general supports this claim. Both women and black people have moved into the middle class primarily by credentialist means or by utilizing petty property.

Of course we do not claim that the delineation of property, bureaucracy and culture is exhaustive, or that these three are symmetrical in their significance. Indeed, it is precisely the lack of symmetricality that makes them interesting not only to researchers, but also to social actors themselves! But we do wish to resist the "legislative" temptation to find *one* crucial template that defines social class.

A crucial point here is that the delineation of class assets is not the same thing as actually being able to distinguish classes defined as social collectivities. From the point of view of class analysis it is as important to consider how processes producing inequalities lead to social collectivities as to multiply the possible axes amongst which such inequalities can be generated. Thus, it could be claimed that right-handed people gain at the expense of left-handed ones, so that "handedness" should be seen as an asset too. And, indeed, there is evidence that the life expectancy of left-handers is markedly lower than that of right-handers, and that some of this difference is due to the way that technologies devised for right-handers are more likely to cause accidents and death to left-handers (notably in road accidents) (see Coren 1992). However, even given this, it would be difficult to claim that handedness has generated distinct social collectivities of left-handed and right-handed people who identify with each other, develop distinct cultural outlooks, organize politically, and so forth. Theoretically such a possibility can perhaps be held open, but we know of little evidence for the existence of such collectivities. Why should this be? Part of the answer is that left-handedness is a relatively "invisible" stigma, not as directly visible as gender, ethnicity or disability. But of course "visibility" is itself socially constructed, and needs explanation as well. Since handedness tends not to be created by social institutions, but appears to be largely the product of factors connected with traumas in pregnancy, there are no social situations that tend to bring people of the same handedness routinely together as there are when more direct social mechanisms produce or are implicated in inequality.

Now of course it can be argued that boundaries between "natural" and "social" mechanisms, never easily determined at the best of times, are becoming increasingly permeable with developments in bio-technology and the like (e.g. Harraway 1990), with the result that there may indeed be interesting changes in the way handedness becomes socially significant. The main point here, however, is to suggest that a key avenue of exploration is the differing propensity of various class assets to give rise to social collectivities, and that a central feature of such a project involves examining, for each asset under consideration, how precisely it may facilitate forms of class formation.

20.3 Occupations, employment and class

This leads us to one of the crucial current issues in class analysis, the link between employment and class. Traditionally in British social science, classes have been defined in occupational, or at least employment-based, terms. Such a view has been consistent with both Marxist and Weberian theoretical emphases and has allowed dialogue between Marxists and Weberians to occur in recent years in terms of debating the best system of grouping occupations and/or employment positions into classes (see Marshall et al. 1988, Wright 1985b, 1989b). However, it is ironic that, just as this exercise has reached unparalleled sophistication, there have been growing claims that actually social classes are not necessarily based simply in employment. One of the general issues discussed in many papers of this book is whether it is useful or helpful to continue to regard classes as primarily employment-based entities. The claim that paid work is becoming a less central feature of contemporary societies is of course a fairly common one today (e.g. Saunders 1990, Beck 1992, Gorz 1989) – although it has been contested (Marshall et al. 1988) – and it may be that, if classes are to be defined in employment terms, their relevance will decline as work itself loses its social and personal significance. Recently, Crompton (1993) has argued that class analysis should not be conceived as concerned only with what she terms "employment aggregates", and contends that other traditions should be given greater prominence.

A number of important issues are relevant here. One, which has been well rehearsed in discussions in this book and elsewhere, is concerned with the complexity of placing a household in a class relation when two or more of its members are employed (see Chs 3, 4 and 18 for some discussion of this point). The paper by Gregson and Lowe (Ch. 9) also shows that many of the middle classes are both employed and employers (of domestic labour). In short, focusing upon work and employment relations may actually produce rather fuzzy and ill-defined classes. But there is a more radical critique, which in this book is found particularly in those papers concerned with place and space. Urry (Ch. 12) points out that as the meaning and nature of work change in contemporary society (and see also Urry 1990), and in particular as growing numbers of people have little, or only indirect, contact to the labour market, class itself becomes less salient. In particular, the traditional view of the countryside as a "rural idyll" defined in contrast to the middle-class workplace becomes less relevant with the development of new sociations and activities. Cloke et al. (Ch. 13) also point to the "cultural textures" of class attitudes, practices and values that the middle classes (as well as other social groups) have towards the countryside. Other contributors also develop arguments that suggest further support for this proposition. Butler (Ch. 11) suggests that identification with inner urban living plays an important cultural role for particular middle-class fractions. Rather than gentrification being the reflex of occupational change, Butler shows that inner urban location is a means of articulating and publicizing identities of a "radical", mature fraction of the middle class. Bagguley's (Ch. 17) emphasis upon how middle-class individuals themselves choose certain jobs to fit in with their political and cultural outlooks also suggests that occupations should be seen as the product, rather than the cause, of the relevant social processes.

It would be premature, however, to claim that this perspective has shown that occupation is of limited significance. Thus, in an area – food consumption – that one might imagine to be increasingly independent of occupational class, Warde and Tomlinson (Ch. 14) in fact show that food consumption appears still very largely correlated with occupationally derived social classes, with hardly any change in recent years towards greater independence. Hamnett (Ch. 15) shows that, although housing tenure and property assets more generally are not simply derived from occupational class, there continue to be clear employment-based differences both in housing tenure and more specifically in the extent of capital accumulation and inheritance prospects over time. Such evidence should also be read along with that suggesting the perpetuation of clear class differences in attitudes, political orientations, and practices documented by Marshall et al. (1988), Heath et al. (1985), and Goldthorpe with Lewellyn & Payne (1987) (see also Crompton 1993).

None the less, although it is premature to write off occupation as a key focus for the study of social class, it would appear that to conflate class with employment is unduly restrictive. The asset approach suggests a resolution to this tension. As we have explained above, the asset approach is not committed to the idea that processes of class exploitation are necessarily based in employment relations, and indeed the idea of cultural assets, derived from Bourdieu's notion of cultural capital, directly points to the ways that forms of social advantage may be constructed in other social fields. None the less, it can be argued that the labour market is still important in crucial ways for constructing and perpetuating class privilege.

First, it is one of the principal ways in which class assets can be translated into material rewards. There are other ways, notably the property market, which tend to have been remarkably ignored in much class analysis (see Scase 1992), but it remains true that most individuals need to activate class assets in the labour market. Admittedly, some sociologists have emphasized the way that the purchase of domestic property allows households to accumulate money in ways that are not directly linked to the labour markets (notably Saunders 1990). One of the merits of

Hamnett's chapter is that it allows some quantitative assessment of the importance of domestic property for securing material rewards to be gauged. If a particularly favourable cohort for the Saunders hypothesis is chosen, those who bought their first house in 1976–7, it would appear that they have accumulated around £5,000 a year in "mean illusory gain". This is a considerable amount, but, set against the salary earned by the same households (possibly with two separate incomes), it is clearly of secondary significance. It also has to be recognized that Hamnett's "mean illusory gain" figure does not take into account the money paid back by households in mortgage and other repayments. In short, although one should not overlook the ways that capital gains can be accrued through owner-occupation, it seems that the majority of people still depend primarily on the labour market. No firm evidence is available on this point, but it is likely that a similar conclusion would apply to the significance of gains through stock dealing (we are, of course, excluding the small, propertied capitalist classes from this analysis).

Secondly, labour markets are key social fields in which people can try to gain or augment assets or try to trade them. Labour markets allow people to make contacts and so develop social networks, gain skills, and elevate their position in organizational hierarchies. They are thus a key field for the deployment and acquisition of class assets. Furthermore, specific jobs have historically been constructed in Britain – as in all other capitalist societies – as being continuous in their nature. That is to say, when an individual is recruited to a job, they are expected to stay in that specific job until such a time as they are moved, or move, to a different job or made redundant. In short, jobs have historically been a primary means of "storing" structured inequalities by offering expectations to their incumbents that in general their current conditions, remuneration, and so forth will be routinely renewed and will not need to be constantly renegotiated and contested.

But this, of course, is dependent upon specific institutional arrangements that are themselves subject to historical change. And here it is possible to argue that current social changes are tending to make some kinds of occupations less robust bearers of class privilege than historically they have been, and are therefore tending to reduce, though unevenly, the salience of the labour market as the crucial axis that underscores class formation. In particular, the restructuring of bureaucratic organizations, notably downsizing, delayering and so forth, linked to the changing dynamics of capitalist accumulation, as well as changing state policy, may be affecting the central role of occupation in middle-class formation. We now turn to consider the evidence on this point directly.

20.4 Labour markets and the changing middle classes?

It should be clear from the foregoing discussion that the asset-based approach should not be seen as concerned with providing an occupational or employment-based class schema to set against alternatives, such as the Nuffield class schema. Occupations are not to be seen as the automatic embodiment of particular assets, for instance where managers are assumed to draw upon organizational assets and professionals upon cultural assets. The extent to which particular occupations may legitimately be seen as drawing upon particular assets varies, and here we also strongly echo Goldthorpe's point concerning the inherent possibility of "slippage between concept and practice". In *Property, bureaucracy and culture*, Savage et al. (1992) argue that in Britain, for reasons to do with the historical development of the middle classes, the distinction between professionals and management has indeed mapped onto a significant difference in the types of assets drawn upon, but it is emphasized that there is no intrinsic reason that this should be so, and they suggest that the situation is different in other countries.

So what, if anything, has actually changed? A common public perception of the middle classes is that they have, in the past five years or so, become increasingly beleaguered. Whereas the early and especially mid-1980s were seen as a period of middle-class expansion and prosperity, the recession of the later 1980s is often thought to have ushered in a period of middle-class anxiety, retreat and retrenchment. Some of the specific features of this apparent shift in middle-class fortunes were the downturn in the housing market, which appeared to leave many middle-class (and other) households with a dwindling asset, and the redundancies of white-collar workers, especially in the financial service industries. But at a more general level it is possible to argue that occupations, as well as "career ladders", have become more diffuse and less secure (see the discussion in Halford and Savage, Ch. 7 in this volume).

Of course, it is easy to exaggerate the extent to which the middle classes have really suffered, compared with other social groups. Although many of the papers do not report research recent enough to cast light on the recession of the later 1980s, the papers by Fielding (Ch. 10) and Hamnett (Ch. 15) give some interesting indications on this matter. Table 10.1 shows that it remained twice as likely for blue-collar workers in 1981 to have become unemployed in 1991 (by which time the supposed white-collar recession was well under way) as it was for white-collar workers. It is, admittedly, difficult to specify the precise impact of the recession because the ten-year period 1981–91 also included a period when the middle-classes flourished. However, at the very least it appears that, even if the recession of the later 1980s caused short-term problems for some middle-class individuals, these do not appear to contradict the long-term expansion of their employment opportunities. Indeed, Fielding's comparison of the 1971–81 period with the 1981–91 period suggests that it was considerably less likely for both men and women to move down into lower social classes in the later compared with the earlier period.

However, Table 10.1 and Table 10.7 of Fielding's analysis also suggest the need to distinguish between the fortunes of professional and managerial employees. Savage et al. (1992) argued that whereas those relying on cultural assets, notably professional workers, were enjoying increased opportunities in the 1980s with the marketization of producer services and the externalization of organizational functions, those relying simply on organizational assets, notably line managers of various kinds, were being hit by the declining salience of bureaucratic organizations as firms restructured to enhance their flexibility. This argument, especially concerning the "squeeze" on middle managers, is of course one that has wide currency (see Scase & Goffee 1989). And, indeed, Fielding's analysis shows that it was nearly twice as likely for managers than professionals to become unemployed between 1981 and 1991, and it was considerably more likely for managers to be downwardly mobile into routine white-collar or blue-collar employment. The rising number of managers moving into self-employment is also striking. Altogether 24% of managers in 1981 had experienced downward mobility (i.e. mobility into manual or routine white-collar work, or unemployment) by 1991, compared with around 14% of professionals.

This observation leads us to one of the most interesting claims arising out of Mills's paper on work-life mobility (Ch. 6). Mills's analysis of Glass's 1949 dataset shows clearly the marked historical differences between professional and managerial careers, but the evidence from the 1986 SCEL study suggests the blurring of such boundaries in the period since the Second World War, an argument which tends to support Goldthorpe's characterization of the service class as becoming more demographically unified as it matures, and the idea that the "situs" distinction between professionals and management is declining. Fielding's analysis, on the other hand, using the OPCS Longitudinal Study, suggests rather different conclusions. He shows that over the period 1981–91 it continued to be much more likely for managers and especially professionals to stay in their situs group rather than to move to the other. Over two-thirds of people in professional employment in 1981 who were still in the labour market in 1991 remained in professional employment – a figure higher than for any other group Fielding distinguishes. Why this apparent difference of opinion? Mills's unit of analysis is the "transition" from one job to another, whereas Fielding's is the mobility of individuals in a fixed ten-year interval (1981–91). Mills's evidence on transitions does not itself indicate how common are transitions of any type in an individual's work life, and therefore should be used carefully for considering questions of demographic class formation. This is so for two reasons. First, transition data may include several transitions by the same individual moving between jobs (possibly from professionals to management or vice versa) and hence may rather skew results towards the careers of possibly unusual, highly mobile, individuals. Although it is of obvious interest to explore such "careers" in their own right, there is a danger that the general or typical patterns are obscured (for further discussions of the complexities of analyzing work-life data, see Abbott & Hrycak 1990). Secondly, those people who do not move jobs will not be included in the analysis at all. On the other hand, Fielding's analysis may be skewed towards stressing stability because he uses data on an individual's job at two moments in time, which means that any intermediate job moves will not be registered. None the less, we would contend that his analysis remains rather more useful for considering aggregate patterns of demographic class formation.

There is a further point to make here. Although the aggregate mobility between professionals and managers is interesting, it would also be important to consider whether such movement is random or whether it is structured in any significant way. Thus, if it is younger rather than older managers who are becoming professionals, this might suggest that, rather than the situs divisions becoming blurred, they are in fact being structured on an increasingly hierarchical basis, with many management positions being simply stepping points to more secure professional ones.

It is for this reason that it is extremely interesting to note that Mills and Fielding do concur on a finding relevant to this issue. Whereas historically it was rather unusual for managers to become professionals, recently it has become much more likely for this transition to occur, and indeed it is now more likely for managers to become professionals than vice versa. It would appear that professional employment is more permeable to those who start their working lives outside it than it has traditionally been. Mills argues that this reflects the changing character of professional employment, and in particular the expansion of professional employment away from the "core", still largely closed, professions such as law, medicine and accountancy. Such findings are also consistent with the idea that professionals are less inclined to move into management as their range of professional opportunities increases with the marketization of welfare services, while managers find the lower rungs of the professions more permeable. Mills's and Fielding's analyses may seem rather different in their arguments, but none the less may be consistent with each other.

Returning to general issues about middle-class formation, one obvious point stands out from the foregoing discussion. Managers as an occupational group are indeed becoming increasingly unstable and volatile. This is something of an historical departure. As Mills (Ch. 6) shows and as Savage et al. (1992: Ch. 3) also discuss, the traditional managerial career involved people being promoted from white-collar or manual positions, but, once they had attained managerial status, having good prospects of remaining in management and enhancing their position through "climbing the ladder". Such prospects do appear to be seriously under question today as growing numbers of managers are either downwardly mobile or move into professional positions. Given that it would appear to be particularly white men who have benefited from such hierarchies, this also raises important questions about the extent to which there may well be significant shifts in the position of ethnic minorities and blacks within the middle classes.

What all these arguments suggest is that the British middle classes are increasingly being re-made around two core groups: a professional middle class and a self-employed group, with others being squeezed between them. An interesting indication of this is to turn (once again!) to Fielding's paper and observe that Table 10.1 shows that the three least common transitions between 1981 and 1991 were, first, from professional employment to unemployment (2.76%), secondly, from professional employment to self-employment (3.4%); and, thirdly, from petit bourgeois status to professional employment (4.11%). These figures are suggestive only, and are affected in various ways by the marginal totals, but are none the less intriguing. Moreover, the marginalization of managerial workers is not confined to the field of employment. Warde and Tomlinson's chapter (Ch. 14) concerning the indistinct-ness of managerial groups in terms of food consumption offers an interesting indication of this point.

For this reason, it appears that Kanter's recent observations about American career patterns may also be increasingly pertinent to the British case. "The locus for careers", she writes, "is not the institution but the person's own professional base and network of contacts. Bureaucratic careers in large organizations are becoming increasingly less prevalent than professional and entrepreneurial careers, in which people count on their own know-how and skill at making connections to provide security, even when they are employed by large organizations" (Kanter 1993: 290). Even allowing for the "management language" evident in the above, there does seem an important argument here – that many sections of the middle classes trust their employers less and instead are turning to build up a personal "portfolio" of skills, contacts, dispositions and the like that they attempt to carry with them. What this points to is the possibility that middle-class formation will increasingly be defined in "civil society", through associational and leisure activity, and also that, as Urry suggests in Chapter 12, this may also change the terrain on which classes form and contest with each other.

Having made these points, it is perhaps worth concluding on one speculative matter (which echoes an observation made by David Lockwood in his Introduction). Although we have argued that many managers have lost out in recent changes, it seems likely that the most senior managers of large organizations actually have enhanced power. Such senior managers are also increasingly likely to be significant property owners of their organizations, through devices such as share options, and also may well come from professional backgrounds. In short, it may be that a new class elite is forming amongst a small cadre who can mobilize organization, property and cultural assets simultaneously. If true, these developments may suggest the emergence of more distinct hierarchical divisions within the British middle class, and the creation of a more cohesive "power elite". But this must be the subject of future research.

Bibliography

Abbott, P. & R. Sapsford 1987. *Women and social class*. London: Tavistock.

Abbott, A. & A. Hrycak 1990. Measuring resemblance in sequence data: an optimal matching analysis of musicians careers. *American Journal of Sociology* **96**(1), 144–85.

Abercrombie, N. & J. Urry 1983. *Capital, labour and the middle classes*. London: Allen & Unwin.

Abercrombie, N. & A. Warde with K. Soothill, J. Urry , S. Walby 1994. *Contemporary British society*, 2nd edn. Cambridge: Polity.

Acker, J. 1973. Women and social stratification: a case of intellectual sexism. *American Journal of Sociology* **78**(4), 936–45.

Ackroyd, S., A. J. Hughes, K. Soothill, 1989. Public sector services and their management. *Journal of Management Studies* **26**(6), 603–19.

Adler, J. 1989. Origins of sightseeing. *Annals of Tourism Research* **16**, 7–29.

Aglietta, M. 1979. *A theory of capitalist regulation: the US experience*. London: New Left Books.

Aldrich, H., T. Jones, D. McEvoy 1984. Ethnic advantage and minority business development. In *Ethnic communities in business: strategies for economic survival* R. Ward & R. Jenkins (eds), 189–210. Cambridge: Cambridge University Press.

Allen, J. & L. McDowell 1989. *Landlords and property: social relations in the private sector*. Cambridge: Cambridge University Press.

Allen, S. 1982. Gender inequality and class formation. In *Social class and the division of labour*, A. Giddens & G. MacKenzie (eds), 137–47. Cambridge: Cambridge University Press.

Althauser, R. P. & A. L. Kalleberg 1981. Firms, occupations and the structure of labor markets: a sociological analysis. In *Sociological perspectives on labor markets*, I. Berg (ed.), 119–49. New York: Academic.

Amin, A. 1994. *Post-Fordism: a reader*. Oxford: Blackwell.

Anderson, P. 1980. *Arguments within English Marxism*. London: Verso.

Anthias, F. & N. Yuval-Davies 1992. *Racialized boundaries*. London: Routledge.

Archer, M. 1987. *Culture and agency: the place of culture in social theory*. Cambridge: Cambridge University Press.

Atkinson, A. B., J. P. Gordan, A. Harrison 1989. Trends in the shares of top wealth holders in Britain, 1923–1981. *Oxford Bulletin of Economics and Statistics* **51**, 315–32.

Atkinson, J. 1984. Manpower strategies for flexible organizations. *Personnel Management*. August, 28–31.

Aygeman, J. 1989. Black people, white landscape. *Town and Country Planning Association* **58**, 338–48.

Badcock, B. 1992. Adelaide's heart transplant, 1970–88: 3. The deployment of capital in the renovation and redevelopment submarkets. *Environment and Planning A* **24**, 1167–90.

—1993. Notwithstanding the exaggerated claims, residential revitalization really is changing the form of some western cities: a response to Bourne. *Urban Studies* **30**, 191–5.

Bagguley, P. 1992. Social change, the middle class and the emergence of "new social movements": a critical analysis. *Sociological Review* **40**, 26–48.

Bagguley, P., J. Mark-Lawson, D. Shapiro, J. Urry, S. Walby, A. Warde 1990. *Restructuring: place, class and gender*. London: Sage.

Bailyn, L. 1978. Accommodation of work to family. In *Working couples*, R. Rapoport & R.N. Rapoport (eds), 159–74. New York: Harper & Row.

Ball, M. 1982. Housing provision and the economic crisis. *Capital and Class* **17**, 60–77.

—1985. Coming to terms with owner-occupation. *Capital and Class* **24**, 15–44.

Banks, J. A. 1954. *Prosperity and parenthood*. London: Routledge & Kegan Paul.

Barbalet, J. M. (1986). Limitations of class theory and the disappearance of status: the problem of the new middle class. *Sociology* **20**, 557–575.

Barlow, J. & S. S. Duncan 1988. The use and abuse of housing tenure. *Housing Studies* **3**, 219–31.

Barrett, M. 1980. *Women's oppression today*. London: Verso.

Bauman, Z. 1985. Social class. Dictionary entry in *Encyclopedia of the Social Sciences*. London: Routledge.

—1987. *Legislators and interpreters: on modernity, post-modernity and the intellectuals*. Cambridge: Cambridge University Press.

—1991. *Intimations of postmodernity*. London: Routledge.

Beck, U. 1992. *The risk society*. London: Sage.

Bell, C. 1968. *Middle class families: social and geographical mobility*. London: Routledge & Kegan Paul.

Bell, D. 1973. *The coming of post industrial society*. New York: Basic Books.

—1974. *The coming of post-industrial society*. London: Heinemann.

Bender, B. 1993. Stonehenge – contested landscapes. In *Landscape: politics and perspectives*, B. Bender (ed.), 245–80. Oxford: Berg.

Benefits Agency. 1992. *Benefits Agency annual report 1991/1992*. London: DSS Benefits Agency.

Benn, T. 1989. *Against the tide, diaries 1973–1976*. London: Hutchinson.

Berens, C. 1993. Tribal Britain. *The Independent*. (London), 12 November.

Berger, P. 1987. *The capitalist revolution*. Aldershot: Wildwood House.

Berger, P. A. & S. Hradil 1990. Die Modernisierung sozialer Ungleichheit – und die neuen Konturen ihrer Erforschung. In *Soziale Welt, Sonderband 7: Lebenslagen, Lebensläufe, Lebensstile*, P. A. Berger & S. Hradil (eds), 3–26. Göttingen: Verlag Otto Schwartz.

Beynon, H., R. Hudson, D. Sadler 1992. *A tale of two industries*. Milton Keynes: Open University Press.

—1994. *A place called Teesside: a locality in a global economy*. Edinburgh: Edinburgh University Press.

Birchall, I., 1974. *Workers against the monolith*. London: Pluto.

Blackburn, R. & M. Mann 1979. *The working class in the labour market*. London: Macmillan.

Blau, P. 1966. *The dynamics of bureaucracy*. Chicago and London: University of Chicago Press.

Blau, P. & O. D. Duncan 1967. *The American occupational structure*. New York: John Wiley.

Blunden, J. & N. Curry 1988. *A future for our countryside*. Oxford: Basil Blackwell.

Bonacich, E. 1973. A theory of middleman minorities. *American Sociological Review* **38**, 583–94.

Bondi, L. 1991. Gender divisions and gentrification: a critique. *Transactions of the Institute of*

British Geographers N.S. **16**, 190–8.

Bourdieu, P. 1984. *Distinction: a social critique of the judgement of taste*. London: Routledge & Kegan Paul.

—1987. What makes a social class? On the theoretical and practical existence of groups. *Berkeley Journal of Sociology* **32**, 1–17.

—1993. Concluding remarks: for a sociogenetic understanding of intellectual works. In *Bourdieu: critical perspectives*, C. Calhoun, E. LiPuma, M. Postone (eds), 263–75. Oxford: Blackwell.

Bourdieu, P. & L. Wacquant 1992. *An invitation to reflexive sociology*. Cambridge: Polity Press.

Bourne, L. 1993a. Close together and worlds apart: an analysis of changes in the ecology of income in Canadian cities. *Urban Studies* **30**, 1293–1317.

—1993b. The demise of gentrification? A commentary and prospective view. *Urban Geography* **14**, 95–107.

Bowman, M. 1993. Drawn to Glastonbury. In *Pilgrimage in popular culture*, I. Reader & T. Walter (eds) 29–62. London: Macmillan.

Boys, J. 1990. Women and the designed environment: dealing with difference. *Built Environment* **16**, 249–56.

Bradley, H. 1990. *Men's work, women's work*. Cambridge: Polity.

Brah, A. & S. Shaw 1993. Working choices: South Asian young Muslim women and the labour market. Employment Department Research Paper no. 91.

Braverman, H. 1974. *Labor and monopoly capital: the degradation of work in the twentieth century*. New York: Monthly Review Press.

Braybon, G. 1980. *Women workers in the first world war*. Brighton: Wheatsheaf.

Brennan J. & P. McGeevor 1990. *Ethnic minorities and the graduate labour market*. London: CRE Publications.

Brennan, T. 1993. *History after Lacan*. London: Routledge.

Brint, S. 1984. "New class" and cumulative trend explanations of the liberal political attitudes of professionals. *American Journal of Sociology* **90**, 30–71.

Bristow, M. & B. Adams 1977. Ugandan Asians and the housing market in Britain. *New Community* **6**, 65–77.

Britten, N. & A. Heath 1983. Women, men and social class. In *Gender, class and work*, E. Gamarnikow, D. Morgan, J. Purvis, D. Taylorson (eds), 46–60. London: Heinemann.

Brooks, C. & J. Manza 1994. The changing middle class voter, 1972–1992. Paper presented to the American Sociological Association, Los Angeles.

Brown, C. 1984. *Black and white Britain*. London: Heinemann.

Bruce Biggs, B. (ed.) 1979. *The new class?* San Diego: Harcourt Brace Jovanovich.

Buck, N., J. Gershuny, D. Rose, J. Scott (eds) 1994. *Changing households: the British household panel study 1990–1992*. Colchester: University of Essex, ESRC Research Centre on Micro-Social Change.

Bulmer, M. (ed.) 1975. *Working class images of society*. London: Routledge.

Bunce, M. 1994. *The countryside ideal*. London: Routledge.

Burawoy, M. 1985. *The politics of production*. London: Verso.

Burnett, J. 1978. *A social history of housing 1815–1970*. London: Methuen.

Burrows, R. & C. Marsh 1992. *Consumption and class, divisions and change*. Basingstoke: Macmillan.

Butler, J. 1990. *Gender trouble*. London: Routledge.

Butler, T. 1992. *People like us: gentrification and the service class in Hackney in the 1980s*. Unpublished PhD dissertation, Open University, Milton Keynes.

Butler, T. & C. Hamnett 1994. Gentrification, class and gender: some comments on Warde's "gentrification of consumption". *Environment and Planning D: Society and Space* **12**, 477–93.

Buzard, J. 1993. *The beaten track: European tourism, literature, and the ways to culture, 1800–1918*. Oxford: Clarendon Press.

Byrd, P. 1985. The development of the peace movement in Britain. In *The peace movement in Europe and the United States* W. Kaltefleiter & R. Pflatzengraff (eds), 63–103. London: Croom Helm.

Byrne, P. 1988. *The campaign for nuclear disarmament*. London: Croom Helm.

Callinicos, A. 1987. The new middle class and socialist politics. In *The changing working class: essays on class structure today*, A. Callinicos & C. Harman (eds), 13–52. London: Bookmarks.

Callon, M. & B. Latour 1981. Unscrewing the big Leviathans. In *Advances in social theory and methodology*, K. Knorr & A. Cicourel (eds), 277–303. London: Routledge.

Cannadine, D. 1990. *The decline and fall of the British aristocracy*. New Haven, Conn.: Yale University Press.

Carchedi, G. 1977. *On the economic identification of social classes*. London: Routledge & Kegan Paul.

Carling A. 1990. *Social division*. London: Verso.

Carr-Saunders, A. M. & P. A. Wilson 1933. *The professions*. Oxford: Oxford University Press.

Carter, B. 1995. A growing divide: marxist class analysis and the labour process. *Capital & Class*, **55**, 33–72.

Cashmore, E. 1992. The new black bourgeoisie. *Human Relations* **45**, 1241–58.

Castells, M. 1977. *The urban question: a Marxist approach*. London: Methuen.

—1993. European cities: the information society, and the global economy. *Tijdschrift voor Economische en Sociale Geografie* **84**, 247–57.

Castles, S. & G. Kosack 1973. *Immigrant workers and the class structure in Western Europe*. Oxford: Oxford University Press.

Central Statistical Office. 1989. *Social Trends*, vol. 19. London: HMSO.

Centre for Contemporary Cultural Studies 1982. *The empire strikes back: race and racism in 70s Britain*. London: Hutchinson.

Charles, N. 1990. Women and class – a problematic relationship. *Sociological Review* **38**, 43–89.

Charles, N. & M. Kerr. 1988. *Women, food and families*. Manchester: Manchester University Press.

Childers, T. 1991. The middle classes and National Socialism. In *The German bourgeoisie*, D. Blackbourne & R. J. Evans (eds), 318–35. London: Routledge.

Clark, C. 1940. *The conditions of economic progress*. London: Macmillan.

Clark, G., J. Darrall, R. Grove-White, P. Macnaghten, J. Urry 1994a. *Leisure landscapes: report*. London: CPRE.

—1994b. *Leisure landscapes: background papers*. London: CPRE.

Clark, J., C. Modgil, S. Modgil 1990. *John H Goldthorpe: consensus and controversy*. London: Falmer.

Clarke, S. (ed.) 1991a. *The state debate*. Basingstoke: Macmillan.

—1991b. Marxism, sociology and Poulantzas's theory of the state. In *The State debate*, S. Clarke (ed.), 70–108. Basingstoke: Macmillan.

Clegg, S. (ed.) 1989. *Organisational theory and class analysis*. New York: de Gruyter.

—1990. *Modern organizations*. London: Sage.

Cloke, P. 1994. Enculturing political economy: a life in the day of a "rural geographer". In *Writing the rural: five cultural geographies*, P. Cloke, M. Doel, M. Phillips, N. Thrift (eds). London: Paul Chapman.

— 1995. Rural poverty and the welfare state: a discursive transformation in Britain and the

USA. *Environment and Planning* A **27**, 1001–1016.

Cloke, P. & M. Goodwin 1992. Conceptualising countryside change: from post-Fordism to rural structured coherence. *Transactions, Institute of British Geographers* **17**, 321–36.

Cloke, P. & P. Milbourne 1992. Deprivation and lifestyles in rural Wales II. *Journal of Rural Studies* **8**, 360–74.

Cloke, P. & N. Thrift 1987. Intra-class conflict in rural areas. *Journal of Rural Studies* **3**, 321–33.

—1990. Class and change in rural Britain. In *Rural restructuring*, T. Marsden, P. Lowe, S. Whatmore (eds), 165–81. London: David Fulton.

Cloke, P., D. Rankin, M. Phillips 1991. Middle class housing choice: channels of and entry into Gower, South Wales. In *People in the countryside* A. Champion & C. Watkins (eds), 38–52. London: Paul Chapman.

Cloke, P., P. Milbourne, C. Thomas 1994. *Lifestyles in rural England*. Salisbury: Rural Development Commission.

Cloke, P., M. Lapping, M. Phillips 1995 [forthcoming]. *The myth and persistence of rural culture.* London: Edward Arnold.

Coates, D. 1980. *Labour in power?* London: Longman.

Cochrane, A. 1993. *Whatever happened to local government?* Milton Keynes: Open University Press.

Cockburn, C. 1983. *Brothers: male dominance and technological change.* London: Pluto Press.

Collins, S. M. 1993. Blacks on the bubble: the vulnerability of black executives in white corporations. *Sociological Quarterly* **34**, 429–47.

Cooper, C. 1976. The house as symbol of self. University of Berkeley Working Paper.

Coren, S. 1992. *The left hander syndrome: the causes and consequences of left handedness.* New York: Free Press.

Corrigan, P. & D. Sayer 1985. *The great arch.* Oxford: Blackwell.

Cotgrove, S. 1982. *Catastrophe or cornucopia.* Chichester: Wiley.

Cotgrove, S. & A. Duff 1980. Environmentalism, middle class radicalism and politics. *Sociological Review* **28**, 333–51.

—1981. Environmentalism, values and social change. *British Journal of Sociology* **32**, 92–110.

Craib, I. 1984. *Modern social theory.* Brighton: Wheatsheaf.

CRE 1988. Report of a formal investigation into St George's Hospital Medical School. London: CRE Publications.

Cressey, P. & I. Scott 1992. Employment, technology and industrial relations in UK clearing banks: is the honeymoon over? *New Technology, Work and Employment* **7**, 83–96.

Crewe, I. 1987. A new class of politics. *Guardian*, 15 June.

Crewe, I. & B. Sarlvik 1981. *Decade of dealignment.* Cambridge: Cambridge University Press.

Crompton, R. 1980. Class mobility in modern Britain. *Sociology* **14**, 117–19.

—1986. Women and the "service class". In *Gender and stratification*, R. Crompton & M. Mann (eds), 119–36. Cambridge: Polity Press.

—1987. Gender, status, and professionalism. *Sociology* **21**, 413–428.

—1989. Class theory and gender. *British Journal of Sociology* **40**, 565–87.

—1990a. Professions in the current context. *Work, Employment and Society* **3**, Special Issue, 147–166.

—1990b. Professions and the "service class". Paper presented to the BSA Conference *Social divisions and social change*, University of Surrey, Guildford.

—1992. Patterns of social consciousness amongst the middle classes. In *Consumption and class*, R. Burrows & C. Marsh (eds), 140–65. Basingstoke: Macmillan.

—1993. *Class and stratification: an introduction to current debates.* Cambridge: Polity Press.

Crompton, R. & J. Gubbay 1977. *Economy and class structure*. London and Basingstoke: Macmillan.

Crompton, R. & G. Jones 1984. *White collar proletariat: deskilling and gender in clerical work*. London: Macmillan.

Crompton, R. & M. Mann (eds) 1986. *Gender and stratification*. Cambridge: Polity Press.

—1994. *Gender and stratification*, 2nd edn. Cambridge: Polity Press.

Crompton, R. & K. Sanderson 1986. Credentials and careers. *Sociology* **20**, 25–42.

—1990. *Gendered jobs and social change*. London: Unwin Hyman.

Crosland, C. A. R. 1956. *The future of socialism*. London: Cape.

Cross, G. 1993. *Time and money*. London: Routledge.

Crozier, M. 1964. *The bureaucratic phenomenon*. London: Tavistock.

Curran, J. & R. Burrows. 1986. The sociology of petite capitalism. *Sociology* **20**, 265–79.

Dahrendorf, R. 1959. *Class and class conflict in an industrial society*. London: Routledge & Kegan Paul.

—1964. Recent changes in the class structure of European societies. *Daedalus* (Winter), 225–70.

Dale, A., N. Gilbert, S. Arber 1985. Integrating women into class theory. *Sociology* **19**, 384–408.

Daunton, M. J. 1987. *A property owning democracy? Housing in Britain*. London: Faber.

Davidoff, L. 1974. Mastered for life: servant and wife in Victorian and Edwardian England. *Journal of Social History* **7**(4), 406–59.

—1983. Class and gender in Victorian England. In *Sex and class in women's history*, J. L. Newton, M. P. Ryan, J. R. Walkowitz (eds), 17–71. London: Routledge & Kegan Paul.

Davidoff, L. & C. Hall 1987. *Family fortunes: men and women of the English middle class, 1780–1850*. London: Hutchinson.

Davies, J. G. & J. Taylor 1970. Race, community and no conflict. *New Society* **406**, 67–9.

Day, G. & D. Robbins 1987. Activists for peace: the social basis of a local peace movement. In *The sociology of war and peace* C. Creighton & M. Shaw (eds), 218–36. London: Macmillan.

Dean, H. 1993 Social security: the income maintenance business. In *Markets and managers: new issues in the delivery of welfare*, P. Taylor-Gooby & R. Lawson (eds), 85–101. Milton Keynes: Open University Press.

De Certeau, M. 1984. *The practice of everyday life*. Berkeley: University of California Press

De Graaf, N-D., P. Nieuwbeerta, A. Heath 1995. Class mobility and political preferences: individual and contextual effects. *American Journal of Sociology* **100** (4), 997–1027.

Delphy, C. 1977. *The main enemy*. London: Verso.

—1981. Women in stratification studies. In *Doing feminist research*, H. Roberts (ed.), 114–28. London: Routledge & Kegan Paul.

Delphy, C. & D. Leonard 1986. Class analysis, gender analysis and the family. In *Gender and stratification*, R. Crompton & M. Mann (eds), 57–73. Cambridge: Polity Press.

Department of Employment et al. 1976. *Family Expenditure Survey 1968* [computer file]. Colchester: ESRC Data Archive.

—1990. *Family Expenditure Survey* [computer file]. Colchester: ESRC Data Archive.

Derrida, J. 1976. *On grammatology*. Baltimore, Md.: Johns Hopkins University Press.

Devine, F. 1992a. Gender segregation in the engineering and science professions: a case of continuity and change. *Work, Employment and Society* **6**, 557–75.

—1992b. Social identities, class identity and political perspectives. *Sociological Review* **40**, 229–52.

Dex, S. 1987. *Women's occupational mobility*. London: Macmillan.

—1990. Goldthorpe on gender and class: the case against. *John H Goldthorpe: consensus and controversy*, J. Clark, C. Modgil, S. Modgil (eds), 135–52. London: Falmer.

Donnison, D. 1987. *The government of housing*. Harmondsworth: Penguin.

Donnison, D. & C. Ungerson. 1981. *Housing policy*. Harmondsworth: Penguin.

Drew, D. et al. 1992. *Against the odds; the education and labour market experiences of black young people*. London: Department of Employment.

Dreyfus, H. & P. Rabinow 1993. Can there be a science of existential structure and social meaning? In *Bourdieu: critical perspectives*, C. Calhoun, E. LiPuma, M. Postone (eds), 35–44. Oxford: Basil Blackwell.

Duckers, W. & H. Davies 1990. *A place in the country*. London: Martin Joseph.

Dunleavy, P. 1979. The urban bases of political alignment: social class, domestic property ownership and state intervention in consumption processes. *British Journal of Political Science* **9**, 403–43.

—1980. The political implications of sectoral cleavages and the growth of state employment: part 2, cleavage structures and political alignment. *Political Studies* **28**, 527–49.

—1989. The end of class politics? In *Politics in transition*, A. Cochrane & J. Anderson (eds). 172–210. London: Sage.

Dupuis, A. 1989. Financial gains from owner occupation: the New Zealand case 1970–88. *Housing studies* **7**(1), 27–44.

Eckersley, R. 1989. Green politics and the new class. *Political Studies* **37**(2), 205–223.

Eder, K. 1993. *The new politics of class*. London: Sage.

Edgell, S. 1980. *Middle class couples*. London: Allen & Unwin.

—1993. *Class*. London: Routledge.

Edgell, S. & V. Duke 1991. *A measure of Thatcherism: a sociology of Britain*. London: HarperCollins.

Edwards, R. C. 1979. *Contested terrain: the transformation of the workplace in 20th century America*. New York: Basic.

Ehrenreich, B. 1989. *Fear of falling: the inner life of the middle class*. New York: Pantheon.

Ehrenreich, B. & J. Ehrenreich. 1979. The professional managerial class. In *Between labour and capital*, P. Walker (ed.), 5–45. Brighton: Harvester Press.

Elias, P. 1995. *Social class and the standard occupational classification*, Institute for Employment Research, University of Warwick.

Emmison, M. & M. Western 1990. Social class and social identity: a comment on Marshall et al. *Sociology* **24**, 241–53.

Erikson, R. & J. Goldthorpe 1988. Women at class crossroads: a critical note. *Sociology* **22**, 545–53.

—1992a. Individual or family? Results from two approaches to class assignment. *Acta Sociologica* **35**, 95–105.

—1992b. *The constant flux: a study of class mobility in industrial societies*. Oxford: Clarendon Press.

Ermisch, J. 1993. Familia oeconomica: a survey of the economics of the family. *Scottish Journal of Political Economy* **40**, 353–374.

Esping Andersen, G. (ed.) 1993. *Changing classes: stratification and mobility in post-industrial societies*. London: Sage.

Evans, G. 1992. Testing the validity of the Goldthorpe class schema. *European Sociological Review* **8**, 211–32.

—1993. Is gender on the new agenda? *European Journal of Political Research* **24**, 135–58.

—1994. An assessment of the validity of the Goldthorpe class schema for men and women. In *Social inequality in a changing world* R. M. Blackburn (ed.), 126–50. Cambridge: Cambridge Social Research Group.

Evans, G., A. F. Heath, C. Payne 1991. Modelling trends in the class/party relationship, 1964–87. *Electoral Studies* **10**, 99–117.

Evetts, J. 1994. Women and career in engineering: continuity and change in the organisation. *Work, Employment and Society* **8**, 101–12.

Fainstein, S., I. Gordon, M. Harloe 1992. *Divided cities: New York and London in the contemporary world*. Oxford: Basil Blackwell.

Fairbrother, P. 1991. In a state of change: flexibility in the Civil Service. In *Farewell to flexibility? Questions of restructuring*, A. Pollert (ed.), 69–83. Oxford: Blackwell.

—1994. *Politics and the state as employer*. London: Mansell.

Fanon, F. 1980. *Black skin and white masks*. London: Paladin.

Farnham, D. & S. Horton 1993. *Managing the new public services*. Basingstoke: Macmillan.

Fendrich, J. M. 1993. *Ideal citizens: the legacy of the civil rights movement*. New York: State University of New York Press.

Ferguson, K. 1984. *The feminist case against bureucracy*. Phildaelphia, PA: Temple University Press.

Fielding, A. J. 1992a. Migration and social mobility: South East England as an escalator region. *Regional Studies* **26**, 1–15.

—1992b. Migration and social change. In *Migration processes and patterns: population redistribution in the 1980s*, J. Stillwell, P. Rees, P. Boden (eds), 225–47. London: Belhaven Press.

—1995. Migration and social change: a longitudinal study of the social mobility of "immigrants" in England and Wales. *European Journal of Population*, forthcoming.

Fielding, A. J. & S. Halford 1993. Geographies of opportunity: a regional analysis of gender-specific social and spatial mobilities in England and Wales, 1971–81. *Environment and Planning A* **25**, 1421–40.

Financial management in government departments 1983. Cmnd 9058, London: HMSO.

Finch, J. 1983. *Married to the job: women's incorporation into men's work*. London: Heinemann.

Fine, B. 1993. *The world of consumption*. London: Routledge.

Forrest, R., A. Murie, P. Williams 1991. *Home ownership: fragmentation and differentiation*. London: Unwin Hyman.

Frazer, E. 1988. Teenage girls talking about class. *Sociology*, **22**, 343–58.

Furbank, R. 1985. *The idea of social class*. Oxford: Oxford University Press.

Gale, D. 1984. *Neighborhood revitalization and the postindustrial city: a multinational perspective*. Lexington, Mass.: Lexington Books.

Gallie, D. 1989. Employment, unemployment and social stratification. In *Employment in Britain*, D. Gallie (ed.), 465–92. Oxford: Basil Blackwell.

Gans, H. 1967. *The Levittowners: ways of life and politics in a new suburban community*. London: Allen Lane, The Penguin Press.

Gardiner, J. 1975. Women's domestic labour. *New Left Review* **89**, 47–71.

Garnsey, R. 1978. Women's work and theories of class stratification. *Sociology* **17**, 223–43.

Gentle, C., D. Dorling, J. Cornfold 1994. Negative equity and British housing in the 1990s: cause and effect. *Urban Studies* **31**, 181–99.

Gershuny, J. 1993. Post–industrial career structures in Britain. In *Changing classes: stratification and mobility in post–industrial societies*, G. Esping Anderson, (ed.) 136–70. London: Sage.

Giddens, A. 1973. *The class structure of the advanced societies*. London: Hutchinson.

—1979. *Central problems in social theory*. Basingstoke: Macmillan.

—1984. *The constitution of society*. Cambridge: Polity Press.

—1991. *Modernity and self identity: self and society in the late modern age*. Oxford: Polity.

—1990. *The consequences of modernity*. Oxford: Polity.

Giddens, A. & G. MacKenzie (eds) 1982. *Social class and the division of labour: essays in honour of*

Ilya Neustadt. Cambridge: Cambridge University Press.

Gilbert, D. 1992. *Class, community and collective action: social change in two British coalfields, 1850–1926.* Oxford: Clarendon.

Gilroy, P. 1987. *There ain't no black in the Union Jack.* London: Hutchinson.

—1994. *The black Atlantic: modernity and double consciousness.* London: Verso.

Glass, D. (ed.) 1954. *Social mobility in Britain.* London: Routledge & Kegan Paul.

Glass, R. 1963. *Introduction to London: aspects of change.* London: Centre for Urban Studies.

Glassner, B. 1989. Fitness and the post modern self. *Journal of Health and Social Behaviour* **30**, 180–91.

Glazer, P. M. & M. Slater 1987. *Unequal colleagues: the entrance of women into the professions, 1890–1940.* New Brunswick, NJ.: Rutgers University Press.

Goldthorpe, J. 1980a. *Social mobility and class structure in Britain.* Oxford: Clarendon Press.

—1980b. Reply to Crompton. *Sociology* **14**, 121–3.

—1982. On the service class, its formation and future. In *Classes and the division of labour: essays in honour of Ilya Neustadt,* A. Giddens & G. MacKenzie (eds), 162–85. Cambridge: Cambridge University Press.

—1983. Women and class analysis: a defence of the conventional view. *Sociology* **17**, 465–78.

—1984. Women and class analysis: a reply to the replies. *Sociology* **18**, 491–9.

—1990. A response. In *John H. Goldthorpe: consensus and controversy,* J. Clark, C. Modgil, S. Modgil (eds), 399–440. London: Falmer.

—1991. The uses of history in sociology: reflections on some recent tendencies. *British Journal of Sociology* **42**(2), 211–31.

—1994. The uses of history in sociology: a reply. *British Journal of Sociology* **45**(1), 55–70.

—1995. *Class and politics in advanced industrial societies.* Mimeo, Nuffield College, Oxford.

Goldthorpe, J. & C. Llewellyn 1977. Class mobility in modern Britain: three theses examined. *Sociology* **11**, 257–87.

Goldthorpe, J. & G. Marshall 1992. The promising future of class analysis: a response to recent critiques. *Sociology* **26**, 381–400.

Goldthorpe, J., D. Lockwood, F. Bechhofer, J. Platt 1968/69. *The affluent worker in the class structure.* [3 volumes]. Cambridge: Cambridge University Press.

Goldthorpe, J. with C. Lewellyn & C. Payne 1987. *Social mobility and class structure in modern Britain,* 2nd edn. Oxford: Clarendon Press.

Goodrich, C. 1975 [1920]. *The frontier of control: a study in British workshop politics.* London: Pluto Press.

Gordon, R., R. C. Edwards, M. Reich 1982. *Segmented work, divided workers: the historical trajectory of labour in the US.* Cambridge: Cambridge University Press.

Gorz, A. 1989. *Critique of economic reason.* London: Verso.

Gouldner, A. 1979. *The future of intellectuals and the rise of the new class: a frame of reference, theses, conjectures, argumentation and an historical perspective.* London: Macmillan.

Gray, A. G. & W. I. Jenkins 1985. *Administrative politics in British government.* Hemel Hempstead: Wheatsheaf.

Gray, R. 1993. Factory legislation and the gendering of jobs in the north of England, 1839–1860. *Gender and History* **15**, 56–80.

Gregson, N. 1988. On the (ir)relevance of structuration theory for empirical research. In *Anthony Giddons and critical theory.* D. Held & J. Thompson (eds). 151–169. Cambridge: Cambridge University Press.

Gregson, N. & M. Lowe 1994a. Waged domestic labour and the renegotiation of the domestic division of labour within dual-career households. *Sociology* **28**, 55–78.

—1994b. *Servicing the middle classes: class, gender and waged domestic labour in contemporary Britain.*

London: Routledge.

Haddon, R. 1970. A minority in a welfare state society: location of West Indians in the London housing market. *The New Atlantis* **1**(1).

Hakim, C. 1991. Grateful slaves and self-made women: fact and fantasy in women's work orientations. *European Sociological Review* **7**, 101–21.

Halfacre, K. 1992. *The importance of spatial representations in residential migration to rural England in the 1980s.* PhD, Geography Department, Lancaster University.

—1993. Locality and social representation: space, discourse and alternative definitions of the rural. *Journal of Rural Studies* **9**, 1–15.

Halford, S. & M. Savage 1995. Restructuring organisations, changing people: gender and careers in banking and local government. *Work, Employment and Society* **9** (1), 97–122.

Halford, S., M. Savage, A. Witz. 1996. *Gender, careers and organisations.* Basingstoke: Macmillan.

Hall, C. 1990. Private persons versus public someones: class, gender and politics in England, 1780–1850. In *British feminist thought*, T. Lovell (ed.), 51–67. Oxford: Blackwell.

Hall, S. 1980. *Drifting into a law and order society.* London: Cobden Trust.

—1992. New ethnicities. In *Race, culture and difference*, J. Donald & A. Rattansi (eds), 252–9. London: Sage.

Hall, S. & M. Jacques (eds) 1989. *New times: The changing face of politics in the 1990s.* London: Lawrence & Wishart.

Halsey, A., A. Heath, J. Ridge 1980. *Origins and destinations.* Oxford: Clarendon Press.

Hamnett, C. 1984a. Housing the two nations: socio-tenurial polarization in England and Wales, 1961–81. *Urban Studies* **21** (3),389–405.

—1984b. Gentrification and residential location theory: a review and assessment. In *Geography and the urban environment: progress in research and applications.* volume VI, D. Herbert & R. Johnston (eds), 283–319. London: Wiley.

—1989. Consumption and class in contemporary Britain. In *The changing social structure*, C. Hamnett, L. McDowell, P. Sarre (eds), 199–243. London: Sage.

—1991a. The blind men and the elephant: the explanation of gentrification. *Transactions of the Institute of British Geographers* N.S. **16**, 173–89.

—1991b. A nation of inheritors? Housing inheritance, wealth and inequality in Britain. *Journal of Social Policy* **20**, 509–36.

—1992. The geography of housing wealth and inheritance in Britain. *Geographical Journal* **158**, 307–21.

—1994. Social polarization in global cities: theory and evidence. *Urban Studies* **31**, 401–24.

Hamnett, C. & W. Randolph 1986. The role of housing and labour markets in the production of geographic variations in social stratification. In *Politics, geography, and social stratification*, K. Hoggart & E. Kofman (eds), 213–46. London: Croom Helm.

—1988. *Cities, housing and profits.* London: Hutchinson.

Hamnett, C. & J. Seavers 1994. A step on the ladder? Home ownership careers in the South East of England. South East Project Working Paper Series 15, Faculty of Social Sciences, The Open University.

—1995. Home ownership, housing wealth and wealth distribution in Britain. In *Income and wealth in Britain*, J. Hills (ed.) (forthcoming). Cambridge: Cambridge University Press.

Hamnett, C., M. Harmer, P. Williams 1991. *Safe as houses: housing inheritance in Britain.* London: Paul Chapman.

Harloe, M. 1984. Sector and class: a critical comment. *International Journal of Urban and Regional Research* **8**(2), 228–37.

Harraway, D. 1990, *Simians, cyborgs and women: the reinvention of nature.* London: Routledge.

Harris, R. & C. Hamnett 1987. The myth of the promised land: the social diffusion of home ownership in Britain and North America. *Annals of the Association of American Geographers* **77**, 173–90.

Harrison, C. 1991. *Countryside recreation in a changing society*. London: TMS Partnership.

Harrop, A. & P. Moss 1994. Working parents: trends in the 1980s. *Employment Gazette* (October), 343–51.

Hartmann, H. 1979. Capitalism, patriarchy and job segregation by sex. In *Capitalist patriarchy and the case for socialist feminism*, Z. Eisenstein (ed.), 206–47. New York: Monthly Review Press.

—1981. The unhappy marriage of marxism and feminism: towards a more progressive union. In *Women and revolution*, L. Sargent (ed.), 1–42. Boston: South End Press.

—1982. Capitalism, patriarchy and job segregation by sex. In *Classes, power and conflict*, A. Giddens & D. Held, (eds), 446–69. London: Macmillan.

Harvey, D. 1985. The geopolitics of capitalism. In *Social relations and spatial structures*, D. Gregory & J. Urry (eds). 202–225. London: Macmillan.

—1987. *The condition of postmodernity*. Oxford: Blackwell.

Heald, T. 1985. *Networks: who we know and how we use them*. London: Hodder & Stoughton.

Heath, A. 1981. *Social mobility*. London: Fontana.

Heath, A. & N. Britten 1984. Women's jobs do make a difference. *Sociology* **18**, 475–90.

Heath, A., R. Jowell, J. Curtice 1985. *How Britain votes*. Oxford: Pergamon.

Heath, A., R. Jowell, J. Curtice, G. Evans, J. Field, S. Witherspoon 1991. *Understanding political change: the British voter 1964–1987*. Oxford: Pergamon.

Heath, A., C. Mills, J. Roberts 1993. Towards meritocracy? Recent evidence on an old problem. In *Social research and social reform*, C. Crouch & A. Heath (eds), 217–244. Oxford: Clarendon.

Heath, A. et al. 1994. *Labour's last chance? The 1992 election and beyond*. Aldershot: Dartmouth.

Hennessy, P. 1990. *Whitehall*. London: Fontana Press.

Herz, T. A. 1990. Die Dienstklasse: eine empirische Analyse ihrer demographischen, kulturellen und politischen Identität. In *Soziale Welt, Sonderband 7: Lebenslagen, Lebensläufe, Lebensstile*, P. A. Berger & S. Hradil (eds), 231–52. Göttingen: Verlag Otto Schwartz.

Hetherington, K. 1993. *The geography of the other: lifestyle, performance and identity*. PhD, Sociology Department, Lancaster University.

—1994. The contemporary significance of Schmalenbach's concept of the bund. *Sociological Review* **42**, 1–25.

Higgs, E. 1983. Domestic servants and households in Victorian England. *Social History* **8**, 201–10.

—1986. Domestic service and household production. In *Unequal opportunities: women's employment in England 1800–1918*, A. John (ed.), 125–50, Oxford: Basil Blackwell.

Hindess, B. 1987. *Politics and class analysis*. Oxford: Blackwells.

Hiro, D. 1973. *Black British, white British*. London and New York: Monthly Review Press.

Hirsch, F. 1978. *Social limits to growth*. London: Routledge.

Hoggett, P. & J. Bishop 1986. *Organizing around enthusiasms*. London: Comedia.

Holloway, J. & Picciotto, S. 1977. Capital, crisis and the state. *Capital & Class* **2**, 76–101.

Holton, R. & B. Turner 1994. Debate and pseudo debate in class analysis. *Sociology* **28**, 799–804.

Hout, M., C. Brooks, J. Manza 1994. The democratic class struggle in the United States, 1948–1992. Paper presented to the International Sociological Association Research Committee on Social Stratification and Mobility, Bielefeld, July.

Hradil, S. 1987. *Sociostrukturanalyse in einer fortgeschrittenen Gesellschaft: von Klassen und Schichten zu*

Lagen und Milieus. Opladen: Leske und Budrich.

Hunt, J. & L. Hunt 1977. Dilemmas and contradictions of status: the case of the dual career family, *Social Problems* **29**, 499–510.

Hunt, J. & L. Hunt 1982. The dualities of careers and families: new integrations or new polarisations. *Social Problems* **29**, 499–510.

Husband, C. 1982. *"Race" in Britain: continuity and change.* London: Hutchinson.

Inglehart, I. 1971. The silent revolution in Europe: intergenerational change in post-industrial societies. *American Political Science Review* **65**, 991–1017.

—1977. *The silent revolution.* Princeton, NJ: Princeton University Press.

—1990. Values, ideology, and cognitive mobilisation in new social movements. In *Challenging the political order*, R. J. Dalton & M. Knechler (eds). Cambridge: Polity.

Jacques, M. 1994. Caste down. *Sunday Times,* Culture Supplement, 12 June, 8–10.

Jager, M. 1986. Class definition and the aesthetics of gentrification: Victoriana in Melbourne. In *Gentrification of the city*, N. Smith & P. Williams (eds), 78–91. London: Allen & Unwin.

Jamieson, L. 1990. Rural and urban women in domestic service. In *The world is ill divided*, E. Gordon & E. Breitenbach (eds), 117–35. Edinburgh: Edinburgh University Press.

Jenkins, K., K. Caines & A. Jackson 1988. *Improving management in government: the next steps.* London: HMSO – The Ibbs Report.

Jenkins, R. 1984. Ethnic minorities in Britain: a research agenda. In *Ethnic communities in business: strategies for economic survival*, R. Ward & R. Jenkins, (eds), 231–8. Cambridge: Cambridge University Press.

Jenkins, S. P. & A. Maynard 1983. Intergenerational continuities in housing. *Urban Studies* **20**, 431–8.

Jessop, B. 1982. *The capitalist state: Marxist theories and methods.* Oxford: Martin Robertson.

—1984. *The capitalist state: Marxist theory and methods*, 2nd edn. Oxford: Blackwell.

—1990. *State theory: putting the capitalist state in its place.* Oxford: Polity.

Jewson, N. et al. 1993. Changes in ethnic minority membership of health authorities 1989–92. *British Medical Journal* **307**, 604–5.

Johnson, R. 1978. Edward Thompson, Eugene Genovese and socialist humanist history. *History Workshop Journal* **6**, 79–101.

Johnson, T. 1972. *Professions and power.* London: Macmillan.

Jones, T. 1993. *Britain's ethnic minorities.* London: PSI.

Jonsson, J. & C. Mills 1993a. Social class and educational attainment in historical perspective: a Swedish–English comparison, Part 1. *British Journal of Sociology* **44**, 213–48.

—1993b. Social class and educational attainment in historical perspective: a Swedish–English comparison, Part 2. *British Journal of Sociology* **44**, 403–28.

Joyce, P. 1990. *Visions of the people.* Cambridge: Cambridge University Press.

Joyce, P., P. Corrigan, & M. Hayes 1988. *Striking out: trade unionism in social work.* Basingstoke: Macmillan.

Kanter, R. 1987. *The change masters.* New York: Simon & Schuster.

—1993. *Men and women of the corporation.* New York: Basic.

Kavanagh, D. 1990. Ideology, sociology and the strategy of the British labour party. In *John H Goldthorpe: consensus and controversy*, J. Clark, C. Modgil, S. Modgil (eds), 171–83. London: Falmer.

Kelly, M. 1980. *White-collar proletariat: the industrial behaviour of British civil servants.* London: Routledge Direct Editions, Routledge & Kegan Paul.

Kemeny, J. 1981. *The myth of home ownership.* London: Routlege.

Kemp, P. 1982. Housing landlordism in late nineteenth century Britain. *Environment and*

Planning A **14**, 1437–47.

Kitschelt, H. & S. Hellemans 1990. *Beyond the European left*. Durham, NC: Duke University Press.

Klingender, F. D. 1935. *The condition of clerical labour in Britain*. London: Lawrence.

Knorr-Cetina, K. 1988. The micro-social order: towards a reconception. In *Actions and structure: research methods and social theory*. N. Fielding (ed.), 20–53. London: Sage.

Kocka, J. 1980. *White collar workers in America 1890–1940*. London: Sage.

Krieger, J. 1983. *Undermining capitalism: state ownership and the dialectic of control in the British coal industry*. London: Pluto.

Kriesi, H. 1989. New social movements and the new class in the Netherlands. *American Journal of Sociology* **94** (5), 1078–116.

Labour Force Survey 1993. Department of Employment, Labour Force Survey Quarterly Bulletin nos 3 & 5, March/September. London: HMSO.

Laclau, E. & Mouffe, C. 1985. *Hegemony and socialist strategy*. London: Verso.

Lamont, M. 1991. *Money, morals and manners: the culture of the French and the American upper-middle class*. Chicago: Chicago University Press.

Landry, B. 1987. *The new black middle class*. Berkeley: University of California Press.

Larson, M. S. 1977. *The rise of professionalism: a sociological analysis*. Berkeley: University of California Press.

Larson, M. 1979. Professionalism: rise and fall. *International Journal of Health Services* **9**, 607–27.

Lash, S. 1990. *Sociology of postmodernism*. London: Routledge.

Lash, S. & J. Urry 1984. The new marxism of collective action. *Sociology* **18**, 33–50.

—1987. *The end of organized capitalism*. Cambridge: Polity Press.

—1994. *Economies of signs and space*. London: Sage.

Latour, B. 1986. The powers of association. In *Power, action and belief*. J. Law (ed.), 264–80. London: Routledge.

Layder D. 1990. *The Realist image in social science*. Basingstoke: Macmillan.

Lean, G. 1994. New green army rises up against the roads. *Observer* (London), 20 February.

Lee, D. J. 1994. Class as a social fact. *Sociology* **28**(2), 397–416.

Leiulsfrud, H. & A. Woodward 1987. Women at class crossroads: repudiating conventional theories of family class. *Sociology* **21**, 393–412.

Lenin, V. I. 1992 [1918]. *The state and revolution*. London: Penguin.

Lewis, R. & A. Maude 1949. *The English middle classes*. London: Phoenix House.

Ley, D. 1988. The social upgrading in six Canadian inner cities. *Canadian Geographer* **13**, 31–45.

—1994a. Gentrification and the politics of the new middle class. *Environment and Planning D: Society and Space* **12**, 53–74.

—1994b. Gentrification and the cultural politics of May 1968. Paper presented to the session "Gentrification: retrospect and prospect" at the Association of American Geographers' meetings, San Francisco, March 1994.

Lieberson, S. 1992. Einstein, Renoir and Greely: some thoughts about evidence in sociology. *American Sociological Review* 57, 1–15.

Lindley, P. 1994. *Labour market structures and prospects for women*. Manchester: EOC.

LiPuma, E. 1993. Culture and the concept of culture in a theory of practice. In *Bourdieu: critical perspectives*, C. Calhoun, E. LiPuma, M. Postone (eds), 14–34. Cambridge: Basil Blackwell.

Little, J. 1987. Gender relations in rural areas: the importance of women's domestic role. *Journal of Rural Studies* **3**, 335–42.

Llewellyn, C. 1981. Occupational mobility and the use of the comparative method. In *Doing feminist research*, H. Roberts (ed.), London: Routledge.

Lloyd, G. 1984. *The man of reason: "male" and "female" in western philosophy*. London: Methuen.

Lockwood, D. 1958. *The blackcoated worker*. London: Allen & Unwin.

—1960. The "new" working class. *European Journal of Sociology* **1**, 248–59.

—1964. Social integration and system integration. In *Explorations in social change*, G. K. Zollschan & W. Hirsh (eds), 244–57. New York:

—1966. The sources of variation in working class images of society. *Sociological Review* **14**, 249–63.

—1981. The weakest link in the chain? Some comments on the marxist theory of action. In *Research in the sociology of work*, I. H. Simpson & R. L. Simpson (eds), 435–81. Greenwich, Conn.: JAI Press.

—1986. Status, class and gender. In *Gender and stratification*, R. Crompton & M. Mann (eds), 11–22. Oxford: Polity.

—1989. *The blackcoated worker: a study in class consciousness*, 2nd edn. Oxford: Clarendon Press.

—1992. *Solidarity and schism: the problem of disorder in durkheimian and marxist sociology*. Oxford: Clarendon.

London–Edinburgh Weekend Return Group, 1980. *In and against the state*, revised and expanded edn. London: Pluto Press.

Lowe, P. & J. Goyder 1983. *Environmental groups in politics*. London: Allen & Unwin.

McAdam, D. 1988. *Freedom summer*. Oxford: Oxford University Press.

McCrone, D. 1992. *Understanding Scotland*. London: Routledge.

McDowell, L. 1982. Housing deprivation in longitudinal analysis. *Area* **14**, 144–50.

McGhie, C. 1988. Lure of the village piles on pressure. *Sunday Times*. (London), 15 May.

MacInnes, J. 1987. *Thatcherism at work: industrial relations and economic change*. Milton Keynes: Open University Press.

McKibbin, R. 1990. *Ideologies of class*. Oxford: Blackwells

McRae, S. 1990. Women and class analysis. In *John H. Goldthorpe: consensus and controversy*, J. Clark, C. Modgil, S. Modgil (eds), 117–34. Brighton: Falmer.

Mallet, S. 1975. *Essays on the new working class*. St. Louis: Telos.

Mann, M. 1986. A crisis in stratification theory? Persons, household/families/lineages, genders, classes and nations. In *Gender and stratification*, R. Crompton & M. Mann, (eds), 40–56. Cambridge: Polity Press.

—1993. *The sources of social power*. Vol. 2, *The rise of classes and nation states, 1760–1914*. Cambridge: Cambridge University Press.

Marsden, T. & A. Flynn 1993. Servicing the city: contested transitions in the rural realm. *Journal of Rural Studies* **9**, 201–4.

Marshall, G. 1988. Classes in Britain: marxist and official. *European Sociological Review* **4**, 141–54.

—1990. *In praise of sociology*. London: Unwin Hyman.

Marshall, G., H. Newby, D. Rose, C. Vogler 1988. *Social class in modern Britain*. London: Hutchinson.

Martindale, H. 1938. *Women servants of the state, 1870–1938: a history of women in the civil service*. London: Allen & Unwin.

Massey, D. 1984. *Spatial divisions of labour: social structures and the geography of production*. Basingstoke: Macmillan.

—1992. Political and space-time. *New Left Review* **196**, 65–84.

—1994. A global sense of place. In *Space, place and gender*, D. Massey (ed.), 146–156. Cambridge: Polity.

—1995a. *Spatial divisions of labour: social structures and the geography of production*, 2nd edn. Basingstoke: Macmillan.

—1995b. Masculinity, dualisms and high technology. *Transactions of the Institute of British Geographers* NS **20**, 487–99.

Massey, D., P. Quintas, D. Wield 1992. *High-tech fantasies: science parks in society, sciences and space*. London: Routledge.

Matless, D. 1994. Doing the English village, 1945–90: an essay in imaginative geography. In *Writing the rural: five cultural geographies*, Cloke et al. (eds), 7–88. London: Paul Chapman.

Mattausch, J. 1989. *A commitment to campaign*. Manchester: Manchester University Press.

Melucci, A. 1989. *Nomads of the present*. London: Radius.

Merrett, S. 1982. *Owner occupation in Britain*. London: Routledge.

Miles, R. 1982. *Racism and migrant labour*. London: Routledge & Kegan Paul.

—1984. Marxism versus the sociology of "race relations". *Ethnic and Racial Studies* **7**, 217–37.

Miliband, R. 1969. *The state in capitalist society*. London: Wiedenfeld & Nicolson.

Mills, C. 1988. "Life on the upslope": the postmodern landscape of gentrification. *Environment and Planning D: Society and Space* **6**, 169–89.

Mills, C. H.1994. Rational choice marxism and social class boundaries. *Rationality and Society*, **6**, 218–42.

Mills, C. W. 1951. *White collar*. New York: Oxford University Press.

—1959. *The sociological imagination*. New York: Harcourt Brace.

Mingay, G. (ed.) 1989. *The rural idyll*. London: Routledge.

Mohan, J. 1989. Unbalanced growth? Public services and labour shortages in a European core region. In *Growth and change in a core region*, M. Breheny & P. Congdon (eds), 33–54. London: Pion.

Molyneux, M. 1979. Beyond the domestic labour debate. *New Left Review* **116**, 3–27.

Morgan, G. 1986. *Images of organization*. London: Sage.

Morris, L. 1994. *Dangerous classes*. London: Routledge.

Morris, R. 1990. *Class, sect and party: the making of the British middle class, Leeds 1820–1850*. Manchester: Manchester University Press.

Morris, R. & R. Murphy 1959. The situs dimension in occupational structure. *American Sociological Review* **24**, 231–9.

Mouzelis, N. 1991. *Back to sociological theory*. Basingstoke: Macmillan.

Mullins, P. 1990. The identification of social forces in development as a general problem in sociology: a comment on Pahl's remarks on class and consumption relations as forces in urban and regional development. *International Journal of Urban and Regional Research* **15**, 119–26.

Munt, I. 1987. Economic restructuring, culture and gentrification: a case study in Battersea, London. *Environment and Planning A* 19, 1175–1197.

Murdoch, J. & T. Marsden 1991. Reconstituting the rural in an urban region: new villages for old? Countryside Change Working Paper 26, University of Newcastle.

Murphy, R. 1984. The structures of closure: a critique and development of the theories of Weber, Collins and Parkin. *British Journal of Sociology* **35**, 547–67.

—1986. Weberian closure theory: a contribution to the ongoing assessment. *British Journal of Sociology* **37**, 21–41.

—1988. *Social closure: the theory of monopolization and exclusion*. Oxford: Clarendon Press.

Newby, H. 1977. *The deferential worker*. London: Allen Lane.

—1979. *Green and pleasant land*. Harmondsworth: Penguin.

Noble, D. 1992. *A world without women: the Christian clerical culture of western science*. Oxford: Oxford University Press.

Northcote, S. H. & Trevelyan, C. E. 1968 [1954]. Report on the Organization of the Permanent Civil Service. Reprinted in Report of the Committee on the Civil Service 1966–68, *The Civil Service*. Cmnd 3638, London: HMSO – Fulton Report.

Oakley, A. 1974. *The sociology of housework*. Oxford: Martin Robertson.

Offe, C. 1985. New social movements: challenging the boundaries of institutional politics. *Social Research* **52**(4), 817–868.

Offe, C. & H. Wisenthal 1980. Two logics of collective action: theoretical notes on social class and organizational form. In *Political power and social theory*, vol. 1, M. Zeitlin (ed.), 67–116. Greenwich, Conn.: Connecticut University Press.

Ohri, S. & S. Faruqi 1988. Racism, employment and unemployment. In *Britain's black population*, 2nd edn, A. Bahat., R. Carr-Hill, S. Ohiri (eds), 147–76. Aldershot: Gower.

OPCS 1980. *Classification of occupations*. London: HMSO.

Ousby, I. 1990. *The Englishman's England*. Cambridge: Cambridge University Press.

Pahl, R. 1965. *Urbs in rure. The metropolitan fringe in Hertfordshire*. London: LSE Geography Department.

—1966. The social objectives of village planning. *Official Architecture and Planning* **29**, 1146–50.

—1984. *Divisions of labour*. Oxford: Basil Blackwell.

—1989. Is the emperor naked? Some questions on the adequacy of sociological theory in urban and regional research. *International Journal of Urban and Regional Research* **13**, 711–20.

—1993. Does class analysis without class theory have a future? *Sociology* **27**, 253–8.

Parkin, F. 1968. *Middle class radicalism*. Manchester: Manchester University Press.

—1974. Strategies of social closure in class formation. In *The social analysis of class structure*, F. Parkin (ed.), 1–18. London: Tavistock.

—1979. *Marxism and class theory: a bourgeois critique*. London: Tavistock.

Parry, N. & J. Parry 1976. *The rise of the medical profession*. London: Croom Helm.

Patel, S. 1988. *Asian retailing in Britain*. PhD thesis, Open University.

Payne, G. 1987. *Mobility and change in modern societies*. London: Methuen.

Payne, J. & G. Payne 1977. Housing pathways and stratification: a study of life chances in the housing market. *Journal of Social Policy* **6**, 129–56.

Penn, R. & H. Scattergood 1992. Ethnicity and career aspirations in contemporary Britain. *New Community* **19**, 75–98.

PEP 1974. *The facts of racial disadvantage*. London: PEP.

Perkin, H. 1989. *The rise of professional society: England since 1880*. London: Routledge.

Peterson, J. J. 1972. The Victorian governess: status incongruity in family and society. In *Suffer and be still*, M. Vicinus (ed.), 75–92. Bloomington: Indiana University Press.

Phillips, M. 1993a. Review, Western Europe: challenge and change. *Journal of Rural Studies* **7**, 341–2.

—1993b. Rural gentrification and the processes of class colonisation. *Journal of Rural Studies* **9**, 123–40.

—1994. Habermas, rural studies and critical social theory. In *Writing the rural: five cultural geographies*, P. Cloke et al. (eds), 89–126. London: Paul Chapman.

Phizacklea, A. (ed.) 1983. *One way ticket: migration and female labour*. London: Routledge & Kegan Paul.

—1994. A single or segregated market? Gendered and racialised divisions. In *The dynamics of "race" and gender*, H. Afshar & M. Maynard (eds), 281–316. London: Taylor & Francis.

Pirani, M. et al. 1992. Ethic pay differentials. *New Community* **19**(1), 31–42.

Pollert, A. 1988. The flexible firm: fixation or fact? *Work, Employment and Society* **2**, 281–316.

Pollitt, C. 1990. *Managerialism and the public services*. Oxford: Blackwell.

Potter, T. 1987. *A temporary phenomenon: flexible labour, temporary workers and the trade union response.* Birmingham: West Midlands Low Pay Unit.

Poulantzas, N. 1973. *Political power and social classes.* London: New Left Books.

—1975. *Classes in contemporary capitalism.* London: New Left Books.

—1978. *State, power, socialism.* London: New Left Books.

Pratt, G. 1982. Class analysis and domestic property. *International Journal of Urban and Regional Research* **6**, 481–502.

Price, R. & G. S. Bain 1988. The labour force. In *British social trends since 1900*, A. H. Halsey (ed.), 162–201. London: Macmillan.

Pringle, R. 1989. *Secretaries talk.* London: Verso.

Przeworski, A. 1977. Proletariat into a class: the process of class formation from Karl Kautsky's "The class struggle" to recent controversies. *Politics and Society* **7**, 343–401.

Ram, M. 1992. Coping with racism: Asian employers in the inner city. *Work, Employment and Society* **6**, 601–18.

Ramsay, H., C. Baldry, A. Connolly, C. Lockyer 1991. Municipal microchips: the computerised labour process in the public service sector. In *White-collar work: the non-manual labour process*, C. Smith, D. Knights, H. Willmott (eds), 35–64. Basingstoke: Macmillan.

Rapoport, R. & R. N. Rapoport 1971. *Dual career families.* Harmondsworth: Penguin.

—1972. The dual career family: a variant pattern and social change. In *Towards a sociology of women*, C. Safilios-Rothschild (ed.), 122–64. Lexington: Xerox College Publishing.

—(eds) 1978. *Working couples.* New York: Harper & Row.

—1980. Three generations of dual-career family research. In *Dual career couples*, F. Pepitone-Rockwell (ed.), 23–48. Beverly Hills, Calif.: Sage.

Reddy, W. 1987. *Money and liberty in Western Europe.* Cambridge: Cambridge University Press.

Reid, I. 1981. *Social class differences in Britain.* London: Grant McIntyre.

Renner, K. 1953. *Wandlungen der modernen Gesellschaft: Zwei Abhandlungen ber die Probleme der Nachkriegszeil.* Vienna: Volksbuchandling.

—1978. The service class. In *Austro Marxism*, T. Bottomore & P. Goode (eds), 249–52. Oxford: Oxford University Press.

Report of the Committee on the Civil Service 1966–68, 1968. *The Civil Service.* Cmnd 3638, London: HMSO – Fulton Report.

Rex, J. & R. Moore 1967. *Race, community and conflict.* Oxford: Oxford University Press.

Rex, J. & S. Tomlinson 1979. *Colonial immigrants in a British city: a class analysis.* London: Routledge & Kegan Paul.

Rigby, B. 1991. *French popular culture in the 1980s.* London: Routledge.

Roberts, E. 1984. *A woman's place: an oral history of working class women 1890–1940.* Oxford: Basil Blackwell.

—1988. *Women's work, 1840–1940.* Basingstoke: Macmillan.

Roberts, H. 1993. The women and class debate. In *Debates in sociology*, D. Morgan & L. Stanley (eds), 55–70. Manchester: Manchester University Press.

Roberts, K., J. Cooke, A. Clarke, E. Semeonoff 1977. *The fragmentary class structure.* Atlantic Highlands, NJ: Humanities Press.

Robinson, V. 1988. The new Indian middle class in Britain. *Ethnic and Racial Studies* **11**, 456–73.

—1992. Move on and up: the mobility of Britain's Afro-Caribbean and Asian populations. In *Migration processes and patterns: population redistribution in the 1980s*, J. Stillwell, P. Rees, P. Boden (eds), 271–91. London: Belhaven Press.

Robson, B. 1969. *Urban analysis: study of city structure.* Cambridge: Cambridge University Press.

Rogers, A. 1992. *English rural communities: an assessment and prospect for the 1990s.* Salisbury: Rural Development Commission.

Rootes, C. 1995. A new class? The higher educated and the New Politics. In *Social movements and social classes*, L. Maheu (ed.), London: Sage.

Rose, D. 1984. Rethinking gentrification: beyond the uneven development of marxist urban theory. *Environment and Planning D: Society and Space* **2**, 47–74.

—1988. A feminist perspective of employment restructuring and gentrification: the case of Montreal. In *The power of geography: how territory shapes social life*, J. Wolch & M. Dear (eds), 118–38. Winchester, Mass: Unwin Hyman.

Rose, M. 1994. Skill and Samuel Smiles: changing the British work ethic. In *Skill and occupational change.* R. Penn, M. Rose, J. Rubery (eds), 281–335. Oxford: Oxford University Press.

Rose, S. 1992. *Limited livelihoods: gender and class in nineteenth century England.* London: Routledge.

Rubenstein, W. D. 1981, *Men of property: the very wealthy in Britain since the Industrial Revolution.* London: Croom Helm.

Rudig W. et al. 1991. *Green Party members: a profile.* Glasgow: Delta Publications.

Rural Development Commission 1992. *Rural development strategies for the 1990s.* Salisbury: Rural Development Commission.

Sarre, P. 1989. Race and the class structure. In *The changing social structure*, C. Hamnett, L. McDowell, and P. Sarre (eds), 124–57. London: Sage.

Sarre, P., D. Phillips, R. Skellington 1989. *Ethnic minority housing: explanations and policies.* Aldershot: Avebury

Sassen, S. 1991. *The global city: London, New York and Tokyo.* Chichester: Princeton University Press.

—1994. *Cities in a world economy.* Thousand Oaks, Calif.: Pine Forge Press.

Saunders, P. 1978. Domestic property and social class. *International Journal of Urban and Regional Research* **2**, 233–51.

—1984. Beyond housing classes. *International Journal of Urban and Regional Research* **8**, 202–27.

—1986. *Social theory and the urban question*, 2nd edn. London: Hutchinson.

—1990. *A nation of homeowners.* London: Unwin Hyman.

Saunders, P. & P. Williams 1986. The constitution of the home. *Housing Studies* **3**, 81–93.

Savage, M. 1987. *The dynamics of working class politics: the labour movement in Preston 1880–1940.* Cambridge: Cambridge University Press.

—1988. The missing link: the relationship between social and geographical mobility. *British Journal of Sociology* **39**, 554–77.

—1991a. Making sense of middle class politics: a secondary analysis of the 1987 British general election survey. *Sociological Review* **39**, 26–54.

—1991b. Career structures and managerial hierarchies: the case of Lloyds Bank, 1870–1950. Mimeo, University of Keele.

—1992. Women's expertise, men's authority: gendered organization and the contemporary middle classes. In *Gender and bureaucracy*, M. Savage & A. Witz (eds), 124–51, Oxford: Blackwell.

—1993. Career mobility and class formation: British banking workers and the lower middle classes. In *Building European society: occupational change and social mobility in Europe 1840–1940*, A. Miles & D. Vincent (eds), 196–216. Manchester: Manchester University Press

—1994. Class analysis and its futures. *Sociological Review* **42**, 531–48.

Savage, M. & A. Fielding. 1989. Class formation and regional development: the "service class" in south east England. *Geoforum* **20**, 203–18.

Savage, M. & A. Miles 1994. *The remaking of the British working class.* London: Routledge.

Savage, M. & A. Warde 1993. *Urban sociology, capitalism and modernity.* Basingstoke: Macmillan.

Savage, M. & A. Witz 1991. *The gendered dynamics of service class formation: beyond the women and class debate.* Mimeo.

—(eds) 1992. *Gender and bureaucracy.* Oxford: Basil Blackwell/Sociological Review.

Savage, M., J. Barlow, P. Dickens, T. Fielding 1992. *Property, bureaucracy and culture: middle class formation in contemporary Britain.* London: Routledge.

Savage, M., P. Dickens, A. Fielding. 1988. Some social and political implications of the contemporary fragmentation of the "service class" in Britain. *International Journal of Urban and Regional Research* **12**, 455–76.

Savage, M., P. Watt, S. Arber 1992a. The consumption sector debate and housing mobility, *Sociology* **24**, 97–117.

Sayer A. 1984. *Method in social science: a realist approach.* London: Methuen.

Scase, R. 1992. *Class.* Milton Keynes: Open University Press.

Scase, R. & R. Goffee 1985. *Women in charge: the experiences of female entrepreneurs.* London: Allen & Unwin.

—1989. *Reluctant managers: their work and lifestyles.* London: Unwin Hyman.

Schulze, C. 1990. Die Transformation sozialer Milieus in der Bundesrepublik Deutschland. In *Soziale Welt, Sonderband 7: Lebenslagen, Lebensläufe, Lebensstile,* P. A. Berger & S. Hradil (eds), 409–32. Göttingen: Verlag Otto Schwartz.

Scott, A. 1986. Industrialization, gender segregation and stratification theory. In *Gender and stratification,* R. Compton & M. Mann (eds), 82–100. Cambridge: Polity.

—1990. *Ideology and the new social movements.* London: Unwin Hyman.

Scott, J. 1982. *The upper classes: property and privilege in Britain.* London: Routledge & Kegan Paul.

—1991. *Who rules Britain.* Oxford: Polity.

—1994. Class analysis: back to the future. *Sociology* **28**.

Seccombe, W. 1974. The housewife and her labour under capitalism. *New Left Review* **83**, 3–24.

—1986. Patriarchy stabilized: the construction of the male breadwinner wage norm in nineteenth century Britain. *Social History* **11**, 53–76.

Sedgemore, B. 1980. *The secret constitution: an analysis of the political establishment.* London: Hodder & Stoughton.

Seyd, P. & P. Whiteley 1992. *Labour's grass roots: the politics of party membership.* Oxford: Clarendon.

Sharpley, R. 1993. *Tourism and leisure in the countryside.* Huntingdon: ELM Publications.

Shavit, Y. & H-P. Blossfeld. (eds) 1993. *Persistent inequality: changing educational attainment in thirteen countries.* Boulder, Colo.: Westview Press.

Short, J. 1991. *Imagined country: society, culture and environment.* London: Routledge.

Short, J., S. Fleming, S. Witt 1986. *Housebuilding, planning and community action.* London: Routledge.

Simpson, M. A. & T. H. Lloyd 1977. *Middle class housing in Britain.* Newton Abbott: David & Charles.

Skellington, R. 1992. *"Race" in Britain.* London: Sage.

Sly, F. 1994. Ethnic groups and the labour market. *Employment Gazette* May, 147–59.

Smart, B. 1992. *Modern conditions, post-modern controversies.* London: Routledge.

Smith, C. 1987. *Technical workers: class, labour and trade unionism.* Basingstoke: Macmillan.

Smith, N. 1979a. Gentrification and capital: theory, practice and ideology in Society Hill. *Antipode* **11**, 139–55.

—1979b. Towards a theory of gentrification: a back to the city movement by capital not people. *American Planning Association Journal* **45**, 538–48.

—1986. Gentrification, the frontier, and the restructuring of urban space. In *Gentrification of the city*, N. Smith & P. Williams (eds), 15–34. London: Allen & Unwin.

Social Security Committee, 1990–91, 1991. *The organisation and administration of the Department of Social Security*. HC 550–1, London: HMSO.

Stacey, M. 1981. The division of labour revisited or overcoming the two Adams. In *Practice and progress: British sociology 1950–1980*. P. Abrams et al. (eds), 172–90. London: Allen & Unwin.

Stanworth, M. 1984. Women and class analysis: a reply to John Goldthorpe. *Sociology* **18**, 159–70.

Stedman-Jones, G. 1973. Notes on the remaking of the working class. *Journal of Social History*. **7**, 460–508.

—1983. *Languages of class*. Cambridge: Cambridge University Press.

Stewart A., K. Prandy, R. Blackburn 1980. *Social stratification and occupations*. London: Macmillan.

Strathern, M. 1993. *After nature*. Cambridge: Cambridge University Press.

Swenarton, M. & S. Taylor 1985. The scale and nature of the growth of owner occupation in Britain between the wars. *Economic History Review* **38**, 373–92.

Taylor-Gooby, P. & R. Lawson (eds) 1993. *Markets and managers: new issues in the delivery of welfare*. Milton Keynes: Open University Press.

Thomas, G. n.d. *Labour mobility in Great Britain 1800–1849*. London: The Social Survey.

Thomas, K. 1973. *Man and the natural world, 1500–1800*. London: Allen Lane.

—1983. *Man and the natural worlds: changing attitudes in England 1500–1800*. London: Allen Lane.

Thompson, E. P. 1968. *The making of the English working class*. London: Penguin Books.

Thompson, J. B. 1984. *Studies in the theory of ideology*. Cambridge: Polity.

—1990. *Ideology and modern culture*. Cambridge: Polity.

Thompson, M., R. Ellis, A. Wildavsky 1990. *Cultural theory, or, why all that is permanent is bias*. Boulder, Colo.: Westview.

Thorns, D. 1981. The implications of differential rates of capital gain from owner occupation for the formation and development of housing classes. *International Journal of Urban and Regional Research* **5**, 205–30.

Thrift, N. 1987. Introduction: the geography of late twentieth century class formation. In *Class and space*, N. Thrift & P. Williams (eds), 207–53. London: Routledge.

— 1987b. Manufacturing rural geography, *Journal of Rural Studies*, **3**, 77–81.

—1989. Images of social change. In *The changing social structure*, C. Hamnett, L. McDowell, P. Sarre (eds), 12–42. London: Sage.

Thrift, N. & R. Johnston 1993. Editorial. *Environment and Planning A*. **32**, 83–85.

Thrift, N. & A. Leyshon 1992. In the wake of money: the City of London and the accumulation of value. In *Global finance and urban living*, L. Budd & S. Whimpster (eds), 282–311. London: Routledge.

Thrift, N. & P. Williams 1987. *Class and space*. London: Routledge.

Tomlinson, M. & A. Warde 1993. Social class and change in the eating habits of British households, *British Food Journal*. **95**, 3–11.

Tonge, R. 1989. Financial management. In *Managing the new public services*, D. Farnham & S. Horton (eds), 78–98. Basingstoke: Macmillan.

Touraine, A. 1974. *The post-industrial society: tomorrow's social history – classes, conflict and culture in the programmed society*. London: Wildwood House.

Treasury and Civil Service Committee, 1988–89, Fifth Report 1989. *Development in the next steps programme.* HC 348, London: HMSO.

—1990–91, Seventh Report. 1991. *The next steps initiative.* HC 496, London: HMSO.

University of Leeds 1992. Developing opportunities for ethnic minority students at the University of Leeds. University of Leeds, Department of Adult Continuing Education.

Urry, J. 1981. *The anatomy of class societies: the economy, civil society and the state.* London: Macmillan.

—1990. *The tourist gaze: leisure and travel in contemporary societies.* London: Sage.

—1995. *Consuming places.* London: Routledge.

Valentine, G. 1995. Out and about: a geography of a lesbian landscape. *International Journal of Urban and Regional Research.* **19**(1), 96–111

Van den Berg, A. 1993. Creeping embourgeoisement? Some comments on the marxist discovery of the new middle class. *Research in Social Stratification and Mobility* **12**, 295–328.

Waddington, D., M. Wykes, C. Critcher 1991. *Split at the seams? Community, continuity and change after the 1984–5 coal dispute.* Milton Keynes: Open University Press.

Walby, S. 1986a. *Patriarchy at work.* Cambridge: Polity.

—1986b. Gender, class and stratification: towards a new approach. In *Gender and stratification,* R. Crompton & M. Mann (eds), 23–39. Cambridge: Polity Press.

—1990. *Theorising patriarchy.* Oxford: Basil Blackwell.

Wallace, A. 1993. *Walking, literature, and English culture.* Oxford: Clarendon Press.

Walton, J. 1983. *The English seaside resorts: a social history, 1750–1914.* Leicester: Leicester University Press.

—1989. *Late Georgian and Victorian Britain.* London: George Philip.

Ward, R. 1985. Minority settlement and the local economy. In *New approaches to economic life,* B. Roberts et al. (eds), 198–212. Manchester: Manchester University Press.

Ward, R. & R. Jenkins (eds) 1984. *Ethnic communities in business: strategies for economic survival.* Cambridge: Cambridge University Press.

Ward, R. et al. 1982. Middle class Asians and their settlement in Britain. In *Migrant workers in metropolitan cities,* J. Solomos (ed.), 176–89. Strasbourg: European Science Foundation.

Warde, A. 1991. Gentrification as consumption: issues of class and gender. *Environment and Planning D: Society and Space* **9**, 223–32.

Watson, W. 1964. Social mobility and social class in industrial communities. In *Closed systems and open minds,* M. Gluckman (ed.), 129–157. Edinburgh: Oliver & Boyd.

Watt, P. 1993. Housing inheritance and social inequality: A rejoinder to Chris Hamnett. *Journal of Social Policy,* **22**(4), 527–34.

Weakliem, D. 1991. The two lefts? Occupation and party choice in France, Italy and the Netherlands. *American Journal of Sociology* **96**, 1327–61.

Weber, M. 1978. *Economy and society.* Berkeley: University of California Press.

Werbner, P. 1980. From rags to riches: Manchester Pakistanis in the textile trade. *New Community* **8**, 84–95.

Westergaard, J. 1992. About and beyond the underclass: some notes on the influence of social climate on British sociology today. *Sociology* **26**, 575–88.

Westergaard J. & H. Resler 1975. *Class in a capitalist society.* London: Heinemann.

Whyte, W. 1957. *The organisation man.* New York: Touchstone.

Wiener, M. 1981. *English culture and the decline of the industrial spirit, 1950–1980.* Cambridge: Cambridge University Press.

Williams, P. 1976. The role of institutions in the inner London housing market: the case of Islington. *Transactions of the Institute of British Geographers* N.S. **1**, 72–82.

—1986. Class constitution through spatial reconstruction: a re–evaluation of gentrification in Australia, Britain, and the United States. In *Gentrification of the city,* N. Smith & P.

Williams (eds), 56–77. London: Allen & Unwin.

Williams, R. 1973. *The country and the city*. London: Paladin.

—1985. *The country and the city*. London: Hogarth Press.

Wilson, W. 1980. *The declining significance of race: blacks and changing American institutions*. Chicago: University of Chicago Press.

—1986. *The truly disadvantaged: the inner city, the underclass and public property*. Chicago: University of Chicago Press.

Witz, A. 1988. Patriarchal relations and patterns of sex segregation in the medical division of labour. In *Gender segregation at work*, S. Walby (ed.), 74–90. Milton Keynes: Open University Press.

Witz, A. 1990. Patriarchy and professions: the gendered politics of occupational closure. *Sociology* **24**, 675–90.

—1992. *Professions and patriarchy*. London: Routledge.

Witz, A. & M. Savage 1992. The gender of organizations. In *Gender and bureaucracy*, M. Savage & A. Witz (eds), 3–62. Oxford: Blackwells/The Sociological Review.

Wolch, J. & J. Dear (eds). 1989. *The power of geography: how territory shapes social life*. London: Unwin Hyman.

Wood, K. & S. House 1991. *The good tourist*. London: Mandarin.

Wood, S. 1989. New wave management. *Work, Employment and Society* **3**, 379–402.

Wright, E. O. 1976. Class boundaries in advanced capitalist societies. *New Left Review* **98**, 3–41.

—1978. *Class, crisis and the state*. London: New Left Books.

—1985. *Classes*. London: Verso.

—1989a. Women in the class structure. *Politics and Society* **17**, 35–66.

—1989b. A general framework for the analysis of class structure. In *The debate on classes*, E. O. Wright (ed.), 3–46. London: Verso.

Wynne, D. 1990. Leisure, lifestyle and the social construction of social position. *Leisure Studies* **9**, 21–34.

Yeandle, S. 1984. *Women's working lives: patterns and strategies*. London: Tavistock.

Youngs, J. 1985. The English television landscape documentary: a look at Grenada. In *Geography, the media and popular culture*, J. Burgess & J. R. Gold (eds), 144–64. London: Croom Helm.

Zimmeck, M. 1988. The new woman and the machinery of government: a spanner in the works. In *Government and expertise: specialists, administrators and professionals 1860–1919*, R. McLeod (ed.), 185–202. Cambridge: Cambridge University Press.

—1992. Marry in haste, repent at leisure: women, bureaucracy and the post office, 1870–1920. In *Gender and bureaucracy*, M. Savage & A. Witz (eds), 185–202. Oxford: Blackwell.

Zukin, S. 1988. *Loft living: culture and capital in urban change*. London: Radius.

Index